Stendhal:
The Red and the Black and *The Charterhouse of Parma*

MODERN LITERATURES IN PERSPECTIVE

General Editor:

SEÁN HAND, Reader, Department of Language Studies, London Guildhall University

Published Titles:

LILLIAN R. FURST, *Realism*

JO LABANYI, *Galdós*

CELIA BRITTON, *Claude Simon*

ROGER PEARSON, *Stendhal: 'The Red and the Black' and 'The Charterhouse of Parma'*

STENDHAL:
THE RED AND THE BLACK
AND
THE CHARTERHOUSE OF PARMA

Edited and Introduced by

ROGER PEARSON

LONGMAN
LONDON AND NEW YORK

Longman Group UK Limited,
Longman House, Burnt Mill,
Harlow, Essex CM20 2JE, England
and Associated Companies throughout the world.

*Published in the United States of America
by Longman Publishing, New York*

First published 1994

ISBN 582 09617.0 CSD
ISBN 582 09616.2 PPR

British Library Cataloguing-in-Publication Data

A catalogue record for this book is
available from the British Library

Library of Congress Cataloging in Publication Data

Stendhal: The red and the black and The charterhouse of Parma /
    edited and introduced by Roger Pearson.
        p.   cm. — (Modern literatures in perspective)
    Includes bibliographical references and index.
    ISBN 0-582-09617-0 (CSD). — ISBN 0-582-09616-2 (PPR)
    1. Stendhal, 1783–1842. Rouge et le Noir. 2. Stendhal.
    1783–1842. Chartreuse de Parme. I. Pearson, Roger. II. Series.
    PQ2435.R72S77 1994
    843'.7—dc20   93-30285
                                                                  CIP

Set by 14 AA in 9/11½ pt Palatino
Produced by Longman Singapore Publishers (Pte) Ltd.
Printed in Singapore

Contents

General Editor's Preface

Modern Literatures in Perspective is a series of collected critical essays on post-1800 European-language authors, works or concepts. It is designed to help the reader study these literatures in isolation and in context by selecting and presenting the most representative and inspiring reactions to the works in question from the time of their first appearance to the present day.

A crucial feature of the series' approach is its open recognition of the critical revolution which has taken place this century and in particular in the last thirty years. Marxist, structuralist, psychoanalytical, deconstructionist and feminist theories have utterly transformed our assessment of literature. *Modern Literatures in Perspective* takes full account of the general issues raised by the revolution in theory, together with the practical effects which these theories have on the reading of the literary canon.

Recognising the need for direction within this plural field of perspectives, each volume offers a high degree of critical guidance and advice in addition to presenting its subject in a methodical and accessible manner.

A substantial introduction outlines the historical and cultural contexts within which the literature in question was produced. It explores and explains the conflicting critical reactions to the literature in perspective and suggests ways in which these critical differences may be put to work. Each essay is prefaced by an introductory headnote setting forth the significance of the piece. A glossary of critical terms and cultural references provides further background information.

Modern Literatures in Perspective offers much more than textual analysis, therefore. It openly examines the relationship between literature and a range of wider issues. At the same time, its approach is more concrete than any history of literature. Rather than impose a synthesis or single methodology, the volumes in this series bring the reader into the heart of a crucial critical debate.

New critical insights, teaching practices and reading publics continue to transform our view of modern European-language writings. *Modern Literatures in Perspective* aims to contribute to this continuous transformation by disseminating and analysing the best modern criticism on the best modern literatures.

Preface

This volume is intended to map out the critical reception of Stendhal's two most widely read novels, *The Red and the Black* (*Le Rouge et le Noir*) and *The Charterhouse of Parma* (*La Chartreuse de Parme*), since their publication in 1830 and 1839 respectively. Part One offers a selection of extracts from well-known and representative nineteenth-century responses to these works, while Part Two presents a cross-section of critical discussion since 1945. The Introduction gives an overview of this reception (including during the period 1900–45) and highlights aspects of the two novels which have given rise to particular controversy.

Constituting the major part of the volume, Part Two consists of chapters, articles, essays, or book extracts from some of the leading critics who have written on Stendhal during the last fifty years. The principles of selection have been, first, to reproduce 'classic' statements of critical position which have influenced subsequent discussion of the novels and, second, to illustrate the main literary-theoretical perspectives from which Stendhal and world literature in general have been viewed in recent decades. It is therefore hoped that the selection will inform the reader reliably and quickly of the entire background to contemporary debate about Stendhal as a novelist and that it will demonstrate the diversity, richness, and—above all—the relativity of twentieth-century critical methods. The order of presentation is largely chronological, and French, British, German, and American writing all finds itself represented. The resulting combination offers a striking image of that very **polyphony** which some recent readers of Stendhal have come to identify as a major feature in his two best-known novels.

The Queen's College, Oxford
23 March 1993

Acknowledgements

We are grateful to the following for permission to reproduce copyright material:

The author, Victor Brombert, for Chapter 6 'La Chartreuse de Parme: the Poetry of Freedom' in Stendhal. Fiction and the Themes of Freedom (University of Chicago Press, 1968), pp. 149–76; Cambridge University Press and the author, Christopher Prendergast, for Chapter 4 'Stendhal: The Ethics of Verisimilitude' in The Order of Mimesis. Balzac, Stendhal, Nerval, Flaubert (1986), pp. 119–47; Librairie José Corti for Georges Blin, Stendhal et les problèmes du roman (1954), pp. 105–12 and extracts from Shoshana Felman, La 'Folie' dans l'œuvre romanesque de Stendhal (1971), pp. 40–3 and 225–30; the Editor of French Forum for extracts from Chapters V and VI from Carol A. Mossman, The Narrative Matrix: Stendhal's 'Le Rouge et le Noir' (1984); pp. 107–12, 125–30 and 132–9; The Society for French Studies for Ann Jefferson, 'Stendhal and the Uses of Reading' in French Studies 37 (1983), 168–83; Editions Gallimard on behalf of the author Michel Crouzet for extracts from Stendhal et le langage (1981), pp. 182–4, 194–200 (© Editions Gallimard, 1981); Hill and Wang, a division of Farrar, Straus & Giroux, Inc., for Roland Barthes, 'One always fails in speaking of what one loves' in The Rustle of Language, translated by Richard Howard (translation copyright © 1986 by Farrar, Straus & Giroux, Inc.); Alfred A. Knopf, Inc. for Chapter 3, 'The Novel and the Guillotine, or Fathers and Sons in Le Rouge et le Noir' in Peter Brooks, Reading for the Plot. Design and Intention in Narrative (copyright © 1984 by Peter Brooks); Les Editions Sociales-Messidor for Pierre Barbéris, 'La Chartreuse de Parme' in Sur Stendhal (1983), pp. 153–71; Princeton University Press for an extract from Erich Auerbach, Mimesis. The Representation of Reality in Western Literature, translated by Willard R. Trask, pp. 454–66 (copyright © 1953 by Princeton University Press, © renewed 1981); Editions du Seuil for extracts from Jean-Pierre Richard, 'Connaissance et tendresse chez Stendhal' in Littérature et sensation (1954), pp. 65–76.

Note on Translation and References

All quotations from *The Red and the Black* (*Le Rouge et le Noir*) are from Catherine Slater's translation in the World's Classics series (Oxford: Oxford University Press, 1991); all quotations from *The Charterhouse of Parma* (*La Chartreuse de Parme*) are from C.K. Scott Moncrieff's translation as published in the Everyman's Library series (London: David Campbell, 1992). Unless otherwise stated in the notes, all other translations are my own.

Potentially unfamiliar terms from literary theory are highlighted in bold when they first occur and are explained in the Glossary at the end, to which readers are similarly referred for the elucidation of further literary, historical, or other allusions.

(. . .) indicates an omission by the author of the piece or quotation reproduced, [. . .] an editorial omission. Other square brackets indicate editorial translation or amended references.

'People see the same thing differently, depending on their own particular standpoint.'

(Preface to Stendhal's *Armance*)

'Every age, in fact, may think that it alone possesses the key to the authoritative meaning of a work, but one has only to broaden the historical perspective a little to transform this singular meaning into a plural one and the closed work into an open one.'

(Roland Barthes, *Criticism and Truth*)

Introduction

'I might write something which would be to my taste alone and which would be recognized as a fine work in the year 2000.'
(*Journal*, 31 Dec. 1804)[1]

'Letters to a friend'

Publishing one's work, Stendhal observed,[2] is like buying a ticket in the lottery of fame. Your number may never come up – or, if it does, only when you are dead and gone. 1880, 1900, 1935, and 2000: these are the years randomly chosen by Stendhal throughout his career to illustrate his firm and well-founded conviction that recognition of his skills as a writer would be delayed. Such predictions may seem immodest, of course, but they simply reflect an open-eyed, resigned acceptance of the fact that his writing was too innovative, too dismissive of accepted values and conventions, to be easily assimilated by a contemporary readership. Hence the dedications of both *The Red and the Black* (1830) and *The Charterhouse of Parma* (1839) to the Happy Few.[3]

Only recently have critics come to consider how much Stendhal cared about his readership. For a long time the prevalent view was of Henri Beyle the egotist,[4] a man so obsessed with himself that he not only wrote diaries, memoirs, and an autobiography but also (allegedly) composed long novels as a form of wish-fulfilment and compensation for his own (principally amorous) disappointments.[5] Such a view has its roots in the biographical approach of the mid-nineteenth century when, following Stendhal's death in 1842 and the publication or republication of many of his works in the mid-1850s by his cousin and literary executor Romain Colomb, obituaries and review articles automatically described the works as reflections of the man. Typical of this tendency was **Sainte-Beuve**, whose review of the newly published *Complete Works* (1854) shows how his personal and political reservations about Henri Beyle as a hedonist, cynic,

1

and agitator lead him to praise Stendhal as a lively critic but to reject him as a bad novelist. In 1869, in case the point had been missed, Sainte-Beuve even went so far as to spread the scurrilous rumour that Stendhal had paid Balzac to write his famous glowing tribute to *The Charterhouse of Parma*.

Between 1888 and 1894, when the writer himself had largely faded from living memory, his more 'personal' works (the diaries, the *Memoirs of an Egotist* (*Souvenirs d'Egotisme*), the *Life of Henry Brulard*) appeared in print for the first time, as did his two unfinished novels *Lucien Leuwen* and *Lamiel*. Together with Colomb's previously published two-volume edition of correspondence (1855), which continued to be supplemented,[6] these 'personal' works gave fresh impetus to the view that Stendhal wrote more to fantasize and speculate about himself than to communicate with others about psychological and political realities: and, despite Marcel Proust's effective critique of biographical criticism in *Against Sainte-Beuve* (posthumously published in 1954), the approach persists even to this day.

But, as I have tried to show in *Stendhal's Violin: A Novelist and his Reader*,[7] Stendhal was acutely conscious of writing to be read (or performed) from the moment when, as an aspirant dramatist in his late teens, he began to attend Parisian theatres, text in hand, in order to note the audience's responses. His celebrated definitions of the novel as a mirror in *The Red and the Black* are disingenuous and question-begging (especially the epigraph to Part I, ch. 13, which is falsely but punningly attributed to the seventeenth-century French historian Saint-Réal); while his keen sense that a novel plays on its reader's reactions is conveyed in his remark that 'a novel is like a bow, the body of the violin *which gives back the sounds* is the reader's soul'.[8]

This quotation comes from the *Life of Henry Brulard*, an autobiography which he knew he would (and could) not publish within his lifetime and in which he comments therefore:

> [. . .] I am writing this, I hope without lying, without deceiving myself, with as much pleasure as if I were writing a letter to a friend. What ideas will this friend have in 1880? How different from our own! [. . .] This is something new for me, to be talking to people about whose turn of mind, education, prejudices and religion one is wholly ignorant! What an encouragement to speak the *truth*, and nothing but the *truth*; that's the only thing that matters.[9]

This shows how attuned Stendhal was to the different factors affecting an individual's interpretation of a given text; for, as he puts it elsewhere: 'that which is felt to be entrancing in Naples will be judged indecent and insane in Copenhagen'.[10] The passage indicates, too, that in the works which he did publish within his lifetime he was knowingly writing against a '**horizon of expectation**'. In the case of *The Red and the Black* and *The*

Charterhouse of Parma this does not mean, though, that Stendhal was ceasing 'to speak the *truth*, and nothing but the *truth*': depiction of 'The truth, the truth in all its harshness'[11] was, with entertainment, one of his principal aims. Yet how was he to convey the 'truth' as he saw it to a reader of late 1830 or of 1839, a French reader in a Catholic country ruled by a reactionary government (despite the so-called Bourgeois Revolution of July 1830) and still in thrall to the safely 'historical' novels of **Sir Walter Scott**? Answer: in the novel, which, like all art in Stendhal's definition, is a 'fine lie'[12]; a fiction that variously challenges and assuages the reader's inevitable prejudices in order to subvert them.

To this end *The Red and the Black* employs shock tactics and *The Charterhouse of Parma* trades on national chauvinism. Both tell tales of ardent young men of imagination and energy who live life and love to the full but come to a grievous end, not least because there seems to be no place in the world for the values which they embody. Imagine a God-fearing, well-to-do French citizen in the 1830s reading about a peasant lad being encouraged above his station, sleeping with the wife of his employer the Mayor, getting a Parisian Marquis's beautiful unmarried daughter pregnant, and returning home to shoot his previous mistress during Mass. The commonest contemporary response to *The Red and the Black* was surely apoplexy – and the real person on whom the story is based was duly executed. But then imagine the same reader faced with the story of a young Italian aristocrat who kills a common man for fear his aristocratic looks may have been disfigured in a brawl and ends up an archbishop in his mid-twenties and the father of a child by a married woman. As both we know and that reader knew, funny things happen abroad.

No writer, therefore, has ever been more aware than Stendhal of the perspective from which his works would be viewed, be it the contemporary perspective of known and manipulable readerly preconceptions, or the future perspective of unpredictable mentalities. Like the *Life of Henry Brulard* (and also the *Memoirs of an Egotist*), Stendhal's two most famous novels are written as 'letters to a friend': texts despatched down the years in the hope that they will reach benevolent readers who will allow their values and desires to mesh sympathetically and creatively with them. As time has passed, the Happy Few have grown rapidly in number, and the tunes played by these reader-violins have been many and various. If the tunes have occasionally suggested a certain warpedness on the part of the violin, that does not take away from the remarkable ability of these two considerable novels to continue to provoke new and interesting readings. As Paul Valéry put it: 'We were never to be able to have done with Stendhal. I can think of no greater praise than that.'[13]

The Red and the Black

Topicality and realism

Stendhal was so concerned about his readers' response that he reviewed *The Red and the Black* himself.[14] Although the Florentine literary review to which he submitted his article (dated 18 October – 3 November 1832) jibbed at printing it, the text survives as testimony to what Stendhal most wanted his readers to cherish in his novel: its topicality. His one previous novel *Armance* (1827) had, at his publisher's behest, been subtitled 'Some Scenes from a Parisian Salon in 1827'; but it gives little insight into the political and social life at the time, concentrating rather on the inner agonies of its hero Octave de Malivert. Now, in his review of *The Red and the Black* (as in its subtitles: 'Chronicle of the Nineteenth Century', 'Chronicle of 1830'), Stendhal stresses this novel's value as an account of contemporary France. The Italian who has read charming eighteenth-century accounts of French life with its sophistication and amiable pleasure-seeking will have no notion how, in post-Revolutionary France, Napoleonic despotism has created a nation in which neighbour spies on neighbour, nor how, since the restoration of the Bourbon monarchy in 1815, the Jesuit order is perpetuating this national network of espionage and corrupt influence. As a result, France has become prudish, cautious, dull: the entertaining world of **Laclos**'s *Dangerous Liaisons* is no more.

So much so that, while the men have abandoned dalliance for more respectable outdoor pursuits, their bored, abandoned wives are left with nothing to do but read novels. Of these there are two kinds, Stendhal informs his Italian reader: 'chambermaid' novels for provincial lower-class women, full of improbable events and absurd heroics (in anticipation of Mills and Boon), or sober narratives for the ladies of Paris who snobbishly disdain even the mildly sensational and have now grown tired even of the 'respectable' excitements provided by the historical novels of Scott and **Manzoni**. 'M. de Stendhal', on the other hand, has 'dared to recount events which took place in 1830.' Moreover he has, for the very first time, depicted Parisian love as it really is: a cerebral 'love-in-the-head' based on vanity, calculation, and self-control. And, most surprising of all, this is not a novel at all: 'Everything he recounts did in fact take place in 1826 near Rennes. [. . .] M. de Stendhal has invented nothing.'[15]

The Red and the Black does indeed offer a comprehensive picture of provincial and metropolitan life in France at this time. Drawing on memories of his own upbringing in the stultifying atmosphere of provincial Grenoble and on the nine years he had just spent immersed in the social, political, and cultural life of the capital, Stendhal offers a harsh indictment of contemporary vanity and hypocrisy. The imaginative energy of Julien Sorel and the unaffected, loving nature of Mme de Rênal stand out against the selfishness, artificiality, and unthinking conventionality of the majority of the other characters. After Italy, which he had first seen with Napoleon's army in 1800 (at the age of seventeen) and where he had lived (in Milan) between 1814 and 1821, Stendhal found France a particularly stuffy place to live. Although he was a participant in the heady 'battle' for Romanticism, which began approximately with the publication of **Lamartine**'s *Méditations* in 1820, continued with Stendhal's own pamphlet *Racine and Shakespeare* (1823, 1825), and culminated in the first night of **Victor Hugo**'s *Hernani* in February 1830, Stendhal's experience of this eventful decade was less one of cultural fervour and innovation than of profound disgust at such a moribund society, desperately afraid of any repeat of 1789 or its bloody aftermath and deeply suspicious of originality and the unconventional.

When the frustrations which he and others felt eventually exploded in the July Revolution, Stendhal was well on the way to finishing *The Red and the Black*, and the Revolution receives no mention in this 'Chronicle of 1830'. Perhaps it was narratively inconvenient that it should; but more likely its author could see that the accession of Louis-Philippe, the Bourgeois King, would change nothing. The dual subtitles of the novel are thus satirically synonymous: France would remain the sclerotic society which it had been since the fall of Napoleon. Julien Sorel, on the other hand, is a representative of its neglected human resources, of the energy and will, as yet unsapped by bourgeois caution, which is still to be found among the peasant class. Like a latter-day Napoleon, but faced with the less glorious armies of snobbery and prejudice, Julien resolves to win fame and fortune: but such is the battlefield upon which he is obliged to fight, both in the provinces and in Paris, that his energy is misdirected into playing society at its own inauthentic games. Like the stream at Verrières upon which his father's sawmill is situated, it has been diverted from its natural course; unlike the stream at Verrières it finally breaks its banks of calculating self-interest in a murderous act of violence which, paradoxically, stands out as the most admirable thing Julien has ever done. A passionate sense of injustice and of honour impugned finds expression in an explosion more authentic than the so-called 'Three Glorious Days' of the July Revolution. And the lady he shoots hastens lovingly to his prison cell when she is sufficiently recovered from her wound.

No wonder, then, that *The Red and the Black* should so have shocked contemporary opinion, and that the *Gazette de France* should have denounced it as a 'shameful production'.[16] The traditional theme of the social climber, or parvenu, making his or her way in the world by charming guile and lucky break had become the exposé of a society in which success at all levels seemingly depends on cold-blooded campaigns of manipulation and exploitation. Worse, the bourgeois goals of wealth, rank, and a 'good' marriage are rejected as sources of happiness in favour of a non-mercenary, adulterous love across class boundaries. No wonder that it took Balzac's breath away: 'the product of a cold and sinister philosophy', he called it, shrewdly observing that (like his own *Physiology of Marriage*) it was 'full of scenes which everyone, from shame, perhaps from self-interest, accuses of being not true to life'.[17]

It is no surprise either that such a novel should have led critics to see Stendhal as a 'father' of Realism. While Ann Jefferson has rightly remarked that he is more like its bachelor uncle,[18] this reputation grew up gradually during the nineteenth century as novelists and theorists looked for famous forebears in their own attempts to represent and analyse reality more closely. **Hippolyte Taine**, rather parochially preferring *The Red and the Black* to *The Charterhouse of Parma* because it is about the French (and because 'the faces of people we know always make for the more intriguing portraits'[19]), describes the psychological portraits of its characters as 'real, because they are complex, many-sided, particular and original, like living human beings'.[20] **Emile Zola** agreed with Taine that Stendhal was principally a 'psychologist',[21] although like Balzac he felt that Stendhal was essentially illustrating a 'theory' rather than proceeding inductively from the facts. Where **Duranty** had rejected Stendhal as a possible ancestor of the Realist school because he was too 'Romantic', Zola counters this view by stressing the way in which Stendhal's writing precisely stands apart from the Romantics and offers a chronological bridge between his own **Naturalism** and the 'psychological realism' of the eighteenth century.

Taken as a whole, however, Zola's comments on *The Red and the Black* display an ambivalent blend of emphatic praise for some passages of psychological accuracy, notably in the depiction of love, and for Stendhal's rejection of convention and rhetorical flourishes, and yet also sheer disdain for various implausibilities and for the transparency of authorial intervention. At the same time he regretted that Stendhal neglected physical description in his novels and that he overlooked both the physiological and the environmental in his analysis of human experience. In other words, he is complaining that Stendhal is not what Zola himself dubbed a 'Naturalist'.

Published two years after Zola's article, **Paul Bourget**'s essay on Stendhal was to set the tone for over half a century. It has often been said by subsequent critics of Stendhal that Bourget's essay proved Stendhal right in his prediction of not being recognized until 1880. This is a distortion.[22] Already in 1854 Sainte-Beuve talks of Stendhal being the object of something like a cult: 'Ten years have scarce elapsed [since Stendhal's death in 1842], and here is a new generation beginning to fall in love with his works, to enquire about him, to study him in every aspect almost like an ancient, almost like a classical writer; it is as if he and his reputation were the subject of a Renaissance. He would have been very surprised.'[23]

Many read Stendhal between 1854 and 1882, and Bourget himself alludes (quite possibly with implicit self-mockery) to a contemporary craze among established writers for quoting half-sentences of *The Red and the Black* at each other to see if the other could remember, for example, the adjectival phrase which followed. Ignorance of a single epithet was an occasion for professional scorn.

If Bourget was not the first to 'recognize' Stendhal, what his essay does do, however, is to redefine Stendhal's 'realism'. He acknowledges the lack of physical description and agrees that Stendhal is above all a psychologist, particularly through the original use of interior monologue. But he challenges the view that the term 'realism' should apply only to what is grotesque and monstrous. Stendhal's main characters are certainly 'superior creatures', possessed, like Stendhal himself, of faculties which raise them above the ordinary. But 'they are not the less real for that':

> Their reality is no more common than the sensibility of their spiritual father itself was. He was right to call them 'my world'. Yes, his world, but also, as we gradually advance, our world. Do not the complex feelings with which Beyle has invested this world created in his own image seem daily less exceptional? If one cares to reflect on the meaning of the term 'superior being', one finds that it embraces one or more advances in our ways of thinking and feeling. Once translated into works of art, these new ways become something for other human beings to imitate.

Bourget is here expanding on Taine, whose essay takes the idea of the 'superior being' as its theme and praises Stendhal's characters for being at once 'real' and exceptional.[24] One notes here also the influence of Bourget's own perspective. Like Zola in his polemical essay *The Experimental Novel*, Bourget sees the novelist as analogous with the scientist, uncovering the truth and presenting discoveries which soon become commonplaces. For Bourget, therefore, Stendhal's realism is more revelatory than reflective; and it reveals not only human nature but also 'several profound truths about nineteenth-century France'.

Bourget's essay ends with lavish praise of *The Red and the Black*, 'this masterpiece'. Its readers should recognize the vigour with which it exposes the inhumanity lurking beneath the smooth surface of 'civilization' and the courage with which the novelist confronts 'the formidable sense of nausea which overtakes the greatest intelligences faced with the vanity of life's efforts'. Thus Bourget turns Stendhal into a master of psychological realism, a profound analyst of France, and a precursor of **Sartre**'s **Roquentin** in his ability to gaze fearlessly into the abyss of the Absurd.

As the topicality of *The Red and the Black* receded into the past, so it became more of a 'historical' novel – just as Stendhal had foreseen in the last sentence of his own review: 'One day, this novel will depict the days of yore like the novels of Walter Scott.' By the time of its centenary **Albert Thibaudet** commented that while it had taken the whole of the nineteenth century to digest *The Red and the Black*, now its 'democratic' thrust (Julien's class-consciousness, his speech to the jury, his desire for a meritocracy) had been blunted by political advance. Similarly, in 1930, acquittal for crimes of passion had become an everyday juridical event: 'today Julien would walk free from the courtroom fined a hundred francs for the unlawful possession of firearms'. For Thibaudet the novel is a cross between **Molière's** *Le Tartuffe* and the Duc de Saint-Simon's memoirs: that is, between a timeless comedy of religious hypocrisy, and the vivid, first-hand account of the politics of a bygone age. Yet, concludes Thibaudet, the novel is still highly relevant: 'Chronicle of 1830. Critique of 1930.'[25]

Thus, by an instructive paradox, the more 'historical' *The Red and the Black* became, the 'truer' it was seen to be. Stendhal's status as a realist was consecrated some fifteen years later in *Mimesis*, Erich Auerbach's monumental study subtitled 'The Representation of Reality in Western Literature' and published in 1946. Consisting of twenty chapters beginning with Homer and ending with Virginia Woolf, the book situates the birth of modern realism in the novels of Balzac and Stendhal. In them, for the first time, the ancients' equation between the social status of the protagonist and a particular stylistic level ('high' tragedy and comedy or 'low' farce and burlesque) was finally broken, and the events and characters of the everyday world could become the subjects of serious, even tragic, art.[26] More particularly, Stendhal was the first to portray a character whose actions were comprehensible only in terms of his historical context:

> Insofar as the serious realism of modern times cannot represent man otherwise than as embedded in a total reality, political, social, and economic, which is concrete and constantly evolving – as is the case today in any novel or film – Stendhal is its founder.[27]

Since Auerbach, Stendhal the Realist has been a familiar figure, and Pierre-Georges Castex's edition of *The Red and the Black* in 1973 epitomizes an essentially **positivist** approach to the novel which seeks to 'explain' it as a mirror of its times. It is but one step beyond this approach to subject the novel's 'political, social, and economic reality' to a political critique; and already in the 1930s the eminent Hungarian Marxist Georg Lukács had begun to do so. For Lukács Stendhal's cult of energy is a nostalgia for the 'heroic' period of bourgeois development which culminated in the Enlightenment and the French Revolution. He concedes that 'as a great realist, he of course sees all the essential phenomena of his time no less clearly than Balzac',[28] but he lacks that 'consciously historical conception of the present [which] is [Balzac's] great achievement'.[29] There is a 'certain abstract psychologism in his important historical portrayals' and, Lukács notes, this is what Paul Bourget praises because Bourget himself is a 'cultivated and intelligent [. . .] reactionary' who was seeking to achieve 'an idealist and reactionary separation of the psychological from the objective determinants of social life, to establish the psychological as a self-contained and independent sphere of human life [. . .] to make the flight from the (abstractly presented) contradictions of contemporary life into religion appear convincing.'[30] While *The Red and the Black* 'exhales a fierce hatred' of the Restoration period, Stendhal interprets the present as a temporary lull in bourgeois glory (whereas for Lukács it marked the beginning of the end of capitalism):

> In Stendhal's view, in pre-revolutionary times there had been a culture and a section of society able to appreciate and judge cultural products. But after the revolution, the aristocracy goes in eternal fear of another 1793 and has hence lost all its capacity for sound judgement. The new rich, on the other hand, are a mob of self-seeking and ignorant upstarts indifferent to cultural values. Not until 1880 did Stendhal expect *bourgeois* society to have reached the stage again permitting a revival of culture – a culture conceived in the spirit of enlightenment, as a continuation of the philosophy of enlightenment.[31]

Bourget's apparent confirmation of Stendhal's prediction that he would be recognized in 1880 is thus argued to be no more than a meeting of reactionary minds.

Plausibility and representation

While *The Red and the Black* was gradually acquiring for its author the reputation of being a realist, the central event in the novel (the shooting of Mme de Rênal) was repeatedly being dismissed as untrue to life – even though it was based on fact! In common with his eighteenth-century predecessors, especially **Diderot**, Stendhal delights in playing with the notion of plausibility in *The Red and the Black*. In the famous passage (in Part II, ch. 19) describing Mathilde's 'mad' love for Julien as she sits up half the night playing the piano, the narrator assures us that as a character she is 'a purely imaginary figure' and moreover 'imagined quite without reference to the social customs which, in the succession of the centuries, will guarantee nineteenth-century civilisation a place of distinction'. Yet the narrator continues by asserting that, since the novel is a mirror, he can but reflect what he sees: if the road is muddy, we should blame neither him nor even the road, but rather the government official who is responsible for the mud. So Mathilde is 'real' after all? 'Now that it is firmly agreed', the narrator continues illogically, 'that Mathilde's character is impossible in our century, which is no less prudent than virtuous, I am less afraid of causing annoyance by continuing to recount the follies of this amiable girl.'

Here Stendhal is simply sending up the pomposity and strait-lacedness of his bourgeois readers by exaggerating their likely reaction and by juxtaposing Mathilde's perfectly plausible 'mad' passion with the quite implausible suggestion that such girls do not exist in 1830. In particular he is putting his readers on their mettle: will they be so conformist as to condemn Mathilde, or will they share the narrator's sympathy? This question poses itself again when Julien comes to shoot Mme de Rênal. In this novel, which devotes so much space to the psychological analysis of its protagonists, explanations of this shooting are glaringly absent. Generally speaking, there have been four principal interpretations of this event: it is implausible and therefore bad novel-writing; Julien is mad; it represents an act of vengeance; it is inexplicable and therefore true to life. While each of these views has had its proponents at various times during the 160-odd years since publication of *The Red and the Black*, it is also broadly true that they have succeeded each other historically. They thus reflect the progression in the novel's reception from incomprehension through admiration for its psychological realism to recognition of Stendhal's 'modern' distrust of coherence and completion and his equally 'modern' doubts about the ability of words to describe things.

The most notorious spokesman for the view that the shooting is implausible was the distinguished academic critic Emile Faguet who, in 1892, declared that 'the dénouement of *The Red and the Black* is very bizarre, and, to tell the truth, rather more contrived than is permissible'. He further observed, with conscious or unconscious humour, that towards the end of the novel 'all the characters lose their heads'. Seeing Julien Sorel merely as a cold-blooded schemer and hypocrite, he found it implausible that Julien should sacrifice all his ambitions in this way. In Faguet's view Stendhal had simply broken off from his own story-line about Julien in order slavishly to copy the real-life shootings of Berthet and Lafargue[32] and had thereby demonstrated his incompetence as a novelist. This view was slightly refined by **Léon Blum**'s argument (in 1914) that it was precisely because the story was true that Stendhal did not bother to make it plausible.[33]

The second theory, that Julien is temporarily insane, has a long history,[34] but its principal spokesman was Henri Martineau who, in 1945, described Stendhal's hero as a psychiatric case, 'a prey to some kind of hypnosis'.[35] In the end, of course, such a view is similar to Faguet's in that the shooting is deemed irrational: it is simply that Faguet blames the inadequacy of the novelist, whereas Martineau blames the state of Julien's mind. Both views were extensively challenged by Pierre-Georges Castex (in 1967 and 1973), for whom the shooting is a lucid act of vengeance.[36] In Castex's argument the vengeance is political in character[37] and stems from thwarted ambition, while many no less eminent critics have seen Julien as avenging a slur on his personal honour.[38] Here, as on many other aspects of the novel, opinion remains divided as to whether contemporary politics or personal values are the novel's principal concern.

The fourth view of the shooting has been that it is inexplicable and therefore true to life. Albert Thibaudet briefly suggested this in 1931, but such an approach was first fully explored in Gérard Genette's essay 'Verisimilitude and Motivation' (1969). For Genette a narrative convinces us of its plausibility in one of three ways: by convention (e.g. cowboy sharp-shooting in Westerns), by generalised reference to supposedly incontrovertible truths about human behaviour, and by being so apparently without motivation that the event in question seems the more true for being beyond the narrator's ability to account for it. For Genette the shooting of Mme de Rênal is the prime example of the latter, which he terms 'arbitrary' narrative.[39]

This approach to the climactic event in the narrative of *The Red and the Black* has acquired new force from the debate concerning 'representation' in realist fiction which has taken place since the 1960s. Where Lukács and later Marxists exposed the naivety of earlier notions of realism by analysing the ideology of nineteenth-century realism – in particular, its often anti-historicist thrust and its status as a bourgeois form of 'production' – more recent theorists, themselves partly guided by this emphasis on realism's lack of ideological 'innocence', have reminded us that the realist novel is not some unproblematic mirror-like reflection of an objective world outside itself but rather a verbal construct producing what Roland Barthes called an 'effect of the real' while subtly engaging with, and then manipulating, the language and received opinions of the reader.[40]

In this debate the many problems and ambiguities involved in what Aristotle and Auerbach confidently called 'mimesis' ('imitation' or 'representation') have been exposed, in particular the fact – as the title of Christopher Prendergast's book *The Order of Mimesis* (1986) indicates and as he himself explains – that 'Mimesis is an order, in the dual sense of a set of arrangements and a set of commands':

> The authoritarian gesture of mimesis is to imprison us in a world which, by virtue of its familiarity, is closed to analysis and criticism, in which the 'prescriptive' and the 'normative' (themselves tacit) ensure that the 'descriptive' remains at the level of the undiscussed, in the taken-for-grantedness of the familiar.[41]

A writer who wishes to 'represent' the world afresh is obliged to use accepted conceptions of reality in order to convince the reader that it is indeed the 'real' world which is being investigated. Yet, if he is in good faith, he will not wish to reinforce these accepted conventions: indeed his primary purpose may well be to modify them, or at least to call them into question. Moreover, he will want to avoid setting up new 'norms' which would simply encourage the reader to settle complacently once more into received patterns of understanding. *The Red and the Black* has proved a fertile source of examples for discussion of this tension at the heart of mimesis, and in the most recent examples of critical perspective collected in the present volume, Christopher Prendergast analyses what he terms the 'ethics of versimilitude', while Ann Jefferson discusses what it means to 'read realism'.

The problem of 'representation' is, at the same time, further complicated by the question of authorial control. To what extent is a novelist the conscious creator of a character or a plot sequence, and to what extent is he driven by unconscious desire during the process of creation? Perhaps, as Peter Brooks suggests, all plots are reflections of a 'masterplot'; and in his essay on *The Red and the Black* included below, he examines its plot in the light of Freudian and Lacanian analyses of desire. And what of the representation of women in supposedly 'realist fiction'? As Naomi Schor has written: 'Realism is that paradoxical moment in Western literature when representation can neither accommodate the Otherness of Woman nor exist without it.'[42] Combining a psychoanalytic approach with her central focus on the role of motherhood and the 'trauma of birth', Carol Mossman's discussion of the 'narrative matrix' in *The Red and the Black* offers new insights into Stendhal's first great novel. Her findings would have greatly surprised Taine and Bourget, but perhaps not Stendhal himself. His mother died in childbirth when he was seven, and he later wrote famously in the third chapter of his *Life of Henry Brulard* of how, when younger, 'I wanted to cover my mother with kisses, and without any clothes on [. . .] I abhorred my father when he came to interrupt our kisses.' How can you have an Oedipus complex when you *know* you hate your father and loved your mother to distraction?

The Charterhouse of Parma

Mirror or myth?

In one of the draft prefaces to *Lucien Leuwen* (1834–5), his unfinished novel about the political world of the 1830s, Stendhal likens his latest work to a mirror liable to be smashed by the sick man who finds in it but a pale and faintly green reflection of himself. For here again the novelist has dared to portray his contemporaries: is it his fault if some of the characters are not of the reader's own political persuasion? Can the writer be held responsible if the reader should dislike what is seen in the mirror? Stendhal's position as French consul in Civitavecchia and the suspension of the freedom of the press (in September 1835) meant that he could not publish *Lucien Leuwen*, even if he could have found a way to end it satisfactorily: the content was simply too explosive.

Such provocative topicality was then abandoned in *The Charterhouse of Parma*, his last completed novel, which was composed (by dictation) with astonishing speed between 4 November and 26 December 1838 and published in April 1839. Based on a malicious early-seventeenth-century manuscript account of the life of Alessandro Farnese (later Pope Paul III), it is nevertheless set in the early nineteenth century. Consequently the curious blend of Renaissance skulduggery, post-Napoleonic reaction, and revolutionary politics (represented by Ferrante Palla) has disconcerted critical efforts to situate this novel within the context of orthodox nineteenth-century realism. The acuity of psychological and political insight and the dark shadows of personal tragedy and a broader pessimism are offset by strong elements of epic, romance, and fairy-tale. Is this a quasi-historical novel, or a veiled account of the present day, or the charming, timeless myth of a lovers' triangle?

Initial reaction to the novel was muted, so that Balzac's extraordinarily generous and detailed eulogy in the *Revue parisienne* on 25 September 1840 does the author of the *Human Comedy* all the more credit.[43] And indeed there remained many after Balzac who were only too ready to damn Stendhal's Italian masterpiece. Sainte-Beuve, for example, quite liked the opening pages but found the rest of the book a thoroughly implausible masquerade and professed himself impatient to move on to something simpler and more wholesome 'in which aunties are not in love with their nephews'.[44] Henry James, writing in 1874, was exceptional in echoing Balzac's marked preference for *The Charterhouse of Parma* over *The Red and the Black*. Somewhat tendentiously describing *The Charterhouse* as being 'now recognised as Beyle's chief title to the attention of posterity', he has no hesitation in considering it 'a novel which will always be numbered among the dozen finest novels we possess'. Although James summarizes the work, with customary high-mindedness, as one in which 'everyone is grossly immoral, and the heroine is a kind of monster', his praise derives from his perception of 'the restlessness of a superior mind' which makes his 'total feeling for Beyle a kindly one': 'We recommend his books to persons of "sensibility" whose moral convictions have somewhat solidified.'[45]

But among its other readers in the second half of the nineteenth century Faguet, for example, thought half of the novel unreadable and considered the principal defect of the whole to be the 'extreme insignificance of the central protagonist'.[46] Zola allowed that it was the only French novel to date which portrayed another nationality convincingly, and indeed that it anticipated Naturalist theories in its depiction of the influence of this Italian milieu on the characters' behaviour.[47] However, he felt that Stendhal was no longer the great psychologist of *The Red and the Black* but simply a 'story-teller', the author of a 'novel of adventure' rather than a 'work of analysis'.[48] Even Stendhal's principal nineteenth-century admirers, Taine and Bourget, tended to comment more on *The Red and the Black*: Taine ostensibly because he felt Balzac had already 'revealed' the later novel to the general public (but also, as already mentioned, from a certain parochialism),[49] and Bourget because *The Red and the Black* better reflected what he perceived to be Stendhal's strengths as a novelist.

Balzac and James apart, therefore, it is really only in this century that *The Charterhouse of Parma* has come to achieve its present status as an undisputed masterpiece, beginning perhaps in April 1913 with **André Gide** who ranked it as the greatest French novel and, in Jamesian vein, as one of only two French novels (the other being Laclos's *Dangerous Liaisons*) which he would include in any list of the world's 'top ten'.[50] Often, as in Gide's case, this admiration has been expressed in hyperbolic terms and accompanied by professions of an inability to state quite why or how the novel has become the object of the critic's admiration. Stendhal himself observed that the Italians seemed to talk only in exclamations, and so it is perhaps appropriate that Thibaudet's account (1931) comprises a series of paragraphs which begin 'And the pleasure! [. . .] The music! [. . .] The intelligence!' But these paragraphs lack the cogency of his pages on *The Red and the Black*. Twenty years after Thibaudet, Jean Prévost writes of the novel's 'rapidity of perfection which is one of the miracles of the literary craft',[51] and he is echoed by two of Stendhal's leading post-war critics: Maurice Bardèche, who professes himself 'inclined to believe in this "miraculous" explanation'[52]; and F.W.J. Hemmings, who argues that 'for once it seems proper to apply the over-used word "miraculous" to this extraordinary eruption of a dense, intricate, dazzlingly poetic masterpiece'.[53] Hemmings, like Bardèche before him and Victor Brombert later, indulges in extended flights of metaphor in order to convey this poetic quality which allegedly defeats conventional critical discourse.[54] Michael Wood spoke for many when he asked 'which other great novel leaves so much work for the critic to do while yet seeming entirely to dispense with his services?'[55]

Balzac, however, was in no doubt where the novel's virtues lay. Already he had stopped Stendhal in the street (appropriately, on the Boulevard des Italiens!) to compliment him on his work,[56] and in his article of 1840 he states: 'M. Beyle [. . .] has written *The Modern Prince*, the novel which Machiavelli would write if he were alive today and living in exile from Italy.' Balzac, too, finds Stendhal's genius extraordinary, imagining him to have rubbed some literary Aladdin's lamp in order to summon forth this vivid, complex tableau of the court of Parma. But as Balzac retells the novel's plot in considerable detail (a procedure then customary in review articles), it becomes clear just how subtle and closely based on first-hand diplomatic experience he believes Stendhal's novel to be. Mosca is a masterly transposed portrait of the Austrian chancellor Metternich, while Parma is the very model of a contemporary northern Italian principality. The Balzac who himself had described the inner workings of French life is fulsome in his appreciation of Stendhal's insights: 'Never before have the hearts of princes, ministers, courtiers, and women been depicted like this.' Stendhal's tableau has the dimensions of a fresco but the precision of the Dutch masters; and the power-struggle between Gina and Ranuce-Ernest IV is described as 'the most thorough, most gripping, most extraordinary, and most accurate drama ever invented (and the most profoundly observant of the human heart), and yet one which has certainly taken place at many points in history, and which will be played out again at the courts of the future, just as Louis XIII and Richelieu, François II and M. de Metternich, Louis XV, la Dubarry and M. de Choiseul have all enacted it already'. Mosca's wisdom makes the book as profound as the maxims of La Rochefoucauld; the structure of the novel is carefully sown together; in short:

> This great work could not have been conceived or carried out by anyone but a man of fifty in all the vigour of his years and in the maturity of all his talents. One sees perfection in everything.

Although Balzac pointed out how Stendhal might have improved on this 'perfection' (by omitting the pages before Waterloo, removing Blanès, and stopping the novel after the return to Parma of Mosca and Gina!) and proceeded even to castigate him for his poor grammar,[57] Stendhal professed himself surprised and delighted at such praise from the foremost novelist of his day.[58] Indeed he claims to have dutifully compressed the first fifty-four pages into four or five. But he rejects the attack on his style, scorning 'fine writing' and preferring clarity and simplicity above flowery periods. He dictated the novel in order to capture the spontaneity of his narrative and to be 'natural' (a practice he disowns in the second and third drafts of his letter). In order to achieve sobriety of tone, he claims to have read passages from the Code civil (Napoleon's three-volume codification of civil law which came into force in 1804). He remembers Metternich from his own younger days at Saint-Cloud working for Napoleon's administration, but such models will be long forgotten by 1880 which is when, Stendhal here repeatedly notes, he will finally be read by those who lack the percipience of Balzac.

While the main tenor of Stendhal's reply is the tactful assertion of his own stylistic originality and 'clarity', he accepts Balzac's compliments about his political analysis (even if he minimizes the importance of contemporary models). In particular he accepts Balzac's perceptive realization that the novel 'could not attack a great state, like France, Spain,

Vienna, because of the details of their administration. Which left the petty princes of Germany and Italy.' And German courtiers, he says, were too abject for his purposes: hence Italy. This suggests, therefore, that Stendhal used the story of Alessandro Farnese as the basis for an indictment of political behaviour at the highest level in the major countries of contemporary Europe. As Harry Levin has acutely observed: '[*The Charterhouse of Parma* . . .] is perhaps the most civilised novel ever written. It was written by a diplomat escaping from his post, whereas [*The Red and the Black*] was written by a dilettante excluded from office.'[59] *The Charterhouse of Parma* is thus as much of a mirror as *Lucien Leuwen* (and *The Red and the Black*), but the sick men of Europe would not recognise themselves so quickly in its distorting glass.

However, whereas *The Red and the Black* came with time to be seen more and more as an accurate record of its day, *The Charterhouse of Parma* has gradually lost some of this contemporary political relevance in the eyes of its readers.[60] Instead attention has focused increasingly on its mythical quality. The idyllic nature of the settings (not least the Farnese Tower!), the exceptional qualities of the central characters (and the almost caricatural defects of their opponents), the uncomplicated forthrightness of their actions (enhanced by the comparative absence of interior monologue and narratorial analysis), the 'magical' accoutrements of omen and astrological prediction, all these aspects of the novel have long contributed to that overriding sense of unselfconscious ease and joy which, for many readers, is the main source of the novel's delights.

However, in the last thirty years, attempts have been made to analyse this 'mythical' quality more precisely. Thus in 1961 Gilbert Durand demonstrated just how many traces of ancient myth are to be found in the novel's plot, suggesting from a **Jungian** perspective that these elements form part of the collective unconscious and write themselves into the novel unbeknownst to the novelist.[61] More recently, Michaël Nehrlich has interpreted the novel as a rewriting of the myth of Eros and Psyche.[62] At the same time critics have concentrated on the ways in which Stendhal has created his own myth of Italy, a marvellous domain exhibiting all the values which he felt France so blatantly to lack (naturalness and spontaneity, passion, courage, energy, creativity, etc.), at once a political statement and an imaginary refuge. Already in 1874 Henry James believed that 'One may say roughly that [Stendhal's] subject is always Italy': 'He had a number of affectations, but his passion for Italy is evidently profoundly sincere, and will serve to keep his memory sweet to many minds and his authority unquestioned.'[63] More recently, and less sweepingly, Michel Crouzet has argued that there is 'an Italian "myth" in Stendhal, a collection of *desires* of which Italy is at once the mirror and the means of expression':

With Stendhal, more than with any one else, the foreign country becomes Me, my world, my private place, my domain, not only somewhere traversed and described but a resting-place, an all-embracing resting-place espoused like some symbolic counterpart of the self, somewhere specially chosen and of which one's moral being becomes a naturalized citizen. It is a case of make-or-break for [Stendhal] the 'Italianist', so strongly does he feel that what lies beyond those mountains is another world, the other world of the self, the world that is most truly one's self.

For Crouzet this 'other world' finds its fullest expression in *The Charterhouse of Parma*: it offers 'a kind of quintessence of Italianness'.[64]

Psychoanalysis and story-telling

The air of improvisation in *The Charterhouse of Parma* and the novel's affiliation to ancient traditions of epic and romance, of fairy-tale and oral narrative, have also led its readers to consider the work in psychoanalytic terms. Already we have seen Gilbert Durand relate its plot to archetypal situations existing in a Jungian collective unconscious. Others, more explicitly than Michel Crouzet, have approached the work in terms of Stendhal's own unconscious. His determination to compose quickly, to speak 'naturally', and not to correct his first formulations have suggested obvious parallels with Freudian attempts to gain access to the unconscious through the free association of words. Robert André has analysed the novel in the light of the psychoanalytic theories not only of **Freud** but of **Melanie Klein**, and – in a new version of the century-old tradition of interpreting the works in terms of the man – argued that 'perhaps no other work of fiction has ever been so directly based on its author's own experiences, and down to the very smallest details'.[65] Similarly, the traditional view of Stendhal's novels as forms of wish-fulfilment is given a Freudian slant in Micheline Levowitz-Treu's contention that the end of *The Charterhouse of Parma* obliges us to welcome its leading characters into our own dream-world with the result that 'Stendhal obtains by transference the seal of amnesty, of justification, and the marks of affection which he was seeking after; at the same time he takes his revenge on the uncomprehending gawpers who refused to take him seriously'.[66]

Of particular interest in this area is Roland Barthes's account of the novel: 'Stendhal's Italy is a phantasm, even if he did in part realize it.' Given the importance of the mother in Barthes's own (later) work, it is easy to hear a personal emphasis in his description of Italy as Stendhal's 'motherland' (as opposed to France the 'fatherland' which Henri Beyle forever associated with his own abhorred father). And Stendhal's relationship to this 'motherland' is like that of a lover: besotted and

The Red and the Black *and* The Charterhouse of Parma

tongue-tied, until in the opening pages of *The Charterhouse of Parma* he is released from blockage by the liberating force of narrative: 'that great mediating form which is Narrative, or better still Myth.'[67] The autobiographical *Life of Henry Brulard* ends, unfinished, with the seventeen-year-old Beyle about to discover Italy in the service of the Napoleonic Army, and ends because the 'subject [in the sense of 'topic'] exceeds the saying of it'. Now, at the beginning of *The Charterhouse of Parma*, the 'subject' has been transposed into fiction, and the conquest of Italy can begin. And the celebrations recorded in those pages, as Milan is released from the grip of Austrian repression, are mirrored in the festival that is Stendhal's final masterpiece.

As with psychoanalytic readings of *The Red and the Black*, one sees how the old biographical approach has been reinvigorated by modern theory, and Barthes's emphasis on the maternal anticipates Carol Mossman's consideration of a narrative 'matrix' in *The Red and the Black*.[68] At the same time Barthes's view of narrative as a liberation relates to other responses to the improvised art of *The Charterhouse of Parma*. C.W. Thompson, for example, has taken the central theme of play and focused on the tensions exhibited at several levels of the novel (plot structure, characterization, verbal style) between order and freedom, between aesthetic imperatives and the ambition for originality and spontaneity of expression.[69]

Language itself and the art of story-telling have been analysed from several points of view. Shoshana Felman has examined the play of shifting semantics (of words like 'madness' and 'intoxication') in both *The Red and the Black* and *The Charterhouse of Parma*[70]; while a number of critics have discussed the ways in which linguistic activity is depicted within the novel itself.[71] Relating the procedures of story-telling to the central depiction of political intrigue, Ann Jefferson in effect deconstructs the novel when she shows how it lays claim to truthfulness by 'reluctantly' including reference to politics (the famous 'pistol shot in the middle of a concert') but then, by demonstrating how political power depends on the use and abuse of story-telling, calls into question this very truthfulness. Once more we are back with the question of representation:

> In representing politics in his text, Stendhal politicises representation by showing that it is liable either to have political motives, or else to have political repercussions in the constructions that may subsequently be put on it. The faithful historian of *Armance* and the mirror tucked into the author's saddle-bag in [*The Red and the Black*] cannot record political reality with impunity, since the object reflected in the mirror will reveal that mirrors are always political – which is to say that they are always implicated in the circumstances which are contained in their own reflections. In the end, therefore, the achievement of this political novel is to show that when politics invade

the mirror which supposedly reflects them, the mirror itself is liable to become entangled in the political contents of its own reflections.[72]

Thus, as with *The Red and the Black*, psychoanalysis and the political and ethical nature of 'representation' (and the reading of representation) are today the principal contexts in which Stendhal's final masterpiece is being most innovatively explored. Yet to come are feminist or gender-oriented readings of a novel which the Foreword itself describes as the 'story of the Duchess Sanseverina'. It cannot be long before someone seeks to challenge the gushing, masculinist assertion of Irving Howe that Gina Sanseverina is 'that superb woman for whom literary critics have been ready to sacrifice everything'.[73]

Perspectives

To trace the reception of two such novels over a period of approximately 160 years is to be reminded of how deeply any given critical approach is rooted in the mental outlook of its age. Sainte-Beuve's Second Empire conservatism is followed by Bourget's 'fin de siècle' pessimism, which in turn is replaced by socialist Léon Blum's anxious search for fellow 'beylistes' on the eve of the First World War.[74] Auerbach's *Mimesis* was written in Istanbul by a Jew who had fled from Nazi Germany, and its story of the gradual accession of the lower social orders to the status of worthy literary subject-matter displays a moving faith in the progress and dignity of humankind, the faith with which its author sought to lighten the darkness of the Holocaust.

In the latter part of this century psychoanalytic and feminist readings continue to reflect widespread preoccupation with the nature of the human subject while seeking to counteract the age-old marginalization both of the unconscious and of female experience. Recent interest in the role of the reader, in **dialogism** and **intertextuality**, and in the potentially repressive nature of literary representation is based on critical thinking which dates back many decades, not least to men like Lukács and **Bakhtin** who were writing in the shadow of Stalinist totalitarianism. But such interest may also reflect a culture overwhelmed by the communications revolution, assailed by voices and images on every side and pressed ever more insidiously into acceptance of received opinion. The need for independent critical thinking has lost none of its urgency, and the diversity and sophistication of contemporary literary theory is testimony to the vigour with which readers and listeners are examining the communications of other readers and listeners in the light of their own values, beliefs, and judgements. The series to which the present volume belongs might also be said to reflect that vigour.

19

One can discern a kind of progress in the critical reception of Stendhal, for there has been a marked advance in subtlety of approach since 1830 and 1839. But one would be wrong to see this as a movement towards any final word. As Peter Brooks has discussed in *Reading for the Plot* (following on from Freud's *Beyond the Pleasure Principle*), to desire an ending is to desire the end of desire, to desire death – in the case of these novels, the death of their readability. It is a commonplace to say that the status of a 'classic' is confirmed with every generation that finds within it a reflection of its own fresh concerns. With Stendhal, however, and with his two most frequently read novels, one is left with the particularly strong sense that they will not quickly lose their capacity to be illuminated, as if for the first time, by future generations and by future avenues of original critical enquiry. The year 2000 is much too modest an estimate of the time it may yet take to exhaust their riches. As Jean-Pierre Richard, one of Stendhal's most attentive readers, has confessed: 'To talk about Stendhal is to condemn oneself every time to the impression that you have said absolutely nothing, that he has eluded you and that everything remains to be said.'[75] One should be thankful that it does.

Notes

1. *Œuvres intimes*, ed. V. del Litto (2 vols, Paris: Gallimard, 1981–2), i. 167.

2. In a letter of 26 Dec. 1828. He repeats the analogy elsewhere (*Œuvres intimes*, ii. 474, 745).

3. The phrase derives not from *Henry V* (IV, iii: 'we few, we happy few, we band of brothers') but from OLIVER GOLDSMITH's *The Vicar of Wakefield*, ch. 2: 'I published some tracts [. . .], which, as they never sold, I have the consolation of thinking were read only by the happy *few*.'

4. HENRI BEYLE first adopted the pseudonym Stendhal for his third published work, *Rome, Naples, and Florence in 1817*, in which it serves the fiction of a German cavalry officer, M. de Stendhal, visiting Italy and composing a guide-book on the basis of his travels. 'Stendhal' is an erudite joke since Stendal was the birthplace of another more famous traveller to Italy, Johann Joachim Winckelmann (1717–68), the centenary of whose birth was being celebrated that year in recognition of his great contribution to aesthetics and the study of ancient monuments.

5. Terms such as 'sublimation', 'compensation', 'imaginary revenge', 'imaginary victory', and even 'self-inflicted punishment' recur regularly in all the 'classic' readings of Stendhal: e.g. HENRI MARTINEAU, *Le Coeur de Stendhal* (2 vols, Paris: Albin Michel, 1952–3), i. 416; JEAN PRÉVOST, *La Création chez Stendhal. Essai sur le métier d'écrire et la psychologie de l'écrivain* (Paris: Mercure de France, 1951), p. 306; VICTOR BROMBERT, *Stendhal et la voie oblique. L'auteur devant son monde romanesque* (New Haven and Paris: Presses Universitaires de France, 1954), pp. 118 ff.; JEAN-PIERRE RICHARD, 'Connaissance et tendresse chez Stendhal', in *Littérature et sensation* (Paris: Editions du Seuil, 1954), p. 105; and JEAN

STAROBINSKI, 'Stendhal pseudonyme', in *L'Œil vivant* (Paris: Gallimard, 1961), pp. 201, 212. GEORGES BLIN, in his *Stendhal et les problèmes du roman* (Paris: José Corti, 1954) and *Stendhal et les problèmes de la personnalité* (Paris: José Corti, 1958), argues that Stendhal not only found solutions to the problems of his personality by imaginatively recreating himself in his characters but also demonstrated, by his authorial intrusions, his superiority over these very characters.

6. COLOMB's edition contained (in heavily bowdlerized form) 272 letters. Ninety-five of Stendhal's letters to his sister Pauline were published in 1892, followed the next year by a further 96 to a variety of correspondents. In ADOLPHE PAUPE's three-volume edition (1908), the total number of letters had grown to 703: in HENRI MARTINEAU's (1933–4), to 1590; in the collaborative edition of HENRI MARTINEAU and VICTOR DEL LITTO (1968), to 1852. The latter has yet to be superseded.

7. Oxford: Clarendon Press, 1988.

8. My translation. See *The Life of Henry Brulard*, trans. Jean Stewart and B.C.J.G. Knight (Harmondsworth: Penguin Books, 1973), p. 163, or *Œuvres intimes*, ii. 699.

9. *The Life of Henry Brulard*, trans. Stewart and Knight, pp. 25–6 (cf. *Œuvres intimes*, ii. 536–7).

10. *Lives of Haydn, Mozart and Metastasio*, trans. and ed. Richard N. Coe (London: Calder and Boyars, 1972), p. 133.

11. *The Red and the Black*, p. 3 (epigraph to Part I, ch. 1).

12. See entry for 1 Feb. 1829 in *Promenades dans Rome*, in *Voyages en Italie*, ed. V. del Litto (Paris: Gallimard, 1973), p. 1136.

13. Last sentence of his essay 'Stendhal' (1927) in PAUL VALÉRY, *Œuvres* (2 vols, Paris: Gallimard, 1957–60), i. 553–82.

14. Extracts are reproduced below, pp. 31–2.

15. See below, p. 32. In fact, of course, *The Red and the Black* is principally based on the story of Antoine Berthet, who attempted unsuccessfully to murder his previous employer's wife, Mme Michoud, in Brangues during Mass on 22 July 1827: he was executed on 23 Feb. 1828. Mme Michoud initially survived (after the removal of two bullets) and on 11 July 1828 gave birth to her eighth child (Léon-Machabée), who himself lived only a day. She died three years later (on 8 Oct. 1831), possibly because a piece of her silk dress had remained lodged in her lungs and made her consumptive. (See René Fonvieille, *Le véritable Julien Sorel* (Paris and Grenoble: Arthaud, 1971), pp. 259–61.)

16. The novel was widely reviewed in the best Parisian newspapers and journals. JULES JANIN, writing in the conservative *Journal des Débats* (26 Dec. 1830), was unusual in commending it as 'worth reading' and 'worthy of further study', but even he 'detested' Julien and considered the novel a 'seriously improbable' portrait of contemporary society.

17. See below, p. 29.

18. *Reading Realism in Stendhal* (Cambridge: Cambridge University Press, 1988), p. 3.

19. From 'Stendhal (Henri Beyle)' (*Nouvelle Revue française*, 1864), extracts from which are reproduced below, pp. 37–40.

20. See below, p. 38.

21. In his 'Stendhal' (*European Herald*, 1880), extracts from which are reproduced below, pp. 41–4.

22. This point has been made by EMILE TALBOT in the introduction to his edition of critical articles on Stendhal, *La Critique stendhalienne de Balzac à Zola* (York, South Carolina: French Literature Publications Company, 1979). His volume has been of great assistance in the compilation of Part One of the present edition.

23. From the opening paragraph of 'M. de Stendhal. His Complete Works', *Le Moniteur*, 2 and 9 Jan. 1854. Cf. below, p. 36. Sainte-Beuve is referring particularly to the enthusiasm generated at the Ecole Normale Supérieure by Paul Jacquinet, who taught French language and literature there between 1842 and 1867 and whose pupils included Taine himself. According to Emile Faguet (whose own comments are reproduced below, pp. 50–4), Jacquinet stressed the precision of Stendhal's psychological analyses and argued that the Stendhalian novel was as much heir to the tragedies of Racine as to the psychological accuracy of MME DE LA FAYETTE's *La Princesse de Clèves* (1678). See JEAN MÉLIA, *Stendhal et ses commentateurs* (Paris: Mercure de France, 1911), p. 238.

24. See below, pp. 38–9.

25. ALBERT THIBAUDET, *Stendhal* (Paris: Hachette, 1931), pp. 127–34.

26. See *Mimesis*, trans. Willard R. Trask (Princeton, N.J.: Princeton University Press, 1953), p. 491, and Lilian R. Furst (ed.), *Realism* (London and New York: Longman, 1992), pp. 5–6.

27. *Mimesis*, p. 463. See below, p. 68.

28. GEORG LUKÁCS, *Studies in European Realism*, trans. Edith Bone (London: Hillway, 1950; repr. The Merlin Press, 1972), p. 80.

29. GEORG LUKÁCS, *The Historical Novel*, trans. Hannah and Stanley Mitchell (Harmondsworth: Penguin Books, 1969), p. 92.

30. *The Historical Novel*, pp. 92, 288.

31. *Studies in European Realism*, pp. 79, 78.

32. The latter being a young cabinet-maker in the Pyrenees so disillusioned by his fiancée's bad character and behaviour that he shot her dead on 21 Jan. 1829 – and was sentenced to a mere five years' imprisonment for 'unpremeditated murder under extreme provocation.'

33. This view has had influential adherents, including Jean Prévost (1942), Michel Crouzet (1964), and Peter Brooks (1984: see below, pp. 171–2).

34. For further details on these four interpretations of the shooting, see my *Stendhal's Violin*, pp. 135–42.

35. See Martineau's edition (Paris: Garnier frères, 1945), p. xxv. With varying emphases, this view has also had some influential adherents, including Jean-Pierre Richard (1954) and Shoshana Felman (1971).

36. '*Le Rouge et le Noir*' de Stendhal (Paris: Cedes, 1967), pp. 133–4, *Le Rouge et le Noir*, ed. Pierre-Georges Castex (Paris: Garnier frères, 1973), pp. liv-lvii.

37. A view shared, from a Marxist perspective, by the poet Louis Aragon in *La Lumière de Stendhal* (1954).

38. E.g. Harry Levin (1963), F.W.J. Hemmings (1964), Michel Crouzet (1964), and Geneviève Mouillaud (1973).

39. This approach has found greatest favour with English critics: e.g. Michael Wood (1971), John Mitchell (1973), Geoffrey Strickland (1974), and Ann Jefferson (1983: see below, p. 212).

40. See Furst (ed.), *Realism*, pp. 10 and 135–41 for comment and Barthes's text in translation.

41. CHRISTOPHER PRENDERGAST, *The Order of Mimesis. Balzac, Stendhal, Nerval, Flaubert* (Cambridge: Cambridge University Press, 1986), pp. 5, 6.

42. *Breaking The Chain. Women, Theory, and French Realist Fiction* (New York: Columbia University Press, 1985), p. xi. Cf. DOROTHY KELLY, *Fictional Genders. Role and Representation in Nineteenth-Century Narrative* (Lincoln and London: University of Nebraska Press, 1989), p. ix: 'There seems to be an essential incompatibility between realism and the feminine'.

43. See below, pp. 33–5.

44. 'M. de Stendhal'.

45. 'Henri Beyle', in *The Nation* (17 Sept. 1874), reproduced in his *Literary Reviews and Essays*, ed. Albert Mordell (New York: Grove Press, 1957), pp. 151–7. Towards the end of this essay James describes *The Red and the Black* as coming nearest, of all Stendhal's works, to being 'absolutely unreadable' and sees in it 'an air of unredeemed corruption – a quality which in the novel amounts to a positive blight and dreariness.'

46. See below, p. 52.

47. Zola here echoes the introduction to TAINE's *History of English Literature* (1863) in which Taine champions Stendhal as the first writer to bring 'scientific procedures' to bear in the analysis of the human heart, and as the first to identify its 'fundamental causal features [. . .] nationality, climate, temperament': 'in short [. . .] he dealt with feelings the way one ought to deal with feelings, that is to say as a naturalist and a physicist, by classifying them and measuring lines of force'.

48. ZOLA, 'Stendhal'.

49. Although, in 1883, Taine professed (in a letter to Bourget) to find *The Charterhouse of Parma* still 'stupefying' and 'enchanting' even though he had now read it 'forty or fifty times'. See Talbot (ed.), p. 210.

50. 'Les dix romans français . . .', in *Œuvres complètes*, ed. L. Martin-Chauffier, Nouvelle Revue Française (15 vols, n.p., n.d.), vii. 449–58. At the beginning of this essay, however, Gide claims to have hesitated for a long time before preferring *The Charterhouse of Parma* to *The Red and the Black*: 'But no: *The Charterhouse* is still the unique book; despite the fact that *The Red and the Black* is more surprising on first reading, *The Charterhouse* is truly magical for this reason: each time one goes back to it, it is always like reading a totally new book [. . .] What grace in its detail! What elegance in its purity of outline! How rarely it labours the point! [. . .] the entire book is written *for pleasure.*' Previously, on 19 Apr. 1897, Paul Valéry had written to Gide describing *The Charterhouse of Parma* as the 'complete book' and as 'deserving of all the praise which [Stendhal] heaped on *Don Quixote*, which, like everything that has dated, leaves me cold'.

51. *La Création chez Stendhal. Essai sur le métier d'écrire et la psychologie de l'écrivain* (Paris: Mercure de France, 1951), p. 432.

52. *Stendhal romancier* (Paris: Editions de la Table Ronde, 1947), p. 418, and cf. p. 401. JEAN PRÉVOST's book, published in 1951, had been a doctoral thesis submitted at the University of Lyon in 1942 and then published in Marseille in the same year. Copies of this had circulated in limited numbers during and immediately after the War.

53. *Stendhal. A Study of his Novels* (Oxford: Clarendon Press, 1964), p. 176.

54. HEMMINGS, *Stendhal*, pp. 200–1; BARDÈCHE, *Stendhal romancier*, p. 365; and VICTOR BROMBERT, *Stendhal. Fiction and the Themes of Freedom* (Chicago and London: University of Chicago Press, 1968), pp. 149–50 (see below, p. 95).

55. '*La Chartreuse de Parme* et le sphinx', *Stendhal Club*, 20 (1977/8), 161–9 (p. 161).

56. As Balzac recalls in his 1840 article (see Talbot (ed.), p. 67). He had also written to Stendhal on two occasions: once (at the end of March 1839 after reading an extracted version of the Waterloo episode in *Le Constitutionnel*) to confess to the sin of envy, and again on 5 April (having read the complimentary copy which Stendhal had sent him) to express – 'without envy, because I would simply be incapable of writing like that' – his conviction that '*The Charterhouse of Parma* is a great and fine book': 'You know what I said about *The Red and the Black*. Well, this time everything is new and original! My praise is unqualified, and sincere.'

57. See below, p. 34.

58. Three drafts of Stendhal's reply to Balzac have survived (dated 16 Oct., 17–28 Oct., and 28–29 Oct. 1840), but it is not known if he ever finally sent a fair copy.

59. HARRY LEVIN, *The Gates of Horn* (New York: Oxford University Press, 1963), p. 131.

60. Notable exceptions are RICHARD N. COE, '*La Chartreuse de Parme*. Portrait d'une réaction', in *Omaggio a Stendhal, II*, Atti del 6° Congresso Internazionale Stendhaliano (Parma: Aurea Parma, 1967), pp. 43–61 (p. 44: 'one of the most profound political novels of all time'); HENRI-FRANÇOIS IMBERT, *Les Métamorphoses de la liberté, ou Stendhal devant la Restauration et le Risorgimento* (Paris: José Corti, 1967); MICHEL GUÉRIN, *La Politique de Stendhal* (Paris: Presses Universitaires de France, 1982); and ALISON FINCH, *Stendhal: 'La Chartreuse de Parme'* (London: Edward Arnold, 1984).

61. *Le Décor mythique de la 'Chartreuse de Parme'. Contribution à l'esthétique du romanesque* (Paris: José Corti, 1961).

62. '*La Chartreuse* est-elle *Le Prince moderne*? Sur l'unité retrouvée du texte stendhalien', in Philippe Berthier (ed.), *Stendhal: l'écrivain, la société, le pouvoir. Colloque du Bicentenaire (Grenoble, 24–27 janvier 1983)* (Grenoble: Presses Universitaires de Grenoble, 1984), pp. 311–27.

63. *Literary Reviews and Essays*, p. 155.

64. *Stendhal et l'italianité. Essai de mythologie romantique* (Paris: Corti, 1982), pp. 2, 9, 287.

65. *Ecriture et pulsions dans le roman stendhalien* (Paris: Editions Klincksieck, 1977), p. 10.

66. *L'Amour et la mort chez Stendhal. Métamorphoses d'un apprentissage affectif* (Aran, Switzerland: Editions du Grand-Chêne, 1978), pp. 185–6.

67. See below, p. 155.

68. See below, pp. 183–98.

69. In his *Le Jeu de l'ordre et de la liberté dans 'La Chartreuse de Parme'* (Aran, Switzerland: Editions du Grand-Chêne, 1982).

70. See below, pp. 129–37.

71. E.g. VIVIAN KOGAN, 'Signs and Signals in *La Chartreuse de Parme*', *Nineteenth-Century French Studies*, 2 (1973/4), 29–38; WILLIAM J. BERG, 'Cryptographie et communication dans *La Chartreuse de Parme*', *Stendhal Club*, 20 (1977/8), 170–82; PETER BROOKS, 'L'invention de l'écriture (et du langage) dans *La Chartreuse de Parme*', *Stendhal Club*, 20 (1977/8), 183–90; and LOIS ANN RUSSELL, 'Les jeux de l'écriture dans *La Chartreuse de Parme*', *Stendhal Club*, 25 (1982/3), 67–77.

72. *Reading Realism in Stendhal*, pp. 179–80.

73. 'Stendhal: The Politics of Survival', in Irving Howe, *Politics and the Novel* (New York: Horizon Press, 1957), pp. 25–50; reproduced in *Stendhal. A Collection of Critical Essays*, ed. Victor Brombert (Englewood Cliffs, N.J.: Prentice-Hall, 1962), pp. 76–94 (p. 90).

74. In the final pages of his *Stendhal et le beylisme* (1914).

75. 'Connaissance et tendresse chez Stendhal', p. 116.

Part One

Nineteenth-Century Views

1 **1831**: Balzac's response to *The Red and the Black**

[. . .] No doubt you have read the *Confession* [by **Jules Janin**]? The idea
behind the book is bold, but it wants for audacity in the execution. **Charles
Nodier** has published his *History of the King of Bohemia*, a delicious literary joke,
full of mockery and disdain: it is the satire of a blasé old man who perceives, at
the end of his days, the awful void at the heart of all intellectual activity and
all literatures. This book belongs to the *School of Disenchantment* [. . .] This
year which began with the publication of the *Physiology of Marriage* [by
Balzac himself] – which you will allow me to say little about – has ended
with *The Red and the Black*, the product of a cold and sinister philosophy: it is
full of scenes which everyone, from shame, perhaps from self-interest,
accuses of being not true to life. These four literary productions contain the
spirit of our age; they reek of the corpse that is our moribund society.

The anonymous author of the *Physiology of Marriage* delights in
dispelling our illusions about conjugal bliss as the principal boon of human
societies. The *Confession* [. . .] proclaims that religion and atheism are both
dead, each killed off by the other, that there is no consolation for the
honourable man who has committed a crime. Nodier comes along, casts an
eye over our city, our laws, our intellectual activity, and, through his
mouthpieces don Pic de Fanferluchio and Breloque, tells us with a huge
laugh: 'Knowledge? . . . Stuff and nonsense! What for? What is all that to
me?' [. . .] Then, in December, Monsieur de Stendhal strips us bare of the
last vestiges of humanity and faith left to us; he tries to demonstrate that
gratitude is only a word, just as *Love*, *God*, *Monarch*, too, are mere words.
The *Physiology of Marriage*, the *Confession*, the *History of the King of
Bohemia* and *The Red and the Black* together represent the intimate
thoughts of an elderly people waiting for youth to come along and
organize it. They are poignant mockeries; and the last of them is like the
laugh of a demon happily discovering that between each person there lies a
chasm of indifference in which the benefits of human society are all
swallowed up.

---

*From his eleventh 'Lettre sur Paris' published in *Le Voleur* on 9 Jan. 1831.

The Red and the Black *and* The Charterhouse of Parma

One day, perhaps, somebody will emerge and sum up these four approaches in a single work, and then the nineteenth century will have its fearsome **Rabelais** to take liberty to task in the same way that Stendhal has here cast doubt upon the human heart.

2 1832: From Stendhal's own draft review of *The Red and the Black**

[...] The 'petites bourgeoises' of the provinces ask only of the author that he provide them with extraordinary scenes sufficient to reduce them to floods of tears; *little does it matter how* he devises such scenes. The ladies of Paris, on the other hand, as consumers of octavo novels,[1] take a devilishly severe view of *extra-ordinary* episodes. The moment an event appears to have been introduced into the plot at a particular point merely to show the hero off to advantage, they put the book down and proceed to regard the author as nothing but a figure of fun.

It is because of these two *opposite requirements* that it is so difficult to write a novel which will be read both in the sitting-rooms of the provincial bourgeoise and in the drawing-rooms of Paris.

This was how the novel stood with the French reading public of 1830. The genius of Walter Scott had made the Middle Ages fashionable, and one was sure of success if one spent two pages describing the view from the hero's room, two more pages describing his manner of dress, and a further two depicting the chair on which he sat. M. de S., bored with all this medievalism, all this talk of ogive arches and fifteenth-century costume, dared recount an adventure which took place in 1830 and yet leave the reader totally in the dark as to the type of dresses worn by Mme de Rênal and Mlle de la Mole, his two heroines (for two heroines this novel has, against all the previous rules of the genre).

The author has dared much more than this; he has dared to depict the character of the Parisian woman who loves her lover only to the degree *that each morning she believes herself to be on the point of losing him.*

Such is the result of the immense vanity which has become almost the only identifiable passion in this city of clever people. Elsewhere a lover can ensure that he is loved by protesting the ardour of his passion, his faithfulness, etc., etc., and by showing his fair lady these laudable qualities in action. In Paris, the more he convinces her that his affections will never

---

*The full French text is given in Pierre-Georges Castex's edition (Paris: Garnier frères, 1973), pp. 712–26.

31

alter, that he *adores* her, the more he ruins his chances in the mind of his beloved. This is something the Germans will never understand, but I am much afraid that M. de S. has provided an accurate portrait. [. . .]

People abroad are quite ignorant of French *moral attitudes*, which is why it has been necessary to point out before dealing specifically with M. de S.'s novel that nowhere could be less like the gay, amusing, rather libertine France which set the tone throughout Europe from 1715 to 1789 than the earnest, moral, morose France we have been left with by the Jesuits, the **congrégations**, and the Bourbons who ruled between 1814 and 1830. As nothing is more difficult in novels than to paint what one sees and not to *copy from books*, no one before M. de S. had yet attempted to portray these forms of behaviour, unappealing as they are but which nevertheless, thanks to the sheeplike mentality of Europe, will end up being the norm from Naples to Saint-Petersburg.

Note also one difficulty which as foreigners we tend not to suspect. By portraying the society of 1829 (when this novel was written), the author was running the risk of offending the ugly faces whose likenesses he drew, and these ugly faces, who were then all-powerful, could perfectly well haul him before the courts and have him sent to the *galleys* at Poissy for thirteen months like Messieurs Magallon and Fontan.[2] [. . .]

This portrait of Parisian love [the relationship between Julien and Mathilde] is absolutely new. It seems to us that it is to be found in no other book. It contrasts nicely with the true, simple, *unselfregarding* love of Mme de Rênal. It is 'love-in-the-head' compared with 'love-in-the-heart'. In any case, this contrast, which is so piquant in France, loses much of its point for people like us who live at three hundred leagues' remove from these nuances of feeling which are so hard to portray. [. . .]

There is one thing which the reader will find surprising. This novel is not a novel. Everything in it actually occurred in 1826 in the vicinity of Rennes. It was in that city that the hero perished after having twice shot at his first mistress, to whose children he had been tutor, and who had prevented him by means of a letter from marrying his second, an extremely rich young lady. M. de S[tendhal] has invented nothing.

His book is lively, colourful, full of interest and emotion. The author has managed to depict tender, naïve love with simplicity.

He has dared to portray Parisian love. No one had attempted this before. Nor had anyone depicted in any detail the kinds of behaviour which the French have been led to adopt by the heavy hand of government during the first third of the nineteenth century. One day, this novel will depict the days of yore like the novels of Walter Scott.

3   1840: From Balzac's review of *The Charterhouse of Parma**

[. . .] M. Beyle has written a book in which the sublime blazes forth from chapter after chapter. He has produced – at an age when men rarely even *think of* large-scale subjects to write about, and having already written some twenty extremely amusing and intelligent volumes – a work which can be appreciated only by people, souls, of a truly superior kind. In short, he has written *The Modern Prince*, the novel that Machiavelli would write if he were alive today and living in exile from Italy.

Hence the great obstacle to M. Beyle acquiring the reputation he deserves is that those clever enough to read *The Charterhouse of Parma* are only to be found among diplomats, ministers, observers of the political scene, the most eminent members of society, and the most distinguished artists, in short, among the twelve to fifteen hundred people at the head of European affairs. Do not be surprised, therefore, that during the ten months since this surprising work was published, not a single journalist has read it, or understood it, or studied it, nor announced its publication, or reviewed it, or praised it, or even made the slightest allusion to it. I who believe myself to have a little expertise in these matters have just read it for the third time: I found it an even better book than before, and I felt in my soul the kind of happiness one derives from seeing a good deed to be done.

And is it not a good deed to try to do justice to a man of immense talent, who will appear a genius only in the eyes of a few privileged people and who is prevented by the transcendence of his thought from achieving that immediate but temporary popularity which is sought after by those who court the public but is scorned by the great of soul? If the average reader knew that he had the opportunity to raise himself up to the level of outstanding people by virtue of understanding them, *The Charterhouse of Parma* would have as many readers as [**Samuel Richardson**'s] *Clarissa* had when it first appeared. [. . .]

---

*First published in the *Revue parisienne* on 25 Sept. 1840.

The Red and the Black *and* The Charterhouse of Parma

The Duchess is like one of those magnificent statues which fill one with admiration for their art while at the same time making one curse nature for being so sparing with the real-life models on which they are based. When you have read the book, Gina will remain before your eyes like a sublime statue: neither the Venus de Milo, nor the Medici Venus, but a Diana endowed with the sensual appeal of a Venus, the sweetness of Raphael's virgins, and the animated vigour of Italian passion. Above all there is nothing French about the Duchess. No, the Frenchman who has made this model and carved and polished the marble has brought nothing of his homeland to this work. Make no mistake, [**Mme de Staël's**] Corinne is a paltry sketch beside this delightful, vibrant creature. You will see greatness in her, you will find her witty and intelligent, passionate, always authentic, and yet the author has carefully concealed the sensual side of her being. There is not a single word in the book to suggest the sensuality of love or to arouse it. Although the Duchess, Mosca, Fabrice, the Prince and his son, Clélia, although the whole book and its characters represent, in one way or another, all the storms of passion, and although this is Italy as she really is, with all the finesse, the play-acting, the cunning, the sang-froid, the tenacity, where the art of high politics is applied in every circumstance, *The Charterhouse of Parma* is a novel more chaste than the most puritan of Walter Scott's. To create someone noble, larger than life, well-nigh irreproachable, out of a duchess who brings happiness to a Mosca and keeps nothing from him, out of an aunt who adores her nephew Fabrice, is that not the work of a master? Racine's Phèdre, *the* sublime role in French theatre, whom even the **Jansenists** dared not condemn, is neither as fine, nor as complete, nor as alive. [. . .]

The weakness of the work lies in the style, that is, in the way the words are combined (for the thought behind them, being eminently French, holds the sentences together). The mistakes which M. Beyle makes are purely grammatical: he is negligent and inaccurate in the manner of seventeenth-century writers.[. . .] Sometimes he uses a wrong tense, sometimes a verb is missing; sometimes it is his repeated use of 'this', 'that', 'that which', 'what', which tires the reader and is somewhat reminiscent of journeying along French roads in a carriage with poor suspension. These rather glaring errors suggest a want of attention to detail. But if the French language is like a coat of varnish applied to thought, then one must be as indulgent towards those in whom the varnish is spread over beautiful paintings as one is severe towards those in whom one sees only the varnish. If in the case of M. Beyle the varnish has yellowed somewhat in places and cracked in others, it nevertheless allows one to make out a sequence of thoughts which follow on from each other according to the laws of logic. His long sentences are poorly constructed, his short ones inadequately rounded off. He writes more or less in the style of Diderot, who was no writer. But the ideas behind it all are substantial and vigorous, and the thinking is original and often well carried through. This is not a system to be imitated: it would be much too dangerous a thing to let authors see themselves as profound thinkers.

What saves M. Beyle is the depth of feeling which animates his thinking. All those to whom Italy is dear, who have studied or understood her, will read *The Charterhouse* with delight. The mentality, the genius, the way of life, the soul of this beautiful country come alive in the pages of this long but always gripping drama, of this vast, skilful, strongly-coloured fresco, which moves the heart to its depths and satisfies the keenest, most demanding intelligence. [. . .]

4 1854: Sainte-Beuve on *The Red and the Black**

Beyle's failure as a novelist stems from the fact that he came to this type of composition only via his critical writing and with a number of fixed, preconceived ideas on the subject. Nature did not endow him with the broad, fertile talent needed for the type of narrative which the characters one has created are able to enter with ease and then to move around in as the action requires; he shapes his characters on the basis of one or two ideas which he considers well-founded and, above all, piquant, and which he spends his whole time repeating. They are not living beings but ingeniously constructed automata; at almost every move they make one can see the working parts which the mechanic has inserted in them and now operates from without. In the case of *The Red and the Black*, Julien, thanks to a few fixed notions with which the author has endowed him, soon appears no better than an odious, impossible little monster, a scoundrel resembling some **Robespierre** condemned to ordinary existence and domestic intrigue: and indeed he ends up on the scaffold. The picture which the author has endeavoured to paint of the cabals and political parties of the time similarly lacks the slow, logical development which alone suggests an authentic picture of society. Shall I be blunt? Having seen too much of Italy, having understood only too well the Rome and Florence of the fifteenth century, having read too much Machiavelli, his *Prince* and his biography of that artful tyrant Castruccio, has all harmed Beyle's capacity to understand France and to present it with portraits of society in the proper manner which it likes and applauds. A perfectly decent and honourable man in his conduct and actions, he did not, as a writer, measure things by the same moral yardstick as we do; he saw hypocrisy in what is simply a legitimate sense of propriety and a reasonable and honest perception of life such as we would like to hold to even in the midst of our desires.

---

*From 'M. de Stendhal: His Complete Works' which appeared in two parts in *Le Moniteur* on 2 and 9 Jan. 1854.

5 **1864**: Hippolyte Taine on characterization and style*

[. . .] Every talent is thus like an eye that is sensitive to one colour only. From the world's infinity, the artist chooses a world of his own. Beyle's contains only feelings, character traits, the vicissitudes of passion, in short, the life of the soul. It is true that frequently he observes how people dress, where they live, the landscape, and he could construct a plot if he wished: *The Charterhouse* proves it. But this is not his aim. He has eyes only for inward things, for sequences of thoughts and emotions. He is a psychologist; his books are simply the history of the human heart. He avoids narrating dramatic events dramatically. 'He does not wish', as he himself says, 'to bewitch the reader's soul by spurious means.' It is well known that a duel, an execution, an escape, are generally a godsend to authors, how they take pains to create and prolong suspense, how they strive to make the deed seem as dark and dirty as can be. We can all remember the last pages of serial episodes or full-length books and how we ask ourselves, breathless and rigid with excitement: Good God, what is going to happen? This is the moment of triumph for all those words like 'suddenly' and similar ominous conjunctions [*sic*] as they ambush us with a cortege of tragic events while feverishly we turn the pages, our eyes aflame, our neck craned to find out more. Here is how Beyle describes an event of this kind: 'The duel was over in an instant: Julien got a bullet in his arm; they bound it up for him with handkerchiefs; they moistened them with brandy and the Chevalier de Beauvoisis begged Julien very politely to allow him to accompany him home in the same carriage that had brought him.'[3] The novel is the story of Julien, and Julien ends up being guillotined; but Beyle would have been aghast at the prospect of treating this like some author of melodrama. He is much too well-mannered to drag us to the foot of the scaffold and show us the blood flowing; such a spectacle, in his view, is for butchers' eyes only. Throughout it all he simply notes three or four inner feelings:

---

*From 'Stendhal (Henri Beyle)' which was published in the *Nouvelle Revue de Paris* in March 1864.

37

> The bad air in the cell was becoming unbearable to Julien. By good
> fortune, on the day he was told that he had to die, the countryside was
> rejoicing in bright sunshine, and Julien was in courageous vein.
> Stepping out in the fresh air was a delicious sensation for him, like a
> walk on land for the sailor who has spent long at sea. Here we go,
> everything's all right, he told himself, I'm not lacking in courage.
> Never had his head [been more full of poetry than] at the moment it
> was due to fall. The sweetest moments he had experienced in those
> early days in the woods [at] Vergy crowded back into his mind with
> great vigour. Everything happened simply, appropriately, and with no
> affectation on his part.[4]

And that is that. Here we have the principal event of the novel, and its
other five hundred pages are no more dramatic than this. [. . .]

Nothing is better conceived than Julien's character. Its mainspring is
inordinate pride, a passionate pride, quick to take umbrage, constantly
injured, prickly towards other people, merciless with himself, together
with an inventive and ardent imagination, that is to say, a capacity to let
the slightest event trigger a whole host of ideas and to absorb himself
totally in them. This accounts for his habitual concentration, his perpetual
reflection on self, the way his attention is constantly focused in on himself,
on forever questioning and examining himself, on creating an ideal model
with whom he then compares himself and by the light of which he judges
himself and decides on his course of action. Conforming to this model, be it
good or ill, is what Julien calls *duty* and is what governs his life. His eyes
fixed on himself, and ever determined to be hard on himself, to suspect
himself of weakness, to reproach himself for his emotions, he makes bold
so as not to want for courage, he risks the greatest dangers for fear of being
afraid. Julien does not look elsewhere for this model, he creates it himself,
and this is the cause of his originality, of his eccentricities and his strength;
in this he is superior, because he *invents* his behaviour, and he shocks the
sheeplike masses, who know only how to imitate others. [. . .]

Such types of character are the only ones deserving of our attention
nowadays. They are quite unlike those epitomes of human passion, those
ideas dressed up as people, which one finds throughout
seventeenth-century literature, and quite unlike the unduly literal copies
we make of our contemporaries today. Such characters are real because
they are complex, many-sided, particular and original, like living human
beings; which means that they are natural and alive and can satisfy our
need for emotion and truth. But, at the same time, they are out of the
ordinary, they take us away from our flat, habitual ways, from our
mechanical lives, from the foolishness and vulgarity which surround us.

They show us great deeds, profound thoughts, powerful or subtle feelings. It is a spectacle of strength, and strength is the source of real beauty. **Corneille** will provide us with models, a contemporary writer with portraits; the one will teach us morality, the other about life. Beyle's heroes, on the other hand, we shall never imitate nor meet in real life; but they will fill and stir our understanding and our curiosity through and through, and there is no higher aim for art than that. [. . .]

'Formal considerations', he used to say, 'are becoming less and less important with every day that passes. Many pages in my book were printed just as I originally dictated them. I try to recount with truth and clarity what is going on in my own heart. As far as I can see, there is only one rule: make yourself clear. If I do not make myself clear, my whole world is destroyed.' Ultimately, style suppressed is style perfected. When the reader ceases to notice the sentences and sees the ideas directly, art has fulfilled its task. A polished style of the kind which calls attention to itself suggests the foolishness or vanity of getting dressed up. On the other hand, a superior mind is so in love with ideas, so happy to follow them through, so uniquely preoccupied with their truth and the logic of their sequence, that he refuses to leave off for a moment in order to select elegant words, or to avoid repetition of sound, or to round out his sentences. That smacks of the rhetorician, and no one thanks **Rousseau** for having 'oft times turned a phrase over in my head for several nights on end' in order to polish it. This intentional casualness gives Beyle's works a charmingly natural air. Reading him is like having a conversation with him. 'One thought to find an author,' **Pascal** once said, 'and one is thoroughly astonished and delighted to encounter a man.' Suppose you are in your room, with a few friends, people of intelligence, and you are obliged to tell them about something that has happened to you. You would hate to sound affected; grand words and sonorous antitheses would be the last thing you thought of using. You would tell it as it was, without exaggeration, without trying to shine, without embellishment. Such is Beyle's manner of narration. He writes without thinking of an audience listening to him, without wanting to be applauded, in intimate contact with the ideas which fill his mind and which 'he needs to *note down*'. Hence a number of singular characteristics which certain literary schools were to reproach him for – for instance, his bareness of style, his aversion to metaphor and colourful expressions. It is amusing to see Balzac claiming that 'Beyle's weak point is his style', on the assumption no doubt that good taste means presenting ideas in illuminated manuscript. [. . .] In this respect Beyle is thoroughly classical, or rather quite simply a pupil of the **Idéologues** and a student of common sense; for it must be said that a metaphorical style is an imprecise style, and is neither rational nor French. When your idea, for want of being properly thought out, is as yet imperfect and obscure, not being able to show it for itself you indicate the things which it resembles; you forsake brief and direct means of expression and cast about for comparisons. It is thus because of your own inability that you pile up the images; for want of being able to state your idea definitely from the outset, you repeat it vaguely several times, and the reader, wishing to understand you, has to make up for your inadequacy or your laziness by translating you back to yourself, by explaining to you what it was you wanted to say and yet did not manage to say. To those who claim that colour illuminates, there is a simple answer: there are no colours in pure light. Beyle is as clear as the Greeks and as our own classical writers, men of pure intellect who drew on the precision of science in their depiction of the moral world and thanks to whom, occasionally, one is actually rather grateful to be a human being. Of these Beyle belongs in the first rank, in the same way and for the same reason as **Montesquieu** and Voltaire; for, like them, he is capable of the incisive witticism or telling phrase that commands our attention, lodges in the memory, and secures our acceptance. Thus he may sum up a whole series of ideas in a striking image or an apparent paradox, which are all the more forceful for being brief and which all of a sudden clarify a situation or a person's character completely. Julien, at the seminary, finally understands why the humble gait, the lowered gaze, the whole ecclesiastical pattern of behaviour, are necessary: 'In a seminary, there is a way of eating a boiled egg which declares the progress made in devotional life. (. . .) What shall I be doing all my life? he would ask himself; selling the faithful their place in heaven. *How is this place to be made manifest to them?* By the difference between my outward appearance and that of a layman.'[5] [. . .]

Is this a writer one can or should imitate? One must imitate no one; it is always wrong to take or ask from others, and in literature borrowing is the road to ruin. Moreover, a man like him occupies a place apart; if everyone was a superior being, like Beyle, no one would be superior, and for there to be people above there have to be people below. – Is he a writer one should read? I have attempted to demonstrate the fact. If at first we find him shocking, we ought before condemning him to consider this definition of intelligence which he places in the mouth of Mlle de la Mole. Beyle himself was an original, which is doubtless why he describes things so well: 'My intellect I do believe in, for it's obvious that I scare them all. If they're brave enough to tackle a serious subject, five minutes of conversation leaves them quite gasping for breath, and seeming to make a great discovery out of something I've been telling them repeatedly for a whole hour.'[6]

6 1880: Emile Zola on Stendhal the psychologist*

[. . .] Stendhal is above all a psychologist. M. Taine accurately defined the scope of his work when he said that Beyle was exclusively interested in the life of the soul. For Stendhal man consists entirely of a brain; the other organs do not count. I am, of course, envisaging feelings, passions, character traits, all as being part of 'the brain', of matter thinking and doing. He does not allow that other parts of the body can have any influence on this noble organ, or at least it seems to him that this influence is neither strong enough nor worthy enough for him to worry about it. What is more, he rarely takes account of surroundings, and by that I mean the air the character lives and breathes. The external world scarcely exists for him; he does not care where his hero grew up nor what horizons bounded his existence. The basic formula of his work, then, may be summarized as the study of the mechanism of the soul for the satisfaction of this same mechanism's curiosity, a purely philosophical and moral study of man, of man considered simply from the point of view of his intellect and his passions, of man separate from nature. [. . .]

For me, Stendhal is not an observer who starts with observation and moves towards the truth in a series of logical steps; he is a logician who starts with logic and often reaches the truth while dispensing with observation altogether.

Stendhal's name is frequently coupled with Balzac's, and yet people seem not to see the huge gulf which lies between them. M. Taine, who compares them, is vague on the subject. To Stendhal he grants psychology, the life of the soul, and on Balzac he adds:

> What did Balzac observe in his *Human Comedy*? Everything, you may say; yes, but as a scientist, as a physiologist of the moral sphere, as a 'doctor in social science' as he used to call himself. Hence the fact that

---

*From 'Stendhal', first published in the *European Herald* in Saint Petersburg in 1880 and subsequently reprinted in Zola's *Naturalist Novelists* (1881).

his narratives are theories, that every so often the reader is met with a kind of university lecture, that discussion and commentary are the bane of his style.

I do not follow the critic's line of argument here at all. A doctor in social science does not need to discuss or comment: all he has to do is present the facts. M. Taine notes the nature of Balzac's literary temperament and presents it without any justification as the fatal flaw in his art. What is true is that Balzac started out in proper scientific fashion by studying his subject; his entire work was based on his observations of the human creature, and he was thus led, like the zoologist, to pay the utmost attention to all its organs as well as to its habitat. One needs to picture him standing in a dissection room, scalpel in hand, observing that man does not only have a brain, realizing that man is like a plant dependent on the soil, and determined henceforth, out of love for the truth, not to leave any aspect of man out of account, to exhibit man in his entirety, in all his true functions and living under the influence of the vast world around him. Meanwhile Stendhal remains closeted in his philosopher's den, tossing a few ideas about, considering only man's head and totting up each impulse of the brain. He does not write novels in order to analyse some corner of reality, its creatures and its physical objects, he writes novels in order to apply his theories on love, to apply **Condillac**'s theory of how ideas are formed. This is the great difference between Stendhal and Balzac. It is a capital one, and does not derive merely from two opposite temperaments but much more from two different philosophies.

In sum Stendhal is the one true link in the chain which connects the novel of today with the novel of the eighteenth century. He was sixteen years older than Balzac, and belonged to another age. It is thanks to him that we can pass over Romanticism and re-establish contact with French genius of old. But what I want to stress in particular is his disdain for the corporeal, his silence on the subject of the physiological aspects of man and the role played by the surrounding milieu. We shall find him taking full account of race in *The Charterhouse of Parma*; he will be the first to show us real Italians and not French people in disguise. Except that landscape, climate, the hour of day, the weather, in short nature, never has a role to play in the action, never has a bearing on the characters. Modern science has evidently not yet reached that stage. It remains determinedly abstract, setting human beings apart within nature and then declaring that since only the soul is noble, then only the soul may be mentioned in literature. And that is why M. Taine, with supposed logic, deems Beyle to be superior. According to him, he is superior because he sticks with the cerebral machine, with pure intellect. That is tantamount to saying that he is the more elevated for disdaining nature itself, for castrating man and shutting him away inside some philosophical abstraction. For me that simply means that his focus is narrower. [. . .]

No one before him ever depicted love with such accuracy. When he is not tying himself in knots with his theories on the subject, he manages to provide evidence which completely confounds received notions and provides sudden insights. Think of all the treatises on love, all the stock material in novels, and then compare how precise and cruel Stendhal's analysis is. This is where his real strength lies. If he is one of our masters, if he does occupy a position at the source of Naturalist developments in the novel, it is not because he was solely a psychologist, but because the psychologist in him was powerful enough to reach the truth despite his theories and without the aid of physiology or our natural sciences. [. . .]

I like *The Charterhouse of Parma* less [than *The Red and the Black*], no doubt because the characters are operating in a milieu which is less familiar to me.⁷ And if you want my opinion, I must confess that I have great difficulty in accepting Stendhal's Italy as a contemporary Italy. In my view, he has depicted instead the Italy of the fifteenth century, with all its poisonings and swordfights and spies and bandits in disguise, all its extraordinary adventures in which love merrily thrives in pools of blood. I do not know what M. Taine thinks about the romance elements in the work, but to my mind the plot could not be more contorted, and nothing could seem less like how I imagine Europe to have been in 1820. To me it is all pure Walter Scott, minus the fine phrases. Perhaps I am wrong.

And indeed I have already said how *The Charterhouse of Parma* is quite definitely the only French novel about a foreign people which actually conveys a real sense of that people. Generally we novelists, even the great ones, are content to splash on some crude local colour, whereas Stendhal has got to the bottom of this race. He finds them less boringly bourgeois, more sensual, less ready to sacrifice everything for money and vanity. I rather suspect him of seeing them through the lense of his own tastes and his own nature. But that has not prevented him from presenting in definitive outline the salient characteristics of this people of free and vivacious temperament for whom the main business of living is to love and to enjoy life and not to care a fig for what people may say. [. . .]

What must also be noted is that while Stendhal affects disdain for the external world, he was the first novelist to observe the law concerning the influence of social and geographical milieus. He has this comment to make in the preface to *The Charterhouse of Parma*, and it is profoundly true: 'it seems to me that, whenever one takes a stride of two hundred leagues from South to North, the change of scene that occurs is tantamount to a fresh tale'. The whole theory of milieu is there. Compare, for example, Mlle de la Mole's experience of love with that of the Duchess Sanseverina. First, their temperaments are quite different, but it is certain also that the differences in the kinds of misfortune brought about by love derive from the differences in the climate and society in which such misfortunes occur. One needs to analyse the two works from this point of view. Stendhal was applying as an abstract thinker theories which we are endeavouring today to apply as scientists. His formula is not yet ours, but our own derives from his. [. . .]

Well, I have finally understood what has been making me feel uneasy. Stendhal, a logician when it comes to ideas, is not a logician in the area of composition or style. That's where the gap is with him, the failing which diminishes him in stature. Is it not surprising? Here is a psychologist of the first order, who can unravel with extraordinary lucidity the complex bundle of ideas to be found beneath the skulls of his characters; he can show how the soul's responses link together, and the order they come in, and he has at his disposal a method of systematic analysis with which to explain each successive state of mind. And then, as soon as it comes to composition, to actual writing, all this admirable logicality goes out of the window. He jots things down at random, sentence after sentence seems to flow from his pen as the fancy takes it. No more method, no more system, no order of any sort; it is a jumble, and an affected jumble at that, one in which he appears to take pride. Yet there is a logic in composition and style which is in the end the same as that which governs facts and ideas. The logic of a given fact dictates the order in which it must be presented; the logic of a given idea in a particular character determines the logic of the words needed to express it. Note that this has nothing to do with rhetoric or having a brilliant and colourful style. I am simply saying that at the heart of Stendhal's superior intelligence there was a lacuna, or worse still, a contradiction. He betrayed his method the moment he passed from idea to language. [. . .]

Stendhal is a great writer each time his admirable logic leads him to some undeniably authentic piece of evidence about the human condition; but his logic is no more than preciosity when he twists the psychology of his characters to try to make them into singular and superior beings. I confess quite frankly that then he leaves me cold; his tone of diplomatic mysteriousness, his pinched irony, these doors he seems to shut on things and yet behind which there lies often nothing but a laboured void, all this gets on my nerves. Like Balzac he is a father to all of us, he brought the art of analysis to the novel, he was unique and exquisite, but he lacked the bonhomie of the really powerful novelist. Life is simpler.

7 1882: Paul Bourget on Stendhal and *The Red and the Black**

This man of letters, who was equally at home in a barrack-room or a diplomat's chancery, had the dangerous privilege to invent for himself an entire new set of feelings and to describe them in a style unknown to tradition. The feelings were not shared, and the style was not to people's taste. He himself gave the reason for this lack of success when he formulated the profound truth that praise between colleagues in the same profession is no more than the award of a certificate of resemblance. [. . .] Henri Beyle was, in the eyes of his contemporaries, like Julien Sorel in the eyes of his companions at the seminary: 'he could not get anyone to like him, he was too different'.[8] Quite the reverse is true today, however, since in some of his most characteristic attitudes he bears a strong resemblance to many of our own contemporaries, who recognize in the author of the **Memoirs of a Tourist** and *The Charterhouse of Parma* an early manifestation of several features of the most modern sensibility. Beyle used to say, with a surprisingly sure instinct for his future reception as an artist: 'I shall finally be understood around 1880.' Forty years ago, that sentence shocked with its arrogant self-confidence; today, it astonishes as a prophetic remark. [. . .]

But with this vigorous temperament went a thoroughly psychological imagination, that is to say, one particularly well equipped to picture to itself other people's states of mind. The contrast is sufficiently intriguing for one to dwell on it a little. When this great believer in the delights of an energetic physical life describes one of his heroes, he precisely omits everything physical and records instead details of the hero's moral existence. The latter, it would seem, was all he could see. If he depicts a face, he does so very rapidly, and almost always to indicate some inner event, and he presents the description in bland terms. He will say of Julien Sorel that he had 'irregular but delicate features, (. . .) a roman nose (. . .)

---

*From Paul Bourget's *Essais de psychologie contemporaine* (1883), first published as separate articles (on Flaubert, Renan, Taine, and Stendhal) in the *Nouvelle Revue* in 1882.

large dark eyes (. . .) a low forehead framed by dark chestnut hair"[9]. . . and then on he goes.[. . .]

Every novelist has one habitual working practice, so to speak, which is closely associated with his particular way of envisaging the nature of his characters. Such a practice indeed could easily serve as a kind of low-water mark when measuring the psychological depth of a writer. One story-teller will always and almost immediately resort to dialogue, while for another it may be description. The reason is that the first focuses above all on how human beings exert influence on each other, while the second sees particularly how a whole host of minute external factors may gradually affect the inner self. A third may divide his narrative up into very short chapters of an insubstantial kind and create his main character from a mosaic of ideas and sensations. This is because he is particularly alert to the tiny agitations that disturb the nervous system and because the lives of especially nervous creatures do indeed consist of momentary experiences and passing perceptions. Stendhal's technique is the monologue.

To be sure, the characters in his narratives are men of action. In *Armance* Octave de Malivert fights a duel and poisons himself. In *The Red and the Black* Julien Sorel, after many dangerous adventures, shoots his former mistress and goes to the scaffold. As we know, the Fabrice of *The Charterhouse* begins by charging into battle at Waterloo. We are not dealing here with a writer who lacks imagination and merely sets up some sort of museum of waxwork figures. Octave, Julien, and Fabrice – and I have specifically chosen the three heroes of Beyle's greatest novels – all come and go, risk their lives, display great daring, undergo endlessly changing circumstances as their lives unfold, . . . and yet throughout the narrative the author shows them constantly taking the pulse of their own sensibility. He makes psychologists of them, sticklers even, who are forever asking themselves why they feel moved, and if they feel moved, who are always examining the nature of their own moral existence in all its most secret nooks and crannies and reflecting on themselves with all the lucidity of a **Maine de Biran** or a **Jouffroy**. And monologue follows monologue. [. . .]

[. . .] Stendhal's method of narration is not only a means of exposition, it is also a means of discovery. I would willingly compare it to the working hypothesis of an experimental scientist.[10] Like all novelists down the ages it is his own faculties that Stendhal the psychologist is studying. His technique consists in endlessly varying the circumstances in which he places these faculties, and then having the character himself note the changes which these circumstances must have wrought. And this is not just a writer's device. The character, being created by Stendhal in his own image, has as the mainspring of his inner workings an analytical turn of mind. The novelist does not need to dismantle a given person's inner motives from without, for it is an essential part of this person that he simultaneously acts and observes his own actions, feels and observes himself feeling. If the narrative is full of specious and complicated explanations, this is because the heroes in question are themselves producing these explanations. There are many different categories of person within the vast supposed unity called humanity. The one studied by Stendhal has as its distinctive trait a capacity and, if you like, a mania for intimate self-dissection. You may dislike this way of being, but to claim that it is factitious, that you cannot; the author would have only to point to himself as an accomplished example of such a category, and the rest of us, who come after him and suffer like him from an excessively acute analytical mentality, would soon be at hand to confirm that the curious specimens, indeed the psychological *cases*, he describes are well and truly our own.[. . .]

I have already said that Beyle's great powers of analysis, his extreme sensitivity, and breadth of experience led him to think and express a number of profound truths about nineteenth-century France. *The Red and the Black* contains the most complete expression of these truths – an extraordinary book which I have seen turn certain young heads in a manner from which they never recover. When this novel is not outraging you, it is bewitching you. It possesses you like the *Human Comedy*. But Balzac needed forty volumes to bring the whole populace of his characters into being. He paints in frescoes and upon a palace wall. There are only five hundred pages in *The Red and the Black*. It is an etching, but an extremely detailed one, and within its limited dimensions an entire universe is contained. [. . .]

[. . .] and he created Julien Sorel. [–] For any character type in a novel to be of particular significance, that is, for it to represent a large number of people similar to it, it needs to have been based on some idea that is fundamental to the period in question. Now it so happens that this sense of isolation felt by the man of superior talents – or who believes himself to be such – is perhaps that most readily engendered by a democracy like ours. At first blush, this democracy seems very much to favour the advancement of merit and indeed, on the basis of the principle of equality, it opens the doors wide to competing men of ambition. But by virtue of this same principle it makes education available to the greatest number. And this excess of logic leads to the strangest of contradictions. For if we look, for example, at what has been going on in this country for the last hundred years, we can see that any adolescent worth anything at all has had no trouble in finding excellent conditions in which to develop. If he shines during his early years at school, he can go on to one of the bigger municipal schools ['collèges']. If he does well there, he can win a scholarship to one of the great lycées in Paris. Parents, teachers, and even willing outsiders all conspire together to ensure that the 'exceptional boy' – as they call him in pedagogical circles – should achieve the highest level of intellectual development of which he is capable. His studies at an end, and his examinations over, there is a complete reversal: the conspiracy begins to work in exactly the opposite direction. For the newcomer finds himself in a society where all the positions are taken, where the competition between men of ambition which I mentioned earlier turns out to be formidable. If the young man of talent but no financial means remains in the provinces, what good will his talents do him, since life there is all governed by established practice and founded on the possession of property? If he comes to Paris, he is friendless. His successes at school, about which people were so fulsome during his childhood, merely allow him to scratch a living in some menial position. What will his thoughts be if his superior talents are not supplemented by the virtues of modesty and patience? While education was equipping him with skills, it was also filling him with aspirations, and he is right to have such aspirations. An adolescent who has read and appreciated the poets will necessarily want to have beautiful, poetic love-affairs himself. If he has a delicate constitution, he will want the finer things in life; if he is of a more robust nature, he will want power. Either way, his is a temperament exactly fitted for literary or artistic work. But if our fellow is neither a man of letters nor an artist – and many a strong personality is incapable of the disinterested wisdom that cures itself of its own dreams and fantasies by giving them expression – then what sinister drama may not be played out within him! He will feel impotent in his actions, yet grand in his desires. He will see people triumphantly succeeding who do not deserve to, and will condemn wholesale a social system which only seems to have raised him up the better to slap him down, like animals that are fattened the more satisfactorily to be slaughtered. First you have the 'déclassé' type, then you have the revolutionary . . . 'It must be admitted', Stendhal says somewhere in *The Red and the Black*, that 'Julien (. . .) had a dreadful look in his eye and a hideous countenance; it exuded unadulterated wickedness. He was the victim of misfortune at war with the whole of society.'[11] [–] This strange war and its mysterious episodes (in which the first heart to bleed is that of the man who started it) constitutes the real subject of Beyle's great novel. A passionate war and a war to stir the passions, especially since the author has been able to endow his hero with a marvellous array of genuinely superior qualities. Julien's intelligence is of the first order. It is quite simply Stendhal's own: clear-minded and anguished, as lucid as an algebraic theorem and as penetrating as a prosecution counsel. [. . .]

Certainly the colouring in his depictions is marvellous. What I find even more admirable, though, is the analytical power which enabled Stendhal to say the definitive word, at the very least, about that whole group of people around 1830 known as the 'children of the age'. Past our eyes it goes, in many works of the time, that legion of melancholy rebels, but all magnificently apparelled, all resplendent in the shining glory of poetry: Victor Hugo's **Ruy Blas** is one, and his **Didier**, and so is **Musset's Rolla**, and **Dumas's Antony**. They all suffer from a longing that seems sublime. Stendhal's Julien Sorel suffers the same longing, but he knows what is really the matter. The cold, cruel desire to rise in society gnaws at his soul, and he admits it to himself. He can recognize in himself the implacable ardour of the 'déclassé' on the verge of crime. The infinite sadness and the vague despair resolve themselves into an unbridled appetite for the pleasures of destruction. To understand the burnings of the Commune and the frightening resurgence of primitive savagery in the gentler midst of our own day, one has only to reread this book, and in particular the discussions which Julien has with himself in prison as he awaits death.

> There's no such thing as 'natural rights': this term is nothing but a bit of antiquated rubbish worthy of the assistant public prosecutor who was hounding me the other day, and whose ancestor was made rich by land which Louis XIV confiscated from the Protestants. There is only a 'right' when there is a law to forbid you doing something on pain of punishment. Before the advent of laws, the only thing 'natural' is the might of the lion or the need of the creature suffering hunger or cold, 'need' in short . . .[12]

From beneath the various notions of propriety with which our brains are burdened, and the rules of behaviour incrusted in our thinking by education, and the inherited caution which makes us like domestic animals, the primitive carnivore can be seen emerging, fierce and solitary, and fully committed to the 'struggle for life' like everything else in nature. You thought he had been subjugated, but he was only sleeping; you thought he had been tamed, but he had only been bound and gagged. The bonds are rent, the beast awakes, and you gaze in horror and amazement that so many centuries of civilization have not suppressed one single seed of ancient savagery. . . .

8   1892: Emile Faguet on *The Red and the Black* and *The Charterhouse of Parma**

Stendhal has left two novels worthy of posterity's attention: *The Red and the Black* (1830) and *The Charterhouse of Parma* (1839). The latter is a second version, at once revised and enfeebled, of the former. I shall deal first with the former. – *The Red and the Black* is a very great work in so far as its general conception and purport are concerned. It has a perfectly comprehensible title, *Red and Black*, that is to say, soldier and priest, in turn military ambition and ecclesiastical ambition, warring energy and scheming diplomacy, with the latter trying to realize the dream of domination originally conceived by the former. Although wide-ranging, the title is still too limited to give a full idea of the work. I would almost prefer it if the book were entitled with its date of publication. 1830, that is the real title of *The Red and the Black*. [. . .] [13]

Such is the typical man of his age, or at least such is Julien Sorel: ambition, willpower, hatred, and the complete absence of any moral sense. He is not an evil person. He likes the people of his own class, as long as they are not totally brutish. He likes his friend the timber merchant. At one point, in the course of a conversation with him, he passes up the prospect of contented mediocrity and feels what it is to be tempted. His is not a vulgar soul: once, in the mountains, as the sun slowly sets, he falls under the deep, intoxicating spell of solitude, under that exquisite enchantment which is nothing less than the liberty of the soul [. . .]. This is in 1818. Wild visions of hope have just swept the world. Every man of the people thinks that he has a marshal's baton in his haversack, or wishes he had one, or is furious that he no longer does. Julien's soul is neither evil nor vulgar: it is depraved. He is determined to succeed at whatever price, and detests with every fibre of his being anyone who comes between him and his goal. He detests them for preserving a state of society which obliges him to defer to them if he is to succeed, to be hypocritical if he is to fulfil his role as a young man of ambition. [. . .].

---

*From 'Stendhal', published in the *Revue des Deux Mondes*; 109 (1892); pp. 594–633.

The dénouement of *The Red and the Black* is very bizarre and, to tell the truth, rather more contrived than is permissible. The French reader of 1890, or even of 1860, is left with the impression that at the end of *The Red and the Black* all the characters lose their heads. [. . .] Not one of them remains recognizable, which says little for their creator. – There are, I think, two reasons for this singular lapse at the end of a story which hitherto had been conducted with such masterly control and such a sharp eye for the truth. First, we are back in 1830, and however impervious Stendhal wishes to be to the influence of fashion, nobody, least of all when they are writing a novel, can avoid it totally. Now in 1830 it was permissible for a novel to be true to life only as far as the dénouement. Then, at least, it had to be 'novelistic', that is, action-packed, extraordinary, and generally tragic. **George Sand** herself, sweet and gentle as she was, used always, until about 1850, to have her amiable and graceful narratives end in melodrama. And I remember, in the days when people used to read **Eugène Sue** and regularly used the more famous expressions from his *Mysteries of Paris* in everyday conversation, a lady saying to me: 'I only read George Sand to the point where they "finally came to blows". That ruins it for me.' From 1830 to 1850 every novel perforce 'finally came to blows'. – Another, more important reason lies in the character and imagination of Stendhal himself, as we now know them. On the one hand Stendhal is a man who loves the truth and is capable of seeing it, while on the other he is someone who adores 'energy', and we know what he means by being 'energetic'. Now in writing *The Red and the Black,* or rather while composing it in his head, his instinct for observation and taste for psychology were fully satisfied, but his worship for 'energy' not so. He could see Julien Sorel being patient, persevering, judicious, tenacious, or bold as and when the situation required, but not 'energetic', that is to say, having at someone with a knife in the traditional Italian manner. And it must have been with real despair that he watched him heading inevitably towards the bourgeois dénouement of worldly success, a good marriage, and charge of a regiment or embassy. So well done is the novel up to this point that this would have been the most fitting dénouement, and in a way its only necessary and inevitable one. It depressed Stendhal. That his beloved Julien should kill no one, that he should fail to do what a Lafargue had done, this was too much to bear. Simply so that Julien could be a Lafargue, Stendhal botched his ending and spoilt the entire novel. For Julien to have the opportunity of shooting someone with a pistol, or at least a pretext to do so, Stendhal suddenly alters the characters of Mme de Rênal, Mathilde, M. de la Mole, and Julien. The cult of energy led Stendhal to say many silly things; here it made him do one. – This is much to be regretted: it gives an accidental ending to a novel that was 'true'. [. . .]

Yet it is a great work, *The Red and the Black,* and it thoroughly deserved for its novelty to go more or less unrecognized, as nearly all great works have done, and then – like all works, even the bad ones, which are based on some great universal truth – to have attracted the attention of posterity.

The Charterhouse of Parma is a kind of copy of *The Red and the Black*: same general idea, same characters, different surroundings and scenery. But the main idea is presented with less force, and the protagonists have, as it were, had their corners softened and their edges smoothed: thoughts and characters all stand out less. It is as if a second impression had been made from a worn woodcut. An ambitious young Frenchman of 1815: *The Red and the Black*; an ambitious young Italian of 1815: *The Charterhouse of Parma*. [. . .] As with Julien, Fabrice's initial enthusiasm for war is followed by the resolve to embark on an ecclesiastical career and to follow the twisting paths of intrigue, as he becomes both hypocrite and diplomat and takes the **cardinal de Retz** as his model. But, being born into the aristocracy and protected by the mistress of a minister, he does not need to make the same effort as [Julien] or to harbour the same feelings: neither the sprung tension of will nor the ardour of envy, hatred, and defiance. Hence he is without meaning, one ought even to say without character; for it was the difficulties of the struggle and the distance from his goal, together with his ambition, which constituted the character of Julien. Julien is always doing things, Fabrice is almost passive. Different things do happen to him. But it is not what happens to someone that is interesting, it is what he does. The major defect of *The Charterhouse of Parma* lies in the extreme insignificance of the central protagonist and the small degree of interest he provokes. – The Duchesse Sanseverina, on the other hand, is strongly drawn as a character and memorable. She is energetic, skilful, but maladroit also and imprudent in the first flush of success because of her excessive confidence in herself and her tendency to become carried away, both of them particularly feminine traits [. . .] What is the meaning underlying the Duchesse and everything she does? That beautiful and intelligent women play enormously important roles in monarchical societies. True, but this is no longer of interest to us. The rise of the lower classes, their struggle to succeed and the feelings which accompany this, were rather more likely to capture our attention. – Finally, just as everything is less brightly coloured, less sharply defined, in *The Charterhouse* than in *The Red and the Black*, so the dénouement is greyer and flatter. One hastens to add, however, that it is also truer to life and more satisfying to our instinct for logic. In *The Red and the Black* everyone lost their wits, while in *The Charterhouse* everyone becomes resigned. Although still in love with her nephew, the Duchesse departs with melancholy calm to take up residence in Naples and to renounce intrigue, as her minister renounces ambition, in favour of bourgeois comfort and well-being. Fabrice, having become a bishop, subsides into the dreary quietude of an habitual love, a slightly furtive and shamefaced love rather reminiscent of an old man's liaison. It is of particular interest, this dénouement, in the study of Stendhal both as a novelist and as a man. We are now in 1839, and no longer in 1830. As a man Stendhal seems to be less keen on his beloved 'energy', on outbursts of vehement, unbridled passion. As a novelist Stendhal is tending now instead, despite all the chivalric or picaresque adventures that pack *The Charterhouse*, to realism. This dénouement, at least, in *The Charterhouse* is fully realist. It seems to be saying: all this enthusiasm, these great hopes, this passion for greatness, this Napoleonic spirit, where – after the great crisis and upheaval that has taken place in Europe – will they all soon lead? To resignation, to the tranquillity to be found in the monotony and selfishness of the bourgeois way of life. This story begins with young Fabrice's escapades at Waterloo and ends in the precautions and discretions of Monseigneur Fabrice del Dongo and Mme Clélia Crescenzi's well-regulated adultery. And so it goes in all our lives: we all start out with our own escapades at Waterloo, and we all have our equivalent of a bishopric in Parma to see us through until, at the end, we each of us make a 'charterhouse' for ourselves, in which to see out our days in silence and in solitude. [. . .]

Stendhal is a realist. And he is realist to the core, despite his taste for 'energy' and knife-fights. He did not always succeed in depicting true-to-life characters, but he intended to, and he did not always fail. He is able to see things, to observe, to analyse. He has the essential gift for this: which is that he can step outside himself, he can enter another person's mind and see things there, sometimes very clearly indeed. In this respect the father of Julien Sorel, of Mme de Rênal, and the Duchesse Sanseverina is chronologically the first of our realist writers. He warrants the title more than Balzac, who had an eye for things too but who was much more of a visionary, and whose realism is encumbered with Romanticism of the most excessive and vulgar kind. [. . .] Typical behaviour throughout the land of France, the characters of average people born of our soil and fashioned by our history, at a given, precise date, without the violent exaggerations of a congested brain, without any cautious transposing, or clever relocation of the action, or ingenious distancing of the point of view: this is what, in the *Memoirs of a Tourist* and *The Red and the Black*, Stendhal had the audacity or frankness, the originality at least, to give us. As Romanticism declined, as the enthusiasms of half of a century were replaced, around 1850, by an unfounded but fatal sense of disaffection, Stendhal came to appear, and rightly so, as the most anti-Romantic writer of that entire Romantic, lyrical, elegiac period. As happens quite naturally in the ebb and flow of literary history, this late-comer turned into a precursor; and a Realist school emerged just at the right time for him to become an ancestor. His imperviousness to fashion thus received its just deserts, which moreover, though with little conviction, he had himself predicted. – And if you add to

53

this the fact that his irreligion in thought and action, which was so unacceptable in his own day, caused no scandal or cooling of enthusiasm among those in the latter half of the nineteenth century who in any case had other reasons to appreciate him, then you will understand this phenomenon, itself quite frequent in the history of literature, of an author being much more widely read, and above all much more widely admired, by the generation who followed him than he ever was by his own.

Editor's Notes to Part One

1. As opposed to novels in duodecimo format, or 'penny dreadfuls'.

2. Respectively, a pamphleteer and the director of a satirical review who were sent to prison for five years in 1824 for their attacks on the government.

3. *The Red and the Black*, p. 282

4. *The Red and the Black*, p. 527. The words in square brackets amend the translation.

5. *The Red and the Black*, pp. 190–1 (Taine's emphasis).

6. *The Red and the Black*, p. 302.

7. Zola here echoes Taine. See Introduction, p. 6.

8. *The Red and the Black*, p. 199.

9. *The Red and the Black*, pp. 19–20.

10. ZOLA's polemical essay *The Experimental Novel* had been published two years earlier in 1880, and Bourget is here both minimizing Zola's claims to originality and also establishing Stendhal's credentials as a forerunner of contemporary trends in the novel.

11. *The Red and the Black*, pp. 337–8.

12. *The Red and the Black*, pp. 518–19.

13. Faguet's interpretation of the title derives from an article in *Le National* on 1 Apr. 1842 by EMILE FORGUES (under the pseudonym 'Old Nick'), who claimed to have heard this explanation from a friend who had consulted Stendhal directly. The equation of black with the Church is persuasive, but the military explanation of red works better if one ignores the blue uniform worn by French Napoleonic soldiers (and the 'red coats' of their opponents at Waterloo) and considers instead the red ribbon of the cross worn by members of Napoleon's recently instituted Legion of Honour (and which is awarded to Julien thanks to the agency of the marquis de la Mole). Connotations of gaming (roulette, playing-cards) are evident, if weakened by the use of 'and' instead of 'or' in the title. Most importantly, red and black flags (signifying a 'fight to the death') had been carried on 16 Aug. 1819 by workers at St Peter's Fields in Manchester protesting in favour of better working conditions: troops intervened and many of the demonstrators met their deaths, the working-class its 'Peterloo'. On 29 July 1830 one such flag was flown from the Vendôme column in Paris during the July Revolution. On 25 Feb. 1830, at the first night of VICTOR HUGO's *Hernani*, red and black tickets were issued in advance to the claque chosen to champion this innovative Romantic drama within the last French bastion of Classical taste, the Comédie Française. In the ensuing 'battle of *Hernani*', the Romantics emerged victorious; and Stendhal's title proclaims, with rich suggestiveness (blood/death, army/church, honour/conspiracy, revolution/reaction, energy/repression, passion/apathy, heart-on-sleeve sincerity/dark hypocrisy, love/tragedy), its author's faith in the new and his radical condemnation of the old. Unbeknownst to Faguet (who was unaware of the red and black flag) the actual title thus carries all the historical and revolutionary charge of his proposed '1830'.

Part Two

Modern Readings

'Realism'

The following extracts illustrate two traditional approaches to Stendhal as an exponent of Realism in the novel. Both have their origins in the positivist criticism of nineteenth-century commentators such as Taine, Zola, and Bourget. The first approach emphasizes the ways in which the Stendhalian novel offers an essentially unproblematic and 'transparent' record of the social, political, and economic circumstances of the age in which it is set: while the second concentrates more on the psychology of the protagonists and the narrative techniques which are employed to create an illusion of reality.

The first extract is taken from Erich Auerbach's *Mimesis. The Representation of Reality in Western Literature*, which was originally published in German in 1946 and then translated into English in 1953. Beginning with Homer and moving historically forward through the major figures of Western literature, Auerbach comes in Chapter 18 (from which the extract is taken and entitled 'In the Hôtel de la Mole') to a consideration of the nineteenth-century French novel, and particularly the novels of Stendhal, Balzac, and **Flaubert**. In the two remaining chapters he discusses the Goncourts, Zola, and Virginia Woolf, before concluding briefly in an epilogue that:

> When Stendhal and Balzac took random individuals from daily life in their dependence upon current historical circumstances and made them the subjects of serious, problematic, and even tragic representation, they broke with the classical rule of distinct levels of style, for according to this rule, everyday practical reality could find a place in literature only within the frame of a low or intermediate kind of style, that is to say, as either grotesquely comic or pleasant, light, colourful, and elegant entertainment. They thus completed a development which had long been in preparation [...] And they opened the way for modern realism, which has ever since developed in increasingly rich forms, in keeping with the constantly changing and expanding reality of modern life.

While the emphasis here is on the different literary treatment which Stendhal gives to the events and personalities of 'daily life', it remains the case, as the extract will show, that Auerbach's principal definition of Realism is founded on the detailed depiction of contemporary social reality of the kind to be found in *The Red and the Black*. His principal reservation about Stendhal's Realism, as the extract also shows, concerns its alleged failure to place 'current historical circumstances' within a broader perspective: 'in particular his representation of events is oriented, wholly in the spirit of classic ethic psychology, upon an "analysis of the human heart", not upon discovery or premonitions of historical forces.' Here Auerbach echoes the opinion of Georg Lukács voiced some ten year earlier (see Introduction, pp. 8–9).

The second extract is taken from Georges Blin's *Stendhal et les problèmes du roman* (*Stendhal and the Problems of the Novel*) published in 1954, which was followed in 1958 by the same author's *Stendhal et les problèmes de la personnalité*. The two studies present the thesis that Stendhal not only found solutions to the 'problems' of his personality by imaginatively recreating himself in his characters but also demonstrated, by his authorial intrusions, his superiority over these very characters.

As Blin states on the first page of *Stendhal and the Problems of the Novel*, this earlier study might also have been entitled *The Limits and Methods of Realism in Stendhal's Novels*. It argues essentially that Stendhal is more of a Realist writer than previously thought because his Realism is not of an obvious, quasi-objective kind (for example, as described by Auerbach), but rather a 'subjective Realism' which 'measures the field of reality from the protagonist's angle of vision'. For Blin such 'point-of-view technique' is the principal method of Stendhalian Realism, or of what, in Part I of his book, Blin calls Stendhal's 'aesthetic of the mirror'. Part I ends with the section included below, which in turn prepares for a detailed examination in Part II of the various limits which are set to narrative viewpoint. Part III analyses the interventions of the author whose intrusive presence threatens to undo the fictional illusion created by 'point-of-view technique' but argues that these interventions serve to establish the narrator as a character in his own right with his own particular viewpoint and ultimately as someone whose story we listen to, therefore, with enhanced interest and credulity.

In advancing this thesis Blin is giving a twist to the old idea that Stendhal's novels are essentially portraits of Henri Beyle himself, while his analyses of 'point-of-view technique' and narratorial intervention reinforce nineteenth-century claims that Stendhal's Realism is essentially 'psychological' rather than social or political. As the extract shows, all reference to the external world in Stendhal's novels is, in Blin's view, subordinate to the depiction of a particular character's desires and of his or her pursuit of happiness. His approach is thus influenced both in its direction and in its vocabulary by **phenomenology**. In this he anticipates the Thematic Criticism of Jean-Pierre Richard, which is illustrated in the next section. His emphasis on the role of desire in perception and interpretation prefigures such subsequent psychoanalytic studies as those of Roland Barthes and Peter Brooks.

1 Erich Auerbach on *The Red and the Black*

Julien Sorel, the hero of Stendhal's novel *Le Rouge et le Noir* (1830), an ambitious and passionate young man, son of an uneducated petty bourgeois from the Franche-Comté, is conducted by a series of circumstances from the seminary at Besançon, where he has been studying theology, to Paris and the position of secretary to a gentleman of rank, the marquis de la Mole, whose confidence he gains. Mathilde, the marquis's daughter, is a girl of nineteen, witty, spoiled, imaginative, and so arrogant that her own position and circle begin to bore her. The dawning of her passion for her father's *domestique* is one of Stendhal's masterpieces and has been greatly admired. One of the preparatory scenes, in which her interest in Julien begins to awaken, is the following, from volume 2, chapter 4:

One morning when the priest was working with Julien in the marquis's library on the never-ending Frilair lawsuit:

'Father,' said Julien suddenly, 'is it one of my duties to dine with her ladyship, or is it a kindness they are showing me?'

'It's a signal honour!' answered the priest, scandalized. 'Not once has M. N—— the academician, who has been assiduous in his attentions for the past fifteen years, been able to obtain it on behalf of his nephew M. Tanbeau.'

'For me, Father, it's the most irksome part of my job. I was less bored at the seminary. I sometimes even see Mlle de la Mole herself yawning, and she at any rate ought to be accustomed to the civility of the family's friends. I'm afraid of falling asleep. I beg you, get permission for me to go and dine for forty sous in some obscure inn.'

Father Pirard, a genuinely self-made man, was highly appreciative of the honour of dining with a great lord. While he was attempting to make Julien understand this sentiment, a slight noise made them look round. Julien saw Mlle de la Mole listening. He blushed. She had come to fetch a book and had heard everything; Julien went up in her esteem. There's a man who wasn't born on his knees, she thought, like that old priest. God, he's ugly!

61

The Red and the Black *and* The Charterhouse of Parma

> At dinner Julien did not dare look at Mlle de la Mole, but she was
> good enough to speak to him. That day they were expecting a large
> party, and she entreated him to stay.

The scene, as I said, is designed to prepare for a passionate and
extremely tragic love intrigue. Its function and its psychological value we
shall not here discuss; they lie outside of our subject. What interests us in
the scene is this: it would be almost incomprehensible without a most
accurate and detailed knowledge of the political situation, the social
stratification, and the economic circumstances of a perfectly definite
historical moment, namely, that in which France found itself just before the
July Revolution; accordingly, the novel bears the subtitle, *Chronicle of 1830*.
Even the boredom which reigns in the dining room and salon of this noble
house is no ordinary boredom. It does not arise from the fortuitous
personal dullness of the people who are brought together there; among
them there are highly educated, witty, and sometimes important people,
and the master of the house is intelligent and amiable. Rather, we are
confronted, in their boredom, by a phenomenon politically and
ideologically characteristic of the Restoration period. In the seventeenth
century, and even more in the eighteenth, the corresponding salons were
anything but boring. But the inadequately implemented attempt which the
Bourbon regime made to restore conditions long since made obsolete by
events, creates, among its adherents in the official and ruling classes, an
atmosphere of pure convention, of limitation, of constraint and lack of
freedom, against which the intelligence and good will of the persons
involved are powerless. In these salons the things which interest everyone
– the political and religious problems of the present, and consequently
most of the subjects of its literature or of that of the very recent past – could
not be discussed, or at best could be discussed only in official phrases so
mendacious that a man of taste and tact would rather avoid them. How
different from the intellectual daring of the famous eighteenth-century
salons, which, to be sure, did not dream of the dangers to their own
existence which they were unleashing! Now the dangers are known, and
life is governed by the fear that the catastrophe of 1793 might be repeated.
As these people are conscious that they no longer themselves believe in the
thing they represent, and that they are bound to be defeated in any public
argument, they choose to talk of nothing but the weather, music, and court
gossip. In addition, they are obliged to accept as allies snobbish and
corrupt people from among the newly-rich bourgeoisie, who, with the
unashamed baseness of their ambition and with their fear for their
ill-gotten wealth, completely vitiate the atmosphere of society. So much for
the pervading boredom.

But Julien's reaction, too, and the very fact that he and the former
director of his seminary, the Abbé Pirard, are present at all in the house of

the marquis de la Mole, are only to be understood in terms of the actual historical moment. Julien's passionate and imaginative nature has from his earliest youth been filled with enthusiasm for the great ideas of the Revolution and of Rousseau, for the great events of the Napoleonic period; from his earliest youth he has felt nothing but loathing and scorn for the piddling hypocrisy and the petty lying corruption of the classes in power since Napoleon's fall. He is too imaginative, too ambitious, and too fond of power, to be satisfied with a mediocre life within the bourgeoisie, such as his friend Fouquet proposes to him. Having observed that a man of petty-bourgeois origin can attain to a situation of command only through the all-powerful Church, he has consciously and deliberately become a hypocrite; and his great talents would assure him a brilliant intellectual career, were not his real personal and political feelings, the direct passionateness of his nature, prone to burst forth at decisive moments. One such moment of self-betrayal we have in the passage before us, when Julien confides his feelings in the marquise's salon to the Abbé Pirard, his former teacher and protector; for the intellectual freedom to which it testifies is unthinkable without an admixture of intellectual arrogance and a sense of inner superiority hardly becoming in a young ecclesiastic and protégé of the house. (In this particular instance his frankness does him no harm; the Abbé Pirard is his friend, and upon Mathilde, who happens to overhear him, his words make an entirely different impression from that which he must expect and fear.) The Abbé is here described as a true parvenu, who knows how highly the honor of sitting at a great man's table should be esteemed and hence disapproves of Julien's remarks; as another motive for the Abbé's disapproval Stendhal could have cited the fact that uncritical submission to the evil of this world, in full consciousness that it is evil, is a typical attitude for strict Jansenists; and the Abbé Pirard is a Jansenist. We know from the previous part of the novel that as director of the seminary at Besançon he had had to endure much persecution and much chicanery on account of his Jansenism and his strict piety which no intrigues could touch; for the clergy of the province were under the influence of the Jesuits. When the marquis de la Mole's most powerful opponent, the Abbé de Frilair, a vicar-general to the bishop, had brought a suit against him, the marquis had made the Abbé Pirard his confidant and had thus learned to value his intelligence and uprightness; so that finally, to free him from his untenable position at Besançon, the marquis had procured him a benefice in Paris and somewhat later had taken the Abbé's favorite pupil, Julien Sorel, into his household as private secretary.

The characters, attitudes, and relationships of the dramatis personae, then, are very closely connected with contemporary historical circumstances; contemporary political and social conditions are woven into the action in a manner more detailed and more real than had been exhibited in any earlier novel, and indeed in any works of literary art except those expressly purporting to be politico-satirical tracts. So logically and systematically to situate the tragically conceived life of a man of low social position (as here that of Julien Sorel) within the most concrete kind of contemporary history and to develop it therefrom – this is an entirely new and highly significant phenomenon. The other circles in which Julien Sorel moves – his father's family, the house of the mayor of Verrières, M. de Rênal, the seminary at Besançon – are sociologically defined in conformity with the historical moment with the same penetration as is the la Mole household; and not one of the minor characters – the old priest Chélan, for example, or the director of the workhouse, Valenod – would be conceivable outside the particular historical situation of the Restoration period, in the manner in which they are set before us. The same laying of a contemporary foundation for events is to be found in Stendhal's other novels – still incomplete and too narrowly circumscribed in *Armance*, but fully developed in the later works: in the *Chartreuse de Parme* (which, however, since its setting is a place not yet greatly affected by modern development, sometimes gives the effect of being a historical novel), as also in *Lucien Leuwen*, a novel of the Louis-Philippe period, which Stendhal left unfinished. In the latter, indeed, in the form in which it has come down to us, the element of current history and politics is too heavily emphasized: it is not always wholly integrated into the course of the action and is set forth in far too great detail in proportion to the principal theme; but perhaps in a final revision Stendhal would have achieved an organic articulation of the whole. Finally, his autobiographical works, despite the capricious and erratic 'egotism' of their style and manner, are likewise far more closely, essentially, and concretely connected with the politics, sociology, and economics of the period than are, for example, the corresponding works of Rousseau or Goethe; one feels that the great events of contemporary history affected Stendhal much more directly than they did the other two; Rousseau did not live to see them, and Goethe had managed to keep aloof from them.

To have stated this is also to have stated what circumstance it was which, at that particular moment and in a man of that particular period, gave rise to modern tragic realism based on the contemporary; it was the first of the great movements of modern times in which large masses of men consciously took part – the French Revolution with all the consequent convulsions which spread from it over Europe. From the Reformation movement, which was no less powerful and which aroused the masses no less, it is distinguished by the much faster tempo of its spread, its mass effects, and the changes which it produced in practical daily life within a comparatively extensive territory; for the progress then achieved in transportation and communication, together with the spread of elementary education resulting from the trends of the Revolution itself, made it possible to mobilize the people far more rapidly and in a far more unified direction; everyone was reached by the same ideas and events far more quickly, more consciously, and more uniformly. For Europe there began that process of temporal concentration, both of historical events themselves and of everyone's knowledge of them, which has since made tremendous progress and which not only permits us to prophesy a unification of human life throughout the world but has in a certain sense already achieved it. Such a development abrogates or renders powerless the entire social structure of orders and categories previously held valid; the tempo of the changes demands a perpetual and extremely difficult effort toward inner adaptation and produces intense concomitant crises. He who would account to himself for his real life and his place in human society is obliged to do so upon a far wider practical foundation and in a far larger context than before, and to be continually conscious that the social base upon which he lives is not constant for a moment but is perpetually changing through convulsions of the most various kinds.

We may ask ourselves how it came about that modern consciousness of reality began to find literary form for the first time precisely in Henri Beyle of Grenoble. Beyle-Stendhal was a man of keen intelligence, quick and alive, mentally independent and courageous, but not quite a great figure. His ideas are often forceful and inspired, but they are erratic, arbitrarily advanced, and, despite all their show of boldness, lacking in inward certainty and continuity. There is something unsettled about his whole nature: his fluctuation between realistic candor in general and silly mystification in particular, between cold self-control, rapturous abandonment to sensual pleasures, and insecure and sometimes sentimental vaingloriousness, is not always easy to put up with; his literary style is very impressive and unmistakably original, but it is short-winded, not uniformly successful, and only seldom wholly takes possession of and fixes the subject. But, such as he was, he offered himself to the moment; circumstances seized him, tossed him about, and laid upon him a unique and unexpected destiny; they formed him so that he was compelled to come to terms with reality in a way which no one had done before him.

When the Revolution broke out Stendhal was a boy of six; when he left his native city of Grenoble and his reactionary, solidly bourgeois family, who though glumly sulking at the new situation were still very wealthy, and went to Paris, he was sixteen. He arrived there immediately after Napoleon's *coup d'état*; one of his relatives, Pierre Daru, was an influential adherent of the First Consul; after some hesitations and interruptions, Stendhal made a brilliant career in the Napoleonic administration. He saw Europe on Napoleon's expeditions; he grew to be a man, and indeed an extremely elegant man of the world; he also became, it appears, a useful administrative official and a reliable, cold-blooded organizer who did not lose his calm even in danger. When Napoleon's fall threw Stendhal out of the saddle, he was in his thirty-second year. The first, active, successful, and brilliant part of his career was over. Thenceforth he has no profession and no place claims him. He can go where he pleases, so long as he has money enough and so long as the suspicious officials of the post-Napoleonic period have no objection to his sojourns. But his financial circumstances gradually become worse; in 1821 he is exiled from Milan, where he had first settled down, by Metternich's police; he goes to Paris, and there he lives for another nine years, without a profession, alone, and with very slender means. After the July Revolution his friends get him a post in the diplomatic service; since the Austrians refuse him an exequatur for Trieste, he has to go as consul to the little port of Cività Vecchia; it is a dreary place to live, and there are those who try to get him into trouble if he prolongs his visits to Rome unduly; to be sure, he is allowed to spend a few years in Paris on leave – so long, that is, as one of his protectors is Minister of Foreign Affairs. Finally he falls seriously ill in Cività Vecchia and is given another leave in Paris; he dies there in 1842, smitten by apoplexy in the street, not yet sixty. This is the second half of his life; during this period, he acquires the reputation of being a witty, eccentric, politically and morally unreliable man; during this period, he begins to write. He writes first on music, on Italy and Italian art, on love; it is not until he is forty-three and is in Paris during the first flowering of the Romantic movement (to which he contributed in his way) that he publishes his first novel.

From this sketch of his life it should appear that he first reached the point of accounting for himself, and the point of realistic writing, when he was seeking a haven in his 'storm-tossed boat,' and discovered that, for his boat, there was no fit and safe haven; when, though in no sense weary or discouraged, yet already a man of forty, whose early and successful career lay far behind him, alone and comparatively poor, he became aware, with all the sting of that knowledge, that he belonged nowhere. For the first time, the social world around him became a problem; his feeling that he was different from other men, until now borne easily and proudly, doubtless now first became the predominant concern of his consciousness and finally the recurring theme of his literary activity. Stendhal's realistic writing grew out of his discomfort in the post-Napoleonic world and his consciousness that he did not belong to it and had no place in it. Discomfort in the given world and inability to become part of it is, to be sure, characteristic of Rousseauan romanticism and it is probable that Stendhal had something of that even in his youth; there is something of it in his congenital disposition, and the course of his youth can only have strengthened such tendencies, which, so to speak, harmonized with the tenor of life of his generation; on the other hand, he did not write his recollections of his youth, the *Vie de Henry Brulard*, until he was in his fifties, and we must allow for the possibility that, from the viewpoint of his later development, from the viewpoint of 1835, he overstressed such motifs

of individualistic isolation. It is, in any case, certain that the motifs and
expressions of his isolation and his problematic relation to society are
wholly different from the corresponding phenomena in Rousseau and his
early romantic disciples.

Stendhal, in contrast to Rousseau, had a bent for practical affairs and the
requisite ability; he aspired to sensual enjoyment of life as given; he did not
withdraw from practical reality from the outset, did not entirely condemn
it from the outset – instead he attempted, and successfully at first, to master
it. Material success and material enjoyments were desirable to him; he
admires energy and the ability to master life, and even his cherished
dreams ('the silence of happiness') are more sensual, more concrete, more
dependent upon human society and human creations (Cimarosa, Mozart,
Shakespeare, Italian art) than those of the *Solitary Walker*. Not until success
and pleasure began to slip away from him, not until practical
circumstances threatened to cut the ground from under his feet, did the
society of his time become a problem and a subject to him. Rousseau did
not find himself at home in the social world he encountered, which did not
appreciably change during his lifetime; he rose in it without thereby
becoming happier or more reconciled to it, while it appeared to remain
unchanged. Stendhal lived while one earthquake after another shook the
foundations of society; one of the earthquakes jarred him out of the
everyday course of life prescribed for men of his station, flung him, like
many of his contemporaries, into previously inconceivable adventures,
events, responsibilities, tests of himself, and experiences of freedom and
power; another flung him back into a new everyday which he thought
more boring, more stupid, and less attractive than the old; the most
interesting thing about it was that it too gave no promise of enduring; new
upheavals were in the air, and indeed broke out here and there even
though not with the power of the first.

Because Stendhal's interest arose out of the experiences of his own life,
it was held not by the structure of a possible society but by the changes in
the society actually given. Temporal perspective is a factor of which he
never loses sight, the concept of incessantly changing forms and manners
of life dominates his thoughts – the more so as it holds a hope for him: In
1880 or 1930 I shall find readers who understand me! I will cite a few
examples. When he speaks of La Bruyère's wit (*Henry Brulard*, chapter 30),
it is apparent to him that this type of formative endeavor of the intellect has
lost in validity since 1789: 'wit, delicious as it is for him who savours it,
does not last. Just as a peach goes off in a matter of days, so wit "goes off"
in the space of two hundred years, and a lot more rapidly than that if there
is a revolution in the relationships between the different classes of society.'
The *Souvenirs d'égotisme* contain an abundance of observations (for the
most part truly prophetic) based on temporal perspective. He foresees
(chapter 7, near the end) that 'at the time when this chatter is read' it will

have become a commonplace to make the ruling classes responsible for the crimes of thieves and murderers; he fears, at the beginning of chapter 9, that all his bold utterances, which he dares put forth only with fear and trembling, will have become platitudes ten years after his death, if heaven grants him a decent allowance of life, say eighty or ninety years; in the next chapter he speaks of one of his friends who pays an unusually high price for the favors of a 'decent woman of the people', and adds in explanation: 'five hundred francs in 1832 will be the equivalent of a thousand in 1872' – that is, forty years after the time at which he is writing and thirty after his death.

It would be possible to quote many more passages of the same general import. But it is unnecessary, for the element of time-perspective is apparent everywhere in the presentation itself. In his realistic writings, Stendhal everywhere deals with the reality which presents itself to him: 'I take things as I find them', he says not far from the passage just quoted: in his effort to understand men, he does not pick and choose among them; this method, as Montaigne knew, is the best for eliminating the arbitrariness of one's own constructions, and for surrendering oneself to reality as given. But the reality which he encountered was so constituted that, without permanent reference to the immense changes of the immediate past and without a premonitory searching after the imminent changes of the future, one could not represent it; all the human figures and all the human events in his work appear upon a ground politically and socially disturbed. To bring the significance of this graphically before us, we have but to compare him with the best-known realistic writers of the pre-Revolutionary eighteenth century: with Lesage or the Abbé Prévost, with the pre-eminent Henry **Fielding** or with Goldsmith; we have but to consider how much more accurately and profoundly he enters into given contemporary reality than Voltaire, Rousseau, and the youthful realistic work of Schiller, and upon how much broader a basis than Saint-Simon, whom, though in the very incomplete edition then available, he read assiduously. Insofar as the serious realism of modern times cannot represent man otherwise than as embedded in a total reality, political, social, and economic, which is concrete and constantly evolving – as is the case today in any novel or film – Stendhal is its founder.

However, the attitude from which Stendhal apprehends the world of events and attempts to reproduce it with all its interconnections is as yet hardly influenced by Historism – which, though it penetrated into France in his time, had little effect upon him. For that very reason we have referred in the last few pages to time-perspective and to a constant consciousness of changes and cataclysms, but not to a comprehension of evolutions. It is not too easy to describe Stendhal's inner attitude toward social phenomena. It is his aim to seize their every nuance; he most accurately represents the particular structure of any given milieu, he has no

preconceived rationalistic system concerning the general factors which
determine social life, nor any pattern-concept of how the ideal society
ought to look; but in particulars his representation of events is oriented,
wholly in the spirit of classic ethical psychology, upon an 'analysis of the
human heart', not upon discovery or premonitions of historical forces; we
find rationalistic, empirical, sensual motifs in him, but hardly those of
romantic Historism. Absolutism, religion and the Church, the privileges of
rank, he regards very much as would an average protagonist of the
Enlightenment, that is as a web of superstition, deceit, and intrigue; in
general, artfully contrived intrigue (together with passion) plays a decisive
role in his plot construction, while the historical forces which are the basis
of it hardly appear. Naturally all this can be explained by his political
viewpoint, which was democratic-republican; this alone sufficed to render
him immune to romantic Historism; besides which the emphatic manner of
such writers as Chateaubriand displeased him in the extreme. On the other
hand, he treats even the classes of society which, according to his views,
should be closest to him, extremely critically and without a trace of the
emotional values which romanticism attached to the word people. The
practically active bourgeoisie with its respectable money-making, inspires
him with unconquerable boredom, he shudders at the 'Republican virtue'
of the United States, and despite his ostensible lack of sentimentality he
regrets the fall of the social culture of the *ancien régime*. 'My goodness, there
is a shortage of wit', he writes in chapter 30 of *Henry Brulard*, 'everyone
devotes all his energies to whatever profession will bring him a position in
the world'. No longer is birth or intelligence or the self-cultivation of the
honnête homme the deciding factor – it is ability in some profession. This is
no world in which Stendhal-Dominique can live and breathe. Of course,
like his heroes, he too can work and work efficiently, when that is what is
called for. But how can one take anything like practical professional work
seriously in the long run! Love, music, passion, intrigue, heroism – these
are the things that make life worthwhile. . . .

Stendhal is an aristocratic son of the *ancien régime grande bourgeoisie*, he
will and can be no nineteenth-century bourgeois. He says so himself time
and again: My views were Republican even in my youth but my family
handed down their aristocratic instincts to me (*Brulard*, ch. 14); since the
Revolution theater audiences have become stupid (*Brulard*, ch. 22); I was a
liberal myself (in 1821), and yet I found the liberals 'outrageously silly'
(*Souvenirs d'égotisme*, ch. 6); to converse with a 'fat provincial merchant'
makes me dull and unhappy all day (*Egotisme*, ch. 7 and *passim*) – these and
similar remarks, which sometimes also refer to his physical constitution
('Nature has given me the delicate nerves and sensitive skin of a woman',
Brulard, ch. 32), occur plentifully. Sometimes he has pronounced accesses of
socialism: in 1811, he writes, energy was to be found only in the class
'which has to struggle in the face of real need' (*Brulard*, ch. 2). But he finds

the smell and the noise of the masses unendurable, and in his books, outspokenly realistic though they are in other respects, we find no 'people,' either in the romantic 'folk' sense or in the socialist sense – only petty bourgeois, and occasional accessory figures such as soldiers, domestic servants, and coffee-house mademoiselles. Finally, he sees the individual man far less as the product of his historical situation and as taking part in it, than as an atom within it; a man seems to have been thrown almost by chance into the milieu in which he lives; it is a resistance with which he can deal more or less successfully, not really a culture-medium with which he is organically connected. In addition, Stendhal's conception of mankind is on the whole preponderantly materialistic and sensualistic; an excellent illustration of this occurs in *Henry Brulard* (ch. 26): 'By *character* I mean a man's habitual manner of undertaking the pursuit of happiness or, in clearer if less descriptive terms, *the sum of his moral habits*'. But in Stendhal, happiness, even though highly organized human beings can find it only in the mind, in art, passion, or fame, always has a far more sensory and earthy coloring than in the romanticists. His aversion to philistine efficiency, to the type of bourgeois that was coming into existence, could be romantic too. But a romantic would hardly conclude a passage on his distaste for money-making with the words: 'I have had the rare pleasure throughout my life of doing pretty much what I pleased' (*Brulard*, ch. 32). His conception of 'wit' and of freedom is still entirely that of the pre-Revolutionary eighteenth century, although it is only with effort and a little spasmodically that he succeeds in realizing it in his own person. For freedom he has to pay the price of poverty and loneliness and his 'wit' easily becomes paradox, bitter and wounding: 'A frightening gaiety' (*Brulard*, ch. 6). His 'wit' no longer has the self-assurance of the Voltaire period; he manages neither his social life nor that particularly important part of it, his sexual relations, with the easy mastery of a gentleman of rank of the *ancien régime*; he even goes so far as to say that he cultivated 'wit' only to conceal his passion for a woman whom he did not possess – 'for ten years, that fear, a thousand times repeated, has in fact been my guiding principle in life' (*Égotisme*, ch. 1). Such traits make him appear a man born too late who tries in vain to realize the form of life of a past period; other elements of his character, the merciless objectivity of his realistic power, his courageous assertion of his personality against the triviality of the rising *juste milieu*, and much more, show him as the forerunner of certain later intellectual modes and forms of life; but he always feels and experiences the reality of his period as a resistance. That very thing makes his realism (though it proceeded, if at all, to only a very slight degree from a loving genetic comprehension of evolution – that is, from the historistic attitude) so energetic and so closely connected with his own existence: the realism of this 'touchy thoroughbred' is a product of his fight for self-assertion. And this explains the fact that the stylistic level of his great realistic novels is much closer to the old great and heroic concept of tragedy than is that of most later realists – Julien Sorel is much more a 'hero' than the characters of Balzac, to say nothing of Flaubert. [. . .]

2   Georges Blin on 'realism' and 'point of view'*

It can scarcely be denied that thanks to this close pictorial detail, these atmospheric qualities, in short this art of enveloping the narrative in the world of the senses, Stendhal provides sufficiently solid references in respect of external reality for him to be regarded as one of the founders, or at least as one of the clearest forerunners, of the modern novel. It only remains to be explained how anyone could ever have thought otherwise: how it is that this colouring, this precision, this suggestive orchestration of concrete detail escape the reader who does not consciously take stock. They do so, first, because this novelist tends to relegate to the background anything that smacks of strict 'realism': the painstaking application to detail that accuracy demands is something he prefers to save for the comic and the odious, whose functioning and portrayal remain of secondary importance, while he uses his own passionate involvement, and hence therefore ours, to breathe life into the lyrical and idealizing passion of his young protagonists: and, of course, it is they, as is only fitting, who receive the largest and most sharply focused share of the limelight. Thus, even when the novelist is led by his instinct for satire to describe things in detail, matters of the heart end up taking precedence over the demands of 'harsh reality'. This co-presence, to varying degrees of effect, of both fantasy and cruelly charged observation, reminds one rather of those painters of old who portrayed the life of Christ by heavily accenting the lifelikeness, even the ugliness, of the minor characters and the executioners, while channelling the observer's gaze towards the extremely idealized figures of Christ and Mary.

Second, even when Stendhal consents to add one or two bold splashes of colour, the overall picture remains grey, and this is because he narrates in a hurry, shaping his sentences like arrows and leaving us little time to identify the tonalities he has employed: movement has no colour, while the pictorial is always static. But this is not all. If such a narrator never stops us in front of a picture, it is not just because of the accelerated way in which

---

*Translated from *Stendhal et les problèmes du roman* (José Corti, 1954), pp. 105–12.

he makes us read, but for the very good reason that he is not painting a *picture*. A commentator assessing the amount of physical data used in *The Red and the Black* or in *Lucien Leuwen* can, by condensing them or listing them in sequence, create the false impression that a considerable measure of concrete reality has been involved in the way these novels treat their fictional stories. But during the telling of the story such touches were not so grouped, and the reader, for whom they were lost to view almost as soon as he encountered them, was never intuitively able to total them in such a way. This explains why, even when Stendhal provides enough physical traits (as accidental or necessary adjuncts of his story-telling) for us to be able to construct a portrait, the physical appearance of his characters is not what strikes us most. And the same goes for the landscapes. It is rare for him to leave us in complete ignorance of the settings, but he only reveals particular details (whether central or incidental) on separate occasions and in the diffuse order of a description whose progression is indistinguishable from that of the action itself. Thus, having never been able to take in the whole setting in one gaze, when we return to it we scarcely recognize it – something, moreover, which does no harm to the narrative since the author has managed to give us a reassuring if false sense of 'déjà vu'.[1] Balzac, on the other hand, who anticipates the Naturalists in this respect, paints his portraits in great set-piece recapitulations, just as he groups together in comprehensive tableaux (where he alternates between simple lists and explanatory linkage) all the descriptive material he needs in order to establish, once and for all, his chosen milieu.[2]

Confirming this difference between the two writers is something which has already been noted and which tends to explain, better than the preceding arguments, why in Stendhal the 'atmospheric' elements do not draw attention to themselves, even though they are carefully specified. The author of *The Red and the Black* has no need to evoke the setting in advance as if he were drawing up some carefully calculated balance sheet for the simple reason that he is not seeking to establish any necessary link between this setting and the human beings whose behaviour he is analysing.[3] Even if he allows elsewhere at a theoretical level (in line with his sensualist mentors, and with Montesquieu or Cabanis) that the physical does condition and therefore explain moral characteristics, as a novelist he champions a kind of parallel philosophy which safeguards the freedom, even gratuitousness, of his heroes' actions, as much in what they decide as in what they actually do. In this respect a character's independence of his hereditary background, of his own past, and of his material or social context represents rather effectively the autonomy which Stendhal the novelist ultimately recognizes to be an essential characteristic of psychological experience. One feels that with him as with the Stoics the inner self can allow sadness and joy to enter only with the assistance and foreknowledge of the imagination and the faculty of judgement; which is why Julien and Fabrice are never so happy as when they are in prison. Blocking all influence from outside, captivity constitutes for them the best of protective shields and safeguards a freedom which for this novelist, as we know, is identical with the freedom to be oneself, is part and parcel of the unfettered pursuance of one's vocation as an egotist. The external world, as long as it does not take the form of a threat, thus counts for very little as far as Stendhal's heroes are concerned. Even if they happen to enthuse about a landscape, it is not the landscape itself which is responsible for the onset of lyricism: the sublime was already there within them, in the form either of a basic prompting or of a particular passion. When, therefore, they cry out in admiration at the sight of a lake or mountain peaks, they are really only using the object of their admiration as a way of exalting themselves: they are simply exclaiming at their own destiny, which explains why the exclamation generally takes the form of a woman's name. As they are in any case acting only at their own behest (almost the only external obstacle to their own freedom being the corresponding freedom of the woman who is singled out in this way), the validity of Stendhal's psychological analysis is in no way reduced if the physical element in a character's actions is not specified, or is merely added as an afterthought and as an author's marginal note. It comes as no surprise to find, therefore, that while the author, on rereading his work, tells himself to add more concrete detail to the original version, he never so much as thinks of altering the logic of the plot or even his account of psychological reactions within it. But one sees also how such descriptive detail – itself so secondary and extraneous as to be superfluous were it not so unobtrusive and were it not as much a guide to understanding as a guarantee of the plausibility of the sense-experiences involved – can be consumed by the reader without his paying very much attention to it, even at moments of closest involvement in the story.

The descriptive novel alternates between a thoroughly Parnassian taste for the pictorial and a desire, in accordance with Naturalist precepts, to explain the internal by the external.[4] In both cases the physical object takes pride of place: in the first as a source of pleasure, in the latter as a provider of meaning. In both cases, it is the physical object which constitutes form: form as something to be admired or form as an active agent. Stendhal, on the other hand, returns the physical object to its status as content or subject-matter, or rather he considers the perceivable world as being nothing other than the scene of the action itself: it is neither a cause nor (as spectacle) an end in itself. The type of vision which his novels propose – and is there a more authentic form of *realism* than this? – is precisely that which we adopt in the course of our daily lives. The external world[5] is seen as exercising a coercive effect only at the level of the 'expedients' to which it reduces us, and as being of pictorial interest only by a process of abstraction (to 'show it to advantage') which thereby removes it from our grasp. To tell the truth, it figures as neither a 'before' nor an 'after' in our actions: and it is the theatre of our actions only to the extent that it is already the means thereof. Neither pure origin, nor end point, but medium and place of passage. To consider the external world in isolation from our undertakings within it in order to set it up either as a principle or as something to be worshipped, is thus always to destroy it, and Stendhal is right not to hypostasize it, right to deny it any transcendental character, right to point to it in his narratives only obliquely, that is, by what it provides in the way of accidents, obstacles, and means for the carrying out of an intention which itself is never presented in isolation, without its 'how' – just as he is right to present the external world as something admired only within the context of individual pursuits of happiness. [6] If it is true that the real is only ever focused upon as the object of a particular intention or ambition[7], the novelist can consider himself exempt from description. Describing is what an ideal witness does, or someone who for the moment is refraining from living his own life. When description interrupts the narrative, far from serving to fix the character in his setting, it in fact thereby removes him from his context, which is always a context of action. It makes him lose interest in himself, as it were, and forces him quite arbitrarily to assume the role of a professional observer or, better perhaps, of the author's surrogate. The concrete is destroyed by being disconnected from existence; and existence – which is always *an* existence, that is to say a being-in-pursuit-of, a need to 'pass beyond', and an inability to 'leave off' from living – does not allow of being separated out, even for the purposes of contemplation. When the novelist makes his picture of reality 'stand out', it is thus from life itself that he is causing the picture to stand out, and he thereby foregoes the right to present it as anything other than a confessedly theoretical reconstruction.[8]

This is what permits Stendhal never to draw up on behalf of his heroes an inventory of their presence in the world which would be tantamount to an inventory of the world itself, but rather one which is invested with their own particular desires, that is to say a world viewed from a particular angle. As far as pictorial detail, setting, and the feeling for nature are concerned (since these are what are at issue), a few examples will suffice to establish that when the author of *The Red and the Black* notes features of the physical world, they are indeed the only ones perceptible from a particular psychological vantage-point. Let us take, for example, a broad vista out of doors: Mme de Renâl, from the top of the dovecot, hears birdsong and the sound of cicadas and gazes out over 'the vast slope of dark greenery, smooth as a meadow, formed by the tops of the trees' when one looks at a forest from a distance.[9] These details are addressed to the senses: but let us look again. Not one is given simply for the fun of it, since Julien's mistress has not 'run up the hundred and twenty steps to the top of the dovecot' just to admire the countryside but rather to send a signal and, possibly, to receive one. Thus she hears the birds only with irritation, cursing them because they may prevent her from hearing a 'shout of joy' from her lover. As for the mass of vegetation, she does not savour it as an artist: she is too busy 'devouring' it with her eyes to see if Julien is replying. She only takes in the uninterrupted patch of colour provided by the magnificent meadow-like expanse of trees because she is scouring it as a background to the signal she hopes to see. On the night when the hero resolves to clamber his way into Mathilde's apartments, 'the moon was so bright', Stendhal carefully informs us,[10] 'that it cast black shadows in Mlle de La Mole's room' – a scene which may stimulate our sensual imagination. But the young man risking his life is not thus stimulated, no more than the author has recorded this suggestive detail of his own accord to lend a Romantic setting to so unsugary a celebration of the bridal-chamber: Julien has only noticed the detail because of his obsessive fear that there may be men lying in wait for him under this particular cloak of darkness, men whose shapes he might not be able to make out. Similarly, in relation to his hero's escape in *The Charterhouse of Parma*, the author mentions that 'towards midnight, one of those thick white fogs in which the Po sometimes swathes its banks, spread first of all over the town, and then . . . '.[11] Certainly this detail establishes the atmosphere, but Stendhal has not simply thrown it in for good measure: he is as precise as this because Fabrice, who is about to slide down the walls of the citadel on a rope, has only ventured out into the void having duly investigated what sort of night it is.

But why look further for examples? One has only to return to the scene criticized by Zola. And if one looks again at the chapter in *The Red and the Black* entitled 'An Evening in the Country', one sees that not one of the details already mentioned has been provided by Stendhal other than from the physical viewpoint or psychological perspective of the protagonists. The darkness caused by the storm clouds is noted via Julien's relieved supposition that his grab for Mme de Renâl's hand will be the better concealed from view. It is via Mme Derville's tiredness that we come to learn that the wind has got up; and this tiredness itself is noticed by Julien, and only because he in turn is afraid of having to be alone with Mme de Renâl, which would happen if her cousin had to retire indoors. We note the rustling of the leaves, as they are sprinkled by the first, refreshing drops of rain, only via Mme de Renâl's feeling of delight, and this delight strikes us simply as a sign of the heroine's decision to give herself up to her love. Only a relaxation of the rules which duty had led her to impose upon herself can have made her so receptive to physical sensations and so open to the world about her. As for the plant-pot knocked over by a gust of wind, this detail is of interest to us solely because Mme de Renâl helped to pick it up, and it was mentioned only because, in order to do so, the young woman had to remove her hand – a fact which in turn is only noteworthy because returning her hand to Julien's afterwards constituted a form of acquiescence. Of course, Stendhal did not need to spell out the links in the chain like this; he has specified the 'circumstance' of the flower-pot being overturned merely to inform us that the heroine has recognized her defeat not just by passive consent but by an initiative of her own. Her gesture may indeed appear all the more deliberate in view of the fact that this temporary attention to a material object must surely, by requiring her to change position, have momentarily broken the spell she was under and so might have allowed her to recover her self-control and master her feelings. This all goes to show, therefore, that the evening of the storm is in fact presented in all its suggestive materiality, but also that the various impressions it affords emerge only within the context of the struggle taking place between two wills, and indeed mostly from the sole perspective of the hero's combative intentions.

We see here, thanks to Stendhal, what might be the task of a novelist who was completely realist. If, in order not to relapse into abstraction, he must refrain from describing that which lies beyond what actually catches the attention of the protagonist concerned; if, in order to remain within the bounds of the real, he is permitted to evoke the external world only as a limited 'field of vision' (and in such a way that the limits themselves continually vary) which is distorted by the to and fro of calculating self-interest, which is traversed by lines of force, which is always anecdotal – that is to say, always sustained by subjective ambitions but always denied final objective resolution (within some historical hierarchy or order of end-results), and which, finally, is always looked beyond in anticipation and cancelled out by the cessation of desire; if this is indeed the world for each person, the world *of* somebody, then the novelist must renounce the convenient ubiquity of the omniscient narrator and enclose himself, at each level of the narrative, within the perspective of whichever protagonist happens to be in question. One of Stendhal's principal merits, and one which has been insufficiently recognized, is to have understood this requirement, and to have convinced himself, with a measure of critical self-awareness which is generally undervalued, that the need for events to present themselves from a particular point of view implied the further need for the narrator to effect 'restrictions in the field of vision'.

Notes

1. JEAN PRÉVOST (*La Création chez Stendhal*, p. 155) indeed points out in respect of *The Red and the Black* that Stendhal, by taking care in advance (and repeatedly) to name the spot where a major scene is going to be set, is already putting our imagination to work and making the particular spot seem familiar, with the result that when the episode finally does occur, we think we have already been shown the place in question, whereas in fact, in the absence of all description, we have hitherto simply been haunting it with our own imaginings.

2. Clearly this assertion would need to be qualified, but it holds for those parts of the *Human Comedy* which are most typical of this novelist.

3. To see the truth of this, one has only to examine the scene which, precisely, Zola criticized in *The Red and the Black*: the evening spent beneath the lime-tree. As mentioned earlier, Stendhal gives more than adequate details of the surroundings, but these do not for a moment explain – that is, they do not determine – either the various stages of this 'duel' or its outcome. One could not maintain, for example, that the stiff breeze, acting as a stimulant, had increased the aggressive daring of the young tutor, nor, conversely, that by causing the heroine to relax, it had helped to disarm the resistance which she might have offered. The specific place and time of day have scarcely any influence on the contingent 'how' of the combat. They simply entail a random set of external features, and the real cause of the conflict has to be sought elsewhere: that is, in the protagonist's own plan of action, for – and Zola's expressed regret at not finding any influence of the environment at work here is all the more misplaced as a result – it was on the previous evening that Julien conceived his move. So it is far from being the case that the situation and the moment might have brought him counsel! One may argue that Zola was thinking especially of the heroine, whose surrender he would like to have seen caused by the damp night air and the wafting scents of August. But that is to forget that at the operative moment the scene is shown almost entirely from Julien's point of view. Since his companion, or rather his opponent, is fully engaged in trying to control her own emotions, and since the young man is not even in a state to observe her properly, Mme de Renâl scarcely exists for us at this point. She appears above all as something encountered in passing as our attention moves out from Julien and then back towards him, as may be seen in the impersonal use of the passive at the crucial moment: 'there was one last attempt to remove it from his grasp, but in the end the hand remained in his' [*The Red and the Black*, p. 57].

4. A concern for pictorial detail points both to the pre-Parnassian ambition of the Romantics to depict external reality and to the principle of realism whereby the reader is seduced into acceptance by aesthetic devices. This means that it is not at all easy to determine in the second quarter of the nineteenth century whether descriptive elements should be attributed to a continuing Romantic taste for local colour or to a tendency, already realist in essence but not yet consciously worked out, to posit a causal role for any given setting.

5. So far is he from being obsessed with the external world that there is never any question of his endowing it, as Balzac and Zola willingly do, with fantastic, mythic, or mythological status.

6. It is good that BAUDELAIRE should have accredited and given prominence to Stendhal's admirable definition of the Beautiful as 'the promise of happiness' [in 'What is Romanticism?', in *The Salon of 1846* and elsewhere: see BAUDELAIRE, *Oeuvres complètes*, ed. Claude Pichois, 2 vols. (Paris, Gallimard (Bibliothèque de la Pléiade), 1975–6), i. 548, ii. 37, 420, 686].

7. In a diary entry of 9 Dec. 1804, having sketched out a 'map of the battlefield', in other words the place where he had met Victorine [Mounier], Stendhal, always very alive to nuance and (being a writer) an alert critic, justified the expression to himself as follows: 'Mante might have said "apartment"; but by saying "battlefield", I am indicating the place where she lives and then also the way in which I envisage it.' Thus setting and intention are systematically combined.

8. Let there be no misunderstanding. It is self-evident that if the character happens

to examine his present experience from an aesthetic or hedonistic point of view, if he proceeds to draw up a survey or inventory of his surroundings, if during some lull he indulges himself or, as it were, takes time off in a dilettante fashion, then the novelist is not only entitled but obliged to accompany him in this reflective and disinterested experience of the world. Clearly our own lives permit of such moments of repose, and we register certain data, in the margins of our 'pursuits', which, being often chanced upon, gradually assume larger proportions as we are led by the aesthetic pleasure they afford to concentrate on them more and more and to confer greater significance upon them. Julien, Fabrice, and all of Stendhal's egotists (including, above all, Stendhal himself) would even seem to be the most liable of all to give themselves up to such moments of enchantment. But it must be noted, first, that such feelings, because value comes to be attached to them, at once become part of the character's ambitions in life, at once imply moral choices in the present of a more or less provisional kind, and, depending on the extent to which they are assimilated, affect the direction of the character's ambitions rather than being simply an incidental feature of them. The novelist is obliged in such cases to take note of the character's impressions, since the character himself 'takes note' of them. But that does not mean that he is allowed in his descriptions to indulge in purple patches or point his telephoto lens when the characters he has created do not themselves relate to the world as painters or detectives. He cannot be explicit about the setting when the hero himself has only a generalized, intermittent or blurred awareness of it without thereby committing himself to some kind of psychoanalysis of his characters, an approach which is not only indiscreet and intrusive but also such as completely to distort the scale of values which has been established in any given instance in respect of the 'interested parties' and their particular outlook. Indeed, the whole nature of the novel as a genre is here at stake. If it permits descriptions which are, as the phrase significantly has it, 'seen in the round', then it must give up any claim to being a 'tale', 'story', or 'narrative'. Its task will no longer be to trace people's activities – their plans, their adventures, their reactions – but to reveal everything that the characters have not understood, even about themselves; or rather to reveal where they have been and what people they have met without their having noticed either, to reveal everything that they might have noticed if they had been as well placed as the novelist, or if they had been more observant, or if they had been in less of a hurry to achieve their aims and thus to bring the book to a close.

9. *The Red and the Black*, p. 138.

10. *The Red and the Black*, p. 351.

11. *The Charterhouse of Parma*, p. 397.

Thematic Criticism

Thematic Criticism was the product of the so-called Geneva School whose main representatives include Gaston Bachelard, Georges Poulet, Jean-Pierre Richard, Jean Rousset and Jean Starobinski. Bachelard's works were published mainly in the 1940s, but the other critics came to prominence during the 1950s and 1960s and have continued to be widely read. This critical approach was influenced by phenomenology as well as by the anti-biographical view of literary criticism proposed by Marcel Proust. Believing, with Proust, that an artist's creative self is something separate from his social self, they saw each creative artist as inhabiting and projecting a distinctive imaginary universe. The critic's task, in their view, was to map such a universe by acting as the 'consciousness of a consciousness'. Moving immediately beyond the author's biographical circumstances, they saw the 'reality' of a text as consisting not in the external world portrayed within it but in the way in which a particular consciousness has structured this world.

Typically, and often paying particular attention to the use of imagery, they chose 'themes', or aspects of human experience (time, space, sensual experience), and investigated how these were represented in literary texts. Thus, for example, in his essay on Stendhal in the fourth volume of *Studies in Human Time* (1968), George Poulet argues that Stendhalian narrative is essentially a series of largely disconnected moments, and he concludes:

> Strictly speaking, the Stendhalian novel lacks temporal continuity. But in the few, discontinuous moments of time which it presents, it offers us by way of compensation – with which to supplement and complete our own happiness as well as that of the person depicted within the extremely narrow context of these brief moments – an opening-out on to *space*. [–] 'A lover', Stendhal tells us, 'sees the woman he loves upon the horizon of every landscape he encounters.' (*Love*, ch. 59)

Jean-Pierre Richard's essay on Stendhal is entitled 'Knowledge and Tenderness in Stendhal' and appeared in his volume of essays *Literature and Sensation* in 1954, a work which also includes pieces on Flaubert, Eugène Fromentin, and the Goncourt brothers. This was followed in 1955 by a further volume on nineteenth-century writers entitled *Poetry and Depth* in which the same critical method is applied to the poetry of Nerval, Baudelaire, Verlaine, and Rimbaud.

The extract given below is taken from the middle of Richard's essay* and illustrates his approach. At the end of his essay he remarks himself that the order in which he has presented his comments has been 'profoundly arbitrary' and that such arbitrariness is an inevitable consequence of his method. This he defines as the ambition to 'locate certain abstract structures' governing Stendhal's 'lived experience' of the world. As the title of Richard's essay indicates, he sees the author of *The Red and the Black* and *The Charterhouse of Parma* as torn between the two opposing tendencies of intellectual abstraction and emotional involvement. Caught thus between these 'two maladies, which are in some respects maladies of a particular epoch, Stendhal endeavoured to fight the one with the other, and less in order to overcome them than to bring each to a point of crisis':

> Stendhal's truth, far from being located in some sensible middle ground, must always be sought in the passionate association of extremes and contradictories.

As the extract illustrates, Richard's own style of writing is characteristic of some Thematic Criticism in its overtly literary pretensions. At the same time, the emphasis on Stendhal's use of particular words anticipates the Structuralist focus on literature as being first and foremost a linguistic phenomenon; while the reference to psychoanalysis and the attempt to map Stendhal's mental world prepare the way, once more, for Barthes and Brooks.

---

*The first part of Richard's essay is available in translation in *Stendhal. A Collection of Critical Essays*, ed. Victor Brombert (Englewood Cliffs, N.J.: Prentice-Hall, 1962) pp. 127–46.

In *The Prisoner* Marcel Proust makes a curious comment about the role of 'altitude' in the Stendhalian universe. 'You will find in Stendhal', Marcel tells Albertine, 'that a certain feeling for altitude is associated with the spiritual life: the high place where Julien Sorel is a prisoner, the citadel at the top of which Fabrice is incarcerated, the church tower in which the abbé Barnès (*sic*) pursues his astronomy and from which Fabrice enjoys such a beautiful view'.[1] Having already been identified as the natural setting for lovers' intimacy, here is space appearing as the very dimension of the spiritual, the concrete domain of the imaginary.

    And indeed it is in terms of space, be it vertical or horizontal, that the purest Stendhalian values find expression. Here is a universe in which souls single each other out according to their greater or lesser degree of 'exaltation', which knows no more ignoble defect than 'baseness', nor finer virtue than 'loftiness' of character, in which, according to Stendhal 'one's duties are in direct proportion to the scope of one's intelligence'[2]: this is a world governed by distinctly 'ascensional' lines of force. Far above 'the mudflats of the real', its inhabitants soar aloft in pursuit of the exhilaration of 'imaginary spaces'. Any psychoanalytic study of Stendhal would have to examine these themes of escape within space, of horizons aerially enjoyed as the eye is held spellbound by that 'magic of far-off vistas' which Stendhal will come to love so much in Correggio. These far-off vistas are magical because the limpidity of the atmosphere has the effect of reducing the realness of objects by covering them, as it were, in a veil of air and so allowing the shifting reflections of reverie to play upon them. This magic is exactly the same as that to be found in love: in love, too, imagination takes over from perception, as the distant image supplants proximate reality. 'Every passion', says Maine de Biran in a text which Stendhal reflected upon, 'is like the superstitious cult of a fantastical object, or of an object the very reality of which is removed entirely from the domain of perception into that of the imagination. The object itself is always presented as being more or less "envelopped", "indefinite"; it appears at a "certain distance" and in a number of different guises . . .'[3] Passion projects its desired object into a space which delivers it from all constraints and frees it from precise, fixed vision: it causes the object to evaporate in some semi-fantastical distance and yet also, oddly, in a distance which some last-minute scruple about precision causes to be delimited by a final line, the line of the horizon. 'A lover sees the woman he loves on the horizon of every landscape he beholds . . .' It is at the vanishing point of perspective that true passion is mostly easily able to delineate its mirages.

And this perspective is as much temporal as spatial: from the church tower at Grianta Fabrice looks out not only over an expanse of countryside, with its mountains and lakes stretching away beneath his gaze, but also over an expanse of time – past, present, and future – which is his entire life. The family castle and the waters of Lake Como which take him back to his childhood, the prophecies of Blanès all at once propelling him forwards towards the events of his future: it is his whole existence which is spread out before him. He sincerely believes that he can discern his future direction in the distant twinkling of the stars which Blanès shows him with his telescope. He feels called, determined, by them, as if beyond all the indeterminacy of space and time (which here merge into one single indeterminacy, a kind of poetic time-space), there were suddenly revealed the precise shape of his future destiny. Stendhal may well have considered such faith in astrology absurd: but this does not stop him from setting great store by it as a form of communion and revelation. Even, he thinks, there can be no great love without the presence of a certain divining magic, without the accompaniment of some groping consciousness that tries to exorcise chance and, to this end, associates feeling with those aspects of reality which seem to be at the furthest possible remove from it. By forecast and connection, by extremely subtle mechanisms of desire and interdict, *superstition* seeks to ward off the formidable uncertainties of love:

> There is no lover on earth, whatever his present happiness, who is entirely free from the fear of a similar catastrophe, or who (. . .) can truly say that he has never once *glimpsed it in the distant dimness of the horizon*; besides, all great passions are fearful and superstitious.[4]

Superstition sees into the temporal distance of love. It causes present fulfilment to open, in timid anticipation, on to a future from which its magical negations try to banish all misfortune. In short, it digs a channel from the present to the future, rather as regret makes the present permeable by the past. Because of the power of superstition Fabrice, Clélia, and Mme de Renâl are prevented from living within the sole limits of their present sensations: each moment of their lives expands and reverberates with the echo, summons, or threat of all other moments. Their life opens out and interconnects. They see it as a destiny.

As to this pleasure in altitude which permits the twin expanses of space and time to spread out beneath a single gaze, let us stop calling it simply 'panoramic': space no longer appears to be simply the negative distance which, by separating consciousness from its object, allows it to perceive a simplified, schematic outline of this object more clearly, but rather space becomes, in a positive and concrete way, like a kind of liquid ether in which feelings are continually growing in some endless process of expansion. 'The intensity and duration of feeling', writes Maine de Biran in particularly Stendhalian vein, 'are always in proportion to the imprecise scope of its perspectives, the distance of its objects, or the indeterminacy of the ideas which accompany it.'[5] With space ultimately embodying the creative freedom of the imagination, it is quite natural that 'height' should assume within the Stendhalian universe – as 'depth', for example, does in Baudelaire's – a spiritual and moral significance. High places encourage lofty thoughts:

> from the *campanile* his gaze shot down to the two branches of the lake, at a distance of several leagues, and this sublime view soon made him forget all the others; it awakened in him the most lofty sentiments . . . Happiness carried him to an exaltation of mind quite foreign to his nature.[6]

In Fabrice's case, therefore, taking pleasure in high places is synonymous with a soaring of the mind.[7] There can be no doubt that the Stendhalian imagination was haunted by dreams of flight. From the Napoleonic sparrow-hawk of *The Red and the Black* to the first thrush downed by Henry Brulard, and which gave him, he tells us, one of the greatest pleasures of his childhood, as well as 'the young crow' he observes on 24 March 1807 'drowned after plummeting into the Ocker, a little river near Brunswick' (a fall in which Stendhal sees 'a fine image of mortality'), a whole series of aerial images lends symbolic shape to the deepest fantasies of ambition, sadistic cruelty, and death. For to live fully is to wrench oneself off the ground, is to know the speed and intoxication of free flight: 'For the first time ever, Mathilde felt what it was to love. Life, which for her had always plodded along like a tortoise, was now on the wing.'[8] A frequenter of peaks, forever borne away to the extremes of his own being, the Stendhalian hero now aspires to leave the summit behind: already imagination had been urging him to make such a break, but he could be seen at the last moment to hesitate and falter. Only a sense of the *sublime* manages then to raise him above the earth and above his condition.

The sublime is what towers above: it is a moral flight, an ethical equivalent of the aerial imagination: and hence it contains several levels of altitude, several levels of authenticity. The *false sublime*, which Stendhal describes as

'unfeeling' ['sec'], offers the ambitious soul a *model* which it endeavours to
live up to. The individual raises himself above himself, but only in order to
identify with an ideal image – which means that this particular form of the
sublime is really little more than a kind of conformism in grandeur.
Mathilde's nobility, for example, seems less pure than Julien's for being
more concerned with the imitation of others. It survives on prejudices
which are just as limiting as the various rules of polite society which
Norbert, Croisenois, Beauvoisis, and all their dandy cousins in gracious
living allow to dictate their merest gesture. In essence, it is anachronism
become a form of snobbery: Mathilde has simply got the wrong century,
and all she is doing is to reject the fashionable mores of her own day in
order to follow those of three centuries past. Intent on imitating the de la
Mole of old who died in the Place de Grève on 30 April 1574, is she really
any different from the girls of 1820 who have read *La Nouvelle Héloïse* so
often that they are no longer capable of love except as a form of recitation?
Like Ranuce-Ernest ensconced beneath the portrait of Louis XIV, she apes
true nobility far more than she actually lives it. And in Julien himself
spontaneous energy flows all too frequently into accepted moulds: it looks
as if he has read the *Mémorial* once too often for him ever to become wary
of what he reads in books. But Julien's hero possesses the great advantage
over Mathilde's that he has not yet been swallowed up by history: sharing
as he does in a living myth, Julien has no need, unlike Mathilde, to worship
at makeshift altars or to wear mourning in honour of ancestral birthdays.
For him, as for all the young men of his age, the stones of Malmaison and
of Marshal Ney's tomb are still warm with the presence of epoch-making
figures, with memories that have scarcely faded, with a history that is more
real than that of the age in which they themselves now have the misfortune
to live. Under the Restoration vitality is still Napoleonic, and that is the
great excuse with which Stendhal provides his hero: for if one is going to
imitate a model come what may, then he prefers that we should follow the
myths of our own epoch rather than hark back to the beliefs of a bygone
age. *Racine and Shakespeare* comes up with the simple idea that
Romanticism suits the taste of the young people of 1820 in the same way as
Classicism suited that of their grandfathers. Despite appearances,
therefore, Stendhal's world sets little store by nostalgia: it wants to be
contemporary and, if possible, contemporary with the future.

The true sublime, on the other hand, cares little for imitating past,
present, or future: it lives solely according to its own promptings. It rises
far above conformism, prejudice, the judgement of others. It is a form of
aerial cynicism. It suggests that our acts fall considerably short of what we
are, and that what we are falls considerably short of what we might have
been, of what we actually were. 'I alone', Stendhal muses, 'I alone know
what I could have done. For other people I am at the very most a
might-have-been . . .' But the sublime does not concern itself with other

people, and it can blossom perfectly well in the face of this obliging 'might-have-been'. The sublime hero feels superior to all his acts: Julien slips in and out of all his roles without any of them rubbing off on him; Fabrice lives at one remove from himself, in a sort of sovereign detachment, in a place to which the eyes of other people can follow him only with difficulty and envy: 'Everything is simple in his eyes, because everything is seen from above . . .' Mosca looks at him from below, as one obliged by his profession to live at ground level and in contact with other men. The sublime, on the other hand, is a form of absence: in Mme de Chasteller's case, for example, it is difficult to tell it apart from nonchalance or ennui. 'What makes souls elevated', Stendhal writes to Pauline, 'is their own sensibility, the enemy within. (. . .) An elevated soul sets itself clearly above certain things that the world provides (. . .).'[9] The sublime soul exiles itself within its own vacuum, from which it looks out with disdain over the false plenitude of human activities. Whether from the top of the Farnese tower or from his pulpit, Fabrice manages to maintain such a regally imposing presence only because he refuses to take himself seriously: detached, slightly indifferent, magnificently natural because also free. Nothing holds him back because he holds nothing in particular awe: neither life, nor ideas. Since he does not even have – and it is Stendhal who emphasizes this – any ideas or system, every thought wells up within him, free and harmonious, like some musical impromptu of the sensibility. Nothing now can break that magnificent spontaneity of his, as if he were a young animal in the wild. His sublime is the natural come fully into bloom.

And his love for Clélia removes him from this state of indifference only to set him even further apart from his fellow-man. Thereafter he parades a soulless body through the salons of society, a sort of frail, gorgeously apparelled phantom whose complete lack of interest in humanity at large passes, in the eyes of the world, for an authentic form of saintliness. And who is to say that the world is wrong? Fabrice in love, it has been written, is already Fabrice in a charterhouse. What is there surprising, what is there sacrilegious even, about seeing Stendhalian passion so frequently offered the protective covering of ecclesiastical dress, when one considers that love and religion represent two closely related forms of detachment and retreat from the world. Love in Stendhal puts forth its most beautiful flowers in secret, in the shadow of the prison-house or amidst the fragrance of the cloister. And if, more often than not, it requires the complicity of the night-time, this is no doubt because of its horror of being observed, of being explicit, but also more especially because the shades of darkness are a realm of departure and secrecy, a kind of sacred dwelling-place which closes its doors as happiness enters. In Stendhal true love thus dedicates itself to silence and to darkness. In their happiness Fabrice and Clélia give both the reader and their own creator the slip; three happy years can be described in ten lines: and they meet with disaster only because they wanted to lighten their darkness, because they succumbed to the temptation of Psyche.[10]

So death remains for them the surest refuge; it steals away with sublime souls, it carries them off. Julien, Fabrice, and Octave do not so much die as slip quietly away. Their creator grants them permission to leave: they depart without a sound, discreetly, graciously, in the bright light of a beautiful sunrise off the coast of Greece, or in the cool air of a glorious morning. One has the impression that for them the day is only just beginning. 'Never had this head been so full of poetry as at the moment when it was due to fall.' Full of poetry, because the poetry of death links with the poetry of the sublime: both place a halo around beings who are half absent, half departed, and who are transfigured by the imminence of their disappearance. This is why there is nothing frightening about death in Stendhal, why it is never accompanied by bodily resistance or anguished awareness. The human being gives himself up to the current which is bearing him away, allows himself to be swallowed up by the void. In order to convey the tranquillity, the instantaneousness, of this abduction, Stendhal provides one of his most cherished spokesmen with a series of admirable metaphors:

> But Duchess, said Roizand, death is a word almost devoid of meaning for most people. It is but a single moment, and generally one that passes unperceived. One is suffering, one is surprised at the strange sensations one feels, and then suddenly one isn't suffering any longer, the moment has passed, one is dead. Have you ever passed in a boat beneath the Bridge of the Holy Spirit which crosses the Rhone outside Avignon? There is much talk of it in advance, there is apprehension, and then there it is in front of you a certain distance away. All at once the boat is taken by the current and in the twinkling of an eye, there is the bridge behind you.
> – Ah, sir, it is the moment of death which I cannot bear to think of.
> – But, madam, the pain of such a moment is sometimes very slight. One can still feel it, which means that one is alive, one is not yet dead, one is as yet merely dangerously ill. All of a sudden, one feels nothing any more, one is dead. Thus, death is nothing. It is a door which is either open or shut, it must be one or the other, it cannot be some third thing.[11]

Through this door the Stendhalian hero makes his exit. For him death is the ultimate form of detachment and, as it were, the definitive taking-off. A taking-off towards some other form of happiness? Stendhal's atheism prevents us from thinking so. But it is disturbing to see how death always brings the lovers together and seems to be preparing a place of reunion for them somewhere else. The optimism of the novelist is so strong in Stendhal that sometimes it even counterbalances the scepticism of the unbeliever. For it is difficult to see how this confident light that happy love casts over the whole of life could be extinguished simply by the brutality of a single moment, and a moment moreover from which Stendhal is careful to banish all pathos. But these are mere hints; what lies in the distance remains and must remain unknown. And since the life of the heart, of tenderness, of love, has been placed entirely beneath the sign of the unknowable, it is a fine thing that it should achieve in the ultimate mystery what is, in every sense of the word, its end.

And yet one must live, which is to say that one must try to be happy. Now the pursuit of happiness presents the Stendhalian hero with a choice between two opposite routes, at the end of both of which only the same anxiety awaits him. For if a life led according to the need for knowledge brings the enjoyment of a world of precision, yet also a world eroded by 'unfeelingness' and emptied of substance, a life devoted to the delights of sentiment will, on the other hand, imprison him in a form of blind enjoyment wherein the object of his pleasure and his very awareness of it will ultimately disappear. 'Your real passion', writes the twenty-year-old Stendhal after reading Maine de Biran, 'is to know and experience things. It has never been satisfied.'[12] An important admission, never subsequently belied, which sets up a fundamental opposition at the heart of Stendhalian experience between knowing and feeling, placing them face to face like enemy worlds separated by an unbridgeable gap, like two separate universes which appear, at the same time as they reject each other, also to exclude the very possibility of happiness.

Stendhal's strength lay in recognizing this opposition and in transforming the breach into a line of demarcation: on each side of this frontier, and despite its deep division, his universe would perhaps manage to orientate itself, to construct itself. For just as in Proust's novel the childhood universe of young Marcel finds its coherence in the belief that the Guermantes way and Swann's way are irremediably separated, so the Stendhalian world assumes shape and certainty by dividing into two enemy 'ways': the French sector and the Italian sector, Henri Gagnon's orchard and Elizabeth's garden, the de la Mole salon and the great woods of Verrières, the Jean-Jacques side and the Helvétius side: central oppositions whereby, in an endless diptych, each of the opposing parties, that of the mind and cool dispassion versus that of the heart and tenderness, endeavours (and always in vain) to exclude the other. This obsessive dualism, which is perhaps suggested by the double titles *Red and Black, Pink and Green, Amaranth and Green*, dominates even his most abstract thinking since there are, Stendhal tells us, 'two ways of explaining the inexplicable, one which persuades the tender soul and one the cool head.

The one is represented by Kant, Schelling, Fichte and all the Germans. Sorry reason, to which one must after all resort when it comes to reasoning, offers us the works of Bayle, Cabanis, Monsieur de Tracy, and Mr Bentham in our arduous quest for the truth.' If Stendhal seems here to align himself with the camp of sorry reason, later he will not fail to excommunicate this same reason in the name of sentiment, Helvétius in the name of Jean-Jacques, Poussin in the name of Correggio. He is forever changing camps.

While reinforcing these oppositions, life in fact obliges him to broaden the range of his experience. No theme is more deeply or more poetically Stendhalian than that of the *mountain crossing*, which symbolically represents this obsessive passing over from one side to the other. A passage – for the young Stendhal who scampers happily down the Alps into Italy with the invading army – from the small-mindedness of Grenoble to the generous spirits of Milan, from childhood to love: a passage geographically reversed for the young Fabrice from life under the thumb to a fantasy world of free and glorious living. And Julien, in order to pass from the Verrières side to the de la Mole side, from Mme de Renâl to Mathilde – these two worlds which are socially and sentimentally sealed off from each other, and which indeed will communicate only the once, in the letter from Mme de Renâl which brings on the final catastrophe – Julien, too, has his own mountain to cross. In a magnificent sentence which seems to make the road stretch into the distance and to push back the horizon, Stendhal shows his traveller looking back to this past that he is leaving behind, his gaze fixed on the church in Verrières which means so many different things to him: 'His soul grieved, and before crossing the mountain, for as long as he could see the church tower, he turned to look.' But at the same time he looks ahead of him; geographically and symbolically his life is contained within two valleys which he can survey from a height and judge. It is a rare virtue to be able, if only for an instant, to arrest the soul in its journey just as it crosses a ridge and to locate in the destiny of men a kind of watershed.

Stendhal did not believe, however, that happiness lay solely in changing camps. Nostalgia and regret pursue the traveller, constantly presenting him with images of a happiness from which he is now separated. To be able to pass so easily from one side to the other, one would need to be able not to remember. But in the company of Mathilde it is the thought of Mme de Renâl that haunts Julien, while it is the thought of Mme de Chasteller that pursues Lucien when he is with Mme de Hocquincourt. No more than he can manage to live life as rigidly separate moments, the Stendhalian hero is thus unable to restrict himself to totally exclusive forms of happiness. And if the Stendhalian world, because of its apparent discontinuity, seems to suffer relatively little from the way in which consciousness and sensibility are constantly disowning each other, the fact remains that the pursuit of happiness would prove impossible in a universe that was irremediably divided. And one can also say that it did indeed prove impossible, that Stendhal's own lived experience ended in failure. The Stendhalian enterprise would then have been successful only at the level of his novel-writing: the dual roles of hero and novelist could be said to have allowed Stendhal both to enjoy, as Fabrice, and to judge, as Stendhal. But one can, precisely at the level of experience, refuse to admit such failure, and we believe Stendhal himself refused to admit it. Between the two basic needs whose contradictory nature he fully recognized within himself, we believe that he managed to establish certain forms of equilibrium, and that between the world of unfeelingness, or knowledge, and the world of tenderness, or sentiment, he discovered a whole area in which it was possible to pass from one to the other, to be here, there, and everywhere. More than that: beyond the unstable compromises in which unfeelingness and tenderness would provisionally combine their advantages, one wonders if, at a more profound level, Stendhal did not practise a kind of inner dialectic whereby passion and knowledge each became the very source of the other.

Notes

1. [*A la recherche du temps perdu* (Bibliothèque de la Pléiade, 1987–9), iii. 879.]

2. [*Love*, trans. Gilbert and Suzanne Sale (Harmondsworth: Penguin Books, 1957), p. 197.]

3. *De l'influence de l'habitude sur la faculté de penser* [*Of the Influence of Habit on the Faculty of Thought*], ed. Victor Cousin (4 vols, Paris: Ladrange, 1841), i. 150.

4. [Stendhal, *Life of Rossini*, trans. and ed. Richard N. Coe, 2nd edn (London: Calder and Boyars, 1970), p. 228.]

5. *De l'influence de l'habitude*, i. 148.

6. [*The Charterhouse of Parma*, p. 171.]

7. Cf. another very significant passage:

   Our young Milanese walked along listening to the silence, his eyes fixed on the trees which marked the horizon of the plain, which is immensely broad at this point. The *depth* of his emotions sent his faculties *soaring* far beyond the lessons of prudence and good sense that a young Norman of his age would have drawn from the merest circumstance. The whole difference lies in the fact that the Norman's soul, if he has one, soon *flounders* as he experiences the first onset of raw vanity; whereas souls like that of Fabrice are not content with being an officer in the local brigade of the national guard or wearing yards of medal ribbon in their buttonhole, but instead soar above such concerns, and sometimes to the point of folly.

   Here again emotion is displayed in spatial terms, seeming like a taking-off, a tearing-away of the self from out of the mire of human mediocrity. The danger

of floundering in the mire is, moreover, clearly defined: it is the danger of *vanity*, which is life lived under scrutiny. In the case of authentic emotion, on the other hand, scrutiny fades into the distance – and this is one of the reasons for the beauty of this text – of the two vast dimensions of the vertical and the horizontal. In this way 'depth of emotion' displays its co-ordinates in concrete terms.
[*Editor's note:* The passage quoted here is from Stendhal's subsequent revisions of *The Charterhouse*, which he made in at least three copies of the first edition (and partly no doubt at Balzac's instigation). This passage occurs in the so-called Chaper copy, in which the original edition had been interleaved with blank sheets for the purposes of revision. The original French may be found in the Bibliothèque de la Pléiade edition, ii. 1389.]

8. [*The Red and the Black*, p. 446.]

9. [24 Mar. 1807 (*Correspondance*, Bibliothèque de la Pléiade, i. 341).]

10. 'Psyche destroyed love by wanting to know it' [see *Œuvres complètes* (50 vols, Geneva: Cercle du Bibliophile, n.d. [1967]–1974), xxxiii. 25].

11. [*Une position sociale*, ch. 2.]

12. [*Œuvres complètes* (Cercle du Bibliophile), xxix. 64.]

Existentialism and Marxism

In the foreword to his *Stendhal. Fiction and the Themes of Freedom* (Chicago and London: University of Chicago Press, 1968) – from which chapter 6 (entitled 'The Poetry of Freedom') is reproduced below – Victor Brombert affiliates his critical approach in this book to that of Thematic Criticism, which he describes as 'valuable when it is ultimately more concerned with the author's art and vision than with any single motif or obsession'. Although he himself has chosen to 'focus on the recurrence and variations of a central, unifying theme' (i.e. freedom), he has endeavoured to do so 'without losing sight of the issues raised by Stendhal's work and of the specific quality of individual texts' and by displaying 'this steady interweaving and counterpoint of social, political, psychological, and ethical preoccupations [which] constitutes, in my opinion, the poetic density of Stendhal's work.'

Brombert's choice of theme, however, owes much to the influence of Existentialist philosophy and its central focus on the implications of human freedom and on the obstacles to it. Drawing on phenomenology (as Thematic Criticism also did), Existentialist thought concerned itself principally with the role of human consciousness, with our anguished awareness of freedom and the accompanying temptation to conceal this freedom from ourselves by accepting as necessary any number of contingent features of living (for example, certain political or moral constraints) and by abdicating our personal freedom in inauthentic role-playing and other acts of 'bad faith'. Rather we should face up to this freedom and exercise it lucidly at every moment of our history (personal and collective): we should commit ourselves to the present, we should achieve 'engagement'.

The 'social, political, psychological, and ethical preoccupations' of Stendhal's work clearly lend themselves readily to an Existentialist perspective. The Stendhalian hero's quest for happiness, which is also a quest for identity, involves him in much soul-searching (Bourget's interior monologue) and regularly confronts him with the dilemma of freedom: whether to be himself (but how can he identify his own 'essence' before he has discovered it during the experience of 'existence'?) or whether to preserve some inner freedom by donning a mask and playing the roles which society, or love, or his own vanity impose upon him. Julien, the self-conscious hypocrite who comes to know himself only when freedom (and a future) is denied him in prison; Fabrice, the unreflecting free spirit who finds himself only within the (enchanted) prison of love and yet must play at being a churchman that he may recover his lost paradise: these paradoxical figures are Existentialist heroes before their time. And Brombert's conclusion is a bleak one: 'The central prison metaphor, which raises Stendhal's two major novels to the level of high romance, invites dreams of liberation: but it also suggests that freedom remains a prisoner's dream, and that man's true vocation is solitude' (p. 185).

For Marxist critics this solitary singularity of Stendhal's heroes equates to a fundamental failure to engage with political and social reality. Irving Howe has remarked of Stendhal that 'No other modern novelist has so consistently approached political life in terms that so consistently evade political categories' ('Stendhal: The Politics of Survival', p. 77), but for some this elusiveness bespeaks an unacceptable hankering after a pre-revolutionary past. As already discussed above in the Introduction (pp. 8–9), the eminent Hungarian Marxist Georg Lukács praises Stendhal for his depiction of contemporary society but perceives the lack of a 'consciously historical conception of the present'. For him there is a 'certain abstract psychologism' which devalues Stendhal's social critiques by its implicit appeal to an eternal, unchanging human nature.

By 'Marxism' is generally meant the body of thought which developed out of the political and economic ideas of Karl Marx (1818–83) and Friedrich Engels (1820–95). Central to this thought is a view of History in terms of Hegelian dialectics, namely that the historical process is a repeated sequence of thesis, antithesis, and synthesis (of the political status quo being modified by radical opposition into a new status quo which then is further modified). Very broadly speaking, Marxists view History as reflecting a necessary progression from feudal society to proletarian rule via an intermediary stage of bourgeois dominance: for them 'class struggle' is vital in the progressive 'liberation' of the masses from bourgeois, capitalist rule and the achievement of a socialist, then ultimately 'communist' society in which the means of production are equally owned by all.

Pierre Barbéris, the author of the second extract reproduced below, is a Marxist critic who has written extensively on Balzac. In 1975 the Livre Club Diderot published several volumes of Stendhal's works with introductions by Barbéris, and these were later reprinted as a separate volume in 1983 to mark the bicentenary of Stendhal's birth. In his foreword Barbéris describes how these introductions were written within a specific political context, namely against the background of a considerable upsurge in support for the left-wing opposition's Common Programme (which eventually brought President Mitterand to power in 1981). Barbéris cautions that these introductions reflect a certain 'euphoria' and optimistic faith in progressive politics which subsequent events have modified (not least the Left's recent

Existentialism and Marxism

accession to power) and calls on his reader to interpret his comments accordingly.

Now, more than a decade later and after left-wing politics have been repudiated by the French electorate, there is even more reason to remember the political context in which Barbéris's introduction to *The Charterhouse of Parma* was written. Rejecting the measured tones of academic discourse, he adopts a jauntier, perhaps more populist register to counter orthodox bourgeois evaluations of the novel (as pleasurably unsubversive) and to show that *The Charterhouse* reveals bourgeois individualism in crisis. For all Barbéris's emphasis on its ephemeral relevance, his essay is still one of the best accounts of the politics of Stendhal's last completed novel, and a salutary reminder that no novel, nor any work of criticism, is ever apolitical.

4 Victor Brombert on freedom in *The Charterhouse of Parma*

A mental landscape

The words 'La Chartreuse de Parme' suffice to conjure up, in the mind of a Stendhalian reader, a recognizable landscape and a specific rhythm. They evoke a fantasy charterhouse, which is not actually mentioned until the very last pages of the book, but is present in the reader's mind from the very beginning, as if to warn him that beyond the scene of political intrigue, savoir-vivre, and cynicism, there exists a privileged and almost inaccessible region: the world of hidden spirituality, the precious world of prison, retirement, and renunciation.

An impressionistic critic might stress the autumnal light of *La Chartreuse*. Distant details are repeatedly brought out in their sharpest outline. Yet this light, allowing for clarity and vast panoramas, does not provide a gay illumination. It has the softness of mellow sadness and resignation. It is a light that somehow suggests the eternity of the fleeting moment.

The opening section of the novel is a dithyramb to youth and impetuous unconcern. The momentum of Bonaparte's soldiers, who are all under twenty-five years of age, the explicit contempt for all that is old and bewigged, the contrast between the zest of this young army and the decrepit imbecilic old generals – all suggests an atmosphere of inebriation and abandon totally devoid of any regret, devoid even of a sense of the past. Thus the grouchy marquis del Dongo, whose reactionary fears make him hate all gaiety, and his young sister Gina, who laughs uncontrollably at the sight of her powdered suitor, belong to different generations; between them there exists, so to speak, a breach of moral and historical continuity. It would seem that even history no longer had any contact with itself.

Timelessness and the imperatives of time – these are indeed the conflicting experiences within the novel. The very structure of the first chapter conveys a scheme of action and reaction. It evokes a new era of happiness, which historic events interrupt and abolish. The French army, which liberates Milan and thus inaugurates a period of happy 'freedom,' is soon again defeated. Laughter is again replaced by morose and unenlightened ideas. But the happy period, precisely because it has vanished, proves to be even more meaningful in retrospect. The interlude colors the events that follow. The entire novel is conceived under the sign of lost youth, which memory and fervor reconquer.

The character who most dramatically embodies this theme of reclaimed youth is Count Mosca. This elegant, middle-aged statesman, who has known the exhilaration of the Napoleonic campaigns but who now submits realistically and ironically to the sordid game of post-Napoleonic politics, retrieves the ardor of his early years through love. As he waits two full hours for Countess Pietranera to appear at La Scala, he comes to the conclusion that old age is really nothing but the inability to surrender to delightful, adolescent emotions. These 'delightful pranks' are fully savored by the hedonistic Mosca. He postpones the moment of presenting himself in Gina's box and appreciates his own unexpected timidity. 'Such a thing has not happened to me in twenty-five years.' (6)* As much as Gina's charm, Mosca admires in himself this process of rejuvenation for which she is responsible.

The ambiguous tone of *La Chartreuse*, which transmutes playfulness into meaning and deals with the most serious events in an almost flippant manner, can easily unsettle the reader. This tone is hard to describe. Unconstrained and irreverent, it seeks out the sophisticated reader, willing and able to follow the author in his mental games and ironic capers. Stendhal's picaresque rhythm and humor are heightened by his mastery of understatement and ellipsis. False conjunctions, misleading parallels, inversions of meaning, and subversive juxtapositions are here used to support themes that the reader must learn to decipher. This allusive technique is essentially that of the conversationalist who seeks to transform his interlocutor into an accomplice. Lively and resilient, Stendhal's voice acts out a game of improvisation. At every point, though carried by the momentum of his story, he pretends not to know what the next episode will reveal. His feigned surprises, his self-induced reactions, stress the freedom of his protagonists. In fact, no novel is more steadily propelled by an inner, almost dreamlike necessity.

Irony and narrative distance are thus the masks for lyric commitment. Stendhal's smile, tender or sarcastic, must not mislead; no writer has used his own wit better to disguise and protect his own affectivity. Irony avenges Stendhal of servitudes to which he is only too happy to submit. The apparent gaiety and carefree tone prove ultimately to be as melancholic as the autumnal light that falls on the marvellous and oppressive Farnese tower.[1]

---

*Numbers in parentheses refer to chapter numbers in *La Chartreuse de Parme*. [The translations are Brombert's own. (*Ed.*)].

Landscapes in *La Chartreuse* are the concrete figurations of Stendhal's lyricism. Ever since his adolescence, Stendhal was tempted by the emotional correspondences between external scenery and private dreams. To reveal the specific affective resonance of the Borromean Islands had been one of his earliest literary ambitions. The 'unique' position of the Dongo castle near Grianta, the view of the 'sublime lake,' the 'admirable forms' of the hills, the secret language of these 'ravishing places' in *La Chartreuse* (2) cannot be dismissed as a yielding to literary fashion. An authentic delight abounds in the Stendhalian evocations: the Lombardy plain, the Parma citadel, the tower of the abbé Blanès – real or imaginary places all of which suggest an Italy that Stendhal, for his own private use, transfigured into a world of revery and energy. As epigraph for *La Chartreuse*, he chose Ariosto's famous lines:

> *Gia mi fur dolci inviti a empir le carte*
> *I luoghi ameni.*
> ['At one time these charming places were sweet invitations for me to fill the pages.']

These *luoghi ameni* – these magic spots of Stendhal's mental topography – conjure up a world of spiritual inebriation in which the very senses are subservient to a delicate poetry.

The privileged place and the privileged moment represent a rare and fleeting conjunction. To attain and remember them justifies all the rest. Stendhal, like Rousseau, develops a cult of those ineffable hours that allow man to forget his contingency and to glimpse the real life of things, moments of grace when suddenly the voice of the world is still. But the privileged temporal and spatial realities in *La Chartreuse* also provide a liberating force. All the eccentricities, all the unforeseeable acts of his non-conventional characters, share the immunity of an enchanted transalpine fairyland – but a fairyland for adults only.

A climate of passion and of madness, disconcerting to literal-minded readers, reigns in this fantasy Italy. Enrico Panzacchi thus protests against the distorted vision of a country with heroic bandits, histrionic priests, and poetic servants composing sonnets.[2] Stendhal's favorite characters in *La Chartreuse* are indeed capable of the most extravagant actions, as though the Italian setting itself inspired extraordinary deeds. Fabrice del Dongo, naïve and superstitious, runs away from home to fight for Napoleon at Waterloo. His aunt, Gina Pietranera, who becomes Duchess Sanseverina, is a woman who scorns prudence and adores her nephew, who kills for his sake and would do 'a thousand times worse,' according to the author. Count Mosca, a Beyliste Metternich, discovers not only the rejuvenating 'folies amoureuses,' but the furor of jealousy, which leads him to the brink of crime. Clélia Conti, whose face seems saddened by the permanent regret of an absent chimera, betrays her jailer-father and, under the most unlikely circumstances, saves the beloved prisoner. Capable of the most attractive crimes, endowed with the most unusual virtues, the Stendhalian heroes know how to despise with passion. Duchess Sanseverina relishes the joys of a shrewdly prepared and slowly savored vengeance. But this capacity to hate also allows the noblest Stendhalian protagonists to experience the raptures of a love so absolute that it ultimately induces them to prefer imprisonment, the refusal of happiness, and even death, to a worse undoing – a life that would erode their capacity to love.

It is this counterpoint of extroverted brio and tender inner music that carries the significant themes of the novel. *La Chartreuse*, like the opera buffa that Stendhal so loved, juxtaposes staccato recitatives and fugitive lyric moments. Prosaic and poetic elements support each other. Illusion and disenchantment, idealism and cynicism, negation and affirmation of values, parody and belief, aloofness and involvement – all these apparent contraries are tightly interlocked. The very unity of *La Chartreuse* rests heavily on its ambiguous nature. Even the last sentence of the book can be interpreted as simultaneously ironic and nostalgic. The order it describes is both the political order that denies life and a spiritual reality that totally transcends the derisive realm of politics.

Ambiguities

The most striking illustration of Stendhalian ambiguities in *La Chartreuse* is the famous Waterloo episode. Stendhal has been praised for his 'realistic' account, for having been the first writer to systematically describe a battle from the point of view of a single consciousness, through the eyes of a single character utterly puzzled by what goes on, and who, instead of dominating the historic event with the perspective and omniscience of a historian, is only able to witness movement and confusion. Stendhal himself, after the Battle of Bautzen (probably the only battle he saw, and at some range at that), remembered that he had glimpsed all there is to be seen of a battle – that is, little, or nothing. With Fabrice at Waterloo, we are far indeed from the Homeric or Virgilian epic slaughters where every participant, weapon, skirmish, and wound is catalogued and described by the poet-strategist.

But if the epic description is debunked by implication, so is the epic hero. Fabrice, in love with the sound of cannons, thirsts for noble sensations. A romantic Candide, he would like to gallop after every one of Napoleon's marshals. He is, in fact, a heroic parasite, inexperienced and totally superfluous on the field of battle. The author treats him with deliberate irony. 'We must confess that our hero was quite unheroic at that moment.' Comments such as these stud the pages of the Waterloo episode. We are invited to laugh at Fabrice's naïveté, his clumsiness, his illusions, and at the deflation of his dreams of heroic comradeship. He discovers that war resembles neither Ariosto's poem nor the proclamations of the Emperor. As the author leads Fabrice from surprise to surprise, from blunder to blunder, from one humiliating experience to another, it becomes quite evident that what these pages propose is not at all a 'realistic' account, but a mock-heroic episode, a parody of epic attitudes and conventions.

Conventional epic elements are in fact repeatedly stressed, but in order, it would seem, to attract attention to obvious discrepancies. A grand spectacle, a hero travelling far from his home country and involved in a series of actions filled with obstacles and dangers, enormous crowds, mysterious omens and predictions, battles pitting entire nations against each other, a collective awareness that the future of an entire continent is at stake – nothing seems to be missing. Yet it is all strangely unauthentic, like a literary game. Fabrice, like Don Quixote, has read too many books. His overexcited imagination attempts to impose the patterns of heroic romance on a banal and recalcitrant reality. Significantly, he considers the heterogeneous group of soldiers he has joined as 'heroic' companions: 'Between them and himself he saw the noble comradeship of Tasso's and Ariosto's heroes.' But he forgets to tell himself that these rough hussars treat him with kindness only because he has just purchased a bottle of spirits.

Reality, vexing or ignoble, is indeed at odds with the epic dream. Thus Fabrice, who rushes gratuitously to the Emperor's defense at Waterloo, is thrown into jail as a suspected spy because of his Italian accent. Thus the grand battle reveals selfishness, cowardice, and the confusion of a humiliating rout. But it is precisely this conflict between a dream reality and the reality of actual experience that provides the interest and the comic mainspring of these pages. For Fabrice, a nineteenth-century Cherubino living out the predictions of Figaro's mocking aria 'Non più andrai,' is only a child who does not even know how to load a rifle. Even more naïve than Tom Jones, a model that haunted Stendhal's imagination, he shows his money to everybody, and is of course thoroughly cheated and robbed. 'You know less than nothing,' is the diagnosis of the benevolent sutler who takes him under her feminine protection. The fact is that Fabrice needs more than four weeks to understand why he has been thrown into jail.

With greater zest than ever, Stendhal deflates his hero and stresses his insufficiencies. Almost with malice, he exposes him to the most trying vexations. He has him walk in rain and in mud, and at that in boots which are not his size. He has him trot on a miserable nag. Fabrice, who is so eager to see Napoleon, misses the occasion at Waterloo simply because he has had too much to drink and the Emperor gallops by too quickly. The entire episode is an exercise in incongruity and lack of synchronization. The worst indignity occurs when Fabrice, ambling proudly along on a good horse, suddenly feels himself lifted up and deposited on the road by a group of soldiers, who unceremoniously confiscate the horse. The incident is doubly ironic, since we are given to understand that the general for whom the horse is confiscated is none other than the former lieutenant Robert, the presumed father of Fabrice.

These humiliations and disheartening adventures might sober up an even greater dreamer than Fabrice. Abandoned by the soldier thieves, he sheds hot tears – from fatigue no doubt, but largely from the sorrow of finding that the world is not filled with tender and heroic comrades-in-arms who die embracing each other while reciting an *ottava rima*. Stendhal explains that his young hero is forced to undo, one by one, every dream of chivalrous friendship inspired by Tasso's *Gerusalemme liberata*. This awakening becomes altogether brutal when, a few pages later, Fabrice is wounded by soldiers who are not even enemies. The episode seems to come to a cruel conclusion as Stendhal observes with a pun:

> Notre héros était ce matin-là du plus beau sang-froid du monde; la quantité de sang qu'il avait perdue l'avait délivré de toute la partie romanesque de son caractère. (5)

The absurd wound suggests a beneficent bloodletting. The Battle of Waterloo seems to function as a special therapy destined to cure Fabrice of his illusions.

Yet it would be a mistake to read these pages simply as a return to lucidity. There is an element of Candide in Fabrice, but there is also a great deal of Don Quixote. One does not recover so quickly from one's dreams. War is not, or no longer is, that generous commitment of brothers-in-arms who thirst for glory. But if the world is not what Fabrice thinks it could and should be, he is nonetheless unable to assume a prosaic view. It is not the nature but the object of his lyric and heroic quest that will change. The war chapters at the beginning of *La Chartreuse* simultaneously devaluate and exalt enthusiasm. Alternating between fervor and irony, Stendhal creates biting contrasts that bring out sharply the essentially 'poetic' spirit of his hero. Fabrice's romantic character affirms itself the more vividly for being set against a background of parody and insignificance.

The paradoxical nature of epic parody is established most clearly in the evocation of Ariosto and Tasso, who, from the very first pages of the novel, are used as symbols of high poetry as well as pretexts for irony. It is indeed with rapture that Countess Pietranera evokes these names as she settles near Lake Como. Her daydream is revealing: 'Among these admirably shaped hills . . . I can keep all the illusions of Tasso's and Ariosto's

descriptions. Everything is noble and tender, everything speaks of love . . .'
(2) In *Vie de Henry Brulard*, Stendhal likewise associates Ariosto with his
most cherished reveries: 'I am still moved, as I was at the age of ten when
reading Ariosto, by any tale of love, of forests (the woods and their vast
silence), of generosity.'³ And the wistful, melancholic smile of the author of
La Chartreuse recalls the delicately saddened smile of the poet who sang

> *Le Donne, i Cavalier, l'arme, gli amori,*
> *Le cortesie, l'audaci imprese . . .*
> [Of ladies and knights, of arms and amours,
> Of courtliness and daring exploits . . .]

There can be no doubt, the lyricism of chivalry, even though treated in an
ironic mode, is not invoked in a derogatory spirit. Far from undermining
the lyric illusion, the elements of parody serve to protect it. They reveal an
oversensitive hero who is forced by the world's coarseness to withdraw
within himself. But the self-exile of an exceptional being in the face of a
hostile environment also impels him to set out in quest of that undefinable
'something' that fills the inner emptiness of the exiled individual and that –
as Camus suggests – marks the simultaneous desire to retrace one's steps
and to attend to the future.

It is in this sense that one could view the Waterloo adventure as a
preliminary stage of a spiritual itinerary.⁴ But the aim of this itinerary is
bound to remain invisible almost until the end. The frustrations and
humiliations of the war chapters are thus part of an evaluation that leads
Fabrice to the discovery of essential values – values that he may vaguely
intuit but that he has to adopt in order to understand. For he was not born
with them, nor does he inherit them ready-made. Thus it is fitting that the
charterhouse remain totally off-stage until the last pages of the book and
that the road to this place of retirement lead through the Farnese prison
tower, a prefiguration of monastic seclusion. Much like other Stendhalian
heroes, Fabrice must wait until he has passed through all the successive
stations of his career and must in the process relinquish many beliefs and
false desires before he can discover what he was really seeking, without
knowing it, from the very beginning.

To be sure, the Stendhalian paradoxes, inversions of meaning, lyrical
parodies, and hidden impertinences are not made to reassure the kind of
reader who wants important subjects to be treated with a tone of
importance. Nothing in this respect can be more unsettling than the
political motif in *La Chartreuse*. For there can be no doubt that the court of
Ranuce-Ernest IV in Parma represents a serious subject. Stendhal
undertook nothing less than a tableau representative of all small and large
courts, in fact of the entire political climate of the reactionary, anachronistic
post-Napoleonic Europe. Yet court life is presented with almost as much

unreality as a comic ballet. We glimpse an operetta palace, crowded with opera buffa characters, the most lucid of whom are, moreover, perfectly aware of 'playing a part'. Duchess Sanseverina enjoys both the 'spectacle' in which she participates and the challenges of assuming a *rôle* beside Count Mosca, who consistently views his own political activities, and politics in general, as a comical game. His official position, he complains with bitter humor, obliges him to dress up like a 'personnage de comédie.' (6)

In this fantasy court, ludicrous types and situations abound. The prince lives in such terror of conspirators and revolutions that special measures have been taken: the eighty-four sentinels of his palace have been ordered to cry out a full sentence every fifteen minutes, all the doors are secured with ten locks, and at the slightest suspicious noise the minister of the Police is summoned to verify in person whether or not a Jacobin is hidden under the prince's bed. At times, the perspective is frankly that of caricature. The kicked buttocks of servile Rassi, the automatic smile of Marquise Balbi, the grotesque thinness of the prince's mistress – these farcical distortions and indignities of the human body contribute to the heavily theatrical atmosphere that reigns at Parma's court. In fact, the word 'theatre,' as well as theatrical metaphors, occurs repeatedly.[5] Amateur *commedia dell'arte* performances are the great pastime among the courtiers. But this comedy is played out at several levels. After a long 'scene' with Ranuce-Ernest IV and his mother, Duchess Sanseverina observes: 'I have played a comedy for one hour on the stage and for five hours in the study.'

Yet this perpetual comedy stands in intimate relation to the profound themes of the book. Parody turns out to be the most suitable means for political critique of the state of affairs after 1815, precisely since much of Europe, according to Stendhal, has turned itself into a pitiful parody of the Ancien Régime. If Ranuce-Ernest attempts to imitate the gesture and the smile of a portrait of Louis XIV, if the princess is pleased to take as a model Marie de Medici, it is not merely to bring out the laughable inadequacies of given characters. What is involved in this political tragicomedy is the very spirit that transforms sunny Parma into a place of tyranny and fear. The otherwise composed Mosca, who tends to view the ebb and flow of political power with a spectator's irony, is not devoid of a sense of tragic indignation. 'We are surrounded by tragic events,' he ominously confesses to Duchess Sanseverina. (10) For he knows better than anyone else that Parma is a city of secret threats and secret measures. The symbolic Farnese tower, with its mysterious geometric patterns, introduces into the smiling Emilian plain an almost Kafkaesque element of nightmare and human alienation.

Mosca's statement to Duchess Sanseverina corresponds to the author's own somber diagnosis. They share, moreover, the same ability to combine irony with passionate indignation. In the same paragraph evoking Fabio

Conti's ludicrous terror at the mere thought of one of his prisoners escaping, Stendhal describes how these humiliated, broken-spirited prisoners, suffering in chains in cells too low to stand up in, pay for a *Te Deum* to celebrate their jailor's recovery. (21) Seen in this light, the citadel becomes an allegorical figuration of human degradation under the despotism of the modern state. Behind the fantasy tower, there is the gloomy silhouette – alas! – of the very real Spielberg fortress where men like Silvio Pellico and Maroncelli, some of them friends of Stendhal, were rotting in the *carcere duro*.

Values

Political satire excludes neither pity nor the glorification of the exceptional being who accepts the rules of a wicked game but does not allow himself to be corrupted. Once again the image of Don Quixote, the eternal prototype of the glorious loser, imposes itself. Count Mosca sums up as follows one of his lessons in political realism: 'At all times the vile Sancho Panchas will in the long run win out over the sublime Don Quixotes.' (10) The political satire, much like the epic parody, is not merely a critical weapon, but an instrument of poetry, which, through contrapuntal effects, stresses all the tender movements, all the flights of generosity, all the potential of passion—and at the same time prevents sentiment from degenerating into undisciplined sentimentality. The rhythm of *La Chartreuse* is that of the music Stendhal loved most, alternating light-hearted brio and lyrical abandon. The law of contrasts is for Stendhal a way of projecting and of protecting his most cherished dreams. In *Vie de Henry Brulard*, he explains his fondness for Ariosto: 'I can be moved to tears *only after a comical passage.*'[6] A remark such as this casts light on the numerous scenes in *La Chartreuse* where comedy, pathos, and musicality echo each other. It is a most exceptional climate where laughter and sarcasm serve the exigencies of the heart.

The Stendhalian paradoxes and inversions of values, so obvious in the political motifs of *La Chartreuse*, are even more striking in the disarming immorality that reigns in the novel. This immorality is not limited to adultery and incest; it is fundamental and seems to characterize the actions and attitudes of the most lovable protagonists. Charles Maurras has called *La Chartreuse* a 'charming manual of political roguery'.[7] But this 'roguery' is by no means limited to the realm of politics. Its manifestations are extremely varied and start with the opening pages of the book. Fabrice, a most unscholarly student, receives five first prizes in his Jesuit college simply because his aunt is an important lady at the court of Prince Eugène. This aunt, in turn, accepts to marry, sight unseen, the decrepit Duke of

Sanseverina-Taxis and to occupy a handsome palace and enjoy the proximity of her lover. Mosca maintains himself in power through flattery and shameless exploitation of the prince's pathological fear. As for Fabrice's choice of an ecclesiastic career, what could be more cynical than Mosca's advice and plans?

> I do not claim to make of Fabrice an exemplary priest of which there are many. No, he is a nobleman first and foremost. He can remain perfectly ignorant if he so chooses. He will nonetheless become bishop and archbishop provided the prince continues to consider me useful.(6)

Mosca, one of Stendhal's most fascinating characters, is an urbane father-substitute for Fabrice. He represents the sophisticated middle-aged figure whom Stendhal, after *Le Rouge et le Noir*, liked to place side by side with his slim, adolescent heroes. The self-indulging and self-punishing tendency was to lead, in *Lamiel*, to the painful caricature of the donjuanesque hunchback, Docteur Sansfin. In *La Chartreuse*, there is no such cruel perspective; yet Mosca is made to feel the specific anguish of his age, as well as the maddening tortures of jealousy. Above all, however, he is the lucid diplomat and tender-hearted professor of cynicism. He knows that politics are a game (and who is foolish enough to object to the rules of a game?), but he also knows that absolute power justifies and sanctifies everything and that tender-heartedness is the greatest self-dupery.

It does not follow that *La Chartreuse* is a breviary of immorality. Quite the opposite. For beyond the apparent absence of conventional ethics, a special morality emerges, a morality not according to the laws and lies of society, but an authentic complex of values founded on truth and merit. Surprisingly, it is the Moscas of this world – that is, the very individuals who play at being cynical and are unable to take themselves seriously – who in their privacy forge for themselves a rigorous moral code, refuse to follow the comfortable and profitable dictates of public morality, and affirm themselves as creators of values. Mosca does not believe in the rosy, liberal formulas of political *arrivistes*. The claim to seek the happiness of the greatest number seems to him naïveté or an imposture. Mosca feels, in the first place, bound to seek the happiness of Count Mosca. But on the other hand, Stendhal explains that Mosca is 'totally honourable,' that not once has he lied to the duchess. (16)

Private and gratuitous, the morality in question rests entirely on a code of honor that freely binds human beings capable of mutual esteem. It is the morality of the Stendhalian 'happy few.' Its first law is not to cheat oneself. Its greatest challenge is how not to lose one's self-esteem. Stendhal's terse assessment of Duchess Sanseverina is characteristic: 'She was above all a woman in perfect good faith with herself.' (6) Unquestionably, it is this same ethic of honesty and severity with oneself – this same abhorrence of all poses and intellectual fraud – that explains why Fabrice, after the experience of Waterloo, unlike so many immorally moral people who never question anything, wonders whether he has really participated in a battle and whether he has really been brave.

It is no doubt for this creative inversion of values that the most fervent lovers of Stendhal are fanatical 'Chartreusistes,' who find in this novel the very essence of Beyliste philosophy, according to which true passion belongs exclusively to an elite. The novel is in fact dedicated 'to the happy few' – those who, together with the author, prize not only passion but also the modest veiling of passion and who, though lucid, love to be the consenting victims of their illusions.

The freedom to become

Some objections might be raised. Readers insensitive to Stendhal's mental pirouettes and to his brand of 'unpoetic' poetry are likely to seek refuge in factual exegesis. They will be tempted to explain the novel as a curious fusion of sources, periods, and subjects, artistic perhaps but not fully convincing – in other words, as a remarkable potpourri. In fact, Stendhal transplanted sixteenth-century mores into the Italy of his day; he utilized the Farnese chronicle, the memoirs of Cellini, the prison accounts of Silvio Pellico and of Andryane; he exploited Renaissance and contemporary history, the resources of parallels and anachronisms, his own personal experiences (Milan, the Napoleonic army, contemporary politics), and, of course, literary models. Among these are Rousseau, quite evidently, but also cardinal de Retz, the bold *libertin* and enemy of Mazarin, who was master-animator of the rebellious Fronde movement, whose real name (Gondi) bears an anagrammatic resemblance to that of Dongo, and who, like Fabrice, was a younger son who also undertook an ecclesiastic career without a religious vocation, had an amorous adventure in jail, successfully escaped, and finally brought an adventurous life to an end in the solitude of a monastery.[8] This extraordinary telescoping of chronicles, memoirs, literary sources, historical facts, and private obsessions would seem to lead to a heterogeneous construction where several possible novels come to meet.

Stendhal has thus been accused of lack of focus, of dilettantism, of indulging in irritating digressions and interventions that discredit his own creation. Humourless readers have complained of elements of melodrama in *La Chartreuse*, of lack of verisimilitude, of absurd coincidences, caprices, and disguises. They have pointed out contradictions and vagueness in the themes, waverings in the conception of the characters, artificialities in the cult of energy. Even Stendhal's treatment of love, a subject of which he makes so much, has disappointed some readers, for although there are mutual attractions, at no point does the novel propose love as the adventure of a couple.

Similar exceptions, though not entirely unwarranted, indicate a lack of response to the specific vision of *La Chartreuse*. The chief difficulty for the reader not yet attuned to Stendhal is that the so-called character psychology as well as the realism of situations are here totally subordinated to the poetic perspective. For it is not a pre-established psychological reality or conceptualization that determines the poetic movement of the novel, but the poetic movement that creates its psychology and ethical substance. In other words: it is not knowledge which begets motion, but vitality, in its sheer gratuitousness, that makes possible the discovery of both the world and the self.

Love, that privileged Stendhalian subject, thus occupies the center of the novel and yet remains elusive. No determination weighs down on what for the author is essentially an élan of the spirit. Physical realities are almost entirely absent. The oppressiveness of desire, the intimacy of the lovers, the satisfaction of the senses, even tenderness persisting and transformed after shared sensual pleasures – all this Stendhal seems to eschew. The reason, however, is not prudery. The disembodiment of love accelerates the momentum of the novel. Thus there is no trace of any Romantic mysticism of the senses: no voluptuous meditations on nothingness, no exaltation of Medusan beauty, no dreams of orgies and exotic tortures. No fatal women or heavily scented temptresses strut through his books. Duchess Sanseverina is far closer to a tragic Phaedra than to a decadent Cleopatra or Salome. As for the very rare love scenes, they are either understated or of an exemplary chastity. The most detailed scene is the one that occurs in a prison cell. It occupies exactly two and a half lines:

> She was so beautiful, half unclad and in this state of intense passion, that Fabrice could not resist an almost unconscious impulse. No resistance was offered him. [trans. Moncrieff] (25)

A physical act is thus convincingly translated into a stylized gesture, and rhythm replaces description and analysis.

It is not fortuitous that the lovers embrace in a cell. Madame de Rênal and Julien also experience their most fervent hours within the confines of prison walls. The myth of difficult and unrealizable love is altogether central to Stendhal's fiction. Hence the repeated images of bounded proximity. Hence also the touching poetry of the 'glance,' that almost Neoplatonic intimacy at a distance. Clélia and Fabrice delight in communicating by means of signs and secret alphabets. This cult of the obstacle and of the separation helps to explain why, toward the end of the novel, Clélia makes the strange vow to the Madonna never again to look at her lover.

In the Stendhalian mythology of love, what counts is neither intimacy nor gratification, but inner tension and the dynamics of a yearning indifferent to the present moment, already in the process of dissolution. Most important is the energy that goes into creating ideal moments. Love is for the Stendhalian heroes, at times without their fully realizing it, the chief preoccupation of their lives. They might well repeat Daphne's words in Tasso's *Aminta*:

> *Perduto è tutto il tempo*
> *Che in amar non si spende.*
> [All time is wasted
> That is not spent in loving.]

But this 'expenditure' of energy in the pursuit of love is worthwhile only because it commits the entire being and projects him into existence. If Stendhalian love never involves possession, this also means that the Stendhalian heroes and heroines remain free – neither possessed, nor humiliated, nor subjugated, nor betrayed. That is why Clélia's enchanting words, 'Enter here, friend of my heart', necessarily announce the end of the novel.

As for the Farnese dungeon where Clélia and Fabrice love each other and which foreshadows the monastic cell into which Fabrice will later withdraw, it symbolizes spiritual freedom and rejection of worldly cares. The prison is thus far more than a melodramatic device. Its most meaningful aspect is suggested in the very title of the book. In fact, references to prisons and images of claustration crowd the pages of *La Chartreuse* from the very beginning, long before Fabrice's actual incarceration in the Farnese tower. Already in the first chapter, we are told of the Italian patriots who are deported to Cattaro and left to die of hunger and exposure in the subterranean caves. Soon after, the famous imprisonment of Silvio Pellico is evoked. Fabrice himself is jailed as soon as he reaches the Belgian frontier. And over the entire opening section of the novel hovers the threat as well as the lyrical prophecy of jail.

For imprisonment is an ambiguous experience in the world of Stendhal. It is, on the one hand, a permanent cause for terror, as well as a concrete figuration of tyranny. The negative references are numerous. General Pietranera is unjustly thrown into jail. (2) Fabrice is warned by the abbé Blanès that he will end his days in a cell (4); the threat of imprisonment hangs over him upon his return from Waterloo (5); the Parma citadel is the 'terror of all of Lombardy,' and only a 'miracle' can bring prisoners out of oblivion (6); nightmarish visions of heavy chains, gangrened limbs, and

107

perpetual immurement bring a 'cold sweat' to Fabrice's forehead (9, 10). 'Anything but the Spielberg,' is his conclusion, as he conjures up horrifying images of the infamous Moravian fortress where Silvio Pellico and Maroncelli had been rotting for years. (11) Finally, reality catches up with his fears. He is arrested, exposed to the humiliation of handcuffs, and a chain, and subjected to the vulgar insolence of the assistant jailer, Barbone. (15)

But, on the other hand, Fabrice's very terror is mixed with a mysterious delight. It is as though Stendhal needed to exorcise the prison obsession by metamorphosing horror into poetry. A secret prison-yearning seems to propel Fabrice and to endow the notion of imprisonment with a singular prestige. Auguries and prophecies of jail seem to point to a meaningful destiny. The abbé Blanès interprets Fabrice's prison experience before Waterloo as a felicitous sign. (8) The monastic cell of Fabrice's last days is clearly prefigured in the belltower scene; so are the poetry of darkness (Blanès tells Fabrice that he must not see him again by daylight) and the notion of spiritual altitude. Blanès's tower, in part an astrological observatory, symbolically reaches toward the firmament. Fabrice, at the top of this tower, experiences the 'highest sentiments' and achieves an unusual 'hauteur de pensées' [loftiness of thought]. (9)

It is no coincidence that the church tower, for a while at least, becomes for Fabrice a protective prison; in it he experiences the characteristic Stendhalian joy of seeing without being seen. All of Stendhal's prisons are thus places of altitude and of privacy, enhanced by extensive views. That the image of happiness is subconsciously linked with the notion of claustration is made very clear by Fabrice's curious proleptic thought, upon first glimpsing Clélia: 'She would make a charming prison companion.' (5) The ambiguities of the terror-jail and the happiness-jail are further stressed when Clélia herself, thinking of Duchess Sanseverina's passion for Fabrice, takes pity on the prisoner's 'awful solitude,' and at the same time imagines his happiness in jail at knowing how much he is loved. (15)

In fact, the 'positive' prison images far outnumber all the others. The prison-wish seems stronger than the prison-fear. When Duchess Sanseverina first visits the Farnese tower, she is delighted by the height and by the freshness of the air, which comes as a relief after the sweltering atmosphere of Parma. (6) As Fabrice climbs the 380 steps leading to the top of the prodigious tower, he can think only of the expression of Clélia's eyes during his arrest. (15) Clélia herself, living at the very summit of the fortress in the midst of a prison atmosphere, enjoys 'the freedom of a convent' and the exquisite pleasures of solitude and of an 'inner life.' (15) In prison, Fabrice actually has no time to think of his unhappiness. Moreover, he undergoes a curious transformation. Imprisonment, which he feared most, now leaves him indifferent, and he even surprises himself by 'laughing in a jail.' (18) 'Never have I been so happy,' he confesses to himself. (19) Now that his heart is 'bound' (16), the other bonds no longer count. And, as if to give imprisonment its fullest symbolic meaning, the governor of the fortress has Fabrice's cell windows obstructed, allowing him only a glimpse of the sky. The Farnese nightmare becomes part of a vast allegory of escape.

The law of contrasts, the dynamics of contempt, and the surprises of self-discovery are all operating here. What Fabrice experiences in essence is a state of happy captivity, which, as Georges Blin puts it, constitutes for the Stendhalian heroes the most efficacious 'preservative' from all noxious external influences.[9] This protection of the self is, in fact, like a rebirth (Fabrice spends exactly nine months in prison). Jungian critics might well be tempted to interpret the entire tower episode as a symbol of regeneration through the analogue of the womb. In any case, this renewal marks a process of spiritualization. The concluding pages of the novel strongly suggest, behind their resigned and ironic sadness, an emancipation from worldly tensions. The final sentence, one of Stendhal's most ambiguous, expresses, at the same time, the detached view of the observer, the bitterness of half-truths, the immense sadness of a world now empty, and the beauty that has sought refuge elsewhere. All seems to withdraw and fade away at the end. Clélia disappears by degrees; her delicate image has the graceful *morbidezza* Stendhal loved so much in the paintings of Correggio. As for Fabrice, he quite literally undergoes a process of disincarnation. Increasingly insensitive to his immediate surroundings, yearning for a conventual retreat, he attains true beauty in his silence and in his ascetic thinness. When Clélia, after her marriage to the Marquis Crescenzi, sees Fabrice again, she is deeply moved by his extreme emaciation and by his expression, which suggests that he is now 'above all that can happen in this world.' (26)

The most important function of the Stendhalian prison is that it restores his heroes to their own selves – or rather, that it allows them to discover the self, and even to create it. The prison thus assumes a protective and dynamic role. It liberates one from the captivity of social existence. Julien Sorel also works out his freedom in jail; his only complaint is that the door of a prison cell cannot be locked from within. Always, this prison dream is bound up with a yearning for altitude and vast panoramas. Marcel Proust once characterized Stendhal's entire vision as 'a certain feeling for altitude associated with the spiritual life'[10] One is indeed bound to recall the many 'elevated' places where Stendhal's heroes discover serenity; Julien's rock, the Gothic tower in Besançon, the belltower of the abbé Blanès, the cell in the Farnese fortress. Isolation and altitude bring about the most intense moments of poetic fervor. The walls of the prison cell become the very symbol of exalted privacy.

The unity of *La Chartreuse* is obviously neither of a 'documentary' nor of an 'analytical' nature in the usual sense of the word. 'Realism' is also a misleading term when applied to an author whose essential achievement, especially in this densely poetic novel, is of a metaphoric order. The psychology of the characters, fluid and unpredictable, is thus not an assessable reality to be demonstrated through the action, but remains subjected to the poetic vision of the whole and to the central themes of freedom in particular. For there exist hardly any a priori definitions of characters in Stendhal's novels. If Fabrice seems naïve at the beginning, if at times he seems to define himself in negative terms, it is in large measure because the author refuses to make him the prisoner of his own 'essence.' The void remains to be filled; and this act of filling is the very act of living. Unlike Balzac, Stendhal proposes fictional figures that are not predetermined. A hundred years before Malraux, Stendhal might have said that man is what he does, not what he hides. This emphasis on choice and action, this disregard for all the forces that may bind and determine, helps explain why Stendhal has been so dear to the Existentialist generation. His great theme, like that of the Existentialist writers, is also the theme of freedom: a freedom discovered in love, in prison, but above all through the protagonists' surprises as they watch themselves live.

Stendhal, instead of defining his characters, grants them the right to self-discovery. His ironic techniques – interventions, commentaries, disapprovals, pretended astonishment, apparent improvisations – seem to encourage them to seek themselves out on their own. It would be easy to show, for instance, that Fabrice's whole adventure is but a succession of self-revelatory glimpses. He sees himself as a volunteer, he sees himself drunk, he sees himself as a soldier who has not fought, he sees himself in a succession of roles – and each role he assumes becomes an instrument of self-understanding. A characteristic rhetoric of surprise is at work. The words 'discovery' and 'surprise' recur with insistence. Fabrice tells himself that he has fallen in love with Clélia, and the author explains that 'he finally made this discovery.' Similarly, the interrogative turn of many internal monologues suggests that the deed precedes knowledge, that action has priority over insight. 'Is this a prison?'–'Is this what I feared so much?'–'Am I a hero unaware?'–'Maybe I have a noble character.' (18) The ethics of freedom and of individuality – the specific Stendhalian 'morality of self to self' implies a pursuit of an elusive identity.

La Chartreuse de Parme is primarily a novel of quest to which all elements and motifs contribute: the thirst for experience, the voyage, the myths of the false father and of the father substitute, the apprenticeship of the world, which is in fact the hero's apprenticeship of his own possibilities, the hard lesson of a difficult and uncomfortable freedom. Time, in Stendhal's novels, is never a prisoner of necessity. To the Romantic obsession with a paralyzing self-analysis, Stendhal opposes that other Romantic obsession, the eternal becoming and the disturbing 'availability' of the individual.

A disquieting note does ultimately characterize all of Stendhal's work. Faced with the self that forever eludes him, Stendhal experiences a constant uneasiness bordering on anxiety. Freedom, as Sartre has reminded us, is not an easy burden to carry. In his autobiographic texts, Stendhal insistently interrogates himself and his past in order to decipher himself – but in vain. One cannot possess oneself. The sleepless hours devoted to the questions 'what am I?' and 'what have I been?' yield no results. The eye needs a mirror to see itself.

But the eye of the 'other,' as Fabrice and all Stendhal's heroes know, has a hostile glance and is truly the enemy of our freedom. Love of freedom and fear of freedom are here complementary. And love of discovery and fear of discovery are equally interlocked. This may well be the secret of that typically Stendhalian shadow, which, like a modest veil, is cast over all precious moments and emotions. This desire to protect and yet to reveal what the author himself fails to penetrate completely is perhaps the secret tragedy behind the Stendhalian creation. Beyond the smile of Stendhal, beyond the movement and fervor of this novel, it is possible to guess the anguish of a man drawn to and at the same time distressed by the mysteries of his personality and who finds it difficult to see himself live otherwise than in the mirror of literary creation.

Notes

1. Some of the ideas developed in this chapter were originally sketched out in my introduction to *Stendhal: A Collection of Critical Essays* (Englewood Cliffs, N.J.: Prentice-Hall, 1962) and were the basis of a paper read at the 'Congrès Stendhalien' held in Parma in May 1967.

2. ENRICO PANZACCHI, 'De Stendhal', *Nuova Antologia* (December 1, 1885), XXIII, pp. 377–95.

3. *Vie de Henry Brulard* (Paris: Le Divan, 1949), I, 233.

4. For a view of *Le Rouge et le Noir* and *La Chartreuse de Parme* as fictional accounts of spiritual pilgrimages, see CLAUDE-EDMONDE MAGNY, *Histoire du roman français depuis 1918* (Paris: Editions du Seuil, 1950), I, 338.

5. For a discussion of the theatrical images in relation to the realism of *La Chartreuse*, see JUDD D. HUBERT, 'The Devaluation of Reality in the *Chartreuse de Parme*', in Victor Brombert, *Stendhal: A Collection of Critical Essays*, pp. 95–100.

6. *Vie de Henry Brulard*, I, 445.

7. On Stendhal as 'docteur d'une nouvelle immoralité', see CHARLES MAURRAS, Preface to *Rome, Naples et Florence en 1817* (Paris: Champion; 1919), I, 34.

8. For echoes of Rousseau in Stendhal's writings, see VICTOR BROMBERT, 'Stendhal, lecteur de Rousseau', *Revue des Sciences Humaines*, 92 (Oct.-Dec. 1958), 463–482. [*Editor's note*: This article has since become available in translation in VICTOR BROMBERT, *The Hidden Reader. Stendhal, Balzac, Hugo, Baudelaire, Flaubert*

The Red and the Black *and* The Charterhouse of Parma

(Cambridge, Mass. and London: Harvard University Press, 1988), pp. 164–82.]
For a discussion of Cardinal de Retz as a possible source for *La Chartreuse*, see
LUIGI MAGNANI, 'L'Idea della Chartreuse', *Paragone*, 38 (Feb. 1953), pp. 5–27.

9. GEORGES BLIN, *Stendhal et les problèmes du roman* (Paris: José Corti, 1954), p. 107.
    Since writing this book, I have read with great pleasure STEPHEN GILMAN's *The
    Tower as Emblem* (Frankfurt: Vittorio Klostermann, 1967), which reaches similar
    conclusions about Fabrice's freedom in captivity.

10. MARCEL PROUST, *A la recherche du temps perdu* (Paris: Bibliothèque de la Pléiade,
    1954), III, 377.

5 Pierre Barbéris on politics in *The Charterhouse of Parma*

Against the novel of the here and now: a novel about happiness and the elsewhere

There is one point on which a whole tradition of critical approach seems to be justified: as a novel about happiness and a novel about pleasure (the happiness and pleasure of the protagonists, but also of the author and reader), *The Charterhouse of Parma* does not easily lend itself to commentary and elucidation and should be left entirely to the person who opens its pages. This time, no preparatory notes . . . Written in six weeks of euphoria, and without the little running battles of self-censorship and self-commentary which had dominated the long and difficult process of writing *Lucien Leuwen*, *The Charterhouse of Parma* is unquestionably a novel if not about liberty then at least about liberation. Some would even say that here, at last, is the 'pure' literary act. There is a lot of mystification in this view, but also a lot of truth. For the reader of this volume, who is beginning to know Stendhal a little better, a somewhat lighter style of introduction will therefore be attempted. When it comes to *The Charterhouse* one has to let the text speak for itself, and if people absolutely must have a commentary, then Balzac's great article on this novel in 1840 could still at a pinch serve such a purpose. Nevertheless, since pleasure and knowledge are not incompatible, one or two clarifications and suggestions are still in order. All the more so as in this novel, and probably more than in those which preceded it (and for reasons which remain to be seen), the snares of conformist reading and dominant ideology are still efficiently set. Our job, once again and perhaps more than ever, is to lift our feet at the right places.

The history of the book is simple. Stendhal undertook the writing of *The Charterhouse* after reading a chronicle about the *Origins of the Most Noble Family of the Farnese* (which provided him with the model for Fabrice making a career in the Church), and with this project he combined a second, *The Vivandière* (military scenes relating to the battle of Waterloo), and then another still, this time relating to the death of Sandrino, the child

113

of Fabrice and Clélia. As to the details, multiple models will provide him with Mosca, Rassi, Ranuce IV and Ranuce V, la Sanseverina and Clélia Conti. From the start he knew where he was headed: a great career as churchman and lover, the encounter with Napoleon, an unhappy ending and withdrawal to the Charterhouse. In six weeks the novel was finished. As it was too long, he had to agree to slight cuts in the final pages, which are very rushed and which Stendhal never had the courage or opportunity to revise, even though he thought of doing so. The novel was published in April 1839. The following year, after an initial exchange of letters, Balzac wrote his famous, enthusiastic article on it for his own *Revue parisienne*. Stendhal momentarily considered making the revisions which his illustrious contemporary had suggested (to begin with Waterloo, for example). But here, too, he desisted.

If the immediate history of the book is simple, its subsequent ideological history is less so. The bourgeois critics' view of the book is clear, only too clear: if *The Red and the Black* had been the unsettling work of an unsettled man, *The Charterhouse* is the reassuring and placatory work of a-man-at-peace-with-the-world-who-has-found-in-art-a-solution-to-his-troubles. So it is a kind of blessing? But the objection comes to mind at once: at peace with the world? this man who has still to write *Lamiel*? and who has just given up writing *Lucien Leuwen* for fear of the police? At peace? this portrayer of villains? No, really, it won't wash. And in fact one can see quite clearly the trap these gentlemen have set: long live art, thanks to which the class struggle is at an end! Long live art, which *single-handedly* solves the problems of the world! André Gide saluted it: 'The book is written entirely for pleasure.' Long live pleasure!, which means, doesn't it, to hell with the 'rest of it', in other words with intellectual enquiry. For all that one may like the novel, one must nevertheless react against this; that is to say, one must read the sense of this *apparent* distancing of class struggle in the Stendhalian novel and of this recourse to some kind of Eden, this *apparent* evasiveness, this *apparent* refusal to talk about France and the reality of the moment, in a novel where money and career no longer *explicitly* play the same role as in Stendhal's previous novels. Bourgeois critics have always jibbed at *The Red and the Black* and the texts which frame it (*Armance* and *Lucien Leuwen*). On the other hand they have always gone into ecstasies over *The Charterhouse*. This is not the fault of *The Charterhouse*, but nevertheless one must try to understand why this is so.

Paul Bourget, novelist and critic of the moral order and ever with the quill between his teeth, saw in Julien Sorel nothing more nor less than 'the murderous psychology of the Terror, the Commune, and the Bolsheviks'. And that was reprinted in 1925 not in some extreme right-wing rag but in the preface to a major scholarly edition of Stendhal's *Complete Works*! In those days the bourgeoisie came clean. Which of them today would dare write such a thing? Today they would be concerned rather to find Julien 'charming'. And yet the bourgeoisie hasn't changed. Indeed it has got worse. But it is no longer able to carry on the struggle in the way it would wish to. Paul Bourget saw in Julien Sorel 'a plebeian transferring from one class to another'. He did not condemn this 'class transfer'. Only, he noted, in the seventeenth century (in Molière, for example) this transfer used to operate at the level of entire families. And so in those days such a transfer endangered neither society nor the individual. On the contrary. It ensured, thanks to the wisdom of 'proceeding step by step',[1] the renewal of the ruling élites. In the nineteenth century, on the other hand – and this is what Stendhal not only realized but also (almost criminal, isn't it?) encouraged – this class transfer is being effected in an uncivilized manner, with families being broken up and individuals let loose on their own, and thus effected in a way which constitutes a threat to order: when an individual goes off on his own, God knows where he'll get to! In Bourget, as far as the causes of this new method of class transfer after the Revolution are concerned, not a word, of course. On the anarchism of social mobility, not a word. One can see why *The Charterhouse* is less troubling, being a novel in which only individuals move, not social types, in which 'rising in society' is not a collective phenomenon, in which intrigue reigns supreme and no 'clear front' of social change or 'revolution' is on the horizon. Granted, there is an alternation between progress and reaction; granted, there is a little riot after the death of the Prince; but there is no movement deep down in society, and hence the undertakings, reactions, and impulses of individuals no longer have the same significance as in the novels of bourgeois 'revolution-in-the-making' in France. These at least contained, for certain readers, some food for thought and something to cheer about. But *why* did Stendhal provide conformist readers with what seem to be mere opportunities for diversion? Why all the licking of critical lips at this apparent 'depoliticization' of the novel? But why, too, this clear depoliticization?

The whole thing stems no doubt from the abandoning of *Lucien Leuwen*. History having reached an impasse, and the hero's journey of education being doomed to sterility, there is only one thing left to do if one wants once more to write a (hi)story, that is to say, to express, in spite of everything, one's inner life, if one wants to do one's 'job' as someone who lives by the pen: namely, to return to a time and place when and where History still opened on to the future, and the blockages of modern bourgeois society were not yet operative. In short, a time and place when and where the evolution of social relations still left free and open a future which in France had now become a past. This is where a rough and ready version of 'Italy' presented itself. Between *Lucien Leuwen* and *The Charterhouse* Stendhal did a lot of work on various *Italian Chronicles*, on the basis of seventeenth-century texts: but his reconversion is not entirely owing to his stay in Italy (some of the *Italian Chronicles* considerably predate the period spent in Civitavecchia), and anyway why did it not

115

happen earlier? In fact it is all a question of finding a new terrain. The small Italian city, human passions within the framework of feudal and pre-monarchical times (when the bourgeoisie did not yet really count either as a social force or as an ideological force), a 'Republican' way of life that had not yet been perverted by monarchical centralization, by the law of 'keeping up appearances', still less by modern democracy, such as these had subsequently manifested themselves in France . . . A sentence from *The Abbess of Castro* says it all:

> In the 15th century, young girls, being more in tune with republican good sense, thought much more of a man for what he had done than for the wealth accumulated by his ancestors or their celebrated actions.

Today's two main qualifications for membership of a supposed 'aristocracy' are being aimed at here, and one is transported to a time when they were not yet operative, when humanity was still free, when modern History, politically, morally, and literarily sterilizing, had not yet begun. But it is the unexpected link with the French Revolution which will make the theme stand out in all its critical force: Milan liberated by Bonaparte in 1796 represents, for a brief, miraculous moment, the coming together of the ancient, natural freedom of Italy and the new freedom of France, of pre-bourgeois and pre-aristocratic freedom and the freedom of the people. A strange, surprising moment: Italy, the land of the natural, becomes even more natural the day that the soldiers of the Revolution, so badly dressed but ever so natural, rid it of the Austrians. At once one finds oneself at a point of double origin, and one is doubly freed: one is far from aristocratic/bourgeois artificiality, and one is far from revolutionary/'revolutioned' society. One finds oneself in an unblocked situation, as if it were the bright morning of the century, whereas *Lucien Leuwen* was the novel of night falling, or about to fall, a novel about the end of an age and its definitive engulfment by the bourgeoisie.

The act of literary escapism has here, therefore, a profoundly political value: one can only write the novel of happiness by swapping literary societies. Being unable to change real society or to envisage that real society will ever change, one adopts a different society in one's writing. And in consequence everything changes in both aspect and significance: the Napoleon, for example, who was one of the people responsible for making France bourgeois again, is once more the young General Bonaparte, who no longer has to be idolized in as illusory a manner and solely by way of expressing opposition to the political right as Julien Sorel used to. One forgets that these simple, heroic officers are the new feudal lords, that men like Lieutenant Robert will become nobles of the Empire, and one remembers only their dazzling beginnings. Etc. The novelist *chooses* with a view to the effect he wishes to create. And the choice, the sifting, of material is so well managed that Stendhal quite forgets one essential feature of his beloved Italy: the 'Italian' way of looking at the question. Bonaparte, the liberator of the Milanese, is indeed presented here in a uniquely positive light; he is the man of the Lodi Bridge, the one who drove out the Austrians. But there is nothing about the man who, in 1797, following his victorious campaign of the previous year, signed the treaty of Campo-Formio which gave Venetia back to the Austrians following shameful negotiations of the most cynically opportunistic and political kind and thus led to the worst kind of repression and the exiling or imprisonment of the sincerest patriots. Yet this aspect of the matter was of capital importance to those Italians who were most attached to the cause of liberty, and Foscolo, in *The Final Letters of Jacob Ortis*, condemned 'the young hero' (for all that he spoke Italian!) who had made this dishonourable pact with absolutism. But at this point in the novel Bonaparte *must* be pure, and so he is presented in a particular way, and Bonaparte, the opportunistic politician when he was negotiating, is seen and allowed to be seen solely as a military figure contrasting with the inadequacies of the Directoire. In this novel one is well and truly in the realm of myth.

But, with myth complementing realism, this allows Stendhal to write of something which is extraordinary to anyone who thinks of the France of 1839 and its divided, individualist society, eaten away by enmities and ambitions: 'a nation madly in love'! Such a thing has long since become impossible in France and in Europe. The same goes, and in a similar sense, for any new politics, any real relaunching of the collective life: such a thing has long become unthinkable, and Leuwen senior could only *play* at making and unmaking a government ministry from within the system; he did not build anything, nor could he build anything, and opposition in *Lucien Leuwen*, as we have seen, meant nothing at all. But it does mean something in Milan in 1796. Because History still has a chance. In *Lucien Leuwen* all the forms which had already begun to seem empty in *The Red and the Black* either continue to diminish in substance or are already completely devoid of it. In *The Charterhouse* they are full of substance once more and in fine fettle. Witness the fact that political victory is at once the victory of art and the victory of expression, and young Gros's cartoon fires the enthusiasm of a people which is able to communicate with each other. We have moved on from little society sonnets, individualist and cold, to the beginnings of a collective art which is synonymous with life itself. Thus creation and enterprise have become, at every level and above all (for a French citizen of 1839) at the level of novel-writing, once more thinkable and possible. Flaubert said how sad one had to be to undertake to bring Carthage back to life! Stendhal does not even need to explain himself: how desperately one must have still had to believe in life to resurrect an Italy liberated by the French Revolution! The difference lies not only in the *character* of the two writers but in the difference between their situations and the ways in which these were internalized: in 1839, despite the blockage in France, people still remain optimistic, if only by continuing to believe in the value of dreaming, whereas dreaming will have become laughable by the time of Flaubert and something he will feel obliged to ridicule or to destroy. It is simply that in the France of 1839, on the eve of Guizot's accession to power, there is a need for an alternative setting. Italy will thus serve as a double Utopia: a geographical and moral Utopia (the land of the natural), and a political Utopia (a land in which certain contradictions are not yet operative). A golden age.

One piece of evidence will suffice; the revolution (?) having failed in Parma after the death of the Prince, the republican Ferrante Palla leaves his country for America, a republican land, a land of the liberty in which he believes, his only mistress, he says, and the only love which can rival in his heart the image of la Sanseverina. In the France of *Lucien Leuwen* people no longer believe in American liberty, are no longer able to believe in it; in the Italy of the great liberal struggles, people do believe in it, and they are still able to believe in it because liberalism has not yet shown its other, hideous face. Fabio Conti arguably belongs to the race of false liberals who are men of the party only to trade themselves and to make a career, and the opposition between Raversi's party and that of la Sanseverina is arguably no more than the opposition of operetta. The one, single figure of Ferrante Palla provides a counterweight, even if only momentarily, to these court games. And so one sees that at his level, as far as the author is concerned, there are no reservations about America or about liberty: what has died in Parma has been born and continues to exist across the Atlantic, *and people are ready to go there*. The reader, and only the reader, can, if he wishes, read Ferrante's comments on America as illusion: for the character himself they are fully meant, and the novelist puts himself in a situation which allows him to write such comments as if he, too, still believed in America, that is, in another place and a future time that are republican. Liberty, in 1796 and in the years that follow the post-Napoleonic reaction, still has a future, and the conservative Prime Minister Mosca, a man of pleasure and taste, scarcely does anything more than *play* at being a right-wing prime minister, undermining Metternich's system from within just as Leuwen senior undermined the banking system from within. A happy situation, a situation of refuge for a man who had just sounded the death knell of a bourgeois republic and bourgeois liberty in *Lucien Leuwen*. The Italy of the *carbonari* and the Risorgimento, the Italy of plots against princes, the Italy of a still possible alliance between the people and those aristocrats or bourgeois who are patriotic and liberal, this Italy is the blessed land of democratic illusionism whose real literary power is in this instance the power of an incantation on liberty's behalf. Now incantation suggests faith. The novel of liberty can no longer be written in France. But as people still believe in liberty, Italy will serve instead. Since his departure from Milan in 1821, Stendhal had made a long detour via France and the 'French' novel. He only came back to his beloved adopted homeland after having established, by his practice as a writer, that there was no other way. But, instead of shutting his reader up in the nightmarish void of a Carthage like Flaubert, he turns him into a Milanese dreamer for whom it is illusion, more than anything else, which proves capable, somehow or other, of describing the real.

Some examples of Stendhalian continuity. But also a break

This novel about happiness is a realist novel insofar as the usual Stendhalian life-pattern continues to unfold: Fabrice dreams only of adventures, splendour, glory, but in the Flemish household where he is lodged after being wounded, beside the little Aniken, he wonders, like Julien in the company of Mme de Rênal: 'Where else could I be better off than here?' And yet he will depart, but only to come face to face with the same problem again: whether to live safely according to the rules of the system, with his horses and his mistresses, or to live dangerously? Does he love Marietta or la Fausta? Not really. But he cannot resist the thrill of taking risks. And on each occasion he sets out in search of adventure and meets only with catastrophe. In his way Fabrice is constantly rejecting the bourgeois way of life. The taste for telling adventure stories does not blot out analysis: adventure does not remake the world, but nor does renouncing adventure. Exactly the same thing happens to la Sanseverina: Mosca provides her with a ready-made situation and ready-made happiness, and repeatedly they both envisage withdrawing to live in isolation and calm; but always there returns the temptation of the pleasure of living. In less dramatic terms one finds here again the dilemma which is at the basis of Balzacian mythology and, more broadly, of the mythology of the Romantic novel: whether to live a slow, safe life on some little island or to spend one's energies and burn life up. There is nothing more despicable, in the eyes of these savourers of existence, than prudence, even though such prudence may periodically ensure the possibility of pleasures to be savoured. But there is also nothing crazier in the end than these undertakings from which nothing lasting can come in this disorderly world, and all possible objections to a well-regulated life are contained in a sentence which might have been uttered by Lucien Leuwen: '"And after ten years of this pleasant life, what would I have achieved", Fabrice asked himself; "what would I be? A mature young man who has to make way for the first handsome adolescent he sees making his debut in the world and, like me, riding a fine English horse."

Another instance of Stendhal's consistency is that the inspiration is still vigorously liberal and continues to manifest itself in satire: the Archbishop of Parma is suspicious of personal merit (which smacks too much of the freethinker and Voltaire) and of all these notions of 'the happiness of the greatest number', that heresy of the nineteenth century; similarly, to succeed one must be colourless, odourless, tasteless; similarly, too, the Prince plays at being Louis XIV and is content to *reign* in little matters. Stendhal here reproduces the reactionary discourse that was current at the beginning of the nineteenth century and counters it with the discourse of progressive satire: esteem for what is original and personal, a sense of the collective rights of man, and a consigning of everything authoritarian to the penumbra of ridicule. But also, as always with Stendhal, the barbs are not aimed only at the conservatism and obscurantism of the nobility: they are aimed at all conservatism, noble *and bourgeois*. All aristocracies hang together, and certain rallying cries which were bourgeois in origin have for a long time been turned against the bourgeois. Good abbé Blanès foresees 'that in fifty years' time perhaps there won't be any place for the life of luxury': this being a Saint-Simonian theme from which Stendhal evidently does not demur. But is he aiming only at the land-owning class here? This is all the more remarkable for the fact that the hero is noble and rich, that his 'dear aunt' reproaches him 'for not withdrawing enough money at the bank'. But that is just it: money, whether it be noble or bourgeois, does not interest Fabrice who, in accordance with Stendhal's text of 1825,[2] is neither noble like the privileged nor rich like the industrialists. There are two ways of indicating the power and harmful effects of money in a novel: by having the hero humiliated and unhappy because he is poor, or having a rich hero who refuses money. If one takes Octave, Lucien, and Fabrice together, it is clear that Stendhal much prefers the second way; and Julien himself, although poor, wishes not so much to become rich as to be recognized. Why? No doubt because his relationship with money (unlike in Balzac) was never of a dramatic kind and because, assured as he is of an indispensable minimum and not much given to spending, his attitude was principally one of detachment? Because also he was less aware of the revolutionary potential of money, of money as a formidable instrument in the transformation of the world? The fact remains that with him money is always, and even increasingly, enemy number one of liberty and truth. The hateful person, the real horror here, like Valenod in *The Red and the Black*, is the fiscal Rassi, a plebeian who has gone over, body and soul, into service with the established order whatever that may be, always ready to sell himself and ready to reach an accommodation with every regime. There are no 'industrialists' in this Italian universe that is singularly lacking in infrastructure, and which is glimpsed only at the level of its domestic staff and its supernumeraries, its 'tertiary sector' and its 'service industries'. But beyond the fact that an Italy which is still largely agricultural and feudal justifies this image, it is evident that a society is apprehended and expresses itself as much in its social and ideological operators as through those who are the real masters of the game. Rassi is much more than the treacherous villain of Gothic novels or melodrama. Rassi is the face of ugliness itself. And Rassi is the man who sits 'below the salt', the type of person against which the most ancient philosophical revolt protests as it transforms itself into a broader form of revolt. Lucien's ministries were full of Rassis. On this point, too, Stendhal continues his critique.

Is this to say that in this Italy which has fallen once more under absolutist domination nothing is left but crazy, romantic dreams of liberty *and* the rottenness and complicities which render it unlikely, impossible? Once more the diagnosis is realistic. In Parma, liberty is not yet mature; the people are capable only of riots: 'It will take this country a hundred years before the idea of a republic ceases to be an absurdity.' Or, as Palla puts it: 'how do you make a republic without the republicans to make it with?' – i.e. *both* without a modicum of serious republican ideology, *and* above all without real social forces able to sustain this republic. The populace of Sacca is still in its infancy, at the stage of infra-history, of non-consciousness. Where would Ferrante find his troops? One can see why Fabrice, the lover of truth and liberty, is no nearer to getting what he wants in his novel than Lucien Leuwen is in his. All the more so as the map, the weapon, the very idea of liberty are to be seen here being used, manipulated, by extremely suspect personages. Does not the Prince, a despot in his own domain, dream in his opposition to Austria of one day being 'the adored liberal leader of all Italy' and later of being 'the constitutional king of Lombardy'? Which means that there is a nationalist constitutionalism which is perfectly compatible with maintaining the privileges of the ruling classes, something the entire history of the Risorgimento will bear out. National liberty as the weapon of national bourgeoisies: it operates against ancient tyrannies; it operates, too, against still dormant peoples. The Prince's plan is in no way a caricature, and its subsequent execution by Cavour and the house of Savoy will provide a fine example of the fact. In Italy too it will be necessary to pass through the stage of bourgeois liberty. A dark future, and one which offsets all the luminosity of the novel's opening pages. But, once again, this is realism. The idyll of a pre-bourgeois historical situation, but also the disintegration of this idyll as one moves away from the great collective light of society's beginnings, and, be it aristocracy or bourgeoisie, in the direction of a return to order. This is the profound dialectic of the novel, and one which prevents it ever being classified with works of the 'rose-tinted democracy' variety.

Here again, then, there is consistency and continuity in the very contradiction itself, that is to say in the expression of the contradictory. One piece of evidence, one example, will serve for all: America. America, for

Ferrante Palla, does not present a problem, but for la Sanseverina, for this aristocratic gaze which is once more a gaze of quality, a gaze which sees straight through bourgeois reality, America is an illusion. The analysis, to be sure, could not here be really and directly *political*; and it is not Stendhal who is speaking but the character. But is it not he also who makes the character speak? On hearing Fabrice, who is looking for something to do with himself and, like Lucien [Leuwen], talking of going to New York, of becoming a republican citizen and soldier in America (which is both true *and* false: Fabrice is right to want to become a republican citizen and soldier, but is there any republic to be found except in one's own country?), the Duchess objects with good reason: 'There won't be any war for you to fight in, and you'll end up leading the life of leisure again, but without elegance, without amorous adventures', and she tells him about 'the worship of the god dollar, and the respect one has to have for the workmen in the street who, with their vote, decide everything'. This is the language of a certain type, certainly, the language of a class. But who would dare maintain that that is all there is to what la Sanseverina has to say? Yes, once more this is the language of unreasonable demand, of quality. The critical function of true aristocracy in a world of mediocrity.

La Sanseverina belongs to no particular party either. What party could it be? She is in Fabrice's party and he in hers. True liberty, she tells herself, exists and may be spoken of only among heroes: Fabrice, who rejects intrigue, money, and paltry ambition; Clélia, who already as a child believed in 'all these liberal ideas' and hates 'the pliant nature of the courtier' – hence that firmness of character ('"I am going to save my husband", she would say to herself'), which makes her Mathilde's sister; the Duchess, so much above the court which she at once knows and yet does not quite know how to manipulate. These three beings, with Mosca as flank-guard and Ferrante Palla as slightly naïve herald, constitute an isolated community, an enclave, a living proof, a *happy few*. But not a vanguard destined for some kind of victory by some prophet or other. *The Charterhouse*, as a novel of idyll, remains far removed from any Messianism, and nowhere in it does one find the promise that History will one day take its full course. Again, the evidence? It is in prison that people are happy, it is in prison that people are free. This discovery dates back to *The Red and the Black*. Men shut us in. But what do they shut in? The body, the outward manifestation. The essential part eludes them. Julien with Mme de Rênal and Fabrice with Clélia are free in the midst of their shackles and surrounding walls, just as in Balzac's *Les Chouans* Marie and Montauran are free in their lovers' nest surrounded by Corentin's police and the rifles of the men in blue. It is in prison that Fabrice – hated by his elder brother, barely loved by his father, yet realizing on two occasions (on the visit to Grianta and when his execution is announced during his stay in prison) that he could have loved this father, that he did perhaps love him, that whatever the case he needed him – that Fabrice in the end finds – and starts – what all Stendhal's heroes lack: a family . . . No bourgeois marriage for him. Only at night will he see the one who bid him 'Enter here, friend of my heart'. He will want to rescue his child from the world of these monsters. The child will die, and all that remains will be for him to shut himself away in the Charterhouse, thus finally justifying the hitherto inexplicable title.

This narrative progression itself, its logic, its coherence, its status as quest, its moments of illumination and failure, all bespeak a liberty forced to internalize itself for lack of the opportunity, despite the hopes and promises of 1796, to realize itself in the world. But this internalization – another important instance of dialectic reversal – is not of a sceptical or pessimistic nature or import. Evidence? The entry of the French into Milan, in fresh and joyful order, as if the curtain had gone up, is counterbalanced by the great confusion of Waterloo viewed from below. But isn't it striking that Waterloo is depicted as a battle and not as a defeat, that the sombre tones of catastrophe are missing? The major contrast with Victor Hugo's Waterloo in *Les Misérables* is not only the contrast between a worm's eye view and a cosmic overview. It is that for Hugo Waterloo represents the spectacular and fatal collapse of a world and of a hero (together with, implicitly, the promise one day of a great victory, of a great light, of all the blessings), while for Stendhal it is a question simply of one particular episode in a young man's life . . . Stendhal's Napoleon is not a man to trouble God. He is simply a man, and the picture which other men have had of him. Neither miracle nor catastrophe attend his origins, but signs. And it is in this world of signs that heroes endeavour to live. Reversal, still: on this point Stendhal continues but also changes. Is not *The Charterhouse* in fact a novel without heroes?

Who, indeed, is the hero of *The Charterhouse of Parma*? The question was meaningless applied to Stendhal's earlier novels, which are both linear (the career of an individual hero) and centred (relating everything to this individual hero). But here? At first the hero is, in a way, Milan after its liberation, together with its populace who have fallen madly in love. Then, for a long time, it is Fabrice, but for a long time too, when he is absent from Parma, it is la Sanseverina. At other times it is Mosca, the jealous lover. Then once more it is Fabrice, and more and more exclusively so, the Fabrice for whom la Sanseverina has been no more than a stage in his development and who finds fulfilment with Clélia. In fact the question never proves susceptible of a totally satisfactory answer. There is no central focus on a unique or exemplary sequence of events in this novel which no longer has a Christian name as its title.[3] This must have been by choice. The Charterhouse of Parma is not only the monastery to which Fabrice withdraws; it is also in a way the enclave that is the city of Parma, in which extraordinary things come to pass. Stendhal has wanted to write, no less than the story of Fabrice, the story of a group and of a collectivity, and in the last line, ironically or not, it is Parma that is in question, and no longer the completed destinies of particular individuals.

The way in which it was written – quickly – and the amateur approach do not therefore totally explain the novel's apparent incoherence and lack of continuity. Stendhal was tempted in turn by the subject of 'Fabrice at Waterloo', then of 'Sanseverina – Mosca – Fabrice', then of 'Fabrice and Clélia', all these 'thens' moreover often being 'at the same times' coming one on top of the other. Ultimately, and if one does not pay too much attention to the focusing on Fabrice and Clélia in the final chapters, *The Charterhouse* is a novel without any real hero or privileged personnel. In this sense, one wonders if the book does not represent, in 1839, a certain crisis in the traditional novel, or at the least a certain questioning of it and hence something of an investigation into the place, function, and value of the individual in the world. The pleasure of recounting episodes and adventures, of analysing situations, proves stronger than the intention to write a coherent narrative: the coherence is to be found elsewhere, and the interest sustained in a new manner. In this respect the chapter on Waterloo points forward: to the crowd novel, the novel dealing with individuals all mixed together and living side by side; the novel of a great, rich tumult in which the individual is but one single point. Think of *Armance*, that novel so exclusively focused on a *case*! The Stendhalian universe has expanded. There are no exemplary heroes any longer. The individual no longer 'is' the novel because the individual no longer 'is' the world. Egotism has come to this: liberation in respect of the 'French model' of the psychological and individualist novel which had been the form appropriate to a particular moment in the evolution of literary knowledge; and transition to the creation in writing of a symbolic world which is no longer a backdrop but the subject itself. In this sense, *The Charterhouse* is an epic. Is that to say – and one has to come to this, to keep coming back to this – that it is Stendhal's masterpiece?

A writer's masterpiece?

What I am about to say will appear to contradict what I said at the beginning. Nevertheless it is necessary to speak without ambiguity and in full awareness of the problems involved. Whoever asks certain questions of this novel – and Stendhal encourages it – must remain somewhat puzzled by this *Charterhouse*, a consecrated text, an arc of the covenant within the tradition of the novel and within our cultural tradition, and which all sorts of more or less silent conspiracies use more or less openly to demote the other three novels to the rank of texts which prepared the way. Well, I will admit it, and at the risk of scandalizing the guardians of our culture: *The Charterhouse*, despite all its importance, has less to say to me than *Armance, The Red and the Black*, and *Lucien Leuwen*. Those three novels speak plainly to me. *The Charterhouse*, on the whole, involves me in too many roundabout ways of saying things. The pleasure of adventure, the charm of the heroes, the world partially preserved, yes. But hadn't Stendhal accustomed us to something else? It would be absurd to 'reproach' *The Charterhouse* for being merely an adventure novel. The fact remains nevertheless that one feels oneself to have taken a step backwards compared with what had gone before, and that something in this text, which, on the basis of certain attributes mentioned earlier, represents an advance, a form of progress, here resigns from office and dissolves itself, leaving itself free to adorn itself in marvellous colours and to work and signify in another way.

Let us go further. It was the powers that be that condemned Stendhal to write *The Charterhouse*. Stendhal made the best of a bad job, and remarkably so. But doesn't one hanker for the *Lucien Leuwen* that might have been if he had been allowed to finish it? And that is why *The Charterhouse* seems to me to be in no way Stendhal's masterpiece, and that is why also, in the end, this text still strikes me as suspect. It is too easy for it to be taken periodically for a novel of universal harmony and a certain deproblematization of the world. Where the three previous novels dipped society's structures in acid, *The Charterhouse* simply pours clean water over them. No more stripping, just a gentle rinse. Tenderness, love, grace, yes. But not enough hard evidence of a time and a place. A miracle of the imagination. Yes. But only because the imaginary is all that remains. And, as I have said, Stendhal was condemned to write *The Charterhouse*. But is it not a matter for regret that he was not free to write something else? *The Charterhouse* seems to me to contain the repressed content – marvellously presented but repressed for all that – of a whole tradition of romance literature which has been forbidden expression. *The Charterhouse* is a knowledge-novel. But can one not imagine and wish that literary knowledge should find other outlets than in the forbidden? Moreover, just one word of advice: having read *The Charterhouse*, read *Madame Bovary*. There, once again, is to be found a France that is hard and real, disenchanted, but true, without opera or ballet, and in which romance has been put in its proper place once more. It is not Stendhal's fault; but *The Charterhouse* shows a man quitting the battlefield and leaving us with no more than a skewed, patchy vision of it, as at Waterloo. Let us not lose sight of this: *The Red and the Black* was Stendhal's Marengo, *Lucien Leuwen* his Austerlitz. And what if *The Charterhouse* were his Waterloo in lace frills?

These remarks do not detract in any way from the positive elements which have already been noted in the novel. Simply, they allow them to be seen in their proper perspective. Can the minor war with liberalism in Italy circa 1820 be of direct relevance to anyone investigating the ways in which the France of 1840 was in the process of becoming the France of 1848 and the France of 1851? And what wizardry of the imagination was ever any use against the power of the gun? *The Red and the Black* and *Lucien Leuwen* (and *Armance*, too, for that matter) are novels which provide arms one has only to reach out and take down from the gun-rack. These novels are acts. With *The Charterhouse*, if the novel still represents an act, it is an act of a different kind. Some sort of era of liberty is coming to a close. Another is opening, for literature always, despite the obstacles, speaks of the real, appropriates it, transforms it. With *The Charterhouse* a certain way of speaking, appropriating, transforming, recedes into the past – one might even say, passes out of fashion. The end of Romanticism? Possibly. The Romantic *I* which had imposed its voice around 1825 is now in crisis. Perhaps that is why one can see in *The Charterhouse*, in 1839, not only a farewell to a whole kind of brilliance and to a certain type of 'novel of education', but also a sign pointing to the inevitable arrival, before too long, of [Flaubert's] *The Sentimental Education*.

Notes

1. *Step by Step (L'Etape)* is the title of a famous 'thesis-novel' by Bourget [published in 1902, (*Ed.*)]. If the grandfather is a peasant, the son a teacher, and the grandson a university lecturer, society and the individual are progressing smoothly. But if people want to move too quickly or to go it alone, then there is breakdown. This is the theory of how, in practical and ideological terms, to integrate children of the people into the ruling classes of society.

2. *Editor's note: D'un nouveau complot contre les industriels (Of a New Plot against the Industrialists).*

3. Note that the original title of *The Red and the Black* was *Julien*.

Structuralism and Language

The following extracts reflect the emphasis on structure and language which was characteristic of literary criticism in the 1960s and 1970s. Structuralism has its origins in the linguistic theories of the Swiss philologist Ferdinand de Saussure (1857–1913), which survived in the notes of his lectures taken by students and were published as the *Course in General Linguistics* (1916). Saussure envisaged any given state of language as essentially a system (or set of systems) of relations between its constituent elements, each of which has a function (and, ultimately, meaning) only by virtue of these relationships. This notion of systematic relations, or structures, has been applied in various fields of intellectual inquiry, notably social anthropology (Claude Lévi-Strauss's *The Elementary Structures of Kinship* was published in 1949, his *Structural Anthropology* in 1958), and the methodology of structural linguistics (developed after Saussure by Roman Jakobson and the so-called Prague School in the 1920s and 1930s) was adopted by other leading French thinkers in the late 1950s (e.g. Roland Barthes's *Mythologies* in 1958) and in the 1960s (e.g. Michel Foucault's *Words and Things* (1966), Jacques Lacan's *Ecrits* (*Writings*) (1966)).

The first set of extracts is taken from Shoshana Felman's book *La 'Folie' dans l'œuvre romanesque de Stendhal* ('Madness' in the Narrative Works of Stendhal), published in 1971. In her opening chapter she asserts that 'it is through words that literature offers itself to us. The literary text is nothing but a linguistic space: words and silences, a spatial disposition of signs, a landscape of verbal forms'. Hence, she continues, 'it was quite natural to look for the *physiognomy* of Stendhal in the verbal landscape of his work. By setting aside from the outset all prejudice, all preconceived notions, all previous knowledge external to the text, we undertook, in the simple, strict sense of the word, to *read* Stendhal. To read, taking each of the words as it comes and waiting for them to give us a sign.'

She goes on to explain how she has sought to trace the itinerary of certain words in Stendhal's writing. Meaning (or 'sens' in French, which means 'direction' as well as 'signification') is constituted by the distance between two uses of the same lexical item, is 'always the product of an encounter, is born of the *contact* between two facts, of the *relationship* between two (or more) terms/termini'. The repeated use of a word (such as 'folie' ('madness' or 'folly') or 'ivresse' ('intoxication' or 'drunkenness')) generates a whole series of 'relationships', and the meaning of such a word in any one instance derives from the location of this single usage within the 'structure' of all its uses in a given text. These uses (in this case, within Stendhal's narrative fiction) are the one true 'dictionary' in which one needs to 'look up' a given word to understand its meaning. To read a literary text is, therefore, not to relate the linguistic signifier to the world beyond the text but to the signifying structures of the text itself, which thus 'shows' one how to read it. In this sense a literary text is 'a network of infinite echoes and allusions, in which writing is forever referring to itself' (p. 30).

The second set of extracts is taken from Michel Crouzet's *Stendhal et le langage* (1981), which was the first part of Crouzet's monumental doctoral thesis on Stendhal to appear in print. Pierre-Georges Castex, Crouzet's thesis-supervisor at the Sorbonne (and his predecessor in the chair which Crouzet now holds), relates how he first beheld an 'enormous suitcase' containing 'approximately five thousand typed pages': it has taken six further volumes to publish the rest (before Crouzet's 800-page biography of Stendhal appeared in 1990).

It was, therefore, appropriate that a man so productive of words should have been the first to offer a comprehensive study of Stendhal and language. Taking his cue from the idea expressed by Felman (and many other structuralist and post-structuralist critics) that the literary text is inherently self-referential, he examines how the problems of linguistic expression are discussed and exemplified not only in Stendhal's own personal and critical writings but also in his fictional work. The passages chosen come from Chapter VII, entitled 'Speech and Silence in the Beylist world', where Crouzet discusses with particular originality and force the paradox inherent in all Stendhal's writings that the spoken (and written) word always threatens to betray the authenticity of the phenomenon or experience which it is intended to convey. His chapter might well have had as its epigraph the entire ninth chapter of Stendhal's *Love*:

> I am making every possible effort to be *dry*. I want to bid my heart be silent, this heart that thinks it has such a lot to say. I always tremble for fear that I have written but a sigh when I thought to have noted a truth.

6 Shoshana Felman on 'madness' and 'intoxication'[1]

'Madness'

That 'madness' for Stendhal is initially no more than 'what people call madness' – that is, a borrowed signifier, a 'manner of speaking' which the author *pastiches* without adopting it as his own– is suggested by many linguistic indicators. And first of all by explicit indications, by warnings about vocabulary: very often the author insists on the fact that he is using other people's language, that he is only *quoting* – and moreover that by quoting he is only reproducing a label, an 'appellation' for which, as it were, there may be insufficient collateral: ' *what she called* her son's *madness*'.[2] 'Quoted speech' (*oratio*) is in fact one of the most noticeable features of Stendhal's writing; his work is full of quotations, false quotations (viz. the epigraphs), and self-quotations, and thanks to this '**mise-en-abyme**' a whole network of discreet ironies is set up between the different speech acts. At the same time the inserted quotations, being messages within messages, become, thanks to the play of subtle linguistic interference, second-order messages: messages about messages. The mania for *italics* is but one of the tricks Stendhal uses to indicate unobtrusively the current of 'quoted statement' flowing through his work, to distinguish the language of the other from his own within the context of his verbal landscape. 'Madness', at least at the outset, is part of this borrowed vocabulary. For Stendhal too, in his way, delights in compiling 'the dictionary of received ideas'.[3]

He does not, of course, subscribe to the clichés he is copying; he just quotes them – without believing a word of them. He reproduces contemporary public opinion while seeing it for what it is: a bundle of prejudices. In fact every fibre of his being, every sinew of his writing, reacts strongly against the ' *vulgarity*'[4] of these commonplace judgements. Why, then, reproduce them?

At this juncture a further aspect of Stendhal's vocabulary of 'madness' comes into play: the way it is aimed at the *receiver*, its *conative function*. 'When speaking to a new interlocutor', says Jakobson, 'everyone always tries, deliberately or involuntarily, to find a common ground of vocabulary: whether simply to make oneself understood, or to please the other person, or just to have done with him, one uses the terminology of the receiver.'[5] Thus Stendhal – by way of shorthand, to please, to make himself understood at a basic level – denounces certain phenomena, certain forms of behaviour, certain gestures, as 'madness', thus employing the presumed language of the receiver, of the average reader, who doubtless shares these accepted notions and commonplace judgements:

> Now that it is firmly agreed that Mathilde's character is impossible in our century, which is no less prudent than virtuous, I am less afraid of causing annoyance by continuing to *recount the follies* of this amiable girl.[6]

However, as may be seen, the conative function of the vocabulary of 'madness' in Stendhal's writing is infinitely subtle, infinitely cunning, since irony is nearly always involved.[7] The receiver is aimed at in two ways, and the more important of these is certainly not the evident one of aiming apparently in the direction of the general public. The mirror which Stendhal holds out for his reader always seems, it is true, to proffer the Hugolian formula: 'Ah! fool, if you think that I am not you!'[8] But this formula is two-edged, like the vocabulary of 'madness' itself indeed. The 'average reader' will recognize himself in the judgement on Mathilde: ' *I am less afraid of causing annoyance* by continuing to *recount the follies* of this amiable girl'; but it is up to the 'happy few' – the real intended audience – to look over the shoulder of the 'typical reader' and spot such a characteristic Stendhalian wink, to reverse the terms, and to understand at a second level of meaning. It is for their benefit that Stendhal is careful to signal the fact – with little clues like italics, an ironic tone, parenthetical comments such as 'which is called', 'in the language of the common man', etc.– that he is not where you think he is, that he is far from being identical with the language he speaks, that he accepts no responsibility for these simplistic judgements on 'madness'.

Aimed thus at the 'happy few' who are the author's fellow-creatures, his brothers,[9] *the conative function itself ends up becoming the expressive function*: writer and reader become one. Stendhal is now simply *reading off* what the 'sensitive soul' *dictates* to him. Even if the term 'madness' drops from the author's lips initially in the guise of 'quoted speech', of a borrowed signifier to which he himself does not subscribe, he none the less ends up recuperating the word, gradually adopting it as his own by investing it with new values, by seducing it into serving his own particular ends. Henceforth, when he uses it, the notion of madness implies both a *way of being* which is special to his particular novelistic world, and a certain *scale of values* by which this world – throughout its length – is measured and judged. 'There are certain words', Valéry says,

> which reveal by their frequency in a given author's work that they
> there assume a resonance and, consequently, an *actively creative power*
> of a quite different order from that which they usually possess. This is
> an example of the *personal systems of value*, of the 'for me the greatest
> value is' kind of statement, which certainly have a leading role to play
> in any mental production.[10]

Although apparently static, the monotony of the same signifier thus in reality
conceals a process of internal evolution of great richness and great dynamism.
In the midst of the same semantic field, Stendhal never ceases to change:
the itinerary mapped out by the different inflexions of the word 'madness'
shows us Stendhal in fact – Stendhal in the process of becoming Stendhal.

This itinerary – which is that of a language in search of itself, of an
attempt to make a private language public by making a public language
private – this process of subscribing to and then revalorizing, certainly
implies *stages*. But if these mark out a space, that space which at once links
and separates the signifier and its signified, they do not also constitute a
chronological sequence, do not succeed each other in time: the ultimate
outcome does not cancel out the phases which preceded it but adds itself to
them – and integrates them into a greater whole.

The result is that in Stendhal's writing all the separate phases are visible
side by side, mingled together, or cutting across one another; all the
functions of 'madness' as a sign – its referential, metalinguistic, conative,
and expressive functions – operate, indeed signify, at one and the same
time. Parallel with the slippage of meaning and semantic contagion taking
place between the figurative and literal senses of the word, a permanent
interaction between the various linguistic functions leads to a permutation
of functions and to contagion between them. Each time it appears, the
word 'madness' seems like a knot of functions each modifying the other.

This is why, illuminating as it may be to distinguish between the
functions of language as a *criterion for the classification* of signifieds, such an
approach also leads to a dead-end. The author cannot be summed up in
terms either of one function or of a number of functions: he is, precisely,
the *system of relationships* between the disparate levels, between the
functional variations, the different values, the diverse points of view. This
is to say that the Stendhalian signified is not *in* the words: it is *between* them.

On 'Intoxication' in *The Charterhouse of Parma*

Such states of heightened emotion, of grace, and intoxication provide only brief moments (and extremely rare ones at that) in Stendhal's novels from *Armance* to *Lucien Leuwen*; but, following on one after the other in a harmonious, tightly knit sequence, they constitute the very substance of *The Charterhouse of Parma*.

Fabrice's career in fact begins in a state of intoxication, which is both physical and moral. Galloping on to the field of battle:

> Fabrice felt *quite drunk*; he had taken too much brandy. He would have done anything in the world for his comrades; *his mind and soul were in the clouds*. Everything seemed to have assumed a new aspect now that he was among friends (. . .) *But I'm still a bit drunk*, he told himself.[11]

Soon afterwards, his new-found comrades steal his horse from him: Fabrice simply substitutes one form of intoxication for another, and becomes 'punch-drunk with anger'.[12] Later he will be 'drunk with joy'.[13]

Now intoxication, like madness, is ambiguous: exaltation is also a form of somnolence. Wine in *The Charterhouse* is not only the key to a world of ecstasy; it is also used as a weapon. On Fabrice's return, Gina makes Ascagne drink in order to put his spying vigilance to sleep:

> This evening, at supper, I condescended to say a few words to him; I had to find some excuse to hide my [mad] joy, which might have made him suspicious. Then (. . .) *I took advantage of his happiness to make him drink a great deal too much*, and I am certain he will never have thought of taking any steps to carry on his profession of spying.[14]

Similarly Clélia, in order to save Fabrice, agrees to get the gaolers drunk:

> Clélia Conti, that pious girl, had betrayed her father since she had *consented to make the garrison drunk* (. . .) 'But', added the Duchessa, beating her breast in desperation, ' *if the garrison had not been made drunk*, all my stratagems, *all my exertions became useless* (. . .)!' [15]

Thus even the clean-living Clélia participates in the general intoxication of the novel and, what is more, causes some of it. The climate of *The Charterhouse* is Dionysian, in Nietzsche's sense of the term: the novel is dominated by the type of individual 'who forgets himself completely', by those 'rare moments of paroxysm', which bring about the 'suspension of all the ordinary barriers of existence':

> Now the slave emerges as a free man; all the rigid, hostile walls which either necessity or despotism has erected between men are shattered (. . .) through [Man] sounds a supernatural power (. . .). He feels himself to be godlike and strides with the same elation and

ecstasy as the gods he has seen in his dreams. No longer the *artist*, he has himself become a *work of art*: the productive power of the whole universe is now manifest in his transport, to the glorious satisfaction of the primordial One.[16]

The Dionysian impetus of *The Charterhouse* is such that intoxication is generalized throughout, becoming a form of universal ecstasy, a *mass* intoxication. Witness, at the beginning of the novel, the intoxication of the Milanese at the entry of the French into Milan. Witness also the intoxication of the citadel guards on the eve of Fabrice's escape:

> in the evening there were fireworks, and in the lower rooms of the 'palazzo' the soldiers received *a quantity of wine four times that which the governor had allowed*; an unknown hand had even sent *several barrels of brandy which the soldiers broached. The generous spirit of the soldiers who were becoming intoxicated would not allow the five of their number who were on duty as sentries outside the 'palazzo' to suffer accordingly*; as soon as they arrived at their sentry-boxes, a trusted servant *gave them wine*, and it was not known from what hand those who came on duty at midnight and for the rest of the night *received also a glass each of brandy, while the bottle was in each case forgotten and left* by the sentry-box (. . .).[17]

Alcohol transfigures and transforms, becomes a phial of sensual delights. The citadel, this redoubtable fortress of order, punishment, and interdict, becomes for one night the orgiastic realm of ecstatic gratification. Intoxication at once arouses and puts to sleep: it puts police vigilance to sleep, and the demands of repression; it arouses, in the 'soldiers who were becoming intoxicated', a 'generous spirit' which 'would not allow the five of their number who were on duty as sentries outside the "palazzo" to suffer accordingly': getting drunk is sanctified by the desire to *give*, to *communicate* with one's fellows, *to forget oneself* in a form of collective joy in which limits are abolished and otherness erased. The whole garrison is moved by one prodigious tremor of happiness. The general intoxication becomes a true Dionysian revel.

This festival of intoxication is not unique in the novel. Another, of greater scope and of an even more delirious kind, will soon echo it: this is the illumination of the castle at Sacca, the orgy of wine, and the flooding of Parma – the signal for the murder of the Prince. It is this grandiose and hallucinating vision of vengeance, conceived by Gina and entrusted to Ludovic, that Stendhal crowns with the title: 'Madness and folly'[18]:

> 'Very well!' the Duchessa went on, in the most winning and light-hearted tone (. . .) '*I wish my good people of Sacca to have a mad holiday* which they will long remember (. . .) you will have my house

illuminated in the most splendid fashion. *Spare neither money nor trouble; remember that the occasion is the greatest happiness of my life.* I have prepared for this illumination long beforehand; *more than three months ago, I collected in the cellars of the house everything that can be used for this noble "festa"*; I have put the gardener in charge of all the fireworks necessary for a *magnificent display*: you will let them off from the terrace overlooking the Po. *I have eighty-nine large barrels of wine in my cellars, you will set up eighty-nine fountains of wine in my park. If next day there remains a single bottle which has not been drunk, I shall say that you do not love [Fabrice].* When *the fountains of wine, the illumination, and the fireworks* are well started, you will slip away cautiously, for it is possible, and it is my hope, that at Parma all these fine doings may appear an insolence.'[19]

While themselves representing the satisfaction of prodigious desire, the celebrations – unbeknownst to the participants – signal the murder of the prince. Life and death are intertwined, they reinforce and affirm each other, beyond the contradiction which they represent. This ecstasy of emotion, this superabundance of life, joy, and underlying pain, already bears the mark of tragedy.

At the heart of the celebrations themselves the joy of being alive, the sensual delight in living, is characterized by destructiveness; reservoirs are opened, there is drinking, flooding, fires are lit, wealth and precious things are expended. If the morality of reason is the morality of being economical, that of intoxication – as of madness – is one of wasting and consuming. In order to feel itself living, life measures itself by a loss of life, confirms itself even as it is consumed; existence is a consuming of existence.

Now, expending is also giving. As dispenser of the celebrations, mistress of the flood and mistress of inebriation, Gina revels in her omnipotence by giving as well as taking (a life), by destroying as well as creating.

Expending, however, is also a means of reaching the other, of *communicating*, of creating a complicity: it is a way of reimmersing oneself in a collective self, of annihilating one's own self, of making oneself participate in an enjoyment that is universal. The celebrations, too, are a language: a discourse of alcohol. The intoxication of vengeance in Gina seeks to propagate itself, to transmit itself to the people through the intermediary of wine: such is the orgiastic mission entrusted to Ludovic.

Intoxication does in fact propagate itself, does communicate, does turn out to be contagious: as Gina's assistant, Ludovic is the first to have his head turned by her mad vision. Now we find laughter and song mingling and infecting each other in consecration of this union in intoxication, in celebration of the happiness of complicity:

'Ah! What an excellent idea of the Signora!' cried Lodovico, *laughing like a madman*; 'wine for the good people of Sacca, water for the cit[izen]s of Parma, who were so sure, the wretches, that Monsignor [Fabrice] was going to be poisoned (. . .)'

Lodovico's joy knew no end; *the Duchessa complacently watched his wild laughter*; he kept on repeating: *'Wine for the people of Sacca and water for the people of Parma! (. . .)'*

– *'And water for the people of Parma', retorted the Duchessa with a laugh. (. . .)*; 'and there must not be a full bottle in my cellars next day.' (. . .)

– *'And water for the people of Parma!' the Duchessa went on chanting (. . .).*[20]

A dream of power at last accomplished, the flooding water beneath the firework display symbolizes the satisfaction – and thirsting – of desire; the diluvian plenitude will turn the gardens of Parma iridescent with the delight of streaming vengeance. The communion of fire and water – bonfires, wine-fountains, the flood – will reflect, in all their sparkling jubilation, the delirium of passion brought to the height of ecstasy.

'Madness' in *The Charterhouse* takes the form of intoxication; but intoxication is also a kind of madness:

Lodovico raised his eyes to the Duchessa and was startled. She was staring fixedly at the blank wall six paces away from her (. . .) 'Ah! (. . .)' thought Lodovico. ' *The fact of the matter is, she is mad.'*[21]

But in Stendhal's eyes, however mad this intoxication may be, as it seeks to express itself symbolically in the orgy it initiates, it still accedes – like madness itself, moreover – to the level of the *sublime*. By stirring up the people, Gina's madness is transformed into one huge, shared fever and becomes a celebration of univeral deliverance:

But in the country, where they know how to appreciate the pleasure of revenge, the illumination and the admirable feast given in the park to more than six thousand 'contadini' had an immense success. (. . .); thus they explained the somewhat harsh reception given to a party of thirty constables whom the police had been so foolish as to send to that small village, thirty-six hours after *the sublime evening and the general intoxication* that had followed it. *The constables, greeted with showers of stones, had turned and fled,* and two of their number, who fell from their horses, were flung into the Po.[22]

From *Armance* to *The Charterhouse* the Stendhalian vision of intoxication – and of madness – has thus evolved. In *Armance* and in *The Red and the Black*, 'madness' – on the linguistic as well as the thematic level – operates in a realm of *disequilibrium*; in *The Charterhouse* it stands resplendent in a world of *excess*. From impotence to intoxication; from inhibition to liberation; from 'madness' as a symptom, a neurosis, to 'madness' which is harmonious, poetic: such is the itinerary which Stendhal's writings seem to follow.

This evolution from one novel to the other is also reflected in the vocabulary. In *Armance, The Red and the Black*, and *Lucien Leuwen*, it is a question of 'fits of melancholy', 'of despair', 'of misanthropy'. 'Madness' is described as 'dark', as a 'state of physical restlessness'. The vocabulary of *The Charterhouse*, on the other hand, depicts a 'sublime madness' that is synonymous with 'grace'. From *Armance* to *The Charterhouse* the state of physical restlessness has become a state of grace.

The tragic ambiguity of 'madness' nevertheless remains. If sexual exile is ended, and impotence and *fiascos*[23] overcome, it is because Dionysian man exorcizes his madness by giving himself up to it and because, in the process of intoxication, he reabsorbs the suffering caused by his own inner contradictions.

Notes

1. *Editor's note:* In this translation 'madness' has almost always been preferred to 'folly' as a translation of 'folie' since the French word connotes insanity more strongly than 'folly'. Similarly, 'intoxication' has been preferred as the usual translation of 'ivresse'. The emphases (in italic) are all Felman's.

2. [*Armance*, ch. 30 (Paris: Bibliothèque de la Pléiade, p. 184)]

3. *Editor's note*: A reference to the *Dictionary of Received Ideas* compiled by Flaubert for inclusion in his final novel *Bouvard et Pécuchet*.

4. Cf. '(. . .) a sensitive, generous, burning spirit – "romantic" – as it is *commonly called*' [*Love*, ch. 3]. Cf. also, on the subject of Octave's 'madness': '*singularities of character* which made him odious in the eyes of *vulgar men*' [end of first paragraph of *Armance*].

5. Roman Jakobson, *Essais de linguistique générale*, ed. Nicolas Ruwet (Paris: Editions de Minuit, 1963), p. 33. *Editor's note*: Jakobson's model of communication distinguishes six functions: the *expressive* (or *emotive*) (denoting the relationship between the 'message' and its sender), the *conative* (message and receiver), the *metalingual* (message and the code used for communication), the *referential* (message and its external context), the *phatic* (message and the means of contact in the communication), and the *poetic* (the relationship of the message to itself).]

6. [*The Red and the Black*, p. 371.]

7. Cf. Victor Brombert, *Stendhal et la voie oblique* (Paris: P.U.F., 54), p. 158: 'Stendhalian irony, in particular, is a provisional, fluctuating process in which things are forever under review, a process which therefore has to be counterbalanced, at every moment, by a translation going on in the mind of the reader.'

8. From the preface to Hugo's *Les Contemplations*.

9. *Editor's note:* A reference to the last line of the introductory poem in Baudelaire's *Les Fleurs du Mal* (*The Flowers of Evil*).

10. [PAUL VALÉRY, *Œuvres*, 2 vols (Paris: Gallimard (Bibliothèque de la Pléiade), 1957–60], i. 1356.]

11. *Editor's note: The Charterhouse of Parma*, pp. 49, 50–1. The last sentence is part of Stendhal's revisions to the text after publication (on the so-called Chaper copy) but not subsequently retained (or, therefore, present in Moncrieff's translation). See Bibliothèque de la Pléiade edition, p. 68 and note 1 (on p. 1391).

12. [For 'punch-drunk with anger' Moncrieff has 'blind with rage' (p. 52).]

13. [*The Charterhouse of Parma*, p. 344 (Moncrieff has 'wild with joy').]

14. [*The Charterhouse of Parma*, pp. 81–2. (Moncrieff has 'frantic joy').]

15. [*The Charterhouse of Parma*, p. 409.]

16. [FRIEDRICH NIETZSCHE, *The Birth of Tragedy*, trans. by Francis Golffing (New York: Doubleday (Anchor Books), 1956), pp. 22, 125, 51 and 23–4.]

17. [*The Charterhouse of Parma*, p. 395.]

18. *Editor's note:* The running page-heads are absent from Moncrieff's translation. The pages corresponding to those which they cover in French editions are roughly pp. 402–6.

19. [*The Charterhouse of Parma*, pp. 404–5.]

20. [*The Charterhouse of Parma*, pp. 405–6.]

21. [*The Charterhouse of Parma*, p. 407.] Cf. p. 403: 'the Duchessa sent for Lodovico. He thought that she had gone mad, so strange was the look that she gave him.'

22. [*The Charterhouse of Parma*, pp. 415–6.]

23. *Editor's note*: Stendhal's word for temporary sexual impotence.

7   Michel Crouzet on language and silence

Silence is thus clearly the language of the self when the self feels itself, whether from self-sufficiency or from a sense of its own powers, to have reached a peak: hence the fact, for example, that once Julien becomes the fateful man of vengeance, he can neither write nor speak a single word. At their extremes individuality and will-power dispense with words; this is the ultimate expression of 'singularity', of loyalty to that unique project which constitutes the self and which is beyond measure. Cut off from common values, the hero falls silent: Julien in the attempted murder of the woman he loves, Fabrice by renouncing everything but reminiscence, prayer, and contemplation.

Moreover, one must distinguish between these silences and contrast the silence or non-language of the person who has not yet acquired the use of language with the silence of the person who renounces language having once possessed it. There is silence by default and silence from excess; a true magnanimity which forgoes what it has, and the false magnanimity which stems, like boredom and melancholy (themselves equally silent), from a kind of impotence. Just as there are real secrets and false secrets (mystification), one form of impotence derives from being ashamed to confess, from a narcissistic embarrassment at speaking and laying oneself bare in language, the other from experiencing the truly ineffable. One sort of silence shirks the task of having to put itself into words and rather too complacently prefers to leave its options open, while the other has passed through language, and the greatness of human experience, and finds itself beyond language.

Stendhal says as much in *Lamiel*[1]: in order to be able to speak, one needs confidence, confidence in oneself, in other people, and, more generally, confidence of a quasi-metaphysical kind. **Joubert**,[2] who was equally interested in the superiority of silence over language, saw clearly that the 'froth of words' compromises the purity of the idea, but that the soul needs words, just as it needs the body; that one is to one's body, and to matter, as one is to language. The divided nature of the man in revolt against society is such that he cannot come to terms with the fact that he depends for the expression of this revolt on something material and social. One's relationship to language and silence is nothing more nor less than the sign of one's well-being or 'ill-being' within human reality. In this respect the silence of the Carthusian monk[3] is not of the same quality as the others: it is that of a man who has always known how to use language with tact and brio, who has always known – be it at Waterloo, or in the presence of petty potentates (or great ones), or with Clélia when he is a prisoner, or when he turns himself into an eloquent preacher, first in order to forget her, then to win her back – how to command his tongue, how to strike a balance between self-revelation and tactical advantage, between wit and diplomacy, in short, how to remain faithful to Mosca's golden rules: 'do not give in to the temptation to shine', 'remain silent',[4] if need be, and speak only with the eyes, at all events hold back when talking, since one's words must be tailored not to the truth they may contain but to the circumstances in which they are uttered. The highest form of opportunism is that of the genuinely sincere person, who, because he has his own language and has not thought himself betrayed by it, can renounce it as the final act of his life among men. Only he that possesses something can be said to make a sacrifice. Though shutting himself away in the silence of his cell, he is not shutting his soul in upon itself; his silence is full of Clélia and of his faith. The contemplative's silent communion with self is quite different from the initial silence of the Stendhalian hero, the 'awkward' silence of the angst-ridden heroes of the time.

As a novelist Stendhal thus has good reason to be attentive to his characters' attitude to language: their relationship to the spoken and the unspoken helps to define their relationship to the world and to themselves, to define the degree of their renunciation of self and world. The problem essentially is how to accede to language and then, once within it, to guard against empty volubility, against the shameless glibness that characterizes the cynics – du Poirier,[5] Sansfin,[6] or Octave during his escapades in the house of ill-repute – while guarding also, on the other hand, against the clumsy and inevitably doomed language of the timid who are bad at talking because they say too much and entrust their very being to speech. The problem lies in managing to be present to oneself and others within language, in managing not to betray oneself by language that is vapid or out of control, in managing not to betray language itself for the sake of a self that has taken fright at its own special value. [. . .]

The case of Julien confirms this. His problem, too, is to find his own way of speaking, to situate himself within language, to accept the bonds of language and the pact with truth which they imply. He, too, is intentionally mute: 'his secret desire not to be spoken to (. . .) was only too apparent'.[7] His uncompromising disdain for debate is such that in the end we see him refusing to negotiate for his release in 'the lengthy discussion he would have to have',[8] just as he refuses to save himself from execution by arguing or pleading his case with the judges. He, too, conceals his secret outside language, though certainly less jealously than Octave, since, when occasionally he tires of having to lie all the time, he does unburden himself to the women he loves. What is more, his secret is just as ambiguous as Octave's since it extends beyond his ambitions for social success and beyond his lack of religious belief, and bears on a more concerted form of duplicity, namely to defy and flout the norms and values of other men. Unlike Octave, he does not hesitate between silence and avowal but has decided instead to use language simply as a counterfeit currency[9]: his intention is to concede it no role as a medium of self-revelation but rather to manipulate it as a form of completely artificial and contrived outward appearance, to falsify it to the point where it ceases to function as a means of two-way communication or contact. He is quite ready to speak, but on condition that he is neither bound by nor held to what he says, that he may dissociate himself from his own language and may dissociate language itself from any form of truth, as from any form of reciprocity. As hero, he is a hero of speciousness: his wager is that he will speak only an empty language that deceives, a mystificatory logorrhoea which is designed to seduce the other and of which he himself would be but the wily, disinterested spokesman.

In this sense, his hypocrisy is akin to a sort of pathology of the word: how can one lie or conceal things indefinitely, withdraw from the pact that is language, speak as if one were not present within the words one utters? Hence we see him adopting the techniques of provincial gossip, its 'knowing obliquities' which bury the point at issue in a welter of talk, or managing with the sub-prefect of Verrières[10] to inflate language to the point of thoroughly vacuous eloquence with rounded period following upon rounded period, an ever-changing kaleidoscope of formulas and clichés, a torrent of words that say nothing at all, or we see him stringing together 'fine phrases' and avoiding delicate issues by taking refuge in intemperate verbal diversions. His talent, to which Stendhal pays hommage, is for being 'able to produce the words that a fervent young seminarist would have used, [. . . to] come up with just the phrases required by a cautious and wily hypocrisy'.[11] More often than not, it is true, he prefers to rely on the simplest of verbal mechanisms: reciting by heart is his speciality and his strong point. With his dupes he does not even bother to invent a special form of discourse: that would still mean there being too much of the discourse that was a part of him, or too much of him a part of the discourse. He wants his words to be purely from memory, purely borrowed, while he simply draws on a prodigious capacity to memorize and repeat.[12] This is the sort of merit Verrières is capable of understanding: the cult of recitation reigns supreme there, the visible manifestation of absolute conformism. Julien's great glory, as one who 'had filled the inhabitants of Verrières with an admiration that may well last a century'[13] is due to his unfailing memory. It is to this that he looks for his self-control and his language: if he can fall back on a ready-made text, be it de Maistre, Rousseau, or Molière,[14] his self-confidence grows, he marks out his own position within language by reference to a type of language which would not be his own way of speaking at all. This he religiously does as a lover,[15] and his initial declarations are no more than declamations of well-known passages from books.

He, too, finds a language: although in Paris he remains above all circumspect in the moves he makes, being sparing with his words and wary of the indiscretion inherent in the spoken and written word,[16] he is nevertheless obliged to learn to speak, to acquire a capacity for 'wit', that supreme, disinterested elegance of the dandy who plays with language, and obliged to achieve the right balance between tactics and sincerity, or rhetoric and spontaneity, thanks to which he will be able to win back his mistresses. In short, the novelist will be able to say of him the day he receives his decoration: 'he spoke much more readily'.[17] At last he is master of the kind of eloquence in which he once used passively to acquiesce without being able to control it. Thus, in the scene where he grabs Mme de Rênal's hand, all at once 'he talked', inspired by some sudden, strange capacity to talk; he talks, yet without being able 'to say the simplest of words to Mme de Rênal'.[18] For such is the ambiguity of silence, and it takes hold of a man whose anxious self-esteem is apprehensive about what kind of welcome he will receive, about the gap between question and answer, about the difference between his perfect self and his real self; it takes hold of him as if he were beyond communication and conflict with other people. So Julien has to find the words, to impose his voice, that is to say his personality, and to move from a silence bred of resentment to a true silence which, from being inferior to others, raises him above them. The progression from one to the other involves a liberation of language. At the outset, he hesitates between a language that is all artifice, and a language that is so authentic that he falls silent for failure to find it; silence at this stage is but the obverse of a language that would be full of him and the equal of the wonder that he is. Thus, with Mme de Rênal: we are told that when Julien is alone with her, she remains deep in silence in a manner which humiliates him 'as if he were to blame personally for this silence'.[19] He says nothing, or nothing worthwhile, because he wants to say too much, he wants to shine, to match up to his nebulous, 'Spanish' notions 'about what a man ought to say when he is alone with a lady'. The ideal of unassailable perfection which he wants to manifest cannot be contained or risked in language; all words are inadequate compared with the perfect words he ought to be saying. 'His soul' is 'in the clouds' or in the perfect image of himself, and his being, his body, flounders in reality, that is to say in the silence of a pride knotted in upon itself: he cannot forget himself, cannot forsake this image of himself, in order to speak and simply be what it is that he can say. This silence is in fact broken by brief flashes of sincerity, moments of heartfelt confession when language pours forth immoderately and with such great confidence in how it will be received that it does not fail to create in the receiver the same opening of the heart as that from which it itself proceeds; then, willy-nilly, souls do speak and attune themselves to each other. But this immoderate language which is, as it were, snatched from him by the delight of a perfect communion of hearts, is also his weakness, either when the interlocutor who has encouraged such fluency and pretended to match it, lays a trap and brutally draws back (as in the seminary examination),[20] or else when Julien is so convinced about something that he forgets that it is worth nothing, or worse than nothing, if he does not also make some effort at persuasion; as with Mathilde when, 'distracted with love and unhappiness', he thinks only of giving vent to pain and entreaty 'in the most tender and heartfelt of tones',[21] when he thinks only of insisting on his love for her that he may demand her love for him in return. Then we have all manner of clumsiness and stupidity about which Stendhal warns his hero, at the same time showing him by way of a lesson what he might have gained had he been able to control his speech and keep a greater distance from her.

Language must not only say what one is, it must also tend to a particular effect, must produce this effect upon another, and not be based on some magical process of contagion. It is oblique because beings are separate and different. It operates with a view to the truth, without relying on the unadulterated power of this truth.[22] It brings souls finally together, even at the cost of a certain duplicity, but it does not mirror them, does not provide some sudden, passive unveiling of them. To learn to turn language into a form of action – with all the compromises which that entails in respect of one's original intentions and of the forms of mediation necessary – is what the Stendhalian hero must steel himself to: this 'hypocrisy' implies that language gives rise to an encounter and does not suppose it already to have taken place. The rhetoric of seduction (of which the Russian [Korasoff]'s letters are a caricatural, mechanical example) locates truth and sincerity in the process of exchange itself or at its end-point, and is far removed from any tendency to suppress the commerce of words and replace it with some blinding mutual recognition of soul-mates in the instant of some ready-made meeting of hearts and minds. Julien is thus, in his proper use of hypocrisy and words, nearer the truth than Octave with his desire for an impossible avowal, in which one can see precisely his impatience with language. Language conditions man's being to the extent that man is involved in the 'world', in conquest and desire. Avowal wants to consume language, not to consummate it.

Julien, on the other hand, discovers that there is an 'art' to everything, or a type of language. It comes to the same thing. If we look again at the example of Julien winning back Mme de Rênal,[23] we see Julien, very much in love, beginning as with Mathilde to invoke by way of argument and justification the fact that he is no longer loved: 'What, is it possible that you don't love me any more, he cried, in that heartfelt tone which it is so difficult to hear with dispassion'. At this point he is sure in the knowledge of his goodness of heart, his unhappiness, and his desire. But subjective, solitary conviction weeps and does not speak; it has to break with itself, go towards the other, plead its cause while admitting that the whole truth as it sees it is less important than the relative truth which it wants the other to share; that love is not what one feels oneself, but what one makes the other person feel. Julien speaks at last: 'do please tell me what you have been doing'. From now on, and not without irony, Stendhal shows how the fortuitous accidents of a dialogue have a profound bearing on the 'moral position' of the protagonists; a chance word may reveal the truth or recall it to mind. Everything happens when one speaks: because Julien and Mme de Rênal have to settle the matter of the 500 francs, 'without realizing it' they are taken up by the dialogue and defined by its progress; Julien can put his arm round his sweetheart and use the diversion of his talk to consolidate his position. So he uses his narrative, drags it out on purpose, surprises Mme de Rênal with the revelation about his departure for Paris, and at the end produces his *coup de théâtre* by pretending to leave. There is a certain cynicism about his discourse, in which quite clearly – if one compares it with Fabrice and the preaching he undertakes with the same object in mind as here – Julien is overdoing things, and at great cost to his happiness. The art of talking is again more important here than sincerity. But the main thing no doubt is that the pain of not being received as he would like, and not being loved as he himself loves, should be overcome through language – language which, while it gives rein to that part of the self calamitously prone to lying and hypocrisy (and yet which cannot be fully absorbed or exhausted by any form of communication), nevertheless has a tendency to exceed the calculations of temporary, artful pretence and to restore the harmonious understanding which had been lost.

But towards the end of the novel, language dies: violence and crime follow in its path, or take its place. After the need for truth and harmony of understanding manifested in language comes the willed silence of the wrong-doer. The pistol-shot and its consequences return Julien to his general war with humanity, and so to silence. Cut off by the crime, and the disapproval, Julien of his own accord adds the separation of absolute silence; the man who is radically other is a mute and absolute will. So, as he refuses to play the part of the accused man, he refuses to play the game of defending himself, either now or later; the silence which he demands of himself and orders Mathilde to keep defines the total non-reciprocity which must be his lot. He is nowhere to be found within the language of men, he must not become posthumous within it, other people have nothing to say to him, nothing to say about him; he will have passed into a different world without leaving a trace. Such is the significance of his letter to

Mathilde[24] in which he adopts the language of Iago, which is the language of the coherent criminal who is not to be reconciled. Evil does not speak of itself; otherwise it becomes the adjunct of goodness. Julien refuses to talk, he does not want others to talk about him, 'silence is the only way of honouring me . . . you must assume a false name and confide in no one'. Even the revenge of posthumous scandal would constitute participation in the affairs of humanity: 'Do not write to me, I would not reply . . . No one shall see me speak or write.' But no doubt the novel shows, as *Crime and Punishment* will, that one cannot always lie, or remain silent, that one cannot carry out for ever the intention to be outside humankind. For Julien is going to speak, going to find his tongue once more,[25] and with it harmony of understanding; for him finally to reach that 'poetic' state in which he dies, which is no doubt not very different from the renunciation of the contemplative and which is true silence, the silence beyond words and not before them, he has to have spoken – to men in order to defy them, to himself in order to see things more clearly, to Mme de Rênal in order finally to discover with her a perfect relationship of mutual transparency. He can only fall silent after having unburdened himself, after reaching the stage of avowal thanks to a liberation of his language. Silence must exceed, subsume, what one says; silence must not fall before language has spoken. Accepting that he has spoken, that he has been present in language, the person in revolt has shown flexibility in his revolt and reached an accommodation with his status as a man in respect of the share in language which he was ready to adopt as his own. For such *separation* from one's fellow man to have any value as the act of a noble and generous spirit, one must have had some fellow men in the first place.

Notes

1. (Lausanne: Editions du Rencontre, 1962), p. 190.

2. See Alain Girard, *Le Journal intime* (Paris: P.U.F., 1963), p. 221, for a discussion of this conflict between the word as sacrifice, as a mutilation of silence, as the limit of ecstasy, and the word as necessitated (as a body is necessitated by the soul) or as a *figure* required by the mind.

3. The silence of the ineffable for Shoshana Felman (*La 'Folie' dans l'œuvre romanesque de Stendhal*, pp. 237–8).

4. [*The Charterhouse of Parma*, p. 128.]

5. *Lucien Leuwen* (Bibliothèque de la Pléiade), pp. 946–7: for example, Lucien's never-ending speech to the doctor to avoid having to speak to Mme de Chasteller.

6. E.g. the 'horrible magnetic power' of the doctor's 'eloquence', in *Lamiel* (Lausanne: Editions du Rencontre, 1962), p. 76. On p. 80 Sansfin says of himself that he can 'destroy any argument with a witticism, and I know how to

manipulate language and ensure that fools – and even, he added with a sigh of satisfaction, the intelligent – think what I want them to think'. Cf. also in *Lucien Leuwen* the fact that, during the confrontation with the workers, 'any officer with a vestige of self-respect remained deep in silence' (p. 991).

7. [*The Red and the Black*, p. 207.]

8. [*The Red and the Black*, p. 474.]

9. Which it is from the very beginning of the novel in the 'deliberately roundabout ways' of the cunning provincial and in the hard bargaining [*The Red and the Black*, pp. 9 and 23].

10. In an 'episcopalian homily' contrasted with the speech of 'an eloquent minister' trying to speed things up at the end of a parliamentary session, followed by a nine-page letter and a further speech to Valenod [*The Red and the Black*, pp. 144–5]; or when he is with the abbé Pirard discussing the incident with Amanda Binet [pp. 193–4]; or with Mme de Fervaques, and his 'appalling' falseness [p. 430].

11. [*The Red and the Black*, pp. 49–50.]

12. Cf. [pp. 22, 25–6, 35–6, 147–8, 197–8, 264, 383–4] (the secret memorandum episode). Julien's father operates in the same way and recites to the mayor 'all the formulas of respect he knew by heart' [p. 17]; and cf. [p. 22].

13. [p. 82.]

14. [pp. 182, 336, 451–3]; and see [p. 444] for the false declaration to Mathilde in which he disowns the genuine things he has just been saying to her as mere 'flowery phrases' previously composed for another woman.

15. [pp. 93, 173, 353.]

16. For fear of the seminary spies [p. 198], or ridicule in Paris [p. 251], or of other rebuffs and humiliations [pp. 276, 326].

17. [p. 291.]

18. [p. 58.] Yet he is inspired by the presence of Mathilde when saying the strangest things to Mme de Fervaques [pp. 425–6], and as a 'sort of Michelangelo prophet' who alarms Mathilde [p. 311].

19. [p. 46.]

20. [p. 209.]

21. [p. 359.] Cf. [p. 365] (during the same episode); [pp. 379, 418, 364]. Even when he is more sure about Mathilde's feelings for him, he still fears that 'the sound of my voice' [p. 441] will betray his intensity of emotion.

22. This being its fundamental rhetorical nature.

23. Cf. [pp. 227–32: 'being thus obtained by skill, they afforded no more than mere pleasure' (pp. 231–2)].

24. [p. 471.] He forbids himself 'to write or utter your name'. Cf. Brice Parain, *Recherches sur la nature et les fonctions du langage* (Paris: Gallimard, 1972), p. 87: 'no one lives without speaking or replying'; in this sense *opinion* can neither be escaped from nor disdained.

25. [pp. 501–2]: addressing the jury 'he unburdened himself of everything he had

bottled up' [p. 502]; and similarly with Mme de Rênal: 'I'm speaking to you just as I speak to myself' [p. 512]. Cf. [p. 471]: 'Unfortunately, my name will appear in the press, and I shall not be able to escape from this world incognito'; and his talking about the priest who is 'repeating my name time and time again' [p. 513].

Psychoanalysis and Narratology

The following two examples of psychoanalytic criticism illustrate different ways of applying psychoanalytic theories to Stendhal's novels and to literary texts in general. Whereas Roland Barthes approaches *The Charterhouse of Parma* from a fairly orthodox Freudian perspective and sees in the text evidence of displacement and transference in its author, Peter Brooks offers a narratological reading which combines Freud and Lacan in an examination of the plot dynamics of the text alone.

Roland Barthes's essay, first published in *Tel Quel* in 1980, was intended as a paper to be delivered in Milan at a conference on Stendhal, but final revision was interrupted by his untimely death in a road accident in Paris in 1980. While he had completed the essay in manuscript form, only the first page had been typed: paper ready for the second was found inserted in his typewriter after his death. Since the one typed page varies slightly from the manuscript, it is likely that he may have revised the remaining text but not to any major extent. Being to all intents and purposes complete, this text is thus the last thing he wrote; and there is a certain poignancy about the subject-matter, since Barthes's later works (*A Lover's Discourse: Fragments* (1977) and *Camera Lucida: Reflections on Photography* (1980)) are themselves an attempt at 'speaking of what one loves': namely, his late mother.

Peter Brooks's account of *The Red and the Black* appeared first as an article in *Publications of the Modern Languages Association* in 1982 (vol. 97, pp. 348–62), and was later included as Chapter 3 of his *Reading for the Plot. Design and Intention in Narrative* (1984). Brooks takes issue with the essentially static nature of Structuralist narratology and goes in search of a more dynamic model, which he finds in Freud. But, he says, 'if we turn toward Freud, it is not in the attempt to psychoanalyse authors or readers or characters in narrative, but rather to suggest that by attempting to superimpose psychic functioning on textual functioning, we may discover something about how textual dynamics work and something about their psychic equivalences' (p. 90). For Brooks, 'plot' (and he prefers the more dynamic term 'plotting') is 'the syntax of a certain way of speaking our understanding of the world' (p. 7), is 'the logic and dynamic of narrative, and narrative itself [is] a form of understanding and explanation' (p. 10). 'Narrative', he says, 'has something to do with time-boundedness, and [. . .] plot is the internal logic of the discourse of mortality' (p. 22).

Taking up Roland Barthes's suggestion (in his 'Introduction to the Structural Analysis of Narrative' (1966)) that readers are animated by 'la passion du sens' (which Brooks translates as both the passion *for* meaning and the passion *of* meaning: p. 19), Brooks conceives of 'the reading of plot as a form of desire that carries us forward, onward, through the text. Narratives both tell of desire – typically present some story of desire – and arouse and make use of desire as dynamic of signification' (p. 37).

His chapter on *The Red and the Black* is presented as an attempt 'to disengage the models of plot and plotting that it appears to propose, and to understand what these have to do with individual biography and collective history' (p. 61). It ends by anticipating the following chapter in which Brooks looks for a model for his 'textual erotics' (p. 37) and, drawing on Freud's *Beyond the Pleasure Principle* (1920) and on Lacan's theory of desire, explores the tension between desire as a desire for an end to desire, on the one hand, and, on the other, the pleasure of deferral through repetition. He finds in Freud's 'masterplot for organic life' (p. 102) a 'dynamic model that structures ends (death, quiescence, nonnarratability) against beginnings (Eros, stimulation into tension, the desire of narrative) in a manner that necessitates the middle as detour, as struggle toward the end under the compulsion of imposed delay, as arabesque in the dilatory space of the text' (pp. 107–8).

8 Roland Barthes on *The Charterhouse of Parma*

One always fails in speaking of what one loves*

A few weeks ago, I made a short trip to Italy. The first evening, in the
Milan station, it was cold, dark, dirty. A train was leaving; on each car
hung a yellow placard bearing the words *Milano-Lecce*. I began dreaming:
to take that train, to travel all night and wake up in the warmth, the light,
the peace of a faraway town. At least that was my fantasy, and it doesn't
matter what Lecce (which I have never seen) is really like. Parodying
Stendhal (my references throughout will be to *Rome, Naples, Florence, The
Life of Henri Brulard, The Charterhouse of Parma*, and *On Love*), I might have
exclaimed: 'At last I shall see *la bella Italia!* A madman still, and at my age!'
For lovely Italy is always farther away . . . elsewhere.

Stendhal's Italy is indeed a fantasy, even if he partially realized it. (But
did he? I shall end by saying how.) The phantasmatic image burst into his
life – it was love at first sight. This explosion assumed the countenance of a
soprano singing in Cimarosa's *Matrimonio segreto* at Ivrea; the singer had a
broken front tooth, but love at first sight is never affected by such things:
Werther fell in love with Charlotte glimpsed through an open door as she
was slicing bread-and-butter for her little brothers, and this first glimpse,
trivial as it was, would lead him to the most powerful of passions and to
suicide. We know that, for Stendhal, Italy was the object of a veritable
transference, and we also know that what characterizes transference is its
gratuitousness: it occurs without any apparent reason. Music, for Stendhal,
is the *symptom* of the mysterious action by which he inaugurated his
transference – the symptom, i.e., the thing which simultaneously produces
and masks passion's irrationality. For once the opening scene is
established, Stendhal constantly reproduces it, like a lover trying to regain
that crucial thing which rules so large a share of our actions: the first
pleasure. 'I arrive at seven in the evening, tormented with fatigue; I run to

---

*This translation by Richard Howard is reproduced from Roland Barthes, *The Rustle
of Language* (Oxford: Basil Blackwell, 1986).

La Scala. My journey was justified,' etc.: like some madman disembarking in a city favorable to his passion and rushing that very evening to the haunts of pleasure he has already located.

The signs of a true passion are always somewhat incongruous, the objects of transference always tending to become tenuous, trivial, unforeseen . . . I once knew someone who loved Japan the way Stendhal loved Italy; and I recognized the same passion in him by the fact that he loved, among other things, the red-painted fireplugs in the Tokyo streets, just as Stendhal was mad for the cornstalks of the 'luxuriant' Milanese campagna, for the sound of the Duomo's eight bells, 'perfectly *intonate*,' or for the pan-fried cutlets that reminded him of Milan. In this erotic promotion of what is commonly taken for an insignificant detail, we recognize a constitutive element of transference (or of passion): partiality. In the love of a foreign country there is a kind of reverse racism: one is delighted by Difference, one is tired of the Same, one exalts the Other; passion is Manichaean for Stendhal, the wrong side is France, i.e., *la patrie* – for it is the site of the Father – and the right side is Italy, i.e., *la matrie*, the space in which 'the Women' are assembled (not forgetting that it was the child's Aunt Elisabeth, the maternal grandfather's sister, who pointed her finger toward a country lovelier than Provence, where according to her the 'good' side of the family, the Gagnon branch, originated). This opposition is virtually physical: Italy is the *natural* habitat, where Nature is recovered under the sponsorship of Women, 'who listen to the natural genius of the country,' contrary to the men, who are 'spoiled by the pedants'; France, on the contrary, is a place repugnant 'to the point of physical disgust.' All of us who have known Stendhal's passion for a foreign country (this was also my case for Italy, which I discovered belatedly, in Milan, at the end of the nineteen-fifties – then for Japan) are familiar with the intolerable annoyance of encountering a compatriot in the adored country: 'I must confess, though it goes against the national honor, that finding a Frenchman in Italy can destroy my happiness in a moment'; Stendhal is visibly a specialist in such inversions: no sooner has he crossed the Bidassoa than he is charmed by the Spanish soldiers and customs officers; he has that rare passion, the passion for *the other* – or to put it more subtly: the passion for that other which is in himself.

Thus, Stendhal is in love with Italy: this is not a sentence to be taken metaphorically, as I shall try to show, 'It is like love,' he says: 'and yet I am not in love with anyone.' This passion is not in the least vague; it is invested, as I have said, in specific details; but it remains *plural*. What is loved and indeed what is enjoyed are collections, concomitances: contrary to the romantic project of *Amour fou*, it is not Woman who is adorable in Italy, but always Women; it is not *a* pleasure which Italy affords, it is a simultaneity, an overdetermination of pleasures: La Scala, the veritable eidetic locus of Italian delights, is not a theater in the word's banally functional sense (to see what is represented); it is a polyphony of pleasures: the opera itself, the ballet, the conversation, the gossip, love, and ices (*gelati, crepe,* and *pezzi duri*). This amorous plural, analogous to that enjoyed today by someone 'cruising,' is evidently a Stendhalian principle: it involves an implicit theory of *irregular discontinuity* which can be said to be simultaneously aesthetic, psychological, and metaphysical; plural passion, as a matter of fact – once its excellence has been acknowledged – necessitates leaping from one object to another, as chance presents them, without experiencing the slightest sentiment of guilt with regard to the disorder such a procedure involves. This conduct is so conscious in Stendhal that he comes to recognize in Italian music – which he loves – a principle of irregularity quite homologous to that of *dispersed love*: in performing their music, Italians do not observe *tempo; tempo* occurs among Germans; on one side, the German *noise*, the uproar of German music, beating out an implacable measure ('the first *tempisti* in the world'); on the other, Italian opera, *summa* of discontinuous and untamed pleasures: this is the *natural*, guaranteed by a civilization of women.

In Stendhal's Italian system, Music has a privileged place because it can replace everything else: it is the degree zero of this system: according to the needs of enthusiasm, it replaces and signifies journeys, Women, the other arts, and in a general manner any sensation. Its signifying status, precious above all others, is to produce effects without our having to inquire as to their causes, since these causes are inaccessible. Music constitutes a kind of *primal state* of pleasure: it produces a pleasure one always tries to recapture but never to explain; hence, it is the site of the pure effect, a central notion of the Stendhalian aesthetic. Now, what is a pure effect? An effect severed from and somehow purified of any explicative reason, i.e., ultimately, of any *responsible* reason. Italy is the country where Stendhal, being neither entirely a traveller (a tourist) nor entirely a native, is voluptuously delivered from the responsibility of the *citizen*; if Stendhal were an Italian citizen, he would die 'poisoned by melancholy'; whereas, a Milanese by affection rather than civil status, he need merely harvest the brilliant effects of a civilization for which he is not responsible. I have been able to experience the convenience of this devious dialectic myself: I used to love Morocco, I often visited the country as a tourist, even spending rather long vacations there; therefore, it occurred to me to spend a year there as a professor: the magic vanished; confronted by administrative and professional problems, I plunged into the ungrateful world of causes and allegiances, I surrendered Festivity for Duty (this is doubtless what happened to Stendhal as consul: Civitavecchia was no longer Italy). I believe we must include within Stendhal's Italian sentiment this fragile status of innocence: Milanese Italy (and its Holy of Holies, La Scala) is literally a Paradise, a place without Evil, or again – let us put matters positively – the Sovereign Good: 'When I am with the Milanese and speak their dialect, I forget that men are wicked, and the whole wicked aspect of my own soul instantly falls asleep.'

This Sovereign Good, however, must express itself: hence, it must confront a power which is not at all innocent, language. This is necessary, first of all, because the Good has a natural force of expansion, it constantly opens out toward expression, seeks at all costs to communicate itself, to be shared; then, because Stendhal is a writer and because for him there is no fulfilment from which the word is absent (and in this his Italian delight has nothing mystical about it). Now, paradoxical as it seems, Stendhal is uncertain how to express Italy: or rather, he speaks it, he sings it, he does not *represent* it; he proclaims his love, but he cannot express it, or, as we say nowadays (a metaphor from driving), he cannot negotiate it. This he knows, this he suffers from, this he complains of; he constantly observes that he cannot 'render his thought,' and that to explain the difference his passion proposes between Milan and Paris 'is the height of difficulty.' Hence, fiasco lies in wait for lyric desire as well. All his accounts of Italian travels are strewn with declarations of love and of failures of expression. The fiasco of style has a name: platitude; Stendhal has at his disposal only one empty word: beautiful (*'beau,' 'belle'*); 'In all my life, I have never seen so many beautiful women together; their beauty made me lower my eyes.' 'The most beautiful eyes I have ever encountered I saw that evening; such eyes are as beautiful and their expression as celestial as those of Mme Tealdi . . .' And in order to vivify this litany, he has only the emptiest of figures, the superlative: 'The women's heads, on the contrary, often reveal the most impassioned finesse, uniting the rarest beauty,' etc. This 'etc.' which I am adding, but which emerges from our reading, is important, for it yields up the secret of this impotence or perhaps, despite Stendhal's complaints, of this indifference to variation: the monotony of Italian travel is quite simply *algebraic*: the word, the syntax, in their platitude, refer expeditiously to a different order of signifiers; once this reference is suggested, Stendhal moves on to something else, i.e., repeats the operation: 'This is as beautiful as Haydn's liveliest symphonies,' 'The men's faces at the ball that night would have afforded magnificent models to sculptors of busts like Danneker or Chantrey.' Stendhal does not describe the thing, he does not even describe the effect; he simply says: *there*, there is an effect; I am intoxicated, transported, touched, dazzled, etc. In other words, the platitudinous word is a cipher, it refers to a system of sensations; we must read Stendhal's Italian discourse like a figured bass. Sade employs the same procedure: he describes beauty very poorly, platitudinously and rhetorically; this is because beauty is merely the element of an algorithm whose goal is to construct a system of practices.

What Stendhal wants to construct is, so to speak, a non-systematic set, a perpetual flow of sensations: that Italy, he says, 'which is in truth merely an occasion for sensations.' From the point of view of discourse, then, there is an initial evaporation of the thing: 'I am not claiming to say what things *are*, I am describing the *sensation* they produce upon me.' Does he really describe it? Not really; he says it, indicates it, and asserts it without describing it. For it is just here, with sensation, that the difficulty of language begins; it is not easy to 'render' a sensation: you recall that famous scene in Jules Romains's play *Knock* in which the old peasant woman, ordered by the implacable doctor to say how she feels, hesitates in her confusion between 'it tickles' and 'it itches' [*ça me chatouille/ça me gratouille*]. Any sensation, if we want to respect its vivacity and its acuity, leads to aphasia. Now Stendhal must go quickly, that is the constraint of his system; for what he wants to note is 'the sensation of the moment'; and the moments, as we have seen apropos of *tempo*, occur irregularly, refractory to *measure*. Hence, it is by fidelity to his system, fidelity to the very nature of his Italy, 'a country of sensations,' that Stendhal seeks a rapid writing: in order to proceed quickly, sensation is subjected to an elementary stenography, to a kind of expedient grammar of discourse in which he tirelessly combines two stereotypes: the beautiful and its superlative; for nothing is faster than the stereotype, precisely because it is identified, alas and invariably, with the spontaneous. We must go still deeper into the economy of Stendhal's Italian discourse: if Stendhalian sensation lends itself so well to an algebraic treatment, if the discourse it feeds is continuously inflamed and continuously platitudinous, this is because that sensation, strangely enough, is *not sensual*; Stendhal, whose philosophy is sensualistic, is perhaps the least sensual of our authors, which is doubtless why it is difficult to apply to him a thematic critique. Nietzsche, for instance – I am deliberately choosing an extreme contrary – when he speaks of Italy, is much more sensual than Stendhal: he can thematically describe the food of Piedmont, the only cooking in the world he enjoyed.

If I am insisting on this difficulty in expressing Italy, despite so many pages which describe Stendhal's 'promenade,' it is because I see in them a kind of suspicion attached to language itself. Stendhal's two loves, Music and Italy, are, one may say, spaces *outside of language*; music is so by status, for it escapes any description, lets itself be described, as we have seen, only by its effect; and Italy joins the status of the art with which it is identified; not only because the Italian language, Stendhal says in *On Love*, 'being much more apt to be sung than spoken, will be supported against the invading French clarity only by music'; but also, for two stranger reasons: the first is that to Stendhal's ears Italian conversation constantly tends to that limit of articulated language which is exclamation: 'At a Milanese soirée,' Stendhal notes admiringly, 'the conversation consists entirely of exclamations. For three quarters of an hour, reckoned by my watch, there was not a single completed sentence'; the sentence, completed armature of language, is the enemy (we need merely recall Stendhal's antipathy for the author of the most beautiful sentences in the French language, Chateaubriand). The second reason, which preciously withdraws Italy from language, from what I should call the militant language of culture, is precisely its lack of culture: Italy doesn't read, doesn't talk, Italy exclaims, Italy sings. This is its genius, its 'Naturalness,' and this is why Italy is adorable. Such delicious suspension of articulated, civilized language recurs for Stendhal in everything that for him constitutes Italy: in 'the profound idleness enjoyed under a splendid sky [I am quoting from *On Love*] . . .; it is the absence of novel reading, and of virtually all reading, which leaves still more to the inspiration of the moment; it is the passion for music which excites within the soul a movement so similar to that of love.'

Thus, a certain suspicion attached to language joins the kind of aphasia which is generated by the excess of love: before Italy and Women, and Music, Stendhal is, literally, *speechless, interloqué*, i.e., ceaselessly interrupted in his locution. This interruption is indeed an intermittence: Stendhal speaks of Italy by an almost daily but enduring intermittence. He himself explains it very well (as always): 'What choice to make? How to paint such insane happiness? My word, I cannot continue, the subject exceeds all expression. My hand can no longer write the words, I shall resume tomorrow. I am like a painter who no longer has the courage to fill in a corner of his picture. In order not to spoil the rest, he sketches in *alla meglio* what he cannot paint . . .' This painting of Italy *alla meglio*, which occupies every account of Stendhal's Italian journeys, is a kind of daubing, a scribbling, one might say, which expresses both love and the impotence to express love, because this love suffocates by its very vivacity. Such a dialectic of extreme love and difficult expression resembles what the very young child experiences – still *infans*, deprived of adult speech – when he plays with what Winnicott calls a *transitional object*; the space which separates and at the same time links the mother and her baby is the very space of the child's play and of the mother's counterplay: it is the still-shapeless space of fantasy, of the imagination, of creation. Such is, it seems to me, Stendhal's Italy: a kind of transitional object whose manipulation, being ludic, produces these *squiggles* which Winnicott notes and which are here any number of travel journals.

To keep to these Journals, which betoken a love of Italy but do not communicate it (at least, such is the judgement of my own reading), we are entitled to repeat mournfully (or tragically) that *one always fails in speaking of what one loves*. Yet, twenty years later, by a kind of after-the-fact which also constitutes part of the devious logic of love, Stendhal writes certain triumphant pages about Italy which, this time, fire up the reader (this reader – but I don't suppose I'm the only one) with that jubilation, with that *irradiation* which the private journals claimed but did not communicate. These admirable pages are the ones which form the beginning of *The Charterhouse of Parma*. Here there is a kind of miraculous harmony between 'the mass of happiness and pleasure which explodes' in Milan with the arrival of the French and our own delight in reading: the effect described finally coincides with the effect produced. Why this reversal? Because Stendhal, shifting from the Journal to the Novel, from the Album to the Book (to adopt one of Mallarmé's distinctions), has abandoned sensation, a vivid but inconstruable fragment, to undertake that great mediating form which is Narrative, or better still Myth. What is required to make a Myth? We must have the action of two forces: first of all, a hero, a great liberating figure: this is Bonaparte, who enters Milan, penetrates Italy, as Stendhal did, more humbly, from the Saint-Bernard pass; then an opposition, an antithesis – a paradigm, in short – which stages the combat of Good and Evil and thereby produces what is lacking in the Album and belongs to the Book, i.e., a meaning: on one side, in these first pages of *The Charterhouse*, boredom, wealth, avarice, Austria, the Police, Ascanio, Grianta; on the other, intoxication, heroism, poverty, the Republic, Fabrizio, Milan; and above all, on the one side, the Father; on the other, Women. By abandoning himself to the Myth, by entrusting himself to the Book, Stendhal gloriously regains what he had somehow failed to achieve in his albums: the expression of an effect. This effect – the Italian effect – finally has a name, which is no longer the platitudinous one of Beauty: it is festivity. Italy is a feast, that is what is ultimately conveyed by the Milanese preamble of *The Charterhouse*, which Stendhal was quite right to retain, despite Balzac's reservations: festivity, i.e., the very transcendence of egotism.

In short, what has happened – what has transpired – between the travel journals and *The Charterhouse*, is writing. Writing – which is what? A power, probable fruit of a long initiation, which annuls the sterile immobility of the amorous image-repertoire and gives its adventure a symbolic generality. When he was young, in the days of *Rome, Naples, Florence*, Stendhal could write: '. . . when I tell lies, I am like M. de Goury, I am bored'; he did not yet know that there existed a lie, the lie of novels, which would be – miraculously – both the detour of truth and the finally triumphant expression of his Italian passion.

9 Peter Brooks on *The Red and the Black*

Le Rouge et le Noir offers an exemplary entry into the nineteenth-century novel, its dynamics, and the interpretive problems these pose. Published a few months after the triumph of the bourgeoisie in the Revolution of 1830 – inaugurating an era of expansive capitalism and the acceleration of social change – *Le Rouge et le Noir* displays an unprecedented concern with energy – the hero's and the text's – and provides a first decisive representation of man constructing his own life's plot in response to the sociopolitical dynamics of modern history, which both shapes the individual career and plays roulette with its most concerted plans. As Harry Levin has written, with Stendhal we undergo 'the rites of initiation into the nineteenth century,' and this is so in good part because Stendhal's novels are inescapably pervaded by a historical perspective that provides an interpretive framework for all actions, ambitions, self-conceptions, and desires.[1] Nowhere is the historical problematic more evident than in the question of authority that haunts *Le Rouge et le Noir*, not only in the minds of its individual figures but in its very narrative structures. The novel not only represents but also is structured by an underlying warfare of legitimacy and usurpation; it hinges on the fundamental question. To whom does France belong? This question in turn implicates and is implicated in an issue of obsessive importance in all of Stendhal's novels, that of paternity.

Upon reflection, one can see that paternity is a dominant issue within the great tradition of the nineteenth-century novel (extending well into the twentieth century), a principal embodiment of its concern with authority, legitimacy, the conflict of generations, and the transmission of wisdom. **Turgenev**'s title, *Fathers and Sons*, sums up what is at stake in a number of the characteristic major novels of the tradition: not only *Le Rouge et le Noir*, but also such novels as **Balzac**'s *Le Père Goriot*, **Mary Shelley**'s *Frankenstein*, **Dickens**'s *Great Expectations*, **Dostoevsky**'s *The Brothers Karamazov*, **James**'s *The Princess Casamassima*, **Conrad**'s *Lord Jim*, **Gide**'s *Les Faux-Monnayeurs*, **Joyce**'s *Ulysses*, **Mann**'s *The Magic Mountain*, **Faulkner**'s *Absalom, Absalom!*, to name only a few of the most important texts that are essentially structured by this conflict. It is characteristic of *Ulysses* as a

summa of the nineteenth- and twentieth-century novel that its filial
protagonist, Stephen Dedalus, should provide an overt retrospective
meditation on the problem:

> Fatherhood, in the sense of conscious begetting, is unknown to man. It
> is a mystical estate, an apostolic succession, from only begetter to only
> begotten. On that mystery and not on the madonna which the cunning
> Italian intellect flung to the mob of Europe the church is founded and
> founded irremovably because founded, like the world, macro- and
> microcosm, upon the void. Upon incertitude, upon unlikelihood. *Amor
> matris*, subjective and objective genitive, may be the only true thing in
> life. Paternity may be a legal fiction. Who is the father of any son that
> any son should love him or he any son?[2]

Stephen's theological musing on the 'apostolic succession' of fatherhood
strikes to the key problem of transmission: the process by which the young
protagonist of the nineteenth-century novel discovers his choices of
interpretation and action in relation to a number of older figures of wisdom
and authority who are rarely biological fathers – a situation that the novel
often ensures by making the son an orphan, or by killing off or otherwise
occulting the biological father before the text brings to maturity its
dominant alternatives. The son then most often has a choice among
possible fathers from whom to inherit, and in the choosing – which may
entail a succession of selections and rejections – he plays out his career of
initiation into a society and into history, comes to define his own authority
in the interpretation and use of social (and textual) codes.

Freud, in his well-known essay 'Family Romances,' develops the typical
scenario based on the child's discovery that *pater semper incertus est*: the
phantasy of being an adopted child whose biological parents are more
exalted creatures than his actual parents, which is then superseded when
the child accepts the actual mother but creates a phantasized, illegitimate
father, and bastardizes siblings in favor of his own sole legitimacy. It may
be significant, as Roland Barthes notes, that the child appears to 'discover'
the Oedipus complex and the capacity for constructing coherent narrative
at about the same stage in life.[3] The most fully developed narratives of the
child become a man all seem to turn on the uncertainty of fatherhood, to
use this uncertainty to unfold the romance of authority vested elsewhere,
and to test the individual's claim to personal legitimacy within a struggle
of different principles of authority. In the nineteenth century, these issues
touch every possible register of society, history, and fiction, and nowhere
more so than in France, where the continuing struggle of revolution and
restoration played itself out in dramatic political upheavals and reversals
throughout the century. Particularly during the Restoration, after the fall of
Napoleon who seemed to incarnate the triumph of energy and youth over

157

The Red and the Black *and* The Charterhouse of Parma

the resistances of age, tradition, and hierarchy, France experienced a relapse into an intense conflict of generations. France was governed by old men who had come of age during the Ancien Régime, Louis XVIII and Charles X (both brothers of Louis XVI), and their ministers. Titles of nobility and certificates of noncollaboration with the Napoleonic regime were necessary to recognition, and the young men of the bourgeoisie (and the people) who had seen the doors of the future open under Napoleon now found them closed. Many of the writers of the period – Stendhal, Balzac, Musset – as well as later historians converge in the diagnosis of a regime and a social structure set in resistance to the real dynamism of the country. The Revolution of 1830 appears in hindsight merely inevitable. In cultural politics, 1830 also appears as an intensely oedipal moment, best symbolized in the famous première of Victor Hugo's *Hernani*, marking the raucous victory of the young Romantics and the forces of movement.[4] And the nineteenth-century novel as a genre seems to be inseparable from the conflict of movement and resistance, revolution and restoration, and from the issues of authority and paternity, which provide not only the matter of the novel but also its structuring force, the dynamic that shapes its plot.

I want now to return from this brief sketch of the issue of paternity and authority to the plot of *Le Rouge et le Noir* by way of the novel's end, by way of the guillotine that so abruptly severs Julien Sorel's life and brilliant career, and thereby threatens our efforts to construct a coherent interpretation of the novel. Just before Julien Sorel's end, the narrator tells us, 'Jamais cette tête n'avait été aussi poétique qu'au moment où elle allait tomber' ('Never had this head been so poetic as at the moment it was about to fall').[5] The next moment of the text – the next sentence – it is all over, and the narrator is commenting on the style with which the head fell: 'Everything took place simply, fittingly, and without any affectation on his part.' In an elision typical of Stendhal, the climactic instant of decapitation is absent. We have the vibrations of the fall of the blade of the guillotine, but not the bloody moment. The elision is the more suspect in that it is not clear that Julien's head needed to fall at all. As a traditional and rationalist criticism of Stendhal used to say, Julien's shooting of Mme de Rênal – which entails his decapitation – appears arbitrary, gratuitous, insufficiently motivated. Engaged to marry the pregnant Mathilde de la Mole, adored of her as she is adored of her father, surely Julien the master-plotter, the self-declared disciple of Tartuffe, could have found a way to repair the damage done to his reputation by Mme de Rênal's letter of accusation. Those other critics who try to explain Julien's act on psychological grounds merely rationalize the threat of the irrational, which is not so importantly psychological as 'Narratological': the scandal of the manner in which Stendhal has shattered his novel and then cut its head off.[6] Still another scandal – and another elision – emerges in this ending because of the novel's chronology, which would place Julien's execution well into 1831. Yet in this novel subtitled 'Chronicle of 1830' we have no mention of the most notable event of the year: the July Revolution. Indeed, Mme de Rênal in the last pages of the novel proposes to seek clemency for Julien by pleading with King Charles X, who had been dethroned for almost a year. The discrepancy is particularly curious in that the whole of Julien's ideology and career – of revolt, usurpation, the transgression of class lines – seems to beckon to and call for revolution. Is the guillotine that executes Julien, the 'peasant in revolt' as he has called himself at his trial, a displaced figure for 'les Trois Glorieuses,' a revolution notable for having made no use of the guillotine? Is the catastrophic ending of *Le Rouge et le Noir* a displaced and inverted version of the revolution that should have been?[7]

Perhaps we have begun to sketch the outlines of a problem in narrative design and intention, in plot and its legitimating authority (including history as plot), and in the status of the end on which, traditionally, the beginning and middle depend for their retrospective meaning. We can come closer to defining the problem with two statements that Julien makes shortly before the arrival of Mme de Rênal's accusatory letter. When the Marquis de la Mole has given him a new name, M. le chevalier Julien Sorel de la Vernaye, and a commission as lieutenant in the hussars, he reflects, 'After all . . . my novel is finished' (p. 639). Yet the novel – if not his, then whose? – will continue for another eleven chapters. Shortly after the statement just quoted, Julien receives twenty thousand francs from the Marquis, with the stipulation that 'M. Julien de la Vernaye' – the Sorel has now been excised – will consider this a gift from his real (that is, natural, illegitimate) father and will donate some of it to his legal father, Sorel the carpenter, who took care of him in childhood. Julien wonders if this fiction of the illegitimate aristocratic father might not be the truth after all: 'Might it really be possible, he said to himself, that I am the natural son of some great noble exiled in our mountains by the terrible Napoleon? With every moment this idea seemed less improbable to him . . . My hatred for my father would be a proof . . . I would no longer be a monster!' (p. 641). The word 'monster,' as we shall see, evokes a network of references to Julien's moments of self-identification as the plebeian in revolt, the usurper, the hypocrite, the seducer, the Tartuffe, he who, in the manner of all monsters, transgresses and calls into question the normal orders of classification and regulation. But can illegitimacy rescue him from monstrosity, when throughout the novel illegitimacy has appeared the very essence of the monstrous? Can hatred for the legal father be a proof of innocence, that is, of the lack of monstrosity, of the lack of a need to act the hypocrite? If so, have we really all along been reading not a 'Chronicle of 1830' but an eighteenth-century novel – by a writer such as Fielding or Marivaux – where the hero is a foundling whose aristocratic origins eventually will out, and will offer a complete retrospective motivation – and absolution – for his desire to rise in the world: usurpation recovered as natural affinity? Legitimized by illegitimacy, Julien's plot could simply be a homecoming, a *nostos*, the least transgressive, the least monstrous of narratives.

Earlier in the novel, M. de Rênal, reflecting on his children's evident preference of Julien to their father, exclaims: 'Everything in this century tends to throw opprobrium on *legitimate* authority. Poor France!' (p. 353). The comment explicitly connects political issues of legitimacy and authority with paternity, itself inextricably bound up in the problem of legitimacy and authority. The shape and intention of the novel are tied closely to this network of issues. The way in which the novel poses the questions of authority and legitimacy might be formulated first of all in the queries: What kind of a novel is this? To what models of plot and explanation does it refer us? There occurs a striking example of this problem early in the novel (Book 1, Chapter 9), in the episode of the 'portrait in the mattress.' Julien has just learned that M. de Rênal and his servants are going to restuff the straw mattresses of the house. He turns to Mme de Rênal and begs her to 'save him' by removing from his mattress, before M. de Rênal reaches it, a small cardboard box containing a portrait. And he begs her as well not to look at the portrait in the box; it is his 'secret.' The narrator, typically cross-cutting from the perceptions of one character to those of another, tells us that Mme de Rênal's nascent love for Julien (of which she is still largely ignorant) gives her the heroic generosity of spirit necessary to perform what she takes to be an act of self-sacrifice, since she assumes that the portrait must be that of the woman Julien loves. Once she has retrieved the box and given it to Julien, she succumbs to the 'horrors of jealousy.' Cutting back to Julien, we find him burning the box, and we learn that it in fact contains a portrait of Napoleon – *l'usurpateur*, Julien names him here – with lines of admiration scratched on its back by Julien. The misunderstanding between the two characters, where neither perceives what is at stake for the other, cannot be confined to the realm of the personal: they are living in different worlds, indeed in different novels. For Mme de Rênal, the drama has to do with love and jealousy, with amorous rivalry and the possibility of adultery. She thinks she is a character in an eighteenth-century novel of manners, **Les Egarements du coeur et de l'esprit**, perhaps, or (as one of its innocents) *Les Liaisons dangereuses*. Julien, on the contrary, is living in the world of modern narrative – post-Revolutionary, post-Napoleonic – which precisely throws into question the context of 'manners' and the novel of manners, subverts its very possibility. Napoleon, the 'usurper' in Julien's pertinent epithet, represents a different order of *égarement*, or wandering from the true path: the intrusion of history into society, the reversal of a stable and apparently immutable world, that of the Ancien Régime, which made 'manners' as social and as literary code possible and necessary. If, as Julien says a few chapters later, the 'fatal memory' of Napoleon will forever prevent young Frenchmen like himself from being happy, the reason is that Napoleon represented the possibility of *la carrière ouverte aux talents*: advancement through merit, the legitimation of class mobility, legalized usurpation. While Julien studies not to appear a disciple of Napoleon, he manages at various times in the novel to resemble first Robespierre, then Danton, both of whom stand behind Napoleon as destroyers of the Ancien Régime who, at the very least, historicized the concept of *le monde*, thus making the novel of manners in the strict definition impossible. The scene of the portrait in the mattress signals the impossibility of the novel of manners as Mme de Rênal understands it: questions of love and interpersonal relations no longer play themselves out in a closed and autonomous sphere. They are menaced by class conflict as historicized in the persistent aftermath of the French Revolution.

In a number of essays and reflections over the years, Stendhal developed an explicit theory of why the Revolution had rendered social comedy – *la comédie de Molière*, in his shorthand – impossible. He explains himself most fully in 'La Comédie est impossible en 1836,' where he argues that social comedy could work only with a unified audience, sharing the same code of manners and comportment, and agreeing on what was deviant and extravagant in terms of this code. The Revolution, in destroying the society of court and salon, and raising to consciousness the claims of different social classes, shattered the unity of sensibility on which **Molière**'s effects were predicated; at a performance of *Le Bourgeois Gentilhomme* in 1836, half the audience would laugh at the would-be gentleman, Monsieur Jourdain – as was Molière's intention – but the other half would admire and approve him.[8] When social class becomes the basis for political struggle, one man's object of ridicule becomes another man's serious social standard. The demonstration applies as well to the novel (as Stendhal noted in the margins of a copy of *Le Rouge et le Noir*)[9]: the novel of manners is itself threatened with usurpation, it cannot exclude from its pages something else, something that had best be called politics. Mme de Rênal has no knowledge or understanding of politics, yet she is living in a world where all other questions, including love, eventually are held hostage to the political, and this is true as well for the novel in which she figures.

Politics in *Le Rouge et le Noir* is the unassimilable other, which in fact is all too well assimilated since it determines everything: nothing can be thought in isolation from the underlying strife of legitimacy and usurpation that polarizes the system within which all other differences are inscribed and that acts as a necessary (though I refuse to say ultimate) interpretant to any message formulated in the novel. A telling illustration of this proposition occurs in chapter 18 of book 1, which describes the king's visit to Verrières and which is rich in representations of the movement from red to black, as Julien first cuts a figure in the mounted Honor Guard and then dons the cassock to assist the Abbé Chélan in the magnificent *Te Deum* at the chapel of Bray-le-Haut, which so overwhelms him that in this moment 'he would have fought for the Inquisition, and in good faith.' It is in the midst of this religious spectacular that the narrator treacherously comments, 'Such a day undoes the work of a hundred issues of Jacobin newspapers.' The reader who has been paying attention will understand that this undoing has been the intent and design of the religious ceremony, staged and financed by the Marquis de la Mole: it is one more political gesture in the continuing struggle to say to whom France belongs.

But if politics is the indelible tracer dye in the social and narrative codes of the novel, the very force of the political dynamic is matched by the intensity with which it is repressed. For to admit to the force of the political is to sanction a process of change, of temporal slippage and movement forward – of history, in fact – whereas the codes of the Restoration are all overtly predicated on temporal analepsis, a re-creation within history of an ahistorical past, a facsimile Ancien Régime that rigorously excludes the possibility of change, of revolution. Hence those who claim to be the legitimate masters of France cannot allow themselves to mention politics: the 'Charter of the Drawing-Room' in the Hôtel de la Mole prohibits mockery of God and the Establishment, bans praise of Voltaire, Rousseau, and the Opposition newspapers, and decrees 'especially that one never talk politics' (p. 457). The result is boredom, for what has been repressed is what interests everyone most passionately, and indeed ultimately motivates those acts that claim ostensibly to belong to the domain of manners, since manners themselves – such an act as changing into silk stockings and slippers for dinner – are political gestures. Politics stands as the great repressed that ever threatens to break through the bar of repression. Politics, as someone calling himself 'the author' puts it in a parenthetical debate with another figure called 'the publisher,' is like a pistol shot in the middle of a concert. Even before Julien's pistol shot shatters the ceremony of the Mass in the church at Verrières, there is a constant threat of irruption of the political into manners, a denuding of the mechanisms governing the relations of power and of persons, an exposure of the dynamic governing history and narrative.

At stake in the play of politics and its repression is, I have suggested, the issue of legitimate authority versus usurpation; and in this opposition we find the matrix of the principal generative and governing structures of the novel. The interrelated questions of authority, legitimacy, and paternity unfold on all levels of the text: in Julien's use of models to conceive and to generate his own narrative, in the problematizing of his origins and his destiny, in the overriding question of who controls the text. To treat only briefly the first of these issues: we know that Julien from his first appearance in the novel moves in a web of bookish models, derived first of all from **Las Cases**'s memoir of Napoleon, the *Mémorial de Sainte-Hélène*, the *Bulletins* of the Grande-Armée, and **Rousseau**'s *Confessions*, which are then supplemented by the New Testament, which Julien has simply learned by heart, and by Joseph de Maistre's book on the papacy; to these one could add occasional references to **Corneille**'s *Le Cid* as model of honor, and continuing citation of **Molière**'s *Tartuffe*, another text memorized. The extent to which Julien believes in his texts of reference varies, but so does the meaning of 'belief,' since he has chosen to be the *hypokrites*, the player of roles. It is significant that the Abbé Pirard will note Julien's complete ignorance of Patristic doctrine: Julien's texts provide individual interpretations of models of behavior but no authoritative tradition of interpretation and conduct.

As a result, Julien continually conceives himself as the hero of his own text, and that text as something to be created, not simply endured. He creates fictions, including fictions of the self, that motivate action.[10] The result is often inauthenticity and error, the choice of comportments dictated by models that are inappropriate. In Julien's 'seduction' of Mme de Rênal, for instance, we are told that his success comes not from efforts to play the role of a consummate Don Juan but from his natural unhappiness at failing to please so beautiful a woman: when he bursts into tears, he achieves a victory his stratagems had failed to win. His sense of 'duty' to 'an ideal model which he proposed to imitate' indeed nearly spoils what is most attractive to Mme de Rênal, and robs Julien of the pleasure he might have experienced. Yet just when the reader is ready to judge that Julien would do better to abandon models and roles, the narrator turns around and points out that the contrived self-conceptions alone have put Julien in a position where his *naturel* can effect results. In a typically dialectical statement, the narrator tells us: 'In a word, what made Julien a superior being was precisely what prevented him from enjoying the pleasure that had come his way' (p. 298).

Julien's fictional scenarios make him not only the actor, the feigning self, but also the stage manager of his own destiny, constantly projecting the self into the future on the basis of hypothetical plots. One of the most striking examples of such hypotheses occurs when, after receiving Mathilde's summons to come to her bedroom at one o'clock in the morning, he imagines a plot – in all senses of the term, including plot as machination, as *complot* – in which he will be seized by Mathilde's brother's valets, bound, gagged, imprisoned, and eventually poisoned. So vivid is this fiction that the narrator tells us: 'Moved like a playwright by his own story, Julien was truly afraid when he entered the dining room' (p. 536). Such fictions may even encompass the political, as when Julien immolates his last vestiges of remorse toward the Marquis – the benefactor whose daughter he is about to seduce – by evoking the fate of MM. Fontan and Magalon, political prisoners of the regime: an evocation that is factually accurate but of the most fictive relevance to his own case, as indeed, we may feel, are all his self-identifications as plebeian in revolt and peasant on the rise, since they do not correspond either to our perceptions of his identity or to his own identifications with more glorious models. Because the scenarist of self-conceptions cannot maintain a stable distinction between the self and its fictions, Julien must unceasingly write and rewrite the narrative of a self defined in the dialectic of its past actions and its prospective fictions.

To Julien's generation of his narrative from fictional models we can juxtapose the seriality of those figures of paternity who claim authority in his career. He is set in relationship to a series of ideal or possible fathers, but in a curious manner whereby each father figure claims authority, or has authority conferred on him, at just the moment when he is about to be replaced. The 'real,' or at least legal, father, Sorel the carpenter, is already well on the way to repudiation when the novel opens; his first replacement, the chirurgien-major who has bequeathed his Legion of Honor to Julien, is dead and his legacy suppressed in the movement from red to black. The paternity of the Abbé Chélan emerges in strong outline only when Julien has left him for the seminary, where the severe Abbé Pirard will eventually address Julien as *filius*. 'I was hated by my father from the cradle,' Julien will say to Pirard, 'this was one of my greatest misfortunes; but I will no longer complain of fortune, I have found another father in you, sir' (p. 444).[11] Yet this moment of overt recognition comes only in Chapter 1 of Book 2, that is, after Julien's translation to Paris and his establishment in the Hôtel de la Mole: precisely the moment when Pirard begins to give way to the Marquis de la Mole, who will complicate the question of paternity and play out its various transformations.

It is at the moment of transition from Pirard's paternity to the Marquis's that the question of Julien's legitimation through illegitimacy is first explicitly raised: the possibility that he might be the natural child of some aristocrat (perhaps hidden in the mountains of Franche-Comté during the Napoleonic wars), which would explain what the Abbé (and later the Marquis) see as his natural nobility. For the Abbé and the Marquis, Julien's natural nobility is something of a scandal in the order of things, one that requires remotivation and authorization through noble blood, be it illegitimately transmitted. If, like the foundling of an eighteenth-century novel or a Molière comedy, Julien were at last to find that he has been fathered by an aristocrat, this discovery would legitimate his exceptionality, his deviance from the normal condition of the peasant, and show that what was working as hidden design in his destiny was, as the Abbé puts it, 'la force du sang' (p. 441). The strength of bloodline would rewrite Julien's narrative as satisfactorily motivated, no longer aberrant and deviant, and rescue Julien's transgressive career, and the novel's dynamic, from the political realm by restoring them to the anodyne of manners.

A curious dialogue between the Abbé and the Marquis, these two believers in paternal authority and the legitimate order, explicitly formulates for the first time the theory of Julien's illegitimate nobility. The dialogue creates a chiasmus of misunderstanding concerning the anonymous gift of five hundred francs to Julien. Each speaker mistakenly infers from the other's words possession of some secret knowledge about Julien's origins and thus makes further unfounded inferences. It is through misinterpretation and the postulation of concealment – of what is 'really,' so far as we know, the absence of anything to be concealed – that Julien's noble illegitimacy begins to achieve textual status, to acquire an authorship based on a gratuitous play of substitutes for the origin. Further retroactive motivations for the origin then fall into line. The next step follows from Julien's duel with the Chevalier de Beauvoisis, who doesn't want it thought that he has taken the field of honor against a simple secretary to the Marquis: the Chevalier hence lets it be known that Julien is the natural child of 'an intimate friend of the Marquis de la Mole,' and the Marquis then finds it convenient to lend, as he puts it, 'consistency' to this version. He will go on to furnish Julien with a blue costume in addition to the secretarial black; wearing the former, he will be the younger son of the old Duc de Chaulnes (who, I note in passing, comes to be an object of hatred to Julien, a representation of repressive authority).[12] The Marquis then authorizes the Abbé Pirard 'to keep no longer the secret' of Julien's birth. The blue costume is followed by the cross (of the Legion of Honor): the cross that the legitimate son, Norbert de la Mole, has been demanding in vain for some eighteen months. This process of seemingly casual ennoblement by way of illegitimacy, motivating and promoting Julien's rise in the world through a hidden authority, will reach its climax when the recuperated and effaced plebeian makes himself – through Mathilde's pregnancy – into the natural son-in-law, himself continuing the bloodline, and stands on the verge of becoming the legal son-in-law, Mathilde's husband, the Chevalier de la Vernaye.

But I have so far said nothing about another figure of paternal authority in the narrative: the narrator. The relation of the narrator to Julien – and of all Stendhalian narrators to the young protagonists of his novels – is patently paternalistic, a mixture of censure and indulgence; the narrator sets a standard of worldly wisdom that the protagonist must repeatedly violate, yet confesses to a secret admiration for the violation, especially for *l'imprévu*, the unforeseeable, the moments when Julien breaks with the very notion of model and pattern. The narrator constantly judges Julien in relation to his chosen models, measuring his distance from them, noting his failures to understand them, his false attributions of success to them, and the fictionality of the constructions he builds from them. As Victor

Brombert has so well pointed out, the Stendhalian narrator typically uses hypothetical grammatical forms, asserting that if only Julien had understood such and such, he would have done so and so, with results different from those to which he condemns himself.[13] To take just one example, which characteristically concerns what did not happen between Julien and Mme de Rênal: 'If Mme de Rênal had had the slightest *sang-froid*, she would have complimented him on the reputation he had won, and Julien, with his pride set at ease, would have been gentle and amiable with her, especially since her new dress seemed to him charming' (p. 290). Constantly referring to the worlds of misunderstanding between his characters, the missed chances and might-have-beens, the narrator repeatedly adumbrates other novels, texts of the might-have-been-written. This obtrusive narrator, master of every consciousness in the novel, claims to demonstrate why things necessarily happened the way they did, yet inevitably he suggests the arbitrariness and contingency of every narrative turn of events, how easily it might have been otherwise.

'Paternalism' is of course a highly charged concept for Stendhal – a man who used a hundred different pseudonyms, who in his letters to his sister referred to their father as 'the bastard,' thereby no doubt indicating his wish to consider himself as illegitimate, and who once remarked that if you notice an old man and a young man together who have nothing to say to each other, you can be certain that they are father and son.[14] Encoded in his novels is always the problem of whether paternity is possible, whether there might be a father and son who could talk to one another. The unfinished *Lucien Leuwen* comes closest to staging a perfect father, yet even he must eventually be rejected: as Lucien says, my father wishes my happiness, but in his own manner.[15] It is a fault inherent to fatherhood that to act toward the son, even with the intent of aiding him in *la chasse du bonheur*, is inevitably to exercise an illegitimate (because *too* legitimate) control, to impose a model that claims authoritative (because authorial) status. All Stendhal's novels record the failure of authoritative paternity in his protagonists' lives, and at the same time demonstrate the narrator's effort to retrieve the failure of being himself the perfect father, he who can maintain the conversation with his son. Yet there comes a point in each novel where the protagonist must slip from under the control of the narrator-father as well.

Julien, it seems, slips from under the control of each of his figures of paternal authority when that control becomes too manifest. The paternal narrator seeks to restrain Julien, to circumscribe him through the deployment of the father's greater worldly wisdom, yet he also admires those moments when Julien kicks at the traces of narratorial control, creates the unforeseen. Julien's slippage from under the exercise of authority – his self-inventing, self-creating quality – typifies the highly metonymic character of the Stendhalian hero, figure of unarrested, unappeasable desire which can never be anchored in a definitive meaning, even retrospectively. The entire narrative mode of Stendhal's novels is in fact markedly metonymic, indeed virtually serial, giving the impression of a perpetual flight forward, a constant self-invention at the moment and of the moment. The Stendhalian novel appears to be a self-inventing artifact. What we know of Stendhal's habits of composition (particularly from the marginalia to the manuscript of *Lucien Leuwen*) suggests that he literally invented his fiction from day to day, using only the most meager of anecdotes as an armature. Each day's writing – or later, with *La Chartreuse de Parme*, each day's dictation – became an extrapolation of what the protagonist should become on the basis of what he had been, and done, the day before. The astonishing sense of rapidity given by these novels was matched in fact by rapidity of invention, a refusal of revision and the return backward: they are the least palimpsestic texts imaginable.[16]

Upon reflection, one sees that Stendhal makes curiously non-retrospective use of narrative, which, I have argued, is in essence a retrospective mode, tending toward a finality that offers retrospective illumination of the whole. The Stendhalian protagonist ever looks ahead, planning the next moment, projecting the self forward through ambition: creating in front of the self, as it were, the circle of the *ambitus*, the to-be-realized. Lucien Leuwen repeatedly refers to himself as *un grand peut-être* ('a great perhaps'), and Julien, too, ever eludes fixed definitions in favor of constant becoming. The narrator generally seems concerned to judge the present moment, or at most the moment just past, rather than to delve into the buried past in search of time lost. Flaubert will epitomize the essentially retrospective nature of his own, and no doubt most, narrative when, in *L'Education sentimentale*, he has Frédéric Moreau, faced with the portraits of Diane de Poitiers at Fontainebleau, experience *concupiscence rétrospective*, desire oriented toward an irrecoverable past.[17] Stendhal's novels, in contrast, seem to be based on *désir prospectif*, desire in and for the future. If, as Georg Lukács claims, *L'Education sentimentale* typifies the novel's organic use of time, Stendhalian time is inorganic, momentary, characterized by abruptness and discontinuity.[18] This quality may well appear paradoxical in a novelist so preoccupied with history, which is necessarily retrospective. Yet it accords with Stendhal's political liberalism, his belief that only the future could reconcile and resolve the contradictions of the present – and, in the process, create readers capable of understanding his novels. His venture into something resembling the historical novel, in *La Chartreuse de Parme*, is indeed accomplished by making the retrospective impulse an object of satire: the powdered wigs of the court of Parma represent Restoration as make-believe, a ridiculous (and doomed) effort to set back the clocks of history. We might say that Stendhal's typical verb tense is the future perfect, that of the will-have-been-accomplished: a tense that allows for the infinite postponement of accomplishment. And this may offer one clue to the need for the arbitrary and absolute *finis* of the guillotine.

Le Rouge et le Noir, in its rapid, evasive, unarrestable narrative movement, and in the narrator's games of containment and outmaneuver with the protagonist, ever tends to suggest that things might be otherwise than they are or, perhaps more accurately, that otherwise is how things are but not how they might have been. Curiously, the apparently stable figure of the triangle, which René Girard found to be the basic structure of mediated desire in the novel – where A desires B because B is desired by C – lends itself to this narrative instability and uncontrollability, since the very abstraction of the triangle figure permits a free substitution of persons at its corners.[19] Thus, when Julien is most profoundly unhappy at his inability to make Mathilde love him with any constancy, the novel suddenly opens up its most comic episode, the courtship of the Maréchale de Fervaques according to the formula provided, along with a volume of manuscript love letters, by the absurd Russian Prince Korasoff – an episode that is an exercise in pure, which is to say empty, style. The Russian prescribes that Julien must make love to another lady – any other lady – of Mathilde's society. Julien chooses Mme de Fervaques and manages to make eloquent speeches to her by arranging himself in the drawing room so that he appears to look at her while he is gazing past her to Mathilde, the third point of the triangle. The love letters that he daily copies and delivers are so lacking in specific pertinence to their referents that when he once forgets to make the substitution of 'Paris' and 'Saint-Cloud' for the 'London' and 'Richmond' of the original, his oversight makes no appreciable difference. Nor is their addressee of much importance: even after Mme de Fervaques has joined the dialogue and begun to answer him, he continues simply to copy Korasoff's letters. The narrator comments: 'Such is the advantage of the grandiloquent style: Mme de Fervaques was not at all astonished by the lack of relationship between his replies and her letters' (p. 613). The grandiloquent style (*style emphatique*) stands for all that Stendhal detested in such Romantic contemporaries as Chateaubriand and Victor Hugo: a grandiose inanity that was the opposite of the penetrating, denuding prose Stendhal had from childhood admired in the *philosophes* and the *Idéologues*. Julien's success in bringing Mathilde to heel is assured when she opens his desk drawer and finds there a pile of Mme de Fervaques's replies in envelopes that he has not even bothered to open. What impresses her most is not simply that he should be the sentimental choice of the grand Mme de Fervaques but that the relation should be void of content – a matter of envelopes rather than of the messages they enclose. When she falls, vanquished, at Julien's feet, her surrender is a tribute to the authority of empty style, style as pure geometry.

The emptiness generates a plenitude, for Julien's courtship of Mme de

Fervaques results in Mathilde's sustained passion for Julien and in her pregnancy, a full meaning that assures the continuity that entails all Julien's future successes – title, fortune, new name. When the Marquis, acting through the Abbé Pirard, suggests that Julien offer a gift 'to M. Sorel, carpenter in Verrières, who took care of him in childhood' (pp. 640–1), he offers overt and final realization of Julien's primordial wish not to belong to his biological father. The 'family romance' has, for once, come true. The elaborate fictions of Julien's legitimation through illegitimacy may correspond to Mathilde's pregnancy from elaborate and empty games of style. The episode of Mme de Fervaques offers a remarkable demonstration of the instability of motivation in relation to result, a figure of the narrative's capacity to generate its significant structures from empty configurations, to institute new, authoritative governing structures in its apparently random flight forward. With Mathilde's pregnancy and Julien's dreams for the future of his son – he never conceives the child *in utero* as anything but a son – the past is made, retrospectively, to take on the dynastic authority that it has always lacked. By transmitting paternity and projecting it into the future, Julien can at last postulate fully the paternity that stands behind him, believe in the illegitimacy that ennobles and legitimates him. Julien by this point belongs to the Restoration, indeed stands as a figure of how restoration is carried out: by using politics to attain a place in a system of manners that then is used to efface politics, pretending that the way things came to be as they are (by revolution and reaction, for instance) does not belong to history, that the place of each thing, and person, in the structure of things is immutable.

We have worked our way back to the end, to the moment where the apparent stability achieved by Julien, his guarantee of a non-political and uneventful future, is catastrophically exploded, shattered by the pistol shot in the church of Verrières, annihilated by the fall of the blade of the guillotine. We need to return here to Julien's tentative belief in his remotivated paternity – a belief expressed in a conditional of probability (translated earlier in this chapter): 'Serait-il bien possible . . . que je fusse le fils naturel de quelque grand seigneur exilé dans nos montagnes par le terrible Napoléon? A chaque instant cette idée lui semblait moins improbable' – juxtaposed to its 'proof' in his hatred for the legal father – 'Ma haine pour mon père serait une preuve' – and the comment that with this realization of the family romance he would no longer be a monster – 'Je ne serais plus un monstre' (p. 641) – and also his remark, a few lines earlier, that his novel is over and the merit is his alone: 'Après tout, mon roman est fini, et à moi seul tout le mérite.' If we can understand how hatred works to guarantee a benign origin, authorizing the political change of place and of class as necessary and nontransgressive, we still need to ask why the novel that claims to be finished continues for another eleven chapters, and why these chapters stage the return of the monster.

The Red and the Black *and* The Charterhouse of Parma

The word 'monster' is used on a few occasions in the text. It appears to refer in particular to ingratitude, especially toward figures of paternal authority, and also to erotic transgression, usurpation, class conflict and the stance of the 'plebeian in revolt,' a stance that Julien tends to assume at moments of crisis (for example, upon Mathilde's declaration of love and at his trial) perhaps because it is simplifying and political, a decisive model for action. The monster figures the out-of-place, the unclassifiable, the transgressive, the desiring, the seductive.[20] The letter that Mme de Rênal writes under the dictation of her confessor will provoke catastrophe because it sketches precisely the portrait of Julien as monster.

> Poor and avid, it is by means of the most consummate hypocrisy, and by the seduction of a weak and unhappy woman, that this man has sought to make a place for himself and to become something. . . . In conscience, I am forced to think that one of his means to success in a household is to seek to seduce the most notable woman there. Covered by an appearance of disinterestedness and by phrases from novels, his sole and overriding object is to succeed in gaining control of the master of the house and his fortune. (pp. 643–4)

The whole letter indeed reads like an outline of *Tartuffe*, the classic story of the usurper who comes to the point of throwing the legitimate masters out of the house:

> C'est à vous d'en sortir, vous qui parlez en maître:
> La maison m'appartient, et je le ferai connaître.
> [It is for you to get out, you who speaks as master:
> The house belongs to me, and I shall make it known.]
> (Act 4, scene 7, lines 1557–8)

This portrait of Julien has a certain truth, not only because it offers an interpretation that an unsympathetic reader might well adopt but also because it corresponds to Julien's occasional portrayals of himself as the monster. If we were looking for psychological explanations, could we not say that Julien, in attempting to kill Mme de Rênal, is seeking to kill the monster, to eradicate the person who has preserved and transmitted the monster image of himself? And perhaps he is seeking to assure as well his own eradication by assuming the monster identity – for if he dies, the monster will die with him. Such an explanation gains plausibility when we find that Julien at his trial publicly assumes this identity, calling himself a 'peasant who has revolted against the lowness of his condition' (p. 674). In raising this political specter that everyone wants repressed, this potential of monstrous usurpation, Julien, as the Abbé Frilair points out, virtually commits suicide. It is as if he were confessing to a guilt deeper than his crime in order to make sure that full punishment would ensure. And that is one way to lay the monster to rest.

But such an 'explanation' seems too easy, too smooth. It covers up and reduces the scandal of the ending, and this strikes me as a mistake, especially since 'ending' is a chronic scandal in Stendhal's narratives: *La Chartreuse de Parme* collapses its set so fast that three of the four major characters are done away with in the space of a few sentences, and two important novels, *Lucien Leuwen* and *Lamiel*, never managed to get finished at all. Like his admirer André Gide, Stendhal dislikes concluding.[21] Would it, then, be more productive to think of the Stendhalian ending as a version of what the Russian Formalists called 'the laying bare of the device,' which here would be the very device of plotting, the need for beginning, middle, and end, which in the laying bare would be shown to be both necessary and arbitrary?

I do not want to use an appeal to what has been called in some recent criticism the *arbitraire du récit*, the gratuitous freedom of narrative, as explanatory in itself. I do, however, want to call attention to a specific and curious intrusion of the arbitrary that we find in the relation between the anecdote that served as source and armature for *Le Rouge et le Noir* and the narrative discourse invented on its basis, between the 'raw material' of story and its elaborations in Julien's plot. This anecdote is strangely contextualized early in the novel itself, in condensed and displaced form, as a weird indicator of things to come. I am thinking of the moment when Julien, on his way to the Rênal house for the first time, stops in the church of Verrières for a show of prayer, and finds a scrap of newspaper, on which he reads: 'Details of the execution and the last moments of Louis Jenrel, executed at Besançon the . . .' The rest of the article is torn off. Turning the scrap over, he reads: 'The first step' (p. 240). That Julien also thinks he sees blood on the pavement (it is in fact water from the font, colored by light coming through the crimson curtains) adds to the sense of a foreshadowing which appears somewhat crude in the context of Stendhalian subtlety. We seem to have the intrusion within the novel of the crime, trial, and execution of Antoine Berthet: the story that Stendhal found in *La Gazette des Tribunaux*, and used as outline for his novel – a *fait-divers* covered by the narrative discourse but only half-accommodated to its new context.[22] That Louis Jenrel is an anagram of Julien Sorel may indicate something about the partially concealed, half-assimilated status of this anecdote in the novel: the anecdote is present in the manner of a statement displaced into a corner of a dream, demanding expansion and relocation in the process of dream interpretation. How do we read the newspaper in the novel?

The ending of the novel appears to mark a new intrusion of newspaper into novel, dictating that Julien must finish in the same manner as the prototype from whom he has so markedly deviated. That is, maybe Julien shoots Mme de Rênal and goes to the guillotine *because* that original monster Antoine Berthet shot Mme Michoud de la Tour and went to the guillotine, and here my 'because' does not belong to the domain of source studies or psychological explanation but to narratology, to a perverse logic of narrative. Julien is handed over to the guillotine because the novel is collapsed back into the anecdote, the *fait-divers*, in which it originated and from which it has diverged.[23] This outcome may on the one hand suggest that Julien's plot finally is not his own, to shape as he wills. On the other hand, it may suggest a more general suspicion of narrative invention, which appears to be subject to interference from outside texts – to the uncontrollable intrusion of a newspaper fragment, for example, that at the last constitutes a mortal intertext.

Saying that Julien attempts murder and suffers execution because he must be made to fulfil Berthet's scenario is, of course, critically perverse, but it has the advantage of not concealing the perverse relations of Stendhal's novel to Julien's. The climactic moment of *Le Rouge et le Noir* may be an instance of what is known in classical rhetoric as a 'metalepsis of the author': assigning to the author's agency an action that should normally have been given an agency in the text, as when one says that Vergil 'makes' Dido die in Book 4 of the *Aeneid*, or when **Sterne** or Diderot invokes the author's power to accomplish (or defer) some event in the narrative.[24] Neither Stendhal nor the narrator so overtly appears to stage-manage events – Julien's fatal act indeed inaugurates a period of diminished narratorial intervention, as we shall see – yet the effect is similar, a denuding of the very act of narrative invention. One cannot get around the problem or the effect by claiming that Julien's narrative fills in the 'details' that are torn off from the newspaper story, thus providing a new, fuller motivation for crime and execution, for it is precisely in the details pertaining to the motives for crime and execution that the text radically frustrates us. Remotivating the text here, to make it a well-behaved, docile narrative, will always require ingenious extrapolation, classically psychological in nature. It may be better to recognize that the *fait-divers* in the novel remains somewhat diverse, resisting assimilation to our usual models of seamless novelistic worlds. Although it may be perverse to read Julien's plot as motivated in its very undoing by Berthet's plot, such a reading at least forces us to face the rhetorical problem of the ending, putting before us the question of Julien's novel – whose end Julien announces before the pistol shot at Verrières – in relation to Stendhal's, with its peculiar leftover, the status of which we need to determine.

We must now knit closer ties between Julien's two remarks, 'My novel is finished' and 'I would no longer be a monster.' We have seen that 'monster' alludes to the irrepressible presence of class conflict and politics, which turn on the ultimate questions: Where does legitimate authority lie? Who shall inherit France? 'Monster' connotes ambition, mobility, the desire to rise and to change places, to be somewhere one doesn't belong, to become (as by seduction and usurpation) something one cannot be by definition (by birth). The monster is the figure of displacement, transgression, desire, deviance, instability, the figure of Julien's project for himself, of his projective plot. In fact, the monster is conjointly the figure of politics and of plottedness, of politics as plot and plot as politics. Plot itself – narrative design and intention – is the figure of displacement, desire leading to change of position. The plotted narrative is a deviance from or transgression of the normal, a state of abnormality and error, which alone is 'Narratable.' What Julien identifies as his 'Novel' at the moment he declares it finished is precisely a deviant trajectory that has led him away from the authority of his legal origins, that has deauthorized origins and all other principles of legitimate authority, to the point where he could postulate a new authority in the theory of natural nobility. Yet, since that nobility, that legitimacy through illegitimacy, has been achieved through the deviance and usurpation of a highly political career, it is *ipso facto* tinged with monsterism. Later in the century, novels by Balzac, Hugo, Eugène Sue, Dickens, Dostoevsky, and others will exploit a world of the criminally deviant, as if the underworld of the transgressive and dangerous social elements were the last fund of 'Narratable' material in an increasingly bland social and literary system. Julien has no connection to the underworld, as yet undiscovered in 1830; yet his plot is already criminally deviant and transgressive, politically usurpatory. Hence what must be punished is not so much any specific act or political stance but rather the fact of having had a plot.

Can we then say that Julien Sorel is handed over to the guillotine because he has had a plot? There must be the guillotine at the end because there has been the novel, that strange excrescence of telling produced by the tissue of living. The telling perpetuates itself through more telling – scenarios for its further development, adumbrations of how it might be told otherwise – and then the simple monstrous anecdote of Antoine Berthet obtrudes again at the end, as Stendhal's reminder (to himself, to us) that to have lived in the divergence of plot, to have lived as the narratable, means somehow to be deviant, hence, in some cosmic narratological court, to be guilty. To frame Julien's novel within his own novel – to continue beyond the end of Julien's novel and take it to pieces – is Stendhal's way of having a plot and punishing it, of writing a novel and then chopping its head off.

The narrative 'leftover' that follows Julien's shooting of Mme de Rênal presents a Julien already castrated of the desiring that creates the novelistic plot: no longer interested in ambition, he judges his whole Parisian experience to have been an error; no longer interested in Mathilde and his worldly marriage, he returns to the explicitly maternal embrace of Mme de Rênal.[25] 'He never thought of his successes in Paris; he was bored with them' (p. 664). His mode of thought and being here passes beyond the self-conceptualization and the invention of roles necessary to the plotted existence; he rejects the mediating figures essential to the creation of scenarios of desire and displacement: 'One dies as one can. . . . What do *others* matter to me?' (p. 667). Not only does Julien appear to renounce his models in these final chapters, he seems also to move beyond the control and guidance of the paternal narrator. There is far less commentary by the narrator in these chapters; indeed his voice nearly falls silent, to leave the stage to Julien's almost uninterrupted monologue. The last four chapters (42–5), following Julien's sentencing, also lack titles and epigraphs, a departure from the rest of the novel that accords with the notable effacement of the narrator's discursiveness and dramatic presence. Julien has simultaneously moved beyond paternal authority and beyond the plotted novel. He is no longer narratable material; his novel has closed shop, and the extranovelistic perspective of its closing chapters serves to underline the disjuncture between plot and life, between Julien's novel and Stendhal's, between authoritative meaning and the subversion of meaning.

It is as if Stendhal had decided to enclose within *Le Rouge et le Noir* the scenario for what he liked to refer to, contemptuously, as a 'Novel for chambermaids.' Not that Julien and his plot have much to do with chambermaids, except in his social origin, and also in the offer made to him early in the novel of Mme de Rênal's chambermaid, Elisa, as a suitable wife – an offer whose acceptance would have effectively arrested the plot of ambition, short-circuited the novel. But we may perhaps take the 'chambermaid's novel' more generally as the figure of seductive literature. To read a novel – and to write one – means to be caught up in the seductive coils of a deviance: to seduce, of course, is to lead from the straight path, to create deviance and transgression. Stendhal seduces us through Julien's story, then he denounces the seduction. With the fall of the blade of the guillotine, he puts an end to the artificiality of the plotted story.

Something similar, though perhaps inverse, happens to the plotting of history in Stendhal's novel. The Revolution of 1830, as I mentioned, never manages to get represented in the novel even though in strict chronology it should; the novel as concert waits in suspense for this true historical pistol shot, which never comes. Yet the entire political dynamic of Julien's career tends toward that revolution: his personal transgression will be played out on the national theater in 1830 – and then again, more savagely, in 1848 and 1871. The whole novel motivates and calls for the Revolution of 1830, as if it should be the forty-sixth chapter of Book 2, the one beyond the last. In refusing to furnish us with that extra chapter, Stendhal performs a gesture similar to his dismantling of Julien's novel, suggesting that one cannot finally allow even history to write an authoritative plot for the novel.

The issue of authority, in all its manifestations, remains unresolved. Julien achieves no final relationship to any of his figures of paternity. It is indeed Sorel the carpenter who re-emerges in the place of the father at the end, and Julien attributes to him the jolly thought that the expectation of a legacy of three or four hundred louis from his son will make him, like any father, happy to have that son guillotined. The fathers inherit from the sons. As for Julien's own paternity, his plan that Mme de Rênal take care of his son – whom Mathilde will neglect – goes for naught when Mme de Rênal dies three days after he does. The fate of this son – if son it be – never is known. The novel rejects not only specific fathers and authorities but the very model of authority, refusing to subscribe to paternity as an authorizing figure of novelistic relationships. Ultimately, this refusal may indicate why Stendhal has to collapse his novels as they near their endings: the figure of the narrator as father threatens domination, threatens to offer an authorized version. He too must be guillotined.

The question, who shall inherit France? is left unresolved. The question, who shall inherit from Julien Sorel? is resolved only on the financial plane; and the victory of Sorel *père* over his son is perhaps an ironic representation of the novelist's ultimate and absolute paternal power to put his creatures to death. But the novel comments further on its close and perverse relation to the guillotine when Julien, in prison, recalls Danton's grammatical musings on the eve of his death: 'It's singular, the verb *to guillotine* can't be conjugated in all its tenses; one can say: "I will be guillotined, you will be guillotined," but one doesn't say: "I have been guillotined" ' (p. 677). For very good semantic reasons, the verb is grammatically defective: one cannot, in the first person, use it retrospectively. We encounter again, even here at the end, Stendhal's typical prospectivity, his predilection for the future perfect: 'I will have been guillotined' – the tense of deferral, the tense that denies retrospective satisfaction. Deferral haunts as well Stendhal's relation to the 'happy few' he designated as the inheritors of his message. In *Vie de Henry Brulard*, he famously inscribes these happy few, his readers, in a future fifty or a hundred years after his time. To do so is to defer the question of readership and to temporalize the spatiality of the dialogue in which readership might be thought to consist. The uncertain reader may then, too late, want to ask of the novel why it should be thus and not otherwise: or, in the words ascribed to Beaumarchais that serve as epigraph to Book 2, chapter 32: 'Hélas! pourquoi ces choses et non pas d'autres?'

Le Rouge et le Noir, perhaps more acutely than more 'normally' plotted novels, makes us aware of both the consonances and the disjunctures of life and its telling, of event and might-have-been, of biological pattern and concerted deviance from it. Julien Sorel's brilliant, brief, transgressive, and truncated career raises in acute form questions about significant ends and their relation to generative structures of narrative. Stendhal's somewhat perverse refusal to end 'naturally' – this postponement of conclusion, superseded by the catastrophic eclipse – places us before the problem of

175

The Red and the Black *and* The Charterhouse of Parma

standard narrative form, the ways in which we usually understand beginnings, middles, and ends. In particular, his obsessive concern with problems of paternity and authority – on the structural and textual as well as thematic levels – makes us ask why we have fictional biographies, what we expect them to do. *Le Rouge et le Noir* solicits our attention and frustrates our expectation because we have some sense of the fitting biographical pattern: one in which sons inherit from fathers and pass on, be it through Stephen Dedalus's 'apostolic succession,' a wisdom gained, a point of understanding attained. Stendhal's perversity may make us realize that such a patterning is both necessary, and suspect, the product of an interpretation motivated by desire, and that we also must acknowledge the work of more negative forces of recurrence and revenge. How we move from beginning to end in a significant way – creating a pattern of transformation in the sequence leading from beginning to end – demands further reflection, and a more fully elaborated model of understanding, which we will find suggested in the most boldly speculative work of Freud.

Notes

1. HARRY LEVIN, *The Gates of Horn* (New York: Oxford Univ. Press, 1963), p. 149. The classic exposition of how representation in Stendhal is pervaded by historical perspective may be found in ERICH AUERBACH, *Mimesis*, trans. Willard Trask (Garden City, N.Y.: Anchor Books, 1957), pp. 400–13.

2. JAMES JOYCE, *Ulysses* (New York: Modern Library, 1961), p. 207.

3. See 'Family Romances' [Der Familienroman der Neurotiker] (1908), in *The Standard Edition of the Complete Psychological Works of Sigmund Freud*, ed. James Strachey (London: Hogarth Press, 1953–74), vol. 9, pp. 237–41; see ROLAND BARTHES, 'Introduction à l'analyse structurale des récits', *Communications*, 8 (1966), p. 27. The 'family romance' as an underlying structure of the modern novel has been well discussed by MARTHE ROBERT in *Roman des origines, origines du roman* (Paris: Grasset, 1972).

4. *Hernani* itself, curiously, stages the eventual victory of the paternal generation over the son, as the aged Don Ruy Gomez reappears on Hernani's wedding night to reclaim Hernani's life, which he previously saved. Hernani has throughout expressed guilt toward his own father, whose memory he was to avenge in killing the king, Don Carlos. Accepting death from the hand of Don Ruy Gomez, he may at the last succumb to the burden of oedipal guilt – as if in token of Victor Hugo's act of compensation for his own oedipal transgression. On Stendhal's attitudes toward the Restoration, see, among others, GENEVIÈVE MOUILLAUD, *'Le Rouge et le Noir' de Stendhal: Le roman possible* (Paris: Larousse, 1973).

5. STENDHAL, *Le Rouge et le Noir*, in *Romans et nouvelles*, ed. Henri Martineau (Paris: Bibliothèque de la Pléiade, 1963), vol. 1, p. 697. Subsequent references are to this edition, and will be given in parentheses in the text. Translations from Stendhal are my own.

6. Henri Martineau summarizes critical objections to the end of the novel and offers his own psychological interpretation in *L'Œuvre de Stendhal* (Paris: Le Divan, 1945), pp. 343–51. For another useful summary of critical commentaries on the dénouement, and an attempt to remotivate Julien's acts on a rational basis, see P.-G. CASTEX, *'Le Rouge et le Noir' de Stendhal* (Paris: SEDES, 1967), pp. 124–55.

7. MARTINEAU establishes a careful fictional chronology of the novel in the Garnier edition (Paris: Garnier, 1957), pp. 533–7. On the problem of chronology, see also CHARLES J. STIVALE, 'Le Vraisemblable temporel dans *Le Rouge et le Noir*,' *Stendhal Club*, 84 (1979), 299–313. Concerning revolution and the guillotine, see Stendhal's account of his joy – at age ten – on learning of the execution of Louis XVI, an event he explicitly contrasts with the failure of the July monarchy to execute the Comte de Peyronnet and the other ministers who signed the 'ordonnances de Juillet,' which touched off the Revolution of 1830. *Vie de Henry Brulard*, in *Œuvres intimes*, ed. Henri Martineau (Paris: Bibliothèque de la Pléiade, 1955), p. 94.

8. See STENDHAL, 'La Comédie est impossible en 1836,' in *Mélanges de littérature*, ed. Henri Martineau (Paris: Le Divan, 1933), vol. 3; and the fuller discussion of the question of social comedy and novel of manners in PETER BROOKS, *The Novel of Worldliness* (Princeton, N.J.: Princeton Univ. Press, 1969), pp. 219–26. Stendhal's argument is already largely adumbrated in *Racine et Shakespeare* (1823; 1825).

9. Rereading the 'Bucci copy' of his novel in 1835, Stendhal noted in the margins of book 1, chapter 21 – where Mme de Rênal has been manoeuvering her husband to the conclusion that the anonymous letters come from Valenod – 'Here is a scene of comedy,' after which he goes on to lament that it cannot be put on the stage, and to explain why. See Pléiade edition, p. 1465.

10. See F.W.J. HEMMINGS's discussion of Julien as a 'dreamer' in *Stendhal. A Study of His Novels* (Oxford: Clarendon Press, 1964).

11. Julien states: 'Je ne me plaindrai plus du hasard, j'ai retrouvé un père en vous, monsieur.' And the Abbé replies: 'Il ne faut jamais dire le hasard, mon enfant, dites toujours la Providence' – 'Never say fortune, my child, always say Providence.' Substituting 'Providence' for 'fortune,' of course, indicates a belief in an overall direction to human plots – that of the Father – which the novel as a whole tends to discredit.

12. The trace of the Duc de Chaulnes in the novel presents many curiosities. The Marquis dubs Julien 'the younger brother of the Comte de Chaulnes, that is, the son of my friend the old Duc' (p. 477). Julien dispels his remorse at seducing his benefactor's daughter by recalling with anger that the Duc de Chaulnes has called him a 'domestic' (p. 509), a remark that Julien recalls again upon receiving Mathilde's declaration of love (p. 524): to be put in the role of Julien's father, even fictively, is to assume the burden of oedipal hatred. Mathilde, reflecting on the dishonour she is courting, mentions the Duc de Chaulnes as father of her official fiancé, the Marquis de Croisenois (p. 529). Yet elsewhere in the novel the Duc de Chaulnes is given as the Marquis de la Mole's father-in-law, and after Mathilde announces her pregnancy and her determination to marry Julien, the Marquis thinks of passing on his peerage to Julien, since the Duc de Chaulnes has 'several times, since his only son was killed in Spain, spoken of his desire to transmit his title to Norbert [de la Mole] . . .' (p. 637). One is tempted to conclude that the shadowy Duc de Chaulnes, representative of the Ancien Régime and of legitimate authority, is par excellence the figure of paternity in the novel,

pressed into service whenever Stendhal needs a reference to paternity. As a figure of legitimation for Julien, he is also alienating, perhaps inevitably; and he may be guilty of putting his biological son to death. And as a figure of paternal authority, he is curiously absent and trivial. The more one probes the mystery of paternity in this novel, the more it appears mysterious.

13. See VICTOR BROMBERT, *Stendhal et la voie oblique* (Paris and New Haven: Yale Univ. Press, 1954).

14. The remark occurs, I believe, in Stendhal's *Filosofia Nova*. On these questions, see also Jean Starobinski, 'Stendhal pseudonyme,' in *L'Œil vivant* (Paris: Gallimard, 1963), pp. 191–240. ROBERT ANDRÉ, *Ecriture et pulsions dans le roman stendhalien* (Paris: Klincksieck, 1977), gives a detailed account of Beyle's oedipal conflict and the forms of hatred for the father presented in the novels, especially *La Chartreuse de Parme*. See also MICHELINE LEVOWITZ-TREU, *L'Amour et la mort chez Stendhal* (Aran: Editions du Grand Chêne, 1978). The relation of Julien's search for a father to political questions is perceptively discussed by HENRI-FRANÇOIS IMBERT in *Les Métamorphoses de la liberté* (Paris: Corti, 1967).

15. 'Oui, mon père est comme tous les pères, ce que je n'avais pas su voir jusqu'ici; avec infiniment plus d'esprit et même de sentiment qu'un autre, il n'en veut pas moins me rendre heureux *à sa façon* et non à la mienne.' *Lucien Leuwen*, in *Romans et nouvelles*, vol. 1, p. 1355.

16. See JEAN PRÉVOST, *La Création chez Stendhal* (Marseilles: Editions du Sagittaire, 1942); and the remarkable essay – touching on a number of the questions that interest me here – by GÉRARD GENETTE, ' "Stendhal" ' in *Figures II* (Paris: Editions du Seuil, 1969), pp. 155–93.

17. GUSTAVE FLAUBERT, *L'Education sentimentale*, in *Œuvres* (Paris: Bibliothèque de la Pléiade, 1952), vol. 2, p. 352.

18. See GEORG LUKÁCS, *The Theory of the Novel*, trans. Anna Bostock (Cambridge: MIT Press, 1971), pp. 124–5. On the nature of Stendhalian temporality, see also GENETTE, ' "Stendhal" ' and GEORGES POULET, *Mesure de l'instant* (Paris: Plon, 1968).

19. RENÉ GIRARD, *Mensonge romantique et vérité romanesque* (Paris: Grasset, 1961).

20. Some examples of the use of 'monster' in the novel: when Julien enters his post at the Hôtel de la Mole, the Abbé Pirard notes the magnitude of what the Marquis is doing for him, and says, 'Si vous n'êtes pas un monstre, vous aurez pour lui et sa famille une éternelle reconnaissance' ('If you are not a monster, you will be eternally grateful to him and his family') (p. 443); when Julien reflects on the calumny his name will receive if he is killed while climbing to Mathilde's bedroom, he says to himself, 'Je serai un monstre dans la posterité' ('I will be a monster for posterity') (p. 537); when the Marquis berates him for seducing Mathilde – and Julien has just cited, in his defence, the words of Tartuffe: 'je ne suis pas un ange . . .' ('I'm no angel') – he calls him 'Monstre!' (p. 629); when the Abbé Chélan comes to visit Julien in his prison cell, the Abbé addresses him: 'Ah! grand Dieu! est-il possible, mon enfant . . . Monstre! devrais-je dire' ('Ah! Lord, is it possible, my child . . . Monster, I should say') (p. 1651). Note also this remark of Stendhal's about his relations with his own father: 'J'observai avec remords que je n'avais pas pour lui une *goutte* de tendresse ni d'affection. Je suis donc un monstre me disais-je, et pendant de longues années je n'ai pas trouvé de réponse à cette objection' ('I observed with remorse that I hadn't a *drop* of tenderness or affection for him. I am thus a

monster, I said to myself, and for many years I found no answer to this objection'), *Vie de Henry Brulard*, in *Œuvres intimes*, pp. 217–18.

21. On the resistance to ending in Stendhal, see the excellent study by D.A. MILLER in *Narrative and Its Discontents* (Princeton, N.J.: Princeton Univ. Press, 1981), pp. 195–264.

22. Using the terms of the Russian Formalists, one could say that the *fabula* (the order of event referred to by the narrative) intrudes into the *sjužet* (the order of event in its presentation by the narrative discourse). But to do so would mean reducing the *fabula* to the bare-bones anecdote from which Stendhal worked, whereas the *fabula* is properly understood as the whole of the story to which the narrative discourse refers, the order of events that a reading of the narrative enables one to construct, an order that, of course, has no existence beyond this construction. What invades the narrative discourse of *Le Rouge et le Noir* is distinctly heterogeneous, another order of discourse, another genre, another story. The account of Antoine Berthet's trial in *La Gazette des Tribunaux* is reprinted in the Pléiade edition, pp. 715–30.

23. Some earlier critics of *Le Rouge et le Noir* – Léon Blum, Henri Rambaud, Maurice Bardèche – noted that Stendhal seems to insist upon returning to his documentary scenario at the end: see the summary of their comments in CASTEX. *'Le Rouge et le Noir' de Stendhal*, pp. 126–7. Here again, I find the more 'traditional' critics closer to the mark: they have noted real problems, though their treatment of them does not fall within the analysis of narrative that interests me here.

24. On the metalepsis of the author, see the discussion by GENETTE (himself referring to Fontanier) in 'Discours du récit', p. 244.

25. Possessing the mother/mistress, Julien may realize a final desired confusion of origins, enacting the oedipal story according to Claude Lévi-Strauss as well as Freud. He has answered the problem of origin by its confusion, 'sowing where he was sown': note that not only does Julien want Mme de Rênal to be mother to his unborn child, Mme de Rênal herself earlier expresses the wish that Julien were father to her children – children who curiously are sometimes three in number, and sometimes two, further confusing the question of generation and perhaps thereby further confirming LÉVI-STRAUSS's view that the Oedipus myth tells the story of an insoluble problem: see 'The Structural Study of Myth', in *Structural Anthropology* (Garden City, N.Y.: Anchor-Doubleday, 1967), pp. 202–28. As with the postulated paternity of the Duc de Chaulnes, we are here faced with a significant confusion. See also LEO BERSANI's remark: 'almost the entire story is an immense detour which Julien takes in order to return, in prison, and this time consciously and with full consent, to the happiness of merely being with Mme de Rênal which he had thought himself ready to sacrifice to his ambition.' *A Future for Astynax* (Boston: Little, Brown, 1976), pp. 111–12.

Feminism and Gender Criticism

In *The Second Sex* (1949) Simone de Beauvoir praised Stendhal for taking the view that women 'are not angels, nor demons, nor sphinxes: merely human beings reduced to semislavery by the imbecile ways of society'.[1] Commenting on his treatment of Mme de Rênal and Mathilde, of Clélia and Gina (as well as of Mme de Chasteller and Mme de Hocquincourt in *Lucien Leuwen*, and Mina de Vanghel in the short narrative which bears her name), she argues that 'it is the ardent quest for valid reasons for living, the search through the darkness of ignorance, of prejudices, of frauds, in the shifting and feverish light of passion, it is the infinite risk of happiness or death, of grandeur or shame, that gives glory to these women's lives' (p. 153). For de Beauvoir Stendhal's attitude 'presupposes that woman is not pure alterity: she is subject in her own right', and thus 'Stendhal never limits himself to describing his heroines as functions of his heroes: he gives them a destiny of their own' (p. 155).

De Beauvoir's approach is characteristic of earlier feminist writing in its emphasis on women's emancipation, and the Existentialist focus on human freedom and on the moral imperative of what might be called an 'authentic becoming' allows her to reconcile Stendhal's Romanticism and his feminism:

> Stendhal demands woman's emancipation not only in the name of liberty in general but also in the name of individual happiness. Love, he believes, will have nothing to lose; on the contrary, it will be the more true as woman, being man's equal, is able to understand him the more completely. No doubt certain qualities admired in women will disappear; but their worth comes from the freedom they express. This will be manifested under other forms, and the romantic will not vanish from the world. Two separate beings, in different circumstances, face to face in freedom and seeking justification of their existence through one another, will always live an adventure full of risk and promise. Stendhal puts his trust in truth. [. . .] Woman according to him is simply a human being: nor could any shape of dreams be more enrapturing. (pp. 155–6)

Such comments today seem remarkably phallocentric (and even ironic, given our current knowledge of de Beauvoir's own relationship with Sartre): for doubtless not all women believe that their destiny is to be fulfilled by understanding men better. And indeed the naivety of de Beauvoir's enthusiasm for Stendhal's feminism has been duly demonstrated by Julia Kristeva.[2] Far from Stendhal's heroines (or the women he describes in his personal writings) being partners whose 'alterity' (or otherness) promotes the heroes' own personal fulfilment, they are secular goddesses: their otherness is a projection of male desires for the maternal, for sexual passion, for death. Note, she says, how the women favoured by this atheist with left-wing sympathies all tend to be either Catholic, or aristocratic ladies enamoured with medieval values, or simply 'irrational Italians' (p. 363). In Kristeva's view, 'feminine' is no more than a metaphorical description of these projected male desires, and Stendhal has 'fetishized' female otherness and turned it into a secular idol. She concludes:

> If there is a Stendhalian feminism, it consists precisely in the worship that suggests that feminism is perhaps our last religion, that of the woman with authority. The primordial mother, absolute mistress, is not dead: she urges us on to love, to death . . . (p. 364)

Among the comparatively few examples of feminist or gender-based readings of individual Stendhalian texts, one of the most interesting has been Naomi Schor's account of Stendhal's last, unfinished novel *Lamiel*.[3] Being, in its first version, the story of an independent-minded orphan girl who determines to find out about the world, this text would seem to enhance Stendhal's feminist credentials; but, as Schor then argues, the radical-feminist thrust of the work is 'unwritten' by Stendhal's subsequent, substantial rewriting of the novel (and later by the novel's critical reception). The 'unleashed forces of female energy' in the original story-line are 'recontained', as the female autodidact is transformed into the 'brilliant pupil of a single [male] professor of cynicism: Sansfin' (p. 143).

In her book on fictional genders,[4] Dorothy Kelly shows how a number of French nineteenth-century texts illustrate and endeavour to eliminate the 'undecidability of gender' (p. 2), that is, the impossibility of distinguishing other than biologically between the sexes. Characters like Balzac's Eugénie Grandet and Cousine Bette or Stendhal's Julien Sorel and Fabrice Del Dongo, who are described in the text as sharing certain characteristics with the opposite sex and thus threaten conventional gender classification, ultimately either die or conform to gender type. For Kelly the 'poetics of gender' in *The Red and the Black* is such that 'Julien represents the woman's place, and his decapitation figures that of women in society' (p. 41). His attempt to escape his class is directly comparable with – and just as doomed as – the attempts of nineteenth-century women to escape their gender roles.

The Red and the Black *and* The Charterhouse of Parma

The most sustained account of a Stendhalian novel from the perspective of gender is that (not mentioned by Kelly) of Carol A. Mossman in *The Narrative Matrix. Stendhal's 'Le Rouge et le Noir'* (Lexington, Ky.: French Forum, 1984), from which the following extracts are taken. In adopting this perspective Mossman combines the psychoanalytic and narratological approaches exemplified above by Barthes and Brooks; on the one hand, she follows Barthes beyond the Oedipal to consideration of the maternal, while, on the other, she imitates Brooks in focusing not on the psyche of the author but on the plot dynamics of his text. Appropriately, in that Barthes talks about 'the Mother' and Brooks about 'Fathers and Sons', their two approaches are combined in Mossman's quest for 'the unborn child' and in her consequent analysis of the 'trauma of birth' as it is figured in the imagery and plot of *The Red and the Black*.

Mossman finds it 'odd that the importance of pregnancy in the work of Stendhal has gone virtually unrecognized' (p. 19), particularly as Henri Beyle's mother died in childbirth. Contending that 'the plotting out of fictions can repair some of the damages done along life's way' (p. 19), she notes that 'the figure of pregnancy manifests itself in various forms in Stendhal's literary masterpieces. [*The Red and the Black*] shuts down on an infant *in utero*, and *Lucien Leuwen* stages a simulated pregnancy. In his last work of fiction, [*The Charterhouse of Parma*], Stendhal does finally manage to deliver, even though little Sandrino's earthly career is cut short soon thereafter' (p. 20). What follows, therefore, is an account of a 'narrative matrix'.

Notes

1. DE BEAUVOIR's comments on Stendhal are reproduced in translation in *Stendhal. A Collection of Critical Essays*, ed. Victor Brombert (Englewood Cliffs, N.J.: Prentice-Hall (Twentieth-Century Views series), 1962), pp. 147–56 (p. 148).

2. 'Stendhal and the Politics of the Gaze: An Egotist's Love', in JULIA KRISTEVA, *Tales of Love* (first published as *Histoires d'amour* (Paris: Denoel, 1983)), trans. Leon S. Roudiez (New York: Columbia University Press, 1987), pp. 341–64.

3. In her *Breaking The Chain. Women, Theory and French Realist Fiction* (New York: Columbia University Press, 1985), pp. 135–46.

4. *Fictional Genders. Role and Representation in Nineteenth-Century French Narrative* (Lincoln and London: University of Nebraska Press, 1989). See especially 'Stendhal's Gender Classes', pp. 23–42.

10 Carol Mossman on *The Red and the Black*

Stendhalian codes: birth in *Le Rouge et le Noir*

1. Cyclical time versus linear time: the narrative pulse

How to apprehend (in a double sense) change is a question we have always put to ourselves. To arrest, thereby to apprise, movement so as to order it into meaningful sequence is as much a cosmogonical business as it is the pursuit of narrative. The limitless combinatory of possibilities set aside, the ways of organizing time ultimately reduce to two: the way of history and the way of myth. Although these correspond roughly to Eliade's distinction between sacred and profane temporality, Kermode's division of time is more pertinent here for its narratological orientation. Against 'chronos,' or passing time awaiting fulfilment already postulated in an apocalypse, he pits 'kairos,' a seasonal time whose every present moment is 'charged with a meaning derived from its end.' If the prospect of an anchorless, cyclical repetition proves too daunting because apparently devoid of structure, one may look instead to a linear, historical mode of explanation which guarantees firm beginnings and definitive ends.

Historicizing time by instilling it with a chronology means postulating a beginning and an end: not to do so would leave a borderless and imponderable between. History, in fact, is precisely the middle, just as narrative is, since beyond beginnings and endings nothing lies to be recounted. The womb and the tomb define the limits of the narratable.

This kinship of history and the plotting of fiction has long been recognized. Indeed, it is scarcely a coincidence that Aristotle was the single sire of the notion of a Prime Mover and the founding treatise on narrative. From out of the chaotic Heraclitean strife of the elements, Aristotle extruded a linear explanation. Now, the Freudian exertions moved in the same direction. What else can the father of psychoanalysis be said to be doing, if not creating plots out of the embarrassing *medias res* of repetition and screen memory he must confront with each new case 'history'? In what other act is he indulging, if not the creation of an intelligible account which resides on a primal event of some sort? The Primal Father of *Totem and*

Taboo reflects a similar penchant for 'narrativizing,' a reaching out, cost what it may, for a beginning.

And yet, as was pointed out earlier, the Patriarch so resolutely set forth in the 1912 work appears considerably more reticent in *Moses and Monotheism*, in which the matriarchy lingers, seductive, in the wings of the argument. By the same token, the primal scenes and deeds whose reverberations were seen to comprise the organism's psychic constitution early on in the Freudian itinerary, had subsequently blurred, first, into fictions wrought in the imaginings of neurosis, and finally into phylogenetic memories, traces of the individual's attachment to species. Not only is event no longer perceived as founding, but it is also no longer unequivocally 'event.'

With much the same assertiveness of Freud's 'official' account of beginnings, certain Biblical versions of origins have crowded others into the margins of orthodoxy. Beyond the Ur-narrative of the Occident, the Bible, so full of its own beginnings and endings (what with the din of the prophets trumpeting the end with the self-same word that authenticates their predecessors) – beyond this account with its *ex nihilo* origins in Eden, we catch glimpses in the Rabbinical apocrypha of 'the other woman,' Lilith. Her ghostly presence, like Freud's matriarchy, is posed there as if to suggest the other way of figuring time – and figuring it out – (by now one cannot help but associate the other solution with the maternal): in terms of meaningful periodicity.

So it begins to appear as though narratives which overtly stage linear and paternal progression may also contain, albeit less visibly, intimations of an alternate cosmogony. This is certainly true of *Le Rouge et le Noir*. Classically, it is the image of the Phoenix which resumes this mythical perspective on the temporal. Consistent with this view of time, the Firebird may be depicted at rest, since this is not its permanent posture, whereas in the linear, historical *Weltanschauung* death (repose) is precisely that which must not be recounted: indeed, its representation suffices to collapse the entire structure. Not only does quiescence invoke the narrative telos, but in the linear vision it also demands to be depicted as a qualitative leap which, as a euphemizing factor, springs it outside the domain of what can be told. It is partly for this reason that the post-mortem description of Emma Bovary's body scandalizes. Flaubert has refused transcendence.

It would, thus, seem that novelistic convention has almost religiously exempted authors of mortuary description, as if the soul of the narrative quits the body of the text on its hero's death. Tradition has sanctioned death in linear narrative as a leap, a supersession of the constraints of its own system: we have only to look at the iconic dead body of Roland being assumed into the celestial spheres.

As for emblems of 'kairos,' Monique Schneider has dealt in some detail with the image of the phoenix:

(. . .) this sojourn among the ruins proved lethal since it was necessary, once brought back out of them, for the phoenix to return to life; but its previous presence allows this event to be seen against the background of a dim and distant past, which dispenses the Archaeopteryx from the need to 'found' the story [of the phoenix]. This is why, supported as it is by this 'humus' of the past, it can be depicted in a state of repose.[1]

But to all appearances the resolutely serial movement in *Le Rouge et le Noir* dims any prospect of such repose. Rarely is the novel's dynamics jeopardized by stasis: however, when action *does* come to a halt, it is inevitable that it occurs over a pregnant evocation of space.

The blade, castration and sons: what trio could be more irrevocably stuck together, sealed, and layered over by decades of Freudianism and its offshoots? Up to now in the present reading of *Le Rouge et le Noir*, the figure of the blade has been outlined as an arm of castration. In corresponding narrative terms, the sharpened edge has claimed responsibility for the on-prodding of plot. In like manner an equivalence has been set up between narrative movement, on the one hand, and fathers versus sons, on the other.

Suppose now that this same blade is a double-edged signifier and that the severance imputed to it refers, in fact, to another psychoconstruct: for it would seem, what with surgeons and sanguineous spaces, that this blade is implicated in a castration, true, but in its primal instance, that is, in an act of parturition.

This does not mean that the Oedipality of Julien's novel dims into a shadow of its former self (like Freud's Primal Father) or that the foregoing analysis might have been dispensed with. There is no question of eliminating: it is here, rather, a matter of complementing. Instead of assigning to the signifier a univocal function in the text, I merely propose that the arc of the blade's downward fall be allowed to speak its plenitude. And it is consistent with this analysis, which deals after all with overlapping texts, to consider that the matrix of the novel resides in an inherent ambivalence.

Our initial reading of *Le Rouge et le Noir* was attentive to the Oedipal drama and, thus, to a model continuously projected, re-staged, mirrored and displaced, repeated with no hope of ceasing, reiterated in the name of the father and of the son and of the surgeon ghost, world without apparent end and strife with no ending – unless it be an arbitrary one.

To such a parade of surrogation, there can be no decisive conclusion, since metonymy and repetition resist containment. It is with a pace ever quickening by the intuition that to remain immobile is to fall victim to the blade, that father and son alike are forcibly subsumed under the aegis of the temporal, of 'chronos.' The legacy of the father/son succession in *Le Rouge et le Noir* is, precisely, the advance of time and its agent, plot. To plot against Time is to contest its outgrowth, the patriarchal system. But this sort of subversion works as well against the text itself: since the narrative traces the blood lines of patriarchy, a halt in its movement represents nothing else than a plot against the plot.

Who, then, shall fall heir to the novel, if not Father Time and his consubstantial delegates, the father and the son? Does there not exist an antidote to unstructured slippage? To put the question another way, how, amid the repetition, can meaning be arrived at? In this second part of what has turned out to be a diptych, I will attempt to show that the novel's issue reverts to the genetrix, who all along has been presiding over the son-rising and paternal shifting. This is the figure which organizes the novel's flux, lending it the coherence of meaningful periodicity and recuperating its metonymy through totalization. While to a certain degree it is true that the Mother is introjected into the narrative, on the whole she remains aloof in a subtending stance, dominating through a resistance to being incorporated and finally through her incorporation of the hero/son.

Now, although Julien's novel certainly sketches the conquest of legitimacy through the assumption of a Paternal Name, it has already been demonstrated that his novel does not represent the text project, which, as will be seen, revolves around a seeking out of the Mother. Inasmuch as Julien's manifest search for authority is an embedded text and not one which is brought to signify *through* ending, the patrilinear circuit must, in this context of frames, be considered as metonymic.

Any association of gender with tropes points to Lacan, whose celebrated correspondences are directly opposed to the ones which will be made here. But putting aside the Lacanian fixed and categoric gender assignation (metaphor = Dead Father), it seems that, if change and movement (metonymy) can be discerned solely with respect to a reference point (metaphor), then the rhetorical figures which are made to correspond to the two genders must vary according to which gender is perceived as totalizing. And the one which is all-subsuming in *Le Rouge et le Noir* remains to be established through demonstration.

Earlier, we witnessed Freud brushing aside the genetrix. Jacques Lacan has since institutionalized this tendency. Accordingly, the function of signifying totalization has fallen to the father. This father, proprietor of the Symbolic, oversees chronology, language, desire and, presumably, narrative. Yet there is about this figurehead who is the apotheosis of paternalism something so encompassing that one begins to suspect the feminine element of being itself encompassed and reinstated behind the veil.

With Lacan, Freud's covert veiling has become explicit. The Freudian 'progress of civilization' can be matched up with the Symbolic, while the retreating matriarchy corresponds, in an anthropological sense, to the Imaginary.[2] And, among other things, what characterizes this Imaginary is the (emergent) subject's inability to differentiate between interior and exterior, itself and other, and an anguish at the perception of absence and disunion: it is, in short, an irreducibly spatial experiencing of the world. If Lacan has proceeded then to hypervalorize the Symbolic and the Dead Father, as Jameson suggests in *The Prison-House of Language*, the dominance of these latter is not necessarily borne out in literature. *Le Rouge et le Noir* is a case in point.

This analysis began by asserting that space constitutes a sort of primal stuff out of which *Le Rouge* comes to be fashioned. However, following the description of Verrières's topography, those claims of spatial primordiality were left unexplored and were abandoned for a discussion of the issues of succession, both narrative and paternal. And, if the subject was broached only to be stilled – if it has remained in suspension – it is because the father and son impose themselves more forcefully on the reader's attention. Spaces, in fact, surface only occasionally, but when they do they merit careful attention. It is this rarification which signals repression, and it is out of this very absence, or abdication, that a narrative has been generated. Of key importance is the fact that the figure of the mother and her spaces are conspicuously missing from the novel's original domestic situation, so that ulterior insistence of these spaces can be construed as reparation through a *mise en texte* ['textual installation']. Let us now proceed to a reading of Stendhal's novel which is, in addition, a re-reading of my preliminary treatment of it. This shift in perspective is really more of a pivot, because I shall remain attentive to sequences already discussed, notably those dealing with the notion of severance. [. . .]

Leaving the Virago's role in *Le Rouge et le Noir* in suspense, let us return to the church scenes[3] and examine the tableaux in the light of Rank's hypothesis.[4] The most telltale similarity among the four is the characterization of the space itself. In each episode the interior of the church is red-hued, and invariably the windows are covered over with crimson curtains; one entrance always remains exposed. A space, then, which can only be said to be uterine in its coloration, in the textual pliancy lent it by drapes and, as well, in the sheer sensuality it evokes, often experienced synesthetically by Julien as an orgy of color, texture and fragrance.

Always somber, quiet and tranquil, the church is usually old ('antique' and 'gothique'). Its age would seem to point to a sort of subterranean past with which it has come to be associated. Typifying the interiors of the two more elaborate cases of Bray-le-Haut and Besançon are feelings of coolness and moistness. Waters and the impression of flowing liquid predominate in the two initial scenes. In Julien's delusional view of the baptismal waters transformed into blood and his accompanying 'terreur secrète' in Verrières, it is difficult not to see an anxiety directly related to birth. The fact that the waters are baptismal links his dread less to the actual place of repose than to the egress from it. (In more metaphorical terms, and since Julien and his plot are identified through a mutual fate of decapitation, the narrative might be said to be undergoing a certain baptism as well, for it also is barely emergent.)

During the adoration of the relic at Bray-le-Haut, once again Julien sees blood flow where none exists. Thus, in both these episodes the reader notes a special emphasis not so much on blood as on the imaginary impression of blood, underlining the subjectivity and hallucinatory quality of Julien's perceptions. Such delusions should be a signal to us that far more is at stake than a hero's social ascent. The *ex nihilo* conjuring up of blood is a certain gauge that the 'realism' of this novel is more than anything else a psychic realism.

Within these churches themselves the ambiance is conducive to reverie during which all chronology becomes obliterated. Time is precisely what inhibits indulgence in those 'imaginary spaces.' And in these spaces where plot is refused advancement one finds oneself in the presence, however fleeting, of a structure which, when bound with others like it, will totalize (and, to a point, *neutralize*) the story of fathers and sons. These church spaces are premonitions of the final metaphor.

Now, as just indicated, presiding over the incident of the oracle is a feeling of terror and anxiety. By comparison, the Bray-le-Haut episode reflects a calmness and sense of repose; it is not completely stripped of anxiety, however, as denoted by the associational tear drop which falls on Julien's hand. And it is worth observing that this entire incident is preceded – indeed, heralded – by a fall from a horse.

The scope of affects elicited by Julien's presence in these churches is broad, ranging from terror to ecstasy: this corresponds to the very ambivalence whose existence with respect to birth Rank had indicated and to which he attributed the binary expression of mother figures so prevalent in literature. Passages do play a predominant role in these simulated delivery sequences. It is as Julien is making his way out of the Verrières church – in fact, at its very portals presided over by ritual holy water – that he experiences his secret terror. At Bray-le-Haut sinuous passages and stairways ever upward-leading must be followed in order to reach the chapel, entrance to which requires passage through 'an extremely small doorway.' (Are we glimpsing the constricting Sphinx?) But, if corridors seem danger-laden, then thresholds are still more problematic. In the Besançon episode Julien must first scramble up ladders, whence he proceeds towards the tabernacle by effecting a hazardous crossing over.

Maternal spaces, then, are spaces of repose, reverie and liberation from movement. The difficulty with which the uterine site is attained is signaled by a proliferation of chambers, each one smaller than the last, each encased within the previous one. The church itself, although uterine in character, is an exterior chamber which harbors an inner sanctum which is always located in the loftiest reaches of the church space.

In Bray-le-Haut the path upward begins in the church body itself, gravitating towards a small chapel ('very small, but very high up') in which the relic is housed. The relic itself consists of bones, and these are in turn buried within the waxen figure of St. Clement. The steady probing towards spaces of decreasing size is echoed in Besançon. Once within the edifice, Julien makes his way upward towards the canopy. Continuing this persistent focalizing trajectory, he reaches the place above the tabernacle wherein, as has already been pointed out, is en-t-wombed another son.[5]

The *mise en abyme* of these successive penetralia follows a pyramidal movement: tendency is always towards height and geometric reduction. Proust was the first to notice Stendhal's penchant for altitudes, and since then hardly a critic has failed to make at least passing mention of his acrophilia. However, it would appear that this figure, which prevails throughout Stendhal's prose works, has rarely been linked to the notion of a return to the womb, and, when it has (as Chaitin did literally and Brombert metaphorically), it has been with respect to *La Chartreuse de Parme* and its celebrated prison.[6] The red chambers and inner sanctuaries which punctuate *Le Rouge et le Noir* and, more important, the efforts to reach them and the pain incurred on their egress seem to have attracted scant critical attention. Wondering at just this sort of lacuna, Hemmings asked: 'Has it ever been observed how, on three crucial occasions, the hero finds himself *in a church hung with red draperies* of one sort or another?'[7] However, his astonishment was easily put to rest through his own answer to the query: 'Both these occasions are no doubt meant to recall the experience Julien had when he was on his way, for the first time, to the Rênals' house.' Geneviève Mouillaud was the first to analyse the series of tableaux as a system which she finally relates to the bedroom of Henri Beyle's mother, whom it is common knowledge that he lost at the age of seven. (But let me comment in passing that it seems more likely that this bedchamber constitutes a screen memory which, thus, would refer to another event or place.)

If what goes up is experienced euphorically, should it follow that what comes down functions contrarily? Within the logic of Stendhal's spatio-affective structurations, such indeed proves to be the case. Uterine spaces being loftily perched, the movement towards them must be one of ascent. It should come as no surprise, then, when we suggest that a downward-falling motion describes the descent of a delivery with all the attendant pain. As it turns out, the figure of falling is one often seen in this author's work, and it is accompanied by the anticipated emotions.

Two of the church scenes entail falls, although the first one does so only peripherally. It is M. Moirod's fall from his horse which does, after all, inaugurate the Bray-le-Haut episode. It emphasizes that, for the time being at least and by way of contrast, Julien's movement will be one of ascent which culminates, in fact, at the elevated site of a small chamber. Special care is taken to describe that very secondary character Moirod's 'horrible fear' of horses. Again, the term 'horrible' is inscribed within the same lexical register of taboo as those other terms 'monstre,' 'terreur' and 'affreuse volupté' ['awful voluptuousness']; thus, it has a less than innocent ring to it. That is, it almost certainly points to the psychic intertext which the novel occasionally allows to intrude. It is the reader's task to pick up such terms, understanding that they are members of an identical vocabulary set which is not that of the manifest text.

In the Stendhalian code, then, falling appears to designate a *mise au monde* ['bringing into the world']. Investing an apparent accident such as falling with a psychic meaning (a parapraxis) may not be unusual, as Freud pointed out in *The Psychopathology of Everyday Life*: 'Similarly, falling, stumbling and slipping need not always be interpreted as purely accidental miscarriages of motor actions. The double meanings that language attaches to these expressions are enough to indicate the kind of phantasies involved, which can be represented by such losses of bodily equilibrium.'[8]

Moreover, the code provides a specification of the concept 'descent', and that is the fall from a horse. That Stendhal has exploited this particular form of falling throughout his opus is no secret, and, as always, the choice of such a construct has scarcely been arbitrary. Aside from the sheer movement of descent evocative of birth, this sort of fall entails (1) force by another agent, (2) an unwillingness on the part of the mounted party to relinquish his seat, and finally (3) the pain produced by the fall itself. In *Le Rouge et le Noir* Moirod is toppled in the Verrières cycle, as Julien will be later in Paris.

At this juncture it is difficult to resist quoting an incident which transpires early in *La Chartreuse* and during which Fabrice is 'delivered' of his horse by his own unrecognized father, the Lieutenant Robert: '[Fabrice] felt himself seized by the feet; they were taken out of the stirrups at the same time as someone caught him underneath the arms; he was lifted over his horse's tail and then allowed to slip to the ground, where he landed sitting.'[9] A more graphic description of a delivery experienced passively can scarcely be imagined. Nevertheless, Chaitin and André have both singled out this very passage as designating the hostility between father and son: while this seems true, it does not seem strictly to the point. In anticipation of the next chapter, I would simply like to recall that Julien's novel opens with the youthful hero seated 'à cheval' ['astride'] some rafters, from which he is soon brought down by the paternal hand.

That all the spaces depicted in this novel are feminine and, more specifically, maternal is indisputable. In most cases Mme de Rênal is directly associated with them. For instance, scarcely has Julien left the scene of the oracle which occurred in the Verrières church than he walks straight into the arms of Mme de Rênal. Later the long description of the decoration of the altar can only be followed by an encounter with Mme de Rênal. Though it is unexpected by Julien, the reader can hardly have failed to anticipate it, for in this birth simulacrum she, the most salient element, was missing. And in the final incident she is conspicuously designated with a gunshot at the same ritual moment at which the son is removed from his tabernacle.

In these preliminary remarks concerning birth as it is articulated in *Le Rouge et le Noir*, we have isolated four static tableaux which all exhibit rather remarkable affinities with birth scenes, each evincing problematic affective composites of dread and desire, an intrigued reticence not dissimilar to the idea of the pleasure principle working in the service of the death drive.

As has been seen, the Oedipal conflict and the urge to return converge over identical manifestations. Whether Freud was correct in considering the figures of birth to be euphemizations of incest, or whether the reverse is true, as not only Rank, but also Eliade claim ('The *regressus ad uterum* is sometimes presented in the form of incest with the Mother'), we cannot say.[10] In either case, there is a perfect superimposition of one analyst's construct onto the other: who is on top is irrelevant. In the end, the divergences of the two can be evaluated in terms of a shift in emphasis. What the possibility of such superimposition entails in narrative terms – that is, the narratological implications of a double-edged blade in this tale with a double ending – remains to be discussed.

Birth and the dynamics of narrative

1. The blade as double-edged signifier

Let us now re-think the function of the Surgeon Major – that master chopper by profession – who haunts the text edge. For it was the Surgeon Major who, to use Julien's own expression, 'had made a man of him.' A key phrase, certainly, and from which one might conclude that, far from unmanning Julien through a castrative act, the old surgeon actually ushered the hero into life. This father who saw Julien into the world had made a man of our hero with a stroke of the sword or a surgical snip of the scissors; in a word, through a blade-fall.

No one would deny that the fall of a blade is a quintessentially divisive act. It severs mother from child and takes the babe out of the timelessness of maternal space, installing him/her in the world of change. This edge is, thus, the irreducible agent of difference (and *différance* ['deferral']): it separates mythic from historic time; in castrative terms, it divides the haves from the have-nots; and, finally, inasmuch as it initiates bio-narrative, the edge staves off – or defers – ending.

Blades are unsheathed and everywhere displayed in *Le Rouge et le Noir*. Now aimed at the father, now at the son, knife edges are always threatening to sever the unspeakable. But, if the dynamics of castration – Julien's novel – hinges on one such mortal edge, these blade surfaces also function to pivot the severance onto another scene. This will be the scene of the metaphor.

Until now, the gesture with which old Sorel nearly topples his son under the sawmill blade at the beginning of Julien's story has been considered as the novel's castration precedent, set there to be repeated ever after. If, however, the meaning of the Julianic text is brought to completion with a stroke of the guillotine, this same masculine caesura leaves certain essential aspects of the narrative in the margins of the text. For instance, what becomes of the conclusion of Mathilde's novel, all the more impossible to dismiss once it has been seen to be doubly buttressed first by Marguerite de Navarre's story and, beyond that, by Salome's? Furthermore, in what way does the blade of castration bring those church scenes, so essential to the novel, to signify?

Let us, then, recalibrate the story line by bracketing the novel of ambition and framing it within the confines of the larger plot structure. To do this, one need only realize that the signifier 'severance' acts as a transformer which mediates *Le Rouge*'s two narrative economies. It functions to modulate the incongruities between the two plots. As an example of how this sort of mediation might operate, recall the passage cited earlier from *La Chartreuse* which portrays Fabrice being robbed of his mount by his father. This passage captures the modulation between Oedipus and birth as it occurs, and gives it the most perfect utterance imaginable: '[Fabrice] felt himself seized by the feet. . . .'

We will now proceed to reassess the conception of this narrative earlier put forth as linear and historical, and often deemed such by the novel's critic/readers. In summary, it was for the following reasons that we held *Le Rouge* to be a serial narrative: the action of the novel is pursued inexorably upward and onward; the social gravitation of all characters is consistently aimed in a motion of ascent, while the story itself moves from point A to point B and ultimately to Z in a resolute vector, seldom lingering. There are neither flashbacks nor backtracking to confound chronology. In fact, the majority of elements conspire to push Julien's tale to the fore. Moreover, as has been seen, the sequentiality of his tale is determined by father figures presented serially and is further characterized by the hero's unceasing efforts to shed each of them in order to accede to the next in line. Just as Julien's novel of ambition always postulates a paternal point of destination, accordingly it closes with an act of politico-paternal chastisement.

Ultimately, however, a continuous toppling of fathers by sons must stand in breach of meaning. The metonymy of overthrow is rendered the more redundant for its resonance on the intertextual registers, and it risks becoming blurred into an unintelligible repetition. What rescues the patrifilial sound and fury from signifying nothing is also what mitigates the linearity of the novel. And it must be conceded that the assertion which held the plot progression of *Le Rouge et le Noir* to be linear is a half-truthful one, even if this is the aspect which imposes itself on the reader with the most insistence. Because, as in any good story, the plot must be endowed with periodicity. Thus, the novel's action may also be grouped into cycles, and these, to rejoin one of the great literary commonplaces, are associated with a maternal order.

While varying considerably in social scope, each of these cycles (Verrières, Besançon, Paris) offers a homology in structure with the other two. Julien arrives, with much trepidation, in a new world, is instructed, and then put to the test. Inevitably he succeeds. After having consolidated the maximum of power possible in a given sphere, he is, in a manner of speaking, spilled over, and the cycle of apprenticeship and mastery begins anew. It is as if the hero, having saturated his potential in one arena, must effect a leap outward. He thereby strays ever farther from his matrix cycle, whose structural kinship with the others still suffices to lend them coherence. Eventually, however, Julien so strains the novel's system of signifying through analogy that a collapse ensues. Everything then centripetally reverts to its point of origin. Something about Julien Sorel's triumphs is redolent of the Grecian hubris: this hero has finally ventured too far afield.

We have gradually been obliged to make way for the Mother, who, arising out of total repression, comes at last to a position of narratological and psycho-thematic prominence. Her presence makes itself felt slowly: while the paternal/filial war was declared at the novel's outset and relentlessly exposed ever after, the Mother unveils herself through cycles, an unveiling at first necessarily imperceptible, since patterns, like plot middles, become recognizable as such solely in retrospect.

In the preceding chapter we examined a series of tableaux depicting enclosures which were construed to be uterine spaces. The maternal womb, at the onset in eclipse, grows increasingly visible in *Le Rouge et le Noir* through the hero's multiple attempts at ingress and egress. If one re-reads those acts of severance earlier treated as castrative punishment, it will be discovered that everywhere reflected off the same surfaces of these blades is the drama of birth.

Taking the cue from the fact that the youngest son Julien is seated 'à cheval' [astride] the rafters of the mill, and that he is brutally forced by his father from a position of elevation into a rapid descent, we can reconstruct this scene which generates the narrative movement as a figural act of genesis. One Julien Sorel has been born and is forthwith delivered into paternal hands. (Rank's remark that it was 'the father who actually initiated the primal severance from the mother and so became the first and lasting enemy' can be pertinently applied here.) The waters flowing beneath the mill evoke the amniotic fluids already seen to be present in the womb tableaux. And, while Julien is delivered into safety through a paternal gesture, he nonetheless finds himself 'all bleeding' as a result of this incident.

As befits a new arrival, the hero's first concern is nourishment. Julien's reaction to his father's announcement that he will be in the mayor's employ is: 'But then who am I going to have my meals with?' (p. 21). During the negotiation which transfers Julien to the Rênal hearth old Sorel goes to the mayor's house to inspect his son's bedroom. Shelter and source of food thus assured, Julien remains, like a newborn, to be clothed. And clothed he is. Immediately on entry into the Rênal household, he assumes the somber vestment of a young cleric: but, more significant, Mme de Rênal soon sees to it that he is well provisioned in linen. In a very short space of text, then, the reader is witness to the hero's figural genesis and the provisioning of his most primordial needs.

A narrative has been born, spawned, like its hero, of a blade. In the first part of this reading, the inaugural action of the novel, which devolved from the menace of the blade, was construed in an Oedipal light to be a punishment for a transgression (in this case the activity of reading), much the same as in a folktale opening. The novel was seen to ensue from a punitive gesture; the course, and indeed suspense, of the narrative corresponded to the blade in suspension, while the story was simply brought to term by an ultimate blade-fall.

Now to conceive of the narrative along different lines, Julien's novel has been born with the same stroke with which he himself is ushered into the world. There exists, then, a congruence of hero/son and his narrative: they are the twin offspring of a single blade. Furthermore, prior to Julien's palingenetic instatement into each cycle, he will effect a return to Mme de Rênal. Each successive cycle will be initiated by a simulated rebirth, as if the novel as well, the farther it strayed from its strong opening, required a structural rejuvenation.

2. The Vergy idyll

His Majesty the Baby, Julien Sorel, has arrived. Now, in order for the drama between mother and son to be properly played out, it must be removed to its own stage. This is achieved when the Rênal family migrates to its mountain residence at Vergy, from which, notably, the father is most often absent.

Here, in a lofty never-never land, is the place of the idyll: in Vergy are mapped out the pristine prenatal spaces, as the name's anagram 'vierge' ['virgin'] would suggest. It is a place of nostalgia, redolent of the past, but equally premonitory of the church scenes to come. Here one is witness to the construction of a model of the intrauterine situation. However, distinguishing this site from the church scenes is its dynamic character. What Julien and Mme de Rênal undertake in conspiracy at Vergy is precisely a fabrication, a reconstruction of the womb, its passages, and the possibility of absorption therein.

Everything about Vergy bespeaks an unquestionable otherness. As a space, it is above all benevolent and protective. And the unconscious signifiers which abound here have been projected and spatialized into larger-than-life allegories of intrauterine existence. Here the lucid *Rouge* comes as close in texture as it will to the vague and oneiric *Chartreuse de Parme*.

It is as if to connect this site with the psycho-structure of the church that the ruins of an 'ancienne église gothique' [a 'former Gothic church'] have been placed in proximity. Ruins well suit a maternal locale and, inasmuch as they point to a vestigial order, they are material tokens of a lost time. Here chronology is also made to stand still in a fashion which typifies topographical depictions in *Le Rouge*: hours fly by like seconds, while happy moments elastically stretch into days. Childhood and maternity become the sole referents: 'Julien, for his part, had lived like a real child since the beginning of his stay in the country, as happy chasing after butterflies as his young charges were' (p. 54). In this very special pursuit Julien becomes equated with the other children, whose constant and conspicuous cavorting only adds to the childish nature of this fantasy and the accompanying 'happiness' and 'ecstasy' of the entire psychic romp amid fields maternal.

It almost goes without saying that Vergy is situated high atop a mountain peak, one of the first indicators that one is confronting a birth construct. Moreover, the sanctum motif naturally makes its appearance here, for cradled in these elevated peaks is the Rênal castle surrounded by walls and four towers. This 'enceinte' ['fortified enclosure'; also 'pregnant'] is, of course, quite pregnable by Julien, and here he resides in uttermost tranquillity.

The reader who is attuned to the extremely marginal quality of this fantasy within the context of the rest of the novel will realize that no single element in so bounteous and overdetermined a garden can be arbitrary. Casting a protective shade over the entire episode are quantities of trees. But these are no ordinary trees: they are apple and chestnut, or again – and more interesting – walnut trees which tower fully eighty feet above the ground. Fruit-bearing vegetation offers a natural emblem of provident maternity. In fact, the telluric tree, like the tabernacle, is an ideal composite of several preferred motifs of the Stendhalian imagination. (And, in connection with this, one thinks of Fabrice's consubstantial attachment to 'his' tree.) Firmly rooted in mother earth, these plants also attain those cherished heights and produce offspring eminently recognizable as such.

At Vergy a whole botanical hierarchy is set forth: the favored trees are, of course, those whose fruit is enveloped in a protective covering. Thus, oranges, acorns and walnuts, presenting as they do the embryonic model, compose the forests of this Edenic passage.

No sooner does the Rênal brood arrive at Vergy than Julien and Mme de Rênal begin some work which takes the form of 'improvements' to 'a little sandy path which would wind through the orchard and under the great walnut trees, allowing the children to go for walks in the early morning (. . .) This idea was carried out less than twenty-four hours after being *conceived*' (my emphasis). Much care is taken to exclude M. de Rênal from this activity, strictly the endeavor of the mother and her son. The father neither knows of it nor funds it, and his cooperation is adamantly denied. A soft passage ('sandy') has been reopened and its entrance renegotiated. It is surely no coincidence that the possession of Mme de Rênal occurs here and that it is subsequent to the construction of this charming pathway.

What is a fitting topic of conversation when one is in residence in the country? The birds and the bees, perhaps, but at Vergy the conversation turns to the subject of butterflies. Julien instructs his willing pupil, Mme de Rênal, as to 'the peculiar habits of these poor creatures'. Together they learn about butterflies, among whose 'peculiar habits,' it might be added, is the spinning of protective cocoons wherein the offspring reside for the duration of gestation. Emphasis here lies on the fact that it is a uterine situation under construction. Later M. de Rênal will inadvertently contribute to this construct by affirming that women are good only for 'catching butterflies.'

Given expression at Vergy is *Le Rouge et le Noir's* most complete and benevolent expression of the birth fantasy. The requisite components of altitude, space and consequent distortion of time are all assembled, along with a Gothic church contiguously evoked and which suffices to trigger an association with those other church/birth tableaux. Emphasis here, however, is on the past and making reparations: once again, the text is pointing to itself as process and a working through, this time via the double figure of a worm spinning and the rebuilding of a path. *Le Rouge et le Noir* can frequently be caught in the act of spinning out miniatures of its own destiny: castration/beheadings and returns are everywhere being re- and pre-enacted.

At Vergy the reader is able to witness an unfettered indulgence in a fantasy of birth, envisioned in all its most pleasurable and heavily overdetermined circumstances. Conjoined as part of a single matrix (Rank and Eliade are borne out here) are the Oedipal possession of the mother and the retrieval of her sanctum. And it will become evident that, wherever it is possible to read the story of Oedipus, the narrative of birth is co-present. These are the zones of the narrative where one may best capture the superimposing of Julien's and Mathilde's novels.

The single most significant aspect of the Vergy birth fantasy as it is distinguished from the others is its absence of blood. It remains dissociated from crime, from pain and from anxiety as well as from their signifier, the color red. Nothing in this uterine depiction menaces, portends or threatens. As an idealization and projection, it is the one and only presentation in *Le Rouge et le Noir* of a maternity solely benevolent, of a mother unconditionally good. As the reader of the novel is aware, there is another feminine figure on whom the negative affects are focused.

Space, when it is evoked, can consistently be associated with the maternal. Since the novel begins with the monolithic 'mons Verrières' and ends with the assumption of Julien's head into a most special space, there is a sense in which the maternal presides over the paternal: the less apparent remains stronger than the only-too-visible. And indeed we may properly speak of a partial repression in the text with regard to the Mother and Space: the return of the repressed converges over a return to the womb, which, in less archetypal terms, takes the form of a restitution of the missing organ.

The Verrières cycle is sprinkled with birth sequences and tableaux. Hinted at everywhere is castration's 'other': a return to maternal origins. However, as the novel progresses along the pathways of patriarchy, uterine references diminish measurably. By the time Paris has been reached, they have been nearly rarified out of existence.

Notes

1. MONIQUE SCHNEIDER, ' "Mon père est dans les douleurs" ', *Etudes Freudiennes*, 15/16 (April 1979), 7–38 (p. 27).

2. Now, although Lacan's gender associations are perhaps too categoric, his divisions of Symbolic and Imaginary could be usefully applied to *Le Rouge et le Noir*. Julien Sorel's conflict with paternal authority translated onto the linguistic plane and his visibly alienated desire for Mathilde both betoken the Symbolic register (as, indeed, must be the case of any story of apprenticeship). And the linking of the maternal Mme de Rênal with space, and the denial of the linguistic element in her regard, suggest that one is in the presence of the Imaginary.

3. *Editor's note*: The four 'church scenes' may be found in *The Red and the Black*, pp. 27, 107–15, 200–5, and 468.

4. *Editor's note:* 'In 1924, in *The Trauma of Birth*, OTTO RANK elaborated a theory which, while outwardly recognizing the Freudian achievement of the Oedipal construct, in reality subverted the latter by relegating it to the status of the less-than-primal. By displacing the source of anxiety at one remove from the Oedipal event onto birth and positing an alternative to Freud's originary model, Rank brought to light various structures touching on the thematics of origins' (MOSSMAN, *The Narrative Matrix*, p. 121).

5. The prisons of *La Chartreuse de Parme* have the same function, although they

offer a less than perfect model because they do not inherently designate a filial place of residence.

6. GILBERT CHATIN, *The Unhappy Few: A Psychological Study of the Novels of Stendhal* (Bloomington: Indiana University Press, 1972) and VICTOR BROMBERT, *Stendhal: Fiction and the Themes of Freedom.*

7. F.W.J. HEMMINGS, *Stendhal: A Study of his Novels* (London: Oxford University Press, 1964), p. 124.

8. FREUD, *The Psychopathology of Everyday Life* ,VI, pp. 174–5.

9. [*The Charterhouse of Parma*, p. 51.]

10. Mircea Eliade, *Initiation, rites, sociétes secrètes* (Paris: Gallimard, 1959), p. 127.

Readers and Representation

The last two extracts in this volume illustrate two further areas of interest which have preoccupied literary criticism in recent years: the role of the reader, and the problematic nature of fictional representation.

The first of these is Ann Jefferson's discussion of *The Red and the Black* and 'the uses of reading', first published in *French Studies* in April 1983 (the version reproduced here) and subsequently incorporated in a slightly modified form in her *Reading Realism in Stendhal* (Cambridge: Cambridge University Press, 1988). In this book Jefferson draws on various aspects of the work of Roland Barthes and on Mikhail Bakhtin's notion of the text as 'dialogic polyphony', and she proposes a fresh approach to realism which focuses less on the relationship between text and world and concentrates more on that between text and reader. In her view 'Stendhal sees [. . .] representation as being determined more by the mental habits and the cultural expectations of the audience for whom it is constructed than by fidelity to the original events which it supposedly portrays' (p. 11). Stendhal's novels, she argues, are not simple mirror-like reflections of the external world but works which highlight the problems of imitation (such as banal conformity to pre-existing models) and which question 'what interests, particularly social and cultural interests, the reading of novels might be reinforcing' (p. 21). For Stendhal the role of the authentic novel must be not only to frustrate platitude and preconception but to prevent itself in turn from becoming yet another model for the conformist reader to live up to. Stendhal's greatest accolade would be to remain 'inimitable'.

Accordingly, in Jefferson's view, Stendhal's novels display 'the discontinuous juxtaposition of a whole variety of different voices and discourses' (p. 100), each of which relativizes the other so that 'in the discursive hierarchy of the narration there is no single level that can be relied upon as a source of truth' (p. 98). This Bakhtinian 'polyphony' in which the voice of received opinion (the '**doxa**') is heard in 'dialogue' with alternative voices, thus also reflects what Barthes calls 'bathmology': 'i.e. the play of the various degrees of involvement or distance from one's own language and utterances' (p. 99). The Stendhalian novel is 'like a kind of salon where, under the régime of the ironic, all languages are treated as enemy languages and stripped of their seriousness in this process of non-purposive quotation' (pp. 107–8). Jefferson's 1983 article is inserted at this point as the third of three short chapters on *The Red and the Black*.

The notion of 'performative' reading on which the article ends is developed later in *Reading Realism in Stendhal* in relation to *The Charterhouse of Parma*. Here Jefferson explores the idea of an 'operatic' text in which 'the truth of an aesthetic representation is guaranteed precisely by this diversity [of the reader's "performative" response], a stark contrast to the *vraisemblable*, where repetition and conformity constitute the guiding principle of what passes for representation' (p. 225). And, in a reworking of the traditional Stendhalian antimony (Jean-Pierre Richard's 'knowledge and tenderness'), she concludes by arguing that Stendhal's novels impose on us 'the impossible task of reading with both sublime responsiveness and ironic discrimination', (p. 232) and that this 'fundamental contradictoriness is a sign that the very reading that allows representation to take place cannot itself be represented': 'Representation is therefore paradoxically guaranteed by the unrepresentability of the medium through which it is enacted: the oxymoronic passion/irony of its reader' (p. 231).

As these quotations indicate, the problems of 'representation' are very much at the heart of Jefferson's approach, as they are also of Christopher Prendergast's more wide-ranging study *The Order of Mimesis*, published in 1986. Four central chapters on Balzac, Stendhal (entitled 'The Ethics of Verisimilitude' and reproduced below), Nerval, and Flaubert are surrounded by three chapters in which the question of mimesis is approached more generally with extensive, helpful reference to literary theory both ancient and modern. As Prendergast states in his first chapter: 'Mimesis is an order, in the dual sense of a set of arrangements and a set of commands. [. . .] the logical matrix of mimesis is formed from the combination, and confusion, of three (heterogeneous) kinds of sentences: a descriptive, a prescriptive and a normative' (p. 5). Confusion is the key word here, for the 'authoritarian gesture of mimesis is to imprison us in a world which, by virtue of its familiarity, is closed to analysis and criticism, in which the "prescriptive" and the "normative" (themselves tacit) ensure that the "descriptive" remains at the level of the undiscussed, in the taken-for-grantedness of the familiar' (p. 6). What is accepted as 'vraisemblable' or 'true-seeming' depends on

> a system of conventions and expectations which rests on, and in turn reinforces, that more general system of 'mutual knowledge' produced within a community for the realization and maintenance of a whole social world. This knowledge is not primarily theoretical; rather it is what the sociology of knowledge refers to as 'pragmatic' knowledge – essentially, a set of socially constructed typifications in respect of which the world is expected to behave in certain more or less regular and predictable ways. (p. 51)

Verisimilitude thus poses an 'ethical' question: how far does any writer reinforce this 'mutual knowledge', and how far does he seek to expand or challenge it? Like Jefferson, Prendergast is interested in the ways in which Stendhal's novels foreground the normative and prescriptive thrust of any appeal to 'realism'. For him, too, the problem of 'voice' is central: 'How to speak to others, in the language of others, is at the heart of the Stendhalian dilemma' (see below, p. 228). Ultimately, he argues: 'What Stendhal rejects is not the idea of representation as such, but outworn forms of representation (the academicist "imitation of the Model"), in the name of an art that should respond to the challenge of its age' (see below, p. 244). As he also suggests, this new art is partly an art of silence.

Coming some forty years after publication of Auerbach's study of representation in *Mimesis*, the work of Jefferson and Prendergast shows how much more complex and nuanced the critical debate about 'realism' has become. At the same time their discussions of Stendhal reflect a continuing interest in aspects of the novels which have been emphasized by other critical approaches: the duality of 'knowledge and tenderness' (Richard), the political subtext of the Stendhalian novel and the question of its subversive function (Barbéris), the status of the authorial voice (Blin), the elusiveness of the linguistic signifier (Felman), the role of silence (Crouzet, Barthes), the logic underlying the 'order' of plot (Brooks, Mossman). As Stendhal noted in the preface to his first novel, *Armance*: 'People see the same thing differently, depending on their own particular standpoint'.

11 Ann Jefferson on reading *The Red and the Black*

Stendhal's fiction is both surrounded and inhabited by the voices of its many readers. Reading is a major preoccupation of the text, and in his 'Projet d'un Article sur *Le Rouge et le Noir*' [his draft review: see above, pp. 31–2] Stendhal defines his novel largely in terms of its readership: as a response to certain kinds of reading, and as an anticipation of others. *Le Rouge et le Noir* thus becomes a dialogue with a host of other voices which serve to create polyphonic effects both as a result of this very dialogue, and through their own heterogeneity. For Stendhal's readers are of many kinds: some are desired, some despised; some are men, some are women; some are Parisian, some are provincial; some are liberal, some are not; some live on the second floor, and some on the fifth; some are contemporary, some are not yet born.[1] But whatever the nature of the reader, the texts are written with a strong interlocutory bias, 'as a letter to a friend',[2] or as a substitute for conversations that can never take place, as witness the opening remarks of *Lucien Leuwen*: 'This story was written for a small number of readers whom I have never met and never shall meet, which I much regret: it would have given me so much pleasure to spend the evenings with them!'[3]

Whether or not one sees the 'benevolent reader' so ardently invoked in *Lucien Leuwen* as one of the *happy few*, the novels are nevertheless also explicitly addressed to a much wider audience than that which comprised the Mme Rolands of 1880 or 1935.[4] Indeed, Stendhal regards his switch from theatre to fiction as a move which enables him to accommodate a much more varied audience. In his view the democratization of theatre audiences since the Revolution was incompatible with the fundamentally monologic basis of comedy, and it is precisely the novel's ability to accommodate a heterogeneous audience that makes it the comedy of the nineteenth century.[5] Comedy in the theatre is limited by the choice it has to make between the 'the crude and vulgar, who are incapable of grasping subtlety' (p. 495) and the 'people of artistic temperament who can understand *subtly-written scenes*' (p. 496). It is thanks to its polyphonic structure (although Stendhal does not, of course, make his claims in these terms) that the novel has the capacity to surmount and contain these contradictions.

Indeed, in his 'Projet d'un Article' Stendhal specifically describes *Le Rouge* as being designed to straddle a split reading audience. This audience, he says, comprises on the one hand provincial women, and, on the other, frequenters of Parisian society. This split, based on differences in both geography and education, has, until 1830, led to the production of two quite different types of novel – 'chambermaid novels and 'drawing-room novels' (p. 714). The 'chambermaid novel' is a different size from the Parisian one (in-12to, as opposed to in-8vo), has a different publisher (Pigoreau as opposed to Levavasseur or Gosselin), has a far bigger audience ('before the commercial crisis of 1831, [M. Pigoreau] made half a million by bringing tears to lovely provincial eyes'), and has its own specific conventions as regards character and style ('the hero is always perfect and extremely handsome, with a *fine* figure and *prominent* eyes'). The authors of these novels are M. le baron de la Mothe-Langon, 'M.M. Paul de Kock, Victor Ducange, etc.', they are quite unknown in Paris and their many works profoundly unsuited to Parisian tastes: 'Nothing seems more insipid, in Paris, than this ever-perfect hero, these wretched, innocent, persecuted ladies, to be found in chambermaid novels'.[6]

In contrast, the main aim of the Parisian author is 'literary merit' and this snobbery is reflected in the expectations of his readers.[7] Stendhal mentions Walter Scott and Manzoni as exponents of this classier genre, but they are also exceptions in that they are read as widely in the provinces as in Paris, although for quite different things:

> The 'petites bourgeoises' of the provinces ask only of the author that he provide them with extraordinary scenes sufficient to reduce them to floods of tears; *little does it matter* how he devises such scenes. The ladies of Paris, on the other hand, as consumers of octavo novels, take a devilishly severe view of *extra-ordinary* episodes. The moment an event appears to have been introduced into the plot at a particular point merely to show the hero off to advantage, they put the book down and proceed to regard the author as nothing but a figure of fun. It is because of these two *opposite requirements* that it is so difficult to write a novel which will be read both in the sitting-rooms of the provincial bourgeoise and in the drawing-rooms of Paris. (p. 715)

Stendhal sets himself the task of bridging this gap and, moreover, of doing so in a way that will not make him the two hundred and first imitator of Walter Scott ('Sir Walter Scott has had approximately two hundred imitators in France'). He professes himself 'bored with all this medievalism, all this talk of ogive arches and fifteenth-century costume', and determines to accommodate the contradictions of his audience by treating novelistic convention with high-handed disdain: in *Le Rouge* 'he dared (. . .) leave the reader totally in the dark as to the type of dresses worn by Mme de Rênal and Mlle de la Mole, his two heroines (for two heroines this novel has, against all the previous rules of the genre)'. Imitation (of Walter Scott) can only be a temporary solution to the problem of the 'opposite requirements', as the works of the two hundred would-be Walter Scotts survive little longer than a year or two and are then completely forgotten. Novelistic innovation and transgression represent a more effective form of polyphony than Walter Scott's. But it will also have to accommodate an even more heterogeneous audience – one that includes the readers of 1880.

Unlike the contemporary provincial and Parisian audiences, this future audience is an unknown quantity. In *Henry Brulard* Stendhal describes himself as talking to 'people about whose turn of mind, education, prejudices and religion one is wholly ignorant',[8] and as a consequence, the addition of this silent voice to the polyphony of the text will serve to relativize the topicality associated with what one might call the first level of polyphony, that is, the one that includes the provincial and the Parisian voices of 1830. Readerly multilingualism appears thus to be associated with two distinct projects in the novel: first, topicality in the description of the society of 1829–30, and second, long-term survival in the hearts of the future equivalents of Mme Roland and M. Gros. These two aims may seem to be incompatible, but essential to both is the linking of the strategy of multilingualism with the determination not to copy from books.[9]

The Parisian reader plays a central role in the construction of Stendhal's portrait of the society of 1830, and it is through him[10] that a topical referential reading is established. It is to a large extent by means of the appeal to the Parisian reader's experience that the veracity of the novel's social portrait is authenticated; for it is only the contemporary reader who can judge whether *Le Rouge* is indeed a chronicle of 1830, and whether it lives up to the claims for truth attributed to Danton in the novel's first epigraph. The Parisian reader knows, like Stendhal, that France has changed beyond recognition in the first thirty years of the century, and that the image of French society and *mœurs* portrayed in the tales of Marmontel and the novels of Mme de Genlis are quite out of date ('Projet d'un Article', p. 713). He is presumed, by implication, to have been a guest at 'the balls this winter' (*The Red and the Black*, p. 370), and more explicitly to be acquainted with the tedium of the salons: 'The full boredom of the uneventful life that Julien was leading is no doubt shared by the reader' (p. 430). His are the standards that are invoked by the author as guidelines for interpretation, and at the outset of the novel author and reader are clearly defined as belonging to the same Parisian world.

It is by this means that Stendhal is able to bring his two envisaged readerships into dialogue. Instead of pandering to both sets of tastes by alternating their preferences (which is how Walter Scott manages to succeed with both camps), Stendhal brings them into confrontation. The Parisian reader is set down in the provinces in the guise of the 'voyageur parisien', a kind of tourist whose concerns and interpretations differ on almost every score from those of the provincials around him. He is *surprised* by M. de Rênal's nail factory, *shocked* by his air of self-satisfaction, *struck* by Sorel's sawmill (pp. 4–5) – a series of small collisions which reveal the disparity in experience and presuppositions that exists between the provincial and the Parisian. Even the Parisian's view of the view, to which he turns in order to forget the asphyxiating provincial obsession with money, differs from that of the provincial; for where the Parisian reader dallies with the author 'musing on the Paris balls I had left behind the day before' (p. 7) and admiring the natural beauty of the landscape, the provincial is shrewdly calculating the revenue that the tourist trade is likely to bring. These misinterpretations and surprises have to be set aright for a Parisian audience over and over again, in a manner that ends up by relativizing the assumptions and conventions of both groups in question.

The Parisian needs to have provincial sayings pointed out to him ('Mme de Rênal [. . .] had been the local beauty, *as they say in the mountains round here*', p. 14, my italics). He needs to be told about local practices with which he is unfamiliar – how they stuff their mattresses, for example. And his ignorance of provincial and cultural *mœurs* appears to be total: '*Bringing in money* is the consideration which settles everything in this little town you found so pretty' (pp. 8–9). He even needs Mme de Rênal herself explained to him: 'Mme de Rênal was one of those provincial women who may well strike you as foolish during the first fortnight of your acquaintance. She had no experience of life, and did not cultivate conversation' (p. 39). These two factors make her incomprehensible to Parisian eyes, since experience of life[11] and the ability to hold one's own in company are the *sine qua non* of Parisian success, as Julien's encounter with the salons of the Faubourg Saint-Germain illustrates. The Parisian reader is assumed to be mystified by his introduction to a character who is both exemplary and topical: in his 'Projet d'un Article', Stendhal claims that 'this kind of woman [would have been] impossible in the context of the ribaldry and high-living which took hold in France after the death of proud Louis XIV in 1715 and lasted until the fateful death of his great-grandson Louis XVI in 1793' (ed. Castex, p. 720).

Through this juxtaposition of provincial and Parisian readings of the provinces Stendhal creates a dialogic effect which, as it is developed, leads to a questioning of the Parisian interpretative system that is established at the opening of the novel. The Parisian reader gradually becomes the object of a second reading.[12] He begins to lose his interpretative authority as his

values are progressively turned against him by the text, and to recede
further and further from its central concerns. This process is begun in the
portrait of Mme de Rênal and is continued in such characteristically ironic
authorial remarks as:

> You mustn't take too dim a view of Julien's future prospects. He could
> come up with just the phrases required by a cautious and wily
> hypocrisy. That is not bad at his age. As far as tone and gesture were
> concerned, he lived among county folk, and had been deprived of
> great models to imitate. Later on, he had only to be given the
> opportunity to associate with such gentlemen and he at once became
> admirable in gesture as well as in word. (p. 50)

This forces the reader to endorse and acknowledge values (hypocrisy)
which vanity normally makes him prefer to deny. In this case he cannot,
since the remark is made with such incontrovertible aplomb by an author
with whom the reader has become so inextricably identified (as a worldly
Parisian).

This kind of remark continues to put the Parisian reader in an
increasingly awkward position until authorial values eventually become
more clearly dissociated from Parisian ones. A well-known instance is the
comment made about Julien's entry into the café at Besançon:

> Imagine the pity our little provincial is going to arouse in those young
> Parisian schoolboys who at the age of fifteen are already adept at
> sauntering into a café with the most distinguished of airs! But these boys
> who have so much style at fifteen become *common* at eighteen. (p. 171)

The Parisian is invited to share his younger brother's patronizing scorn for
Julien's inexperience, but is then roundly punished for having done so by
being called common. On this occasion, provincial qualities are
unequivocally preferred to Parisian ones.

The Parisian's role in the interpretation of the text virtually ceases to
function in this explicit way beyond the end of Part I. In Part II it is the turn
of the provincial (largely in the figure of Julien) to make what he can of the
Parisian world. In this reversal of roles the Parisian is still the loser, for by
presenting Paris through the eyes of Julien, Stendhal creates an effect
similar to that of Montesquieu's *Lettres Persanes*: Parisian customs are
rendered arbitrary by Julien's introduction to them. The split between
Julien's view and that of the Parisian reader is made explicit at the
beginning of what Chapter II calls Julien's 'Entry into society':

> The rooms which these gentlemen [Julien and the abbé Pirard] went
> through on the first floor before reaching the marquis's study would

have seemed to you, my good reader, as dismal as they were magnificent. Were you to be offered them just as they are, you would refuse to inhabit them; they are a land of yawns and of dreary argument. They increased Julien's delight. How can anyone be unhappy, he thought, who inhabits so splendid a realm! (p. 250)

Here the Parisian's experience of the world is directly relevant to the world described (Paris), unlike the provincial world of Part I. It is a world which he recognizes and understands.[13] But as Julien gains in experience and loses his initial naïvety, he seems to move further and further away from, and not closer to, this Parisian view of things. He learns to speak the 'Foreign language' of the salons,[14] takes fencing lessons, dancing lessons, and, in short, becomes a dandy. But it is not these accomplishments that endear him to Mathilde or which make him the hero of Stendhal's novel. A split between provincial and Parisian readings thus gives way here to a split between actions and characters which are repeatedly defined as 'singular' on the one hand, and Parisian interpretations of them on the other.

The word 'singulier' [singular] is used to describe Julien in all the different milieux in which he finds himself, but in Paris this singularity poses a serious threat to the Parisian reader's interpretative capacity. It is Parisians themselves who find Julien 'most singular' in the de la Mole salon (p. 262. [Slater translates as 'most peculiar'].) Singularity in Stendhal is generally synonymous with a failure or an inability to comply with the reigning 'proprieties', and in this case those 'proprieties' are the Parisian reader's main point of reference for interpretation. Mathilde too (for all that she is also baffled by Julien) shares this quality of singularity, and her exceptionality is indeed frequently alluded to in the second part of the novel. Croisenois notes that 'Mathilde is very idiosyncratic' (and adds, 'it's a disadvantage', p. 300). The author himself mentions that 'she is a character who constitutes an exception to the mores of this century', although he does so in order once more to turn the novel's values against Parisian ones when he goes on: 'Lack of prudence is not generally a reproach to be levelled at pupils of the noble convent of the Sacred Heart' (p. 321). This crisis in reading comes to a head during Mathilde's night of *folie*.

Here the author creates further bewilderment by invoking the Parisian reader once more, only to confront his values with a character who refuses to conform to them: 'She is a purely imaginary figure, and besides, imagined quite without reference to the social customs which, in the succession of centuries, will guarantee nineteenth-century civilization a place of such distinction' (p. 370). The reader figure is described as one of the 'unresponsive among you' who are likely to take offence at this portrait, and the author goes on elaborately to dissociate them ('the unresponsive [Parisians] among you') from the supposedly un-nineteenth-century behaviour of Mathilde: 'This page will be detrimental to the unfortunate author in more ways than one. The unresponsive among you will accuse him of impropriety. But he isn't insulting the young women who dazzle the Paris salons by supposing that a single one of them is capable of the mad impulses which spoil Mathilde's character.' This move seems at first to be designed to save the Parisian reader's face, but it does just the reverse, for in the next breath the author says that in fact Mathilde is part of the real world that he is portraying:

> You see, sir, a novel is a mirror going along a main road. Sometimes it reflects into your eyes the azure of the sky, sometimes the mud of the quagmires on the road. And the man carrying the mirror in the basket on his back gets accused by you of being immoral! His mirror shows the mire, and you accuse the mirror! You'd do better to accuse the road where the quagmire is, and better still the inspector of roads who allows the water to stagnate and the quagmire to form. (p. 371)

The Parisian's reading fails not only in its response to what lies outside his world (singularity), but, more seriously, in its response to certain aspects of his own. His touchiness on matters of decency seems to blind him to a part of the reality for which he was supposedly the key and the guarantor. Readerly 'properties' are part of a representation which they are incapable of recognizing. But without the Parisian reader to authenticate the portrait of the society of 1829–30 (a society to which he himself belongs) how is this portrait to be read?

Before answering this question, more must be said about Mathilde's topicality. Some (real) contemporary readers seem to have recognized the reality of the portrait of Mathilde. Count Alexis de Saint-Priest wrote a dialogue in which one of the speakers claims to recognize the type and says: 'If you want an accurate portrait of high society, then read *The Red and the Black*. Meet Mlle Mathilde, the typical young lady from the Faubourg Saint-Germain. There is truth for you! There is accuracy! There you really do have an author who knows what he's talking about, and a book written in good faith!'[15] And Stendhal himself appears to regard the depiction of Mathilde's 'love-in-the-head', or 'Parisian love' as a major realist achievement in his novel: 'This portrait of Parisian love is absolutely new. It seems to us that it is to be found in no other book.'[16] So that the assertion in the text that Mathilde is 'imagined quite without reference to the social customs' of the time would appear, at least in part, to be a dig at the Parisian reader's ticklishness in matters of taste. Like the pistol shot of politics she may 'mortally offend' half the readership, even if she does not bore the other half (p. 391). Good taste (or what the author calls *grâce*) is thus incompatible with the mirror principle, for just as the exclusion of politics from the novel would ruin the portrait of France in 1830, so too would the exclusion of Mathilde and her 'love-in-the-head'. The harsh truths of the day (promised in the novel's first epigraph) prove to be too much for the reader of the day. There seems, in a way, to be no reader capable of recognizing the truth of Stendhal's portrait. Referentiality becomes caught in a double-bind whereby the reader is asked to recognize his own world, and at the same time is shown that this world provides an inadequate framework for that recognition. The nature of the society represented prevents that representation from being fully perceived within it.

Returning now to the question of how this partially unrecognizable representation of 1830 is to be read: the novel itself contains suggestive accounts of different uses of reading which may have a bearing on the problem. There are many readers in *Le Rouge*, and reading takes many different forms. Broadly, though, reading falls into two categories: private or clandestine reading, and socially useful reading. It is this socially useful reading that characterizes the Parisian, and leads one to suspect that Stendhal's Parisian reader would not in any case be reading referentially, but strategically, as a means to further his own social advancement.

First and foremost, however, reading, according to Stendhal, is an antidote to boredom. This boredom is part of his portrait of contemporary *moeurs*, for he attributes it to social changes that have taken place since 1789 ('Projet', p. 713). Reading itself is thus an activity made necessary by the society described in the text read. It compensates for the absence of social gatherings and conversations that made life in eighteenth-century France such a pleasure, and which, according to Stendhal, still existed in the Italy of his day (witness the remarks to this effect made in *De l'Amour*). Nineteenth-century French society, however, not content with simply making reading necessary, goes so far as to adapt it to its own purposes: reading is made the passport to social acceptability, even social success. There is censorship not only in what is read, but also in how it is read.

René seems to be the set text for entry into the de la Mole salon. It saves its young readers from ridicule, and provides them with the necessary model to imitate. Julien fails to read quite the right texts (despite the fact that he reads more than anyone else in the novel),[17] and with the exception of the 'unparalleled volume' of *La Nouvelle Héloïse* makes the (socially) crucial omission of fiction. Nevertheless, his initiation into society in the de la Mole household is effected by means of a testing of his reading. His time at the seminary has already taught him the social uses of reading: reading the wrong texts for the exam gets him a poor result, although his knowledge of the same texts on the occasion of his meeting with the archbishop wins him the admiration of the old man and a fine edition of Tacitus. These two events, then, prepare him for the first social hurdle encountered over the dinner table in the Faubourg Saint-Germain – a discussion of Horace. Here his response shows him in a good light for a provincial, but a poor one for a Parisian. His learning is evidently superior, but his style lamentable:

> In his replies Julien improvised ideas, and he lost enough of his
> nervousness to display not wit – something impossible for anyone
> who doesn't know the idiom used in Paris – but fresh ideas, even if
> they were lacking in polish and inappositely presented. And everyone
> saw that he knew Latin perfectly. (p. 256)

Julien fails to conform with Parisian norms because he invents his ideas, rather than repeating the orthodoxy, and because he doesn't speak 'the idiom used in Paris', a language which, to judge by other cases, is best learned parrot-fashion. Croisenois and Norbert are probably some of the best practitioners of this language – Croisenois because he is clearly such an elegant copy of René, and Norbert, because he makes no bones about wrapping up his reading in a series of 'ready-made ideas'. The abbé Pirard suggests to Julien that he is likely to be asked to teach Norbert 'a few stock phrases on Cicero and Virgil' (p. 246). In any case, Norbert regularly comes to the library to mug up topics for the evening's conversation: 'Norbert (. . .) used to come and study a newspaper so as to be able to talk politics that evening.'[18] Society seems, then, to determine the form that reading should take and the uses to which it should be put: imitation and repetition. Under these circumstances, *Le Rouge et le Noir* itself seems particularly unsuitable for a Parisian reading. It constantly offends standards of decent amusement (e.g. Mathilde's night of 'folie'), renders its culminating action inimitable, and, as the next part of the argument will show, invites another kind of reading which more or less precludes any repeatable 'stock phrase'.

The second form of reading that the text represents is clandestine reading, which is offered as an alternative to social reading. Mathilde and Julien are the main secretive readers in the text. Their self-imposed secrecy is partly the result of censorship, for both read politically unacceptable texts: Julien reads Napoleon at night in the Rênal household, his lamp hidden in an upturned vase, and Mathilde, whose clandestine reading is mainly political, comes by her texts through theft.[19] She steals books from the library, and indeed theft itself seems to become a main motive for reading in her case. For example, the private collection of 'titillating new titles' which Julien is responsible for buying on the Marquis's behalf, is regularly purloined: '[Julien] was soon quite certain that these new books only had to be hostile to the interests of throne and altar, and they would disappear in no time. And it was scarcely Norbert who was the reader' (p. 331). Nevertheless, neither Mathilde's nor Julien's motives are genuinely political; for both of them, reading offers models which happen to be socially unacceptable: Napoleon for Julien, Marguerite de Navarre for Mathilde. This type of reading is subversive to the extent that its texts are censored, its heroes unorthodox and its mode clandestine. But it shares with Parisian habits the aim of imitation, and thus belongs ultimately to that camp.

The alternatives to the impossible referential reading of *Le Rouge* are not limited to these socially more or less acceptable repetitions and imitations. A rather different experience of reading is indicated by Saint-Giraud in the mail-coach that takes Julien to Paris: 'a good book is an event in my life' (pp. 239–40), he says on his brief appearance which, in many ways, constitutes one of the novel's densest moments of reflexivity. This 'performative' mode of reading contrasts significantly with the socially utilitarian and imitative readings which are far more frequently evoked in the novel. And if this performative mode does indeed represent a serious and viable alternative, the question of referentiality may, for the time being, be suspended.

In *Henry Brulard* reading is represented almost exclusively as event. It is very similar to Mathilde's sixteenth-century ideal of love: 'it wasn't just one of life's amusements, it actually made a difference to her life'.[20] Brulard's reading is a series of decisive events which leave a permanent effect on his life and personality. The discovery of *Don Quixote* was 'perhaps the greatest period of my life' (p. 106); Ariosto 'formed my character' (p. 107); and without Horace and Euripides he would have succumbed to the tyranny of Raillane and become 'an excellent Jesuit (. . .) or a dissolute soldier, never out of the bar and always chasing skirt' (p. 114). The intervention of books in his life is of unsurpassed importance for two reasons: first, because these books become the grid through which he constructs and interprets his experience (this factor is, of course, not without its dangers); and second, because the reading of them constitutes a kind of experience which is matched by very few other things.

Le Rouge itself does not offer its ('real') reader any model of a performative reading to follow, not least perhaps because to do so would be to introduce imitation into this reading process and so undermine its essential status as event. Instead it elicits such a reading through its repeated use of the 'unpredictable' and through comedy. *Rêverie* and *hilarité*, the two main reader responses that these strategies instigate, are the two inseparable experiential forms that a performative reading of *Le Rouge* would take.

As the novel moves towards its finish, the incidence of what it calls 'madness' and 'the unpredictable' significantly increases. The shooting episode as a whole is 'unpredictable', and is composed of largely inexplicable elements. In the Castex edition the notes to Chapters XXXV (the shooting) and XXXVI (Julien's imprisonment) consist mainly of explanations to fill out the elliptical utterances of the narrative. For instance, the brusque 'Adieu' with which Julien parts from Mathilde is felt to require expansion and clarification. So is the following sentence: 'Julien leaped down out of the cab and ran to his post-chaise' (p. 468), where the lack of clear motive needs, apparently, to be compensated for. The reason why Julien is unable to form the words of a letter to Mathilde gives rise to further editorial intervention and a discussion of divergent scholarly responses: according to Martineau, Julien is in the grip of 'a nervous trembling which prevents him from writing', whereas Castex suggests that the problem may be due to the poor suspension of the post-chaise in which Julien is travelling (p. 637). In either case it is clear that this is an instance of what Wolfgang Iser would call a blank or a gap that needs to be filled by the reader.[21] The number of blanks at this point is extremely high, and the question is: what sort of procedure should be used to fill them?

On this the text is not nearly so directive as Iser's model would suggest, and the reader is confronted with a thoroughgoing indeterminacy concerning the appropriate level of reading. Castex, in accordance with the principles of good scholarship, has gone for a purely referential reading of the particular blank under discussion: stage-coaches of 1830 offered a far smoother ride than the faster post-chaises. Martineau's reading at this point is based on the conventions of psychological realism associated with a certain kind of fiction. It assumes that the hero's feelings and emotional responses are the main object of the text. Neither reading, however, explains why the blank should be there in the first place, and, in a sense, the alacrity with which they rush to fill the gap gives them a certain resemblance to Mme de la Mole and the other *grandes dames* who are so offended by Julien's unconventional behaviour on his arrival in the salon: 'Great ladies are appalled by the *unpredictable* behaviour that heightened sensitivity [in this case Julien's] produces; it is the very opposite of propriety' (p. 277). The 'unpredictability' of Julien's actions at the climax of the novel is, precisely, a flouting of reading 'propriety', be [it] scholarly, psychological or what.

Even Stendhal himself seems to have bridled somewhat at the degree of 'unpredictability' in his text – at least on the level of style. He complains of it in *Henry Brulard* (p. 225), and it is a recurrent theme in his notes in the Civita-Vecchia copy of the text: the style, he says, is 'too abrupt, too staccato', and he recommends to himself, 'fill things out (. . .) to help the imagination picture things' (p. 493). But it does seem that it is the impoverished imagination of the 'unresponsive souls' that he has in mind, and there are two marginalia in Chapter XVII of Part I which would support this view: 'Not sufficiently developed. What is this battle all about? *the dim-witted* will ask'; and 'What speed! Won't it seem too dry to *the half-wits*?' (p. 495, my italics). 'Sensitive souls' can presumably cope with the 'unpredictable' and the reason for this may well be their mode of reading, which is not dependent on 'propriety'. Certainly no convention-bound reading can deal with the increase of 'madness' that occurs towards the end of the novel. As Shoshana Felman remarks, 'madness' tends to appear with gathering frequency towards the end of each of the novels, and *Le Rouge et le Noir* is no exception.[22] And, as she also points out, the mark of the 'madman' is his lack of a common language with others (including, in this instance, the reader), and his inability to make his 'solitary language' understood (Felman, p. 162). 'Madness' and its cognate 'singularity' are terms which are associated first with Mathilde, and then, more extensively, with Julien[23]; this characteristic indicates that the conventional assumptions which form the basis of most readings may not be adequate to their task in this last part of the novel.

If 'sensitive souls' succeed in making sense of the final pages of the novel, this is because their reading is not grounded in any particular kind of language, or any particular set of conventions. Their reading must necessarily be conducted in a state of hilarity and reverie, and they will be profoundly moved by it. In Stendhal's world, these three things (hilarity, revery and 'tenderness') tend to go together, and laughter is an essential prerequisite for being moved. In *Henry Brulard* he claims that his love of *opera buffa* is due to the fact that only in this genre can he be moved to tears: 'I cannot be moved to the point of tenderness *except following some passage of comedy*' (p. 389, Stendhal's italics).

There are many kinds of laughter in Stendhal, but this particular and vital form depends on a freedom from both convention and referentiality.[24] Of all Stendhal's heroes, Lucien Leuwen is probably the most prone to laughter, and this tendency can probably be correlated with the particularly hide-bound nature of the society in which he moves. Nancy is obsessed with 'propriety', and Lucien's first outburst of laughter is provoked by his encounter with the utterly proper and utterly self-important prefect, M. Fléron. The effect of the man's appearance is enough to produce an uncontrollable explosion of laughter in Lucien, which is echoed time and again in the novel. *Le Rouge* represents an equally sober world where laughter is proscribed by 'propriety'. It is explicitly forbidden in the de la Mole salon where 'it was not seemly to joke about anything' (p. 318). But precisely because of the hold of these rules, there is statistically more laughter in this part of the novel than in any of the others.[25] Julien himself has two notable moments of this 'mad laughter': once in Verrières (in a chapter significantly entitled 'Modes of behaviour in 1830') after his Jesuitical conversation with Maugiron, the sub-prefect ('M. de Maugiron had hardly left before Julien burst into uncontrollable laughter' (p. 144)); and once in Paris when Mme de Fervaques enquires about the references to London and Richmond in Julien's latest letter to her. No one is more hide-bound than she, nothing more conventional than the letters that Julien writes to her, so that his response is inevitably to '[break] into helpless laughter' (p. 429). The element of 'madness' in these outbursts is what makes them genuine moments of hilarity, and not instances of 'the affected laughter' which is the social conformist's response to all that he regards as 'ridicule'.[26]

The only other moment of this sort of hilarity occurs on the visit of the singer Geronimo to the Rênal household. As a singer and an Italian, he is the antithesis of all that provincial France stands for. The exaggeratedly foreign accent in which he tells his comic tale has the children in fits of laughter, and the comic aria he sings reduces everyone to tears through laughing (pp. 161–2). The prime feature of this laughter is its essential gaiety, its total lack of malice and self-interest. The effectiveness of laughter as an antidote to propriety lies in this gaiety and the element of 'madness' that it implies. It is the laughter of the *opera buffa* and the only possible prelude to 'tenderness'.

Stendhal devotes a number of pages to comedy and its attendant 'mad laughter' in his essay *Racine et Shakespeare*. Borrowing from Hobbes he defines laughter as 'the physical convulsion (. . .) brought on by unexpectedly seeing our superiority over others' (p. 63), and he lays considerable stress on the element of the 'unpredictable' in this process. The 'unpredictable' takes comedy out of any context of convention or conformity which preclude genuine laughter. Falstaff is the epitome of 'mad laughter' because of his capacity for gaiety (p. 65). Molière, in contrast, is associated with a false laughter, 'affected laughter', which is based on revenge. His comedy is therefore essentially not comedy at all, but satire, a product of the society in which he wrote and which was obsessed with the imitation of a certain model (p. 67). Imitation and reference are incompatible with 'gay laughter'. Laughter is a reprieve from the obligation to imitate: 'if I go to the theatre, it's because I want to be made to laugh, and I have no thought of imitating anyone' (p. 70). Equally, hilarity has to be dissociated from the referential mode of satire which is always directed at targets in social reality. If the *happy few* who read *Lucien Leuwen* are to participate in Lucien's outbursts of laughter, it must be at the expense of all reference to contemporary France:

> Satire on people, amusing as this is, is thus not, unfortunately, appropriate in the narration of a story. The reader is too busy comparing my portrait with the grotesque, or even odious, original with whom he is perfectly familiar. (p. 1067)

In other words, both modes associated with a Parisian reading of Stendhal (referential and imitative) are unequivocally excluded from the hilarious performative reading that is elicited from the *happy few*. That hilarity is an appropriate response to *Le Rouge* can be inferred from a prophetic remark that Stendhal makes in *Racine et Shakespeare*:

> Ultimately, if someone wants to make me laugh despite the profound seriousness to which the Stock Exchange, and politics, and party

hatreds, reduce me, then I have to see persons of a passionate nature taking the wrong route, in an amusing manner, in their pursuit of happiness.

This would seem to describe exactly the story of *Le Rouge et le Noir*.

The novel should, therefore, be seen as a Stendhalian kind of *opera buffa*, in which any hilarity provoked would be accompanied by 'tenderness'. It certainly alternates moments of comedy with moments of more emotive appeal, and perhaps nowhere more strikingly so than in its representations of love. Each affair is initiated by an irresistibly comic *quid pro quo* as each partner misinterprets the motives of the other. And yet, at the same time, love is clearly a matter to be taken seriously and properly responded to. As the first of the 'Projets de préface' to *De l'Amour* makes clear, reading about love depends on the reader's experience of love: 'It is necessary, if he is to follow with interest a *philosophical examination* [or, in the case of *Le Rouge*, a novelistic portrayal] of this feeling, for the reader to be not simply intelligent; it is absolutely vital that he should have seen love for himself'.[27] The reading of a text is, in Stendhal's view, only possible if the experiences that it represents are re-evoked and recreated *within* the reader. They cannot simply remain on the page.

This emphasis on experiential reduplication gives the question of referentiality a rather different twist. Representational accuracy in the text itself has no necessary link with readerly experience which is the only basis for guaranteeing the truth of the text. According to Stendhal, no representation can ever be fully realistic because it is never taken or mistaken for reality.[28] If we admire a landscape by Claude Lorrain, 'it is not that we suppose the trees we are looking at to be capable of providing us with shade, or that we are thinking of drawing water from these purest of springs'. The effect of the painting depends rather on the pleasure it elicits, in which case, 'we have a *vivid picture* in our mind of the pleasure we would take in walking beside these pure springs and in the shade of these beautiful trees' (p. 159). The illusion of reality is not in the text but in the reader, and it is the product of the text's power to move him or her (since Mme Roland is, so to speak, the incarnation of the 'sensitive soul' or the happy reader in question, the introduction of the feminine pronoun is timely). An 'unresponsive soul' will remain unaffected by the most poignant depictions of love and persist in seeing in them only folly. The painters of the *beau idéal*, as Stendhal calls them (Raphael and Correggio) are in themselves neither more nor less realistic in this sense than the 'mirror-painters', such as Guaspre, Poussin and the Dutch school. In both cases,

All at once one finds oneself plunged into a deep reverie, as at the prospect of forests and *their vast silence*. One muses deeply on one's dearest illusions; already they seem less implausible, and soon one is revelling in them as if they were realities. One talks to the person one loves, one dares to question them, one listens to their replies. (179)

Performative readings become the only relevant index of life-likeness however improbable or *invraisemblable* the issues in question.

It is therefore the readers whom Stendhal never met, those who were ten or twelve years old when he wrote *Souvenirs d'égotisme*, those of 1880, those of 1935, perhaps even those of 1980, who have the best chance of achieving such a reading. They are less likely to be seduced by the irrelevance of referentiality, and are assumed to be less bound by propriety, less likely to be in search of a model to imitate.[29] In *Henry Brulard* Stendhal is delighted at the thought of writing for this unknown audience: 'To be talking to people about whose turn of mind, education, prejudices and religion one is wholly ignorant! What an encouragement to speak the *truth* and nothing but the *truth*; that's the only thing that matters' (p. 33). When the performative reading becomes the only possible reading, only then can the text's truthfulness be properly assessed. Stendhal gains the place he hoped for alongside the 'immortal *Tom Jones*' by resisting the temptation to conform to the 'proprieties' of his day,[30] and by not writing like the Jesuit that he could so easily otherwise have become.

This performative reading has a dual standing within the text. At one level it forms part of the polyphony of reading which the novel activates, a voice among many other voices. But at a second level, it is the only reading that can itself accommodate the disjunctions and contradictions of that polyphony. Through it Stendhal manages to resolve and reassess the problems of representation in fiction: being set up as an alternative to a simple referential mode, it serves to relativize that mode, and to question the basis on which it functions (the vanity of the Parisian reader). As both an element of, and a recipient of, the whole polyphonic spectrum of readings in *Le Rouge et le Noir* it has the effect of also relativizing that spectrum, and so bringing them to consciousness as object discourses that can be perceived as such. Finally, by placing the criterion of realism in the reader and not in the text, it raises the question of what kind of writing is required of realist fiction if, as Stendhal writes in the *Vie de Henry Brulard*: 'A novel is like a bow, the body of the violin *which gives back the sounds* is the reader's soul' (180).[31]

Notes

1.   The Parisian reader invoked at the beginning of *Le Rouge et le Noir* presumably shares the same liberal opinions as the author with whom he is in every other way so strongly identified. 'The readers of this book must live on the second

floor or the sixth', a note on the Civita-Vecchia copy of the text, is quoted in P.-G. Castex's edition of *Le Rouge et le Noir* (Paris: Classiques Garnier, 1973), p. 499.

2. *Vie de Henry Brulard* (Collection Folio), Paris, 1973, 32 [*Editor's note:* See above, 'Introduction', p.2.]

3. *Lucien Leuwen*, in *Romans et nouvelles de Stendhal*, ed. Henri Martineau (Paris: Pléiade 1959), vol. I, p. 767. All further references to *Lucien Leuwen* will be to this edition.

4. In his *Souvenirs d'égotisme*, Stendhal writes: 'I confess that I would not have the courage to write if I did not think that one day these pages would be published and that they would be read by someone like Mme Roland or M. Gros, the geometer', *Œuvres intimes de Stendhal*, ed. Henri Martineau, (Paris: Pléiade 1961), p. 1393. All further references to the *Souvenirs d'égotisme* will be to this edition.

5. 'I regard the novel as the nineteenth-century equivalent of theatrical comedy', notes on the Civita-Vecchia copy, *Le Rouge et le Noir*, p. 495. See also p. 496.

6. The ladies of Paris may regard themselves as above this kind of thing, but its importance for Emma Bovary is notorious. Stendhal and Flaubert seem to concur in their characterization of these novels: ['They were concerned only with affairs of the heart, with lovers and their lasses, with persecuted damsels for ever swooning in solitary pavilions, with outriders meeting a violent death on every journey, and horses foundering on every page, with dark forests and agonies of sentiment, with vows, sobs, tears, and kisses, with moonlit gondolas, with groves and nightingales, with cavaliers who were always as brave as lions, gentle as lambs, and virtuous as real men never are, always elegantly dressed and given to weeping with the copious fluency of stone fountains.' *Madame Bovary*, trans. Gerard Hopkins (Oxford: Oxford University Press, 1981), p. 34.] Emma also reads Walter Scott. Another avid reader of 'chambermaid novels' is Molly Bloom who asks Bloom to get her 'another of Paul de Kock's. Nice name he has'. *Ulysses*, (London: Cape, 1949), p. 57.

7. STENDHAL was, apparently, proud of being published in-8vo by Levavasseur who also published an in-12to edition of the novel. BALZAC, who until 1830 had been published exclusively in the in-12to format, was upgraded to in-8vo status with his *Physiologie du mariage*. See note, *Le Rouge et le Noir*, p. 728.

8. GENEVIÈVE MOUILLAUD points out that, although Stendhal's novels are ultimately addressed to the *happy few*, the only readers explicitly addressed in *Le Rouge* are contemporary and largely hostile. *Le Rouge et le Noir de Stendhal: Le roman possible* (Paris: Larousse, 1973), pp. 32–5. *Vie de Henry Brulard*, p. 33.

9. This was a major concern of Stendhal's. See his draft review, where he remarks that 'Nothing is more difficult in novel writing than to paint after nature, and not to *copy books*', *Le Rouge et le Noir*, p. 716.

10. This reader is, on the whole, defined as a man. See MOUILLAUD, p. 32.

11. Mme de Rênal never reads a novel, and with the exception of a single volume of *La Nouvelle Héloïse*, nor does Julien. To Parisian eyes this constitutes a serious omission in their education: 'You can see that Julien had no experience of life, *he hadn't even read any novels*', p. 364, my italics.

12. There is, in other words, a slight shift in the diegetic status of this reader. He remains at all times, however, a characterized rather than an implied reader. For an account of the different statuses of different readers, see W. DANIEL WILSON, 'Readers in Texts', *PMLA*, 96 (1981), 848–63.

13. For an account of the accuracy of the representation of this world, see P.-G. CASTEX, 'Réalités d'époque dans *Le Rouge et le Noir'*, *Europe*, 519–21, (1972), 55–63. However, he makes no mention of the role of the Parisian reader in the authentication of this representation, and the entire drift of my argument goes against his conclusion: 'It is evident how necessary it is, in order to understand *The Red and the Black* properly, to situate the work within its historical context' (p. 63). The Parisian reader shows just how problematic this comprehension is.

14. On his arrival in Paris this language of the salons 'was like a foreign language which he could understand but not speak', p. 266.

15. See CASTEX on 'L'Accueil des contemporains', *Le Rouge et le Noir*, p. 691.

16. See 'Projet d'un Article sur *Le Rouge et le Noir'*, p. 724.

17. Julien's reading includes Napoleon's memoirs, Rousseau, St Jerome, Cicero, Horace, Virgil, Tacitus, Martial, Livy, a history of the Revolution, *Othello*, Rotrou, Voltaire, and La Fontaine.

18. Newspapers are often described by Stendhal as texts that lend themselves to parroting of this kind. He says, for instance, of *Le Constitutionnel* that it is 'the catechism of all Frenchmen born around 1800' (*Promenades dans Rome*), quoted in the Castex notes to *Le Rouge et le Noir*, p. 564. In Stendhal the catechism is always recited parrot-fashion.

19. In the course of the novel Mathilde reads 'Nine or ten volumes of new poetry' (*The Red and the Black*, p. 294), *Le Contrat Social*, Vély's *Histoire de France*, d'Aubigné, Brantôme, Etoile's *Mémoires*, *Manon Lescaut*, *La Nouvelle Héloïse*, the *Lettres d'une religieuse portugaise*, Voltaire, and some of the 'titillating new titles' (p. 331) from her father's collection. She is forbidden by her mother to read Walter Scott.

20. Addition in the notes of the Civita-Vecchia copy, *Le Rouge et le Noir*, p. 502.

21. WOLFGANG ISER, *The Act of Reading* (London: Routledge and Kegan Paul, 1978). See in particular Chapter 8.

22. SHOSHANA FELMAN, *La 'Folie' dans l'œuvre romanesque de Stendhal* (Paris, Corti, 1971).

23. See *The Red and the Black*, pp. 482, 483, 488, 491, 492, 493, 511, and 521.

24. See LÉON CELLIER, 'Rires, sourires et larmes dans *Le Rouge et le Noir'*, in *De Jean Lemaire de Belges à Jean Giraudoux: Mélanges d'histoire et de critique littéraire offerts à Pierre Jourda* (Paris: Nizet 1970), pp. 277–97.

25. See CELLIER, p. 278.

26. '*That* sort of laughter is neither here nor there, and must not enter into our analysis', *Racine et Shakespeare* (Paris: Garnier-Flammarion, 1970), pp. 65–6. All further references are to this edition.

27. *De l'Amour*, ed. Henri Martineau (Paris: Classiques Garnier, 1959), p. 325.

28. *Racine et Shakespeare*, p. 157.

29. There is, nevertheless, something unavoidably Parisian about reading Stendhal in 1982 in order to write an article, and an unpleasant whiff of the seminary in teaching him as a text in the university. These form part of the 'turn of mind, education, prejudices' which Stendhal knew he could not possibly foresee.

30. Conformity seems to lead to early oblivion. 'Is the novel essentially an ephemeral composition? If you want to give infinite pleasure today, you will have to resolve to look ridiculous twenty years from now.' Notes on the Civita-Vecchia copy of *Le Rouge et le Noir*, pp. 494–5.

31. This article is part of a larger study of polyphony and realism in Stendhal. For further discussion of polyphonic fiction, see M.M. BAKHTIN, *The Dialogic Imagination*, tr. C. Emerson and M. Holquist (Austin, Texas: University of Texas Press 1981).

12 Christopher Prendergast on the ethics of verisimilitude

Writer and public

Balzac's novels show that the logic of mimesis is a 'socio-logic',[1] and that the 'fiduciary' conventions which support that logic reach deep into the language and culture of the age. But they also show that their most immediate and practical form turns on the relation between the writer and his public: in *Illusions perdues*, for whom you write is a question inseparable from what you write and how you write. The 'value' of the signs used to represent the world depends crucially on securing the agreement of the reader as to their 'worth'; the text is like a bill of exchange or a promissory note (promising among other things the pleasures of intelligibility, the 'hidden meaning' of reality), the guarantee of which stems from a system of public 'confidence'. We have seen how Balzac's texts undermine that confidence at the very moment of apparently presupposing it. And that shifting, unstable stance brings us to the even more oblique relation to these matters maintained by Stendhal's novels. Stendhal is a writer who never takes his 'public' for granted. Indeed, as he himself was well aware (projecting utopically forward to an ideal readership in the late nineteenth century or dedicating his novels to the *happy few*), the response of his contemporary public appears to have been for the most part either bewildered or hostile. A naive reader of today, unencumbered by background knowledge or unalive to the ironies and ambiguities of the text, might be excused for thinking otherwise. For, through the voice of the narrator, Stendhal's fiction seems to institute and proclaim a concord with the values and attitudes of those very readers excluded elsewhere from the privileged band of true sympathizers. But this, as is now common knowledge, is misleading, part of the Stendhalian ruse, a cosy embrace concealing a dagger. Moreover, the historical facts suggest that the ruse may not have been entirely effective (despite Stendhal's own love of disguise), and lend support to Georges Blin's thesis that Stendhal's ironic masks and subterfuges are almost wholly transparent.[2] The voice, it appears, did not deceive the nineteenth-century reader, who knew that many of his cherished assumptions were under attack, and who reacted with a corresponding counter-attack.

In itself this reaction is in no way remarkable, and belongs to a common pattern of writer-public relations in the nineteenth century. What is interesting, however, are the terms of that reaction, or rather the forms in which they can be seen to interconnect. The study of Stendhal's reputation in the nineteenth century reveals that two main themes stand out with monotonous, if instructive, regularity.[3] The first is the shrill repetition of the charge of immorality (the *Journal des débats* sets the tone and speaks for many in its account of 'a frenzied imagination' whose sole objective is 'to insult the soundest principles of morality').[4] The second is the recurrent accusation of the fundamental *invraisemblance* of many of Stendhal's major creations. Thus, the critic of *Le Globe* found Octave, the hero of *Armance*, to be not only 'a prodigiously bizarre being', but – introducing the critical theme of 'madness' – a being so bizarre as to resemble a character escaped from the lunatic asylum at Charenton.[5] Similarly, the critic for the *Revue des deux mondes* found that 'Julien's character is thus false, contradictory, in places incomprehensible'.[6] The *Revue de Paris* commented on the relationship between Julien and Mathilde: 'one would be particularly inclined to take him to task for the strangeness of his lovers'.[7] In the *Journal des débats*, Jules Janin (again introducing the theme of 'madness') wrote of Mathilde de la Mole: 'This Mathilde is mad (. . .) no one ever imagined a girl like that.'[8] Even Mérimée, Stendhal's friend and colleague, remarked of Julien Sorel: 'Why did you choose someone with such an implausible character? (. . .) I thought I had understood Julien, and yet there is not a single one of his actions which did not contradict what I believed him to be like.'[9]

The list could be substantially extended, but the general shape of the predominant critical attitude should be clear. What has, I believe, gone unnoticed, however, are the important relations of overlap and interdependence between these two themes. For although normally proffered as distinct and discrete evaluations, the judgement of 'immorality' and the judgement of *invraisemblance* issue in large measure from the same ideological space, one in which the two are functionally inter-related, or, rather, where the latter often acts as a kind of cover for the former. By means of a tacit strategy of transference, the moral critique is converted (and thereby strengthened) into a naturalistic critique, in terms of which transgressions of the moral order are seen as violations of the natural order. According to the class-bound morality of the nineteenth century, what could be more scandalous than that the aristocratic Mathilde should take the plebeian Julien as her lover? But what more effective way of rationalizing that sense of scandal, and consolidating that morality, than by accusing her creator of stepping outside the limits of mimetic representation itself, by making of the moral scandal a scandal of representation itself? Emile Faguet remarked, imperturbably erecting prejudice into a criterion of literary realism, that it was 'difficult to allow' that Mathilde should have an affair with 'this little secretary, a sawyer's son'.[10] The irony is that he was probably right, but only by virtue of that self-fulfilling circularity through which prejudice is socially translated into 'fact'. The codes of nineteenth-century behaviour were indeed such as to make a love affair between an aristocratic woman and a man of lower rank appear exceedingly improbable, and could accordingly be appealed to with a good conscience as the empirical basis on which to judge the representation of Mathilde's behaviour as a literary aberration. This is a classic instance of the recursive agency of Opinion in the social construction of reality and its representations; in a closed circuit, 'opinion' and 'reality' model each other, in such a way that the given 'facts' of the latter serve as the irrefutable proof of the legitimacy of the former.

At certain moments of his career, Stendhal appears to have believed that things might have been otherwise in the nineteenth century. In the *Vie de Rossini* he advances the argument that new 'democratic' conditions might lead to the emergence of a new kind of 'public', in which the ossified norms of the past might be broken by the pluralistic spirit of controversy and debate.[11] But as early as *Rome, Naples et Florence en 1817*, we find a quite different recognition: 'I despair of the arts now that we are moving towards being governed by public opinion.'[12] Consensual politics entail the impoverishing prospect of consensual art, regulated by the conformist pressures of Opinion and no less oppressive than the normative culture of autocratic monarchy. To the extent that *Le Rouge et le Noir* works against those pressures, it reflects back an image to society in which the latter, or its critical spokesman, can see only a travesty and a perversion, a wilful secession from the 'common language' of an agreed way of seeing the world. In this respect, the author of the long review-essay on Stendhal in the *Revue des deux mondes* got, if only in a complacently unexamined way, the crucial emphasis absolutely right: 'Here, we must confess, the author and ourselves are no longer speaking a *common language*, and we are unable to understand the one which he is speaking.'[13] It is an emphasis, moreover, provocatively confirmed by Stendhal himself on those various occasions when he remarks that, from the point of view of that kind of definition of the 'common language', his own works will be read as if written in a 'foreign tongue'.[14]

The issue, it will be seen, is profound, and goes far beyond the ordinary scholarly concern with the history of critical reputations and reading publics. Fully elaborated, it touches on entrenched assumptions within early nineteenth-century culture and society (on the terms of what is construed as the 'common language'), and, in that context, on the relation of the internal economy of Stendhal's narrative to the theory and practice of mimesis. In particular, it returns us to the formal description of literary *vraisemblance* given in an earlier chapter,[15] to that reading of Aristotle's

Poetics whereby the literary *eikos* is seen as a function of the *doxa*: what will be accepted as 'probable' or 'likely' in a literary representation will depend on presuppositions embedded in common opinion, in the 'common language', or – since relations of power and interests are importantly determining factors here – in a notion of the common language, as this is defined and protected by those groups and institutions with considerable investment in the ideological appropriation of that notion. One of the clearest examples of that appropriation we have already seen in the context of seventeenth-century poetics, especially the prescriptions, and proscriptions, brought to bear on Corneille's *Le Cid* (it is no accident that Stendhal's most vitriolic literary and cultural criticism is reserved for the Court culture of the seventeenth century). The clamour of nineteenth-century orthodoxy around Stendhal's representation of Mathilde de la Mole's behaviour reminds us of the close link between *vraisemblance* and *bienséance*, plausibility and propriety, in seventeenth-century judgements of *Le Cid*. In her affair with Julien, Mathilde crosses the threshold of intelligibilty for the nineteenth-century conservative imagination in the same way that the seventeenth-century establishment found Chimène's marriage to Rodrigue to be unthinkable. In both cases, the application of criteria of *vraisemblance* in adverse judgement of the text reveals a strategy of censorship at work in the field of desire. Desires which are socially problematical, which threaten the social structure (familial in *Le Cid*, class in *Le Rouge et le Noir*) are coped with by querying or denying the 'plausibility' of the text which presents them. They are removed from that area of society's classification system which articulates the moral order (what is permitted and what is forbidden) to that area which organises the division between the normal and the abnormal, the typical and the aberrant; and, following Aristotle's distinction between the contingently 'true' and the poetically 'probable', although the aberrant may belong to life and to history, it has no place in the representational project of literary mimesis. The seventeenth-century critic, Rapin, declared that the *vraisemblable* rests on 'everything which is consonant with public opinion'.[16] Nearly two hundred years later Balzac remarks, in *Lettres sur la littérature*, that the verisimilitude of a fictional character 'must be supported by the consent of all'.[17] Changed historical circumstances clearly redefine the terms on which that consent can be solicited and given. But both cultures impose limits, the general principle or logical form of which appears to be the same. *Le Rouge et le Noir* is scandalous because it takes us to, and beyond, those limits.

I do not propose to recapitulate here the complex web of cultural and ideological relations engaged by the code of *vraisemblance*. But a convenient shorthand for regaining purchase on them is through John Bayley's unusual yet suggestive adaptation to the novel of the notion of 'pastoral'. 'By pastoral', writes Bayley, 'I mean the principle of making everything in a work of art characteristic.'[18] 'Pastoral', in this account, falls therefore into the category of the 'typical', and hence of the *vraisemblable*; it answers to a system of expectancies centred on likelihoods and predictabilities. As Bayley remarks, taking Balzac's heroine, Eugénie Grandet, as an example of pastoral characterisation, the mark of Eugénie's pastoral status is her predictability, the knowledge that we 'will always find her doing the right thing'.[19] Yet, like those other terms which aid and abet the hidden transactions between *vraisemblance* and the *bienséances*, the phrase 'the right thing' is suitably ambiguous. The 'right thing' is the expected thing, but in two senses: in the sense of what is logically appropriate, consistent with a given psychological model of conduct; but beneath this sense there is also the sense of what is morally 'right', proper rather than appropriate. 'Pastoral', in this definition, responds simultaneously to, or rather gathers into one convention, ideas concerning both what the world is and what it *should* be; the fusion is brought out clearly in Bayley's discussion of pastoral stereotypes in Socialist Realism, where the model of 'realistic' representation derives in part from moral assumptions about an ideal state of affairs.

In these terms, the most striking feature of Stendhal's narrative universe is its resolutely anti-pastoral character. The decisive moments of the narrative are, precisely, its 'a-typical' moments. Indeed, adapting a suggestion by Leo Bersani,[20] one might say that the mass of strictly 'mimetic' material in *Le Rouge et le Noir* (the representation of contemporary social reality by means of a series of interlocking types: the bourgeois of Verrières, the aristocrats of the de la Mole salon) exists mainly in order to focus, by way of contrast, those acts or experiences which subvert the models of 'reality' illustrated and endorsed by these various social types. These acts are, of course, primarily transgressions of moral codes, prompted by impulses and desires forbidden or unacknowledged by society: Julien's crime, Louise's adultery, Mathilde's passion. But the deeper meaning of these acts is in the way they are often received, within the novel itself, not just as defiances of the rules of morality but, more radically, as a departure from 'reality' itself. The rebellion against moral standards is also a rebellion against taken-for-granted standards of intelligibility. Julien not only offends, he also *surprises* his society, and the two are profoundly interconnected. Whence the importance in the text of the motif of the 'unpredictable', the way Julien (like the other 'noble souls') repeatedly eludes and disturbs the 'internalized probability system' of the other characters, to whom he consequently appears, in the term that recurs throughout the novel to mark other people's perception of Julien, as 'singular': strange, unplaceable, infinitely more complex and mysterious than the simple stereotype of the ambitious parvenu.

But it is not only the characters of *Le Rouge et le Noir* who view Julien as 'singular'; as we have seen, this appears also to have been the case with many of its contemporary readers. And in terms of the relation of

Stendhal's novel to nineteenth-century conventions of verisimilitude and their social context, the instructive perspective here is that opened up by this convergence between the reactions and judgements of character and reader (at least to the extent that those of the latter can be reliably inferred from the critical record of the period). Julien is, of course, the main focus for this overlap of 'internal' and 'external' viewpoint. But an equally notable example concerns the respective responses to the behaviour of Mathilde. I have already cited Jules Janin's remark, 'No one ever imagined a girl like that'. But Janin could arguably have taken his cue from what is said about Mathilde within the novel itself, from, for example, M. de la Mole. For, in a sense, he is only echoing the latter's opinion, according to which Mathilde's conduct in taking Julien as her lover is not only outrageous, but unthinkable, emphatically not the 'right thing', in both the prescriptive and the predictive senses of the term:

> Who could have foreseen it? he said to himself. A daughter with such an arrogant character, with such a superior cast of mind, more proud than I am of the name she bears! Whose hand had been requested of me in advance by all the most illustrious nobles in France! (p. 456)

Jules Janin and M. de la Mole speak in what is virtually the same voice from within a common framework of assumptions: what is threatening to both in Mathilde's desire is simply pushed off the map of the intelligible; it literally beggars the 'imagination'. Mathilde is thus the occasion of a double disturbance: for both character and critic (father and censor: two figures of the 'Law'), she disturbs a system of expectations, embedded at once in the novel and in the contemporary society (or at least in those sectors of the society exercising greatest influence over what will be admitted to the canon of the *vraisemblable*). That disturbance is a sign of the text pitting itself against the authority of the *doxa*, seen in its dual role as guardian of the moral order and source of what is naturalistically known as 'reality'.

Evidently there are many difficulties in proposing this type of parallelism between character and reader. There are difficulties of a theoretical kind (we have to avoid the crude reductionism of 'reflection' theory), and of an empirical kind (what is the status of the journalistic critical record as evidence of forms of understanding diffusely at work in society at large; on what grounds, for example, can we assume Janin's to be a representative voice?). Posed in empirical terms, the problem is identical to that which bedevils all attempts at an historical sociology of knowledge: 'opinion' is difficult to investigate, the evidence is often thin, and the temptation to spread it wide very great. Some of these difficulties can, however, be partly met by considering the implications of a third element in the equation – the position of the narrator. For the reactions of M. de la

Mole and Jules Janin find a precise, although deceptive, echo in the magnificently ambiguous intervention of the narrator:

> The outcome of this night of folly was that she believed she had succeeded in triumphing over her love. (This page will be detrimental to the unfortunate author in more ways than one. The unresponsive among you will accuse him of impropriety. But he isn't insulting the young women who dazzle the Paris salons by supposing that a single one of them is capable of the mad impulses which spoil Mathilde's character. She is a purely imaginary figure, and besides, imagined quite without reference to the social customs which, in the succession of centuries, will guarantee nineteenth-century civilization a place of such distinction. (. . .) Now that it is firmly agreed that Mathilde's character is impossible in our century, which is no less prudent than virtuous, I am less afraid of causing annoyance by continuing to recount the follies of this amiable girl.) (pp. 370–1)

Everything in this famous passage is deeply equivocal, and I shall return to some of its more unsettled and unsettling features. In certain respects, however, it does suggest an apparent coincidence of view between character, critic and narrator. The narrator at once pre-empts and concedes the very criticisms of his creation that will be made by others inside and outside the novel. More exactly, it could be said that the narrator, in echoing his character and speaking to his reader, acts as a bridge between the value-systems of each. Of course, the narrator and his implied audience are problematical notions: who and what they stand for are complicated matters. Just as it would be wrong to confuse narrator with author, so it would be naive entirely to identify the implied audience with an actual public. At one level, the 'reader' here is every possible reader, not only those who have read Stendhal, but also those who will read him. We might say that the audience addressed by the narrator is an imaginary audience, a persona whose status is less referential than structural – in Structuralist terms, a functional role corresponding to the category 'narratee' and complementing the role 'narrator'.

Yet the familiar criticism of the Structuralist approach is pertinent here: that, in its insistent concern with abstract categories, it de-contextualizes and de-historicizes its object. That there is a specific historical basis both to the utterances of the Stendhalian narrator and the audience to which they are addressed is unmistakable. The voice appeals to a set of public values and beliefs, rooted in the collective, or consecrated, 'wisdom' of the age. It draws upon attitudes represented, within the novel, by those characters who speak in the name of what the text calls 'public opinion' (p. 156), and communicates with the reader outside the novel on the implicit assumption that these attitudes are shared by the reader. Thus, the empirical thinness of the evidence from the critical writings of the period [is], as it were, compensated by the logically necessary implications of the narrator's role; the very act of appealing to the reader in this way carries with it the presumption of a correspondence between belief-systems within the novel and outside it. Or, to take up Stendhal's own analogy for the project of the mimetic novel, the narrator acts as a kind of 'mirror', reflecting 'doxic' images back and forth between reader and text; as a mediator of *doxai*, he opens a channel of communication, makes possible a 'contract' of intelligibility which, in its most important task, is the confirmation of the 'mimetic contract' itself. We of course know that, through submerged patterns of meaning, Stendhal secretly reneges on all the major clauses of that contract. But the question of the more guarded meanings of the novel is not, for the moment, the immediate point at issue. Rather it is a question of the intervention of certain *forms*, in both the technical sense of a form of discourse and the idiomatic sense of a series of purely formal gestures (without substantial content), designed to sustain the pretence of solidarity with the reader, of endorsing a system of shared meanings against which the 'bizarre' behaviour of Stendhal's heroes and heroines can then be adequately interpreted and assessed. That gesture of solidarity is an illusory and ironic construct, which throws into even sharper relief the forces which break the chain of exchange between writer and reader, and tear the contract of agreed meanings to pieces.

Recitations

Tearing up the contract and withdrawing from the *doxa* is not, however, a straightforward undertaking, and it is only a naive version of a particular romantic ideology of language that will pretend otherwise. That attempted secession is, on the contrary, one of the acutest difficulties faced by both Stendhal and his major characters, and it carries important implications for Stendhal's relation to mimetic notions of narrative, in particular those encapsulated in the conception of the novel as 'chronicle' or 'mirror'. Stendhal and his heroes and heroines often dream and speak of freedom. Freedom here, as Brombert shows,[21] means many things, but pre-eminently freedom from the prison-house of Opinion, even when, paradoxically, the condition of such freedom becomes literal incarceration: to be locked away, 'far from the gaze of other people', is for Julien Sorel and Fabrice del Dongo the supreme mode of individual felicity, the habitat of the untouchable Self. This is, of course, a fantasy. Yet, however much Stendhal's critical intelligence surrounds it with equivocating irony, he was in some respects seduced by it, and it furnishes a coda to his novels (with the exception of *Lucien Leuwen*, which is one of the reasons why that novel remains unfinished, its essential predicament unresolved). The Stendhalian 'self', elusive and perhaps finally unknowable, can be located in at least one negative respect: its committed resistance to incorporation by the idioms of Opinion, or its progressive disengagement from the obsession with self-validation through others. How to outplay the Others is the name of the Stendhalian game.

That enterprise is to a considerable extent animated by what nowadays would be seen as a pure fiction: the notion – largely Rousseauist in its origins – of a unique and precious subjectivity which, in finding its own unique voice, a language fully present to self, will achieve true freedom, miraculously delivered from the social contract of meaning, discarding the currency, the 'well rubbed coins' – in Stendhal's quotation from Sterne[22] – of social exchange (the monetary image is as important for Stendhal as it is for Balzac). 'Mr. Myself', as Stendhal refers to himself in his private jottings, says it all: the paradox of securing the integrity of the self by speaking of it in a foreign tongue. It is the most revealing example of that effort of self-concealment manifested in Stendhal's passion for foreign languages and cryptic codes, and his heroes' frequent preference for secret sign systems and indirect modes of communication. The best, of course, is not to speak at all, and in *Le Rouge et le Noir* 'silence' of a sort will be an optimal, if fragile, solution for both hero and narrator alike. Stendhal himself knew at bottom that it was a fiction,[23] which is presumably one of the reasons why his two major heroes die young; beyond society and its languages there is nowhere else for them to go. But, even as fiction, it gives the terms for the tensions lived by his heroes within the fictions, as well as for some of the problems experienced by Stendhal in the writing of Fiction. How to speak to others, in the language of others, is at the heart of the Stendhalian dilemma.

The problem of living in society and of writing novels for a public is, then, the problem of the *doxa*, and it is primarily a problem of language. The *doxa*, as the sociologists remind us, is fundamentally a matter of language, a corpus of linguistic stereotypes through which a body of 'sedimented meanings' is deposited and maintained in the collective consciousness.[24] The sociological notion of 'sedimentation' corresponds exactly to a key emphasis in Stendhal's own reflections on language, as these have been summarized, in their specific bearing on the relation between writer and public, by Michel Crouzet in his magisterial *Stendhal et le langage*: 'Social, or literary, communication, when it is perfectly attuned to its audience, tends to "sediment" itself in a repertoire of utterances which are purely for consumption, rather than being living language.'[25] In its most reduced and simplified form, Stendhal's linguistic imagination revolves around an opposition between two kinds of speech: 'living language', as the site of authentic subjectivity, versus 'dead language', as the form of the 'social pact'[26] of language, grasped precisely as a kind of mimesis whereby speech moulds itself, in a phrase which in varying guises recurs continually in Stendhal's writings, to what is 'learnt, recited, known by heart'.[27] Social discourse is a repetition of what has been learnt by heart, taken from elsewhere. It is a comedy of 'recitation'; its speakers do not so much speak as recite from a socially consecrated and socially memorised text; they are locked into a linguistic automatism, a petrified code of proprieties and commonplaces, subservient to the *convenu* ['proper', 'appropriate'; lit. 'agreed upon' (Ed.)] and fearful of the *imprévu*.

Much of Stendhal's thinking about language turns on the notion of the *convenu*. Language, Stendhal frequently tells us, is a matter of agreements: in *Racine et Shakespeare*, language is 'a matter of convention'[28]; in *Rome, Naples et Florence en 1817*, it is a system of 'signs agreed upon ["convenus"] for the representation of ideas'.[29] In these remarks the status of the *convenu* is entirely neutral. It registers what Stendhal took from eighteenth-century accounts of the conventional basis of language (largely as encountered through his readings in the work of the *idéologues*). As such, the *convenu* merely states a theoretical fact of language: that linguistic agreements are a condition of mutually intelligible utterance (and hence with the implication that the idea of an autonomous subject exempting itself from those agreements is a myth). But in both his aesthetic and his political writings, the *convenu* also attracts emotionally and ideologically loaded meanings, and often becomes the object of unremitting attack. For something else that Stendhal may have inherited from the more anxious side of the eighteenth-century linguistic imagination – perhaps from Diderot, but more likely from Maine de Biran – is the sense of language as the site of self-alienation, along with the corresponding dream of a form beyond the arbitrarily coded linguistic sign, in which mind, body and sign will be at one. Music often presents itself as a candidate for this role (for Stendhal music is to the soul what for Diderot gesture and expression are to the body); and it is therefore not surprising that it is when Stendhal writes on music that his questioning of the linguistic contract is at its sharpest. In *Vie de Métastase*, for example, language is described once more in terms of the *convenu*, but this time in unequivocally negative vein: 'It is not surprising that our common languages, which are simply a sequence of signs that have been agreed upon for the expression of widely familiar things, should have no signs for the expression of feelings like these, which perhaps only twenty people out of a thousand have ever experienced.'[30] Language, in this account, is that which is shared by all, which ensures the circuit of exchange, but at a level of generality and commonplaceness from which the intimate and infinitely unpredictable inflections of Mr. Myself are wholly excluded. Stendhal, in short, engages critically with the notion of language-as-contract from an intellectual and political perspective quite different from that in which Balzac opposes it. The terms in which Balzac rejects the contractual basis of language derive from the theocratic doctrines of the political right, and in particular from Bonald's theory of the divine origins of language, as something God-given and therefore not dependent on merely human conventions. Stendhal's objections stem rather from the libertarian arguments of Maine de Biran, whereby the unique 'sensations' of the individual cannot find expression in the public stock of agreed forms.[31]

It is from that context that the *convenu* is regularly identified by Stendhal as pure ritual, as 'conventional' discourse in the disabling sense of the stereotyped, the mechanical and the inert. The paradigm of this discourse is Conversation. 'Conversation' is one of the section-headings of Stendhal's most sustained inquiry into the state of the language (*Racine et Shakespeare*), and he returns persistently to the idea that the quality of conversation is the index of the literary and political health of society. This emphasis forms the basis in *Racine et Shakespeare* of his rejection of the legacy of the seventeenth century, and of his attempt to promote an aesthetic of 'modernity'. Though doubtless of real polemical urgency in the early nineteenth century, Stendhal's battle with the neo-classical Academician is in some ways a side issue. For Stendhal's refusal of seventeenth-century literary forms is not just based on the familiar relativist arguments proposed by Romantic cultural historicism: what is right for the 'spirit of the age' in the seventeenth century cannot possibly be right for the culturally different circumstances of the nineteenth century. It stems rather from a deep intellectual and political hostility to the seventeenth century as such, and in particular to what Stendhal sees as the pernicious influence on literature exercised by the language of polite conversation at the Court of Versailles, the language of *le bon ton* and *le bel usage*. The conversation of the Court is pure *doxa*, the ceaseless imitation of a model autocratically imposed by the King as a means of political censorship and control. Hence the impossibility of Stendhal making up his mind properly about Racine: Racine is a great writer – indeed, on the relativist assumptions, a great 'Romantic' writer – but his work remains nevertheless vitiated by the severe constraints imposed by the norms of court exchange (Stendhal's true position is revealed in that bizarre throw-away remark, according to which Racine would have been an even greater tragedian if only he had had the good fortune to have lived in the nineteenth century).[32]

But what really matters in this provocative and often wayward account of the seventeenth century lies more in its bearing upon Stendhal's analysis of the position of the writer and his relation to language in the nineteenth century. 'Conversation' in the nineteenth century is in principle a very different affair; it has, at least potentially (if it were not blocked by the efforts of the Academicians and the salons), a certain vitality; it is linked to a 'torrent of passions' which 'threaten to overturn all proprieties ["convenances"] and to scatter the frequenters of salons to the four winds'.[33] The early nineteenth century offers, or offered, a possibility of healing the rift between public and private, language and action. It is the era ushered in by the Revolution, emancipated from the past, free of the dead weight of the stereotype and the model, and the language appropriate for the artistic representation of the decisive experiences of the age should be, precisely, a language suitable 'for children of the Revolution'.[34] This is the context in which Stendhal tries to re-invent the notion of an authentic 'common language', notably through his interventions, in *Racine et Shakespeare* and elsewhere, in the contemporary debate about modern 'Italian'. Echoing the Jacobin argument that linguistic unity is a condition of political equality, Stendhal, in the Italian debate, sides with the 'modernists' against the 'purists', with the demand for a modern Italian projected as a rationalized 'public' language in which all its subjects will communicate as equal citizens of the republic.[35] *Racine et Shakespeare* also gives the social and political context for Stendhal's related attempt to rework the eighteenth-century concept of the *beau idéal* into what, in *Histoire de la peinture en Italie*, he calls the *beau idéal moderne*.[36] Modern literature will hold a 'mirror' up to the age, but in terms of what is most forceful, uplifting and energizing in the age; its language will be that of the 'children of the Revolution' in that it will be consumed by the famous 'thirst for energy', the aesthetic equivalent, or indeed one of the very forms, of what Stendhal describes in *Racine et Shakespeare* as 'courage civil'[37]: the spirit of innovation, liberty, independence, risk-taking, passionate action.

But by 1823 (the publication of the first part of *Racine et Shakespeare*) this programme, although militantly argued for, is already perceived as in many ways a dead letter. It reflects more a nostalgic memory of possibilities seen as inherent in the heady and dangerous days of the Napoleonic campaigns, a cultural possibility where literature and action could conceivably be posed as mutually informing, where the former might mean something 'to people who were engaged in the Moscow campaign and saw at close hand the strange goings-on of 1814'.[38] By 1823 that possibility seems definitively lost. The return of the Bourbons, the restoration of the authority of the Church, the influence of the Académie and the salons, the proliferation of censors and spies, all conspire to re-imprison discourse within the orthodox grip of Opinion. Stendhal's career as a novelist, and that of his heroes within the novels, are indelibly marked by that loss. Their aversion from the idioms of the time is notorious: Stendhal's pronounced reluctance in *Le Rouge et le Noir* to recount the terms of provincial conversation (p. 9); Julien's disdain for the banalities of every milieu in which he finds himself. Yet for the author of *Le Rouge et le Noir*, the reproduction of these idioms is indispensable to the notion of the novel as a 'chronique du XIXe siècle', and their mastery a necessary condition of the hero's progress. The stake, and the ruse, of both author and hero in *Le Rouge et le Noir* is how to retain some vestige of freedom while negotiating what threatens that freedom: how Julien speaks to the other characters and how Stendhal speaks to his readers are two faces of the same dilemma and the same game.

One way of describing *Le Rouge et le Noir* is as an ensemble of discourses or, in Barthes's term, 'sociolects',[39] each of which corresponds to a particular social group, and which together furnish the different 'scripts' with which Julien acts out his various roles. Leaving aside the more marginal forms – for example, the restricted code of the Congregation, that world of Jesuit conspiracy and high politics whose esoteric language strikes Julien as a source of immense power and influence – there are essentially three such forms: the discourse of Verrières and the provincial bourgeoisie, of the Church and the Besançon seminary, and of the aristocratic salon in Paris. Julien's 'journey' is a movement through this sociolectal universe in a determined, if somewhat discontinuous, process of adaptation and accommodation. For, contrary to his Napoleonic fantasy of a self realized in action, Julien makes his way in the world less through deeds than through words, and it is precisely his education in these terms that gives one of the novel's ironic comments on the fact that in the society of the Restoration significant forms of action are no longer available ('this kind of eloquence, which has replaced the swiftness of action found under the Empire', p. 145). Most of the advice Julien receives (from Abbé Pirard, Prince Korasoff) centres not so much on what he should do as on what he should say (and not say), while many of his own self-admonitions are reflections on the importance of specifically verbal strategies ('Heavens above! who do they take me for? he said to himself. Do they think I can't *read between the lines*?' p. 185). His conquest of society consists largely in learning to manipulate social codes of speech, in acquiring arts of verbal dissimulation through which an accommodating and acceptable public self can be presented to the world ('Julien who had committed himself to the line of only ever saying things that seemed false to him', p. 150). Through a series of studied verbal 'performances', modelled on the socially recognized idioms, he constantly seeks, though sometimes fails, to adjust his visible self to the expectations of others, and, in this way, to forge a secure place for himself in the world.

'Performance' can be taken here in a quite literal sense. Julien's basic relation to the standard discourses of his society is one of *recitation*, parodied in that grotesque recital from memory of long stretches of the Bible which so impresses the Valenod family. The emphasis of Julien's prowess in recital is usually discussed in moral and psychological terms (around the question of the 'hypocrisy' of Julien's conduct). But it can perhaps also be linked emblematically to the more general arguments about society, language and literature sketched in *Racine et Shakespeare*, and in particular to the connection Stendhal makes there between the doxal languages of society and exhausted forms of literary representation:

namely, their character as pure repetition. Julien mechanically repeats, or mimes, what is itself already a language of repetition, and the success of the repetition is a condition of the convincingness (the *vraisemblance*) of the public self presented to others. I do not mean to suggest that there is here a conscious device of *mise-en-abyme* at work in the text of *Le Rouge et le Noir*. It is, however, arguable that, in the verbal mechanics of Julien's self-presentation to the social world of the novel, there is an implicit statement about the novel's own relation to the received idioms of narrative representation. That implication is at its strongest in the exchanges that take place in the salon of M. de la Mole. Of the salon conversations the narrator observes, in a rare moment of absolute candour:

> Provided there was no joking at the expense of God, the clergy, the king, the powers that be, artistic and literary figures currently enjoying favour at Court, or indeed any part of the establishment; provided that no good word was spoken for Béranger, the opposition press, Voltaire, Rousseau, or anything venturing to be in any way outspoken; provided above all that there was never any mention of politics, it *was* permissible to discourse freely on any subject. (p. 263)

Embodied in figures such as le baron Bâton ('this man holds forth, he doesn't converse', p. 268) and M. de Fervaques ('as he could only produce elegant phrases instead of ideas', p. 308), the discourse of the salon is essentially a ritual discourse; it is composed largely of 'phatic' utterance, and devoted to the preservation of a social order by excluding all those other utterances which might threaten its closed system of meanings. It is the nineteenth-century equivalent of the language of seventeenth-century Versailles denounced as a form of cultural and moral death in *Racine et Shakespeare*. In contrast to the 'living' speech of the proscribed Comte Altamira (or the robust political dialogue between the occupants of the carriage in which Julien travels up to Paris), the salon discourse is a 'dead' language, a moribund code within which no real energy or individuality is possible. It is a language of pure 'pastoral' images, where everyone says what everyone expects to hear, always the 'right thing'. Even in matters of life and death, as in Mathilde's acerbic reflection on the conventions of the duel, the bland surface of discursive homogeneity is never ruffled: 'Every bit of it is known in advance, even down to what you have to say as you succumb' (p. 340). Confronted with the new, on the other hand, it reacts as if before an alien life form with which it simply cannot cope; the discourse turns in on itself, breaks the circuit of communication, retreats into mute resistance: 'If you allow yourself to say something true and novel, they are astonished, they don't know what to answer' (p. 290).

Nowhere is the grip of orthodoxy more powerful in *Le Rouge et le Noir* than in the conversation of the aristocrats. Conversation here is not simply a way of passing the time. It is a 'sociolect' operating from a *vraisemblable* of speech, whose purpose is to ensure that all interchange acts as a continuous reproduction of the order of 'reality' consecrated by Opinion. As such, the language of the salon may be said to provide an analogue of one way of constructing the task of mimesis: namely, the negative definition we have already encountered, whereby mimesis turns on a relation between the literary *eikos* and the public *doxa*, in which the former repeats and reinforces the versions of reality proposed by the latter. The discourse of the salon enacts a self-perpetuating cycle of repetitions in which all the participants appear, in the words of the text, as 'all exact copies one of another' (p. 369), as derivatives of a 'common pattern' (p. 341) that is itself the copy of another model (the idea of the pre-Revolutionary aristocracy). Reproducing in and through language forms of social interaction that are themselves already reproductions, they generate an unbroken chain of imitations and duplications that corresponds directly to the idea of mimesis as the imitation of a language that is itself an imitation; as, in Barthes's phrase, the 'copy of a copy'.[40]

It is therefore no surprise that the mode in which Julien engages with those discourses is that of 'recitation', his own interventions in them constituting, as it were, a mimesis at a triple remove, a copy of a copy of a copy. For Julien, mastering the speech of the salon is like mastering a 'competence' with zero generative power and total redundancy, with which the speaker simply recycles a fixed stock of learnt phrases and *idées reçues*. This theme is realized above all in the comic episode of Julien's attempted seduction of Madame de Fervaques by means of the collection of stock love letters lent to him by Prince Korasoff. The importance of Madame de Fervaques lies in her status as pure type, pure pastoral, as the character in whose eyes the aristocratic 'decencies' are identified with a natural and immutable order of things; for whom the 'unpredictable' and the 'unsuitable' are synonyms. For Madame de Fervaques, the unexpected not only surprises, it scandalizes, not only offends but induces a kind of existential terror; to depart from the norms of 'proper' behaviour is literally to take leave of one's senses, to succumb to 'moral inebriation' ('The slightest outward sign of emotion would have struck her as some kind of *moral inebriation*', p. 420).

What more appropriate occasion, then, for illustrating, and parodying, a system of social relations based on a language of pure repetition? Julien faithfully copies out the text of the letters (which, in yet another image of the 'copy of a copy', have already been copied out from the originals), making only minor emendations at the level of circumstantial details. Madame de Fervaques replies, presumably in her own hand, but in exactly the same style. The exchange is, precisely, like a sustained formal recitation from a known, stereotyped text. So mechanical is the transaction, that inevitably certain discrepancies arise; literally copying out the Prince's

letters in the prescribed sequence, Julien does not actually 'reply' to
Madame de Fervaques. Yet the gap seems in no way to perturb the great
lady: 'Gradually, the lady adopted the sweet habit of writing almos+ every
day. Julien answered with faithful copies of the Russian letters, and such is
the advantage of a bombastic style that Mme de Fervaques was not in the
least astonished at the lack of connection between the answers and her
letters' (p. 433). Indeed at one point Julien's transcription of the letters is so
mechanical that, through inadvertence, he forgets to emend the place
names London and Richmond to Paris and Saint-Cloud. Madame de
Fervaques raises the point, with a slightly puzzled air, but does not pursue
it; Julien gives a hopelessly unsatisfactory reply, but, since the reply falls
within the convention of the agreed discourse, does not blow his cover. The
reason is clear: what matters is not the production of the message, but the
reproduction of the code; since the code is 'empty', void of individual
substance, discrepancies and inconsistencies which would otherwise
betray the insincerity of the message, do not in fact matter; the general
message is so strongly presupposed by the code that attention to its actual
articulation becomes unnecessary.

Silences

Julien's slip in the correspondence with Madame de Fervaques is
nevertheless symptomatic of a more general insecurity with regard to the
demands of his various performances. Julien plays the required verbal
game, but not in a manner that is uniformly successful. The slips, or
interruptions, in the performances are fairly frequent, and what they evoke
is a radical interior distance from the public forms of exchange with which
he outwardly engages. Julien adopts, but unlike Madame de Fervaques,
never internalizes the role; Julien merely plays a part, whereas Madame de
Fervaques *is* the part. At a critical level, Julien always stands back from the
role, and it is one of the main functions of Stendhal's version of the interior
monologue to bring out Julien's deeply estranged relation to his own
dissimulating manoeuvres. Behind the discourse of the Other and the
public self, there is another discourse and another self, at odds with what is
being transacted by the socially presented persona. Many of the most
important moments of *Le Rouge et le Noir* are built around the troubled
co-existence in Julien of public and private. There is, for instance, the
occasion of his first social invitation (the Valenod dinner party), at which
Julien pursues an inner meditation not only cut off from, but actively
opposed to the social patter in which he is outwardly involved.
Conversation and monologue run concurrently, but in a relation of total
antagonism; Julien 'performs' at the same time as inwardly despising the
performance; the contradiction produces the potentially tell-tale sign of

pain and protest (the tear induced by Valenod's suppression of the pauper's song in the adjoining debtors' prison); but it is hastily effaced in a violent recall to the required role: 'Julien was brought back to his role with a violent jolt. It wasn't to indulge in daydreaming and sit in silence that he had been invited to dine in such good company' (p. 147).

The gap between 'daydreaming' and 'speaking', inwardness and speech, and the concomitant notion that to cross that gap is to do 'violence' to the self, is a recurring theme of the novel. In the salon of M. de la Mole there are moments when it cannot be crossed, when the game becomes impossible: 'He often laughed with all his heart at the things that were said in this little group; but he felt incapable of thinking up anything comparable' (p. 266). More dramatically still, there is the episode in the library with Mathilde (pp. 436–40), in which the stratagems of seducer's discourse enter into violent conflict with the intensities of concealed feelings. Here the experience of self-estrangement in language is complete, as Julien listens to himself speaking as if he were uttering a foreign tongue ('as he listened to the sound of the idle words his mouth was uttering just as he would have done an extraneous noise'). The whole episode works as a bewilderingly rapid shifting of vocal registers, whereby any sense of a unified speaking voice splinters into a series of heterogeneous and dissociated fragments: the inward voice ('Ah! (. . .) he exclaimed inwardly') becomes detached from the speaking voice ('Meanwhile his voice was saying'); the latter struggles against the force of the former ('the innermost recesses of his heart'), but at a physical and emotional cost that threatens articulation itself ('in a barely audible voice,', 'his voice faltered even more'). The co-existence of the two competing voices is thus far from peaceful. Although for the most part of the novel Julien negotiates the contradictions, he lives in a state of acute tension in which the two voices perpetually threaten to clash with each other; the private voice is the object of continued repression and self-censorship ('the sound of my voice will betray me', p. 441; 'I may lose everything by a single word', p. 434); on the other hand, that repressed voice will not cease in its efforts to make itself heard. And, at the vital moments, it is of course the private voice which wins the contest: in the relationship with Louise, in the Besançon seminary, in the tortured affair with Mathilde, in the speech of denunciation to the court – all so many occasions when the pressures of the inward self lead Julien to say exactly the opposite of the 'expected' thing.

Yet perhaps the mode in which Julien most effectively transcends these self-traducing discourses lies less in the usurping of public performance by 'private' language than in the refusal of language as such, in the opting for silence. Criticism has commented extensively on the symbolism of the 'happy prison' in *Le Rouge et le Noir*, on the paradox of incarceration as liberation, as the moment when Julien abandons the mask to be at one with himself. What has rarely been remarked upon, however, are the implications of that withdrawal for Julien's attitude to language itself. The refusal of the world is also in part a refusal of the word. The leave-taking from society is marked by a silence which provides the novel's own epitaph to the epigraph placed at the head of one of its chapters: 'Speech was given to men to conceal their thoughts' (p. 143). From his prison cell Julien writes to Mathilde: 'You must never speak of me, even to my son: silence is the only way to honour me (. . .) I shall none the less echo [Iago's] words: *From this time forth I never will speak word.* I shall not be observed to speak or write further; you will have had my last words together with my last acts of adoration' (p. 471). That declaration will of course not in fact be Julien's last word. Yet, despite the theatrical quotation, it would be misleading to put this down to being just another instance of the kind of theoretical bravado that so often intervenes in the relationship with Mathilde. For Julien the prison represents above all a withdrawal from the Other ('What do I care about *other people*? My ties with *other people* are going to be abruptly severed', p. 494), a withdrawal from the communicative situation and hence from the language of social exchange. (The exception to this self-appointed exile is Louise, and it is significant that it is in the interchange with her that the 'true' discourse, the language of inwardness, finds its way for almost the first time into a genuine intersubjective encounter: 'I'm speaking to you just as I speak to myself', p. 512.)

The rule, however, is silence, and necessarily so, since the inner resources discovered by Julien in the prison are not communicable within the public forms which have hitherto mediated his relations with society. But perhaps the most important aspect of Julien's choice of silence concerns not so much our interpretation of the hero, as our interpretation of the position of the narrator and his relation to the given discourses of narrative representation. I have suggested that the deeper meaning of Julien's rebellion against the stereotyped morality and language of his society is the questioning by Stendhal of the order of mimesis and the conventions of *vraisemblance* which sustain that order. That connection is, I think, powerfully reinforced by the convergence of hero and narrator on the question of their respective attitudes to language. The parallel can be constructed on various levels. Both hero and narrator impose upon themselves a principle of self-censorship: the constraints Julien places on himself are matched, for example, by the self-censoring footnotes through which, in the political passages of the novel, the narrator proclaims his orthodoxy. Both disguise themselves in the clothing of the *doxa*, the narrator donning a self-protective mask before the reader which corresponds to the mask displayed by Julien to the other characters of the novel. For both this produces various kinds of tension and contradiction, and calls into play various strategies for dealing with them.

In this respect, however, there is a major difference between them:

whereas the hero is allowed to compensate for his outward social deceptions by means of the freedom of the interior monologue, the perpetually exposed narrator can cope with his duplicitous involvement with the codes of his readers only by displacing it into irony. The ironic reversals and pirouettes of the Stendhalian narrator, the masking of implicit negotiations in explicit affirmations, are already the subject of an extensive critical literature.[41] My point here concerns the way these ironic interventions produce a secret sabotaging of the 'contract' with the reader. That sabotaging gesture is nicely illustrated by returning to the example cited at the beginning of this chapter of the narrator's comment on Mathilde. The overt intention is to make a gesture of reassurance to the reader by endorsing those interpretations of her conduct issuing from a shared system of meanings and values. In these terms, not only is Mathilde 'immoral' (an immorality from which the narrator dissociates himself by disclaiming all 'responsibility' for it), but – a far more decisive gesture of recuperation – she is also 'a-typical': she is an 'exception', purely a creature of the 'imagination' (Janin went further in asserting that she was strictly 'unimaginable'); she is 'imagined quite without reference to [our] social customs' she is 'impossible in our century'; in short, her behaviour is not only unrepresentative, it is inexplicable, *invraisemblable*, except as a psychological aberration, as a moment of 'madness'.

It is, of course, the incongruity of the word 'madness' here (it occurs three times in the passage) that gives the game away. As Shoshana Felman has demonstrated in her remarkable study, the lexical adventure of the word 'madness' takes us to the very heart of Stendhal's ironies and ambiguities.[42] 'Madness' is one of the most unstable terms in the constitutively unstable Stendhalian lexicon, the perfect example of a word whose meaning varies from one context to the next, which conjures up and brings into conflict rival systems of connotation in such a way as to play havoc with the *doxa*. Stendhal uses the term in order to show that, as a stable item in the vocabulary of a culture, 'madness' is always defined according to the prevailing norms of 'reason' and 'common sense', as the extreme form through which the consensus deals with what is outside and alien to its system of intelligibility; and that to de-stabilize the term by ironic means is therefore to place great pressure on that system. This is exactly what takes place in the passage about Mathilde, largely by means of the device (later exploited systematically by Flaubert) that Barthes has aptly called 'the quotation without quotation marks'.[43] The narrator here does not so much repeat the commonplaces of the culture as self-consciously *quote* from them, thereby at once instituting an ironic distance and a perspective of negation. The underlying meaning of the commentary depends on a recognition of its 'citational' nature, of the way the narrator signals it as belonging to a discourse with which the narrator is by no means necessarily identified. The commentary thus subtly turns against its own source, provokes a reading that, in fundamental ways, reverses the received meanings (a reversal reinforced elsewhere in the novel by the appearance of the word 'madness' in contexts whose associations of contiguity directly challenge the conventional wisdom of society – 'it was madness, it was [grandeur of soul]', p. 482). Describing Mathilde's behaviour as a 'fit of madness' is not, therefore, the occasion of a negative interpretation. Underlining the fact that she is a-typical, that she acts outside the expectation system of society, and the probability system of the novel, is in no sense a classification of her as 'unnatural'. If anything, it is the contrary; it is the conformity to 'bon sens' that represents the denial of 'nature' (*le naturel*); it is the modelling of one's life on the *doxa*, adaptation of self to the dead forms of the stereotype, that is the mark of inner atrophy and impoverishment. In short, it is precisely the degree to which Stendhal allows his character to be 'mad' in society's terms and *invraisemblable* in the novel's terms, that Mathilde is at her most compelling as a fictional creation. It is at just these points that she becomes the incarnation of the energizing force of 'moral courage', in contrast to the 'moral asphyxia' that dominates the salon (although that description of Mathilde has also to be tempered by the extent to which she too is caught in the 'mimetic trap', imitatively basing her desires and actions on heroic images of her sixteenth-century ancestors).

Irony, then, is one of the narrator's means for secretly withdrawing from the contract. The other, and more powerful, is simply silence, where the narrator joins with his hero in a common refusal of available forms of explanation and self-explanation. Stendhal's 'silences' are famous, and subject to varying interpretations. The most common sees them as deriving from Stendhal's innate 'modesty', his extreme reluctance to expose the most cherished moments of his narrative to the gaze of the hostile Other (as in the example of the three year idyll between Fabrice and Clélia, passed over in a single sentence). The issue, however, may be less one of authorial psychology than one of language and discourse. Leo Bersani has suggested that Stendhal's reticence at key moments of his narrative springs from the hero's profound commitment to a fantasy of withdrawal and regression which is fundamentally incapable of verbal realization, a condition 'about which, finally, there is very little to say',[*] and which therefore can exist in the text only as that which is missing, which can be evoked only through a perpetual deferral. In other words, its unsayability is a sign of its impossibility, its status as myth and illusion, the untenable dream of a return to an undifferentiated unity of self and world; it is the point at which Stendhal allows himself to be seduced, and hence paralysed, by the Rousseauist myth of a unique, pre-social, pre-linguistic self. Such an interpretation is by no means implausible, and would moreover connect with some of the themes we have seen at work in Stendhal's own reflections on the gap between language and subjectivity. My own claim here, however, would be not so much that the hero's interior distance from the world is, as it were, ontologically unsayable, as that it encounters a difficulty of representation that is social and historical in character; that it resists and exceeds nineteenth-century schemes of *vraisemblance* and intelligibility.

This surely is the sense of the most spectacular instance of Stendhalian silence, the episode of Julien's crime. For Julien's attempted murder of Louise is not an instance of regressive fantasy, but a concrete act, the sudden and unexpected surfacing of the energy and passion hitherto repressed beneath the role-playing performances. It is the moment at which we find him categorically not doing the 'right thing'. It is the triumph of spontaneity over calculation, of the immediacy of action over the mediations of language, through which Julien not only places himself outside society but, far more importantly, outside society's frame of meanings. Of all his unexpected acts, this is the most bewildering. Apart from an official insistence on the 'premeditated' nature of the deed, Julien himself says virtually nothing about it, rejects all invitation to self-explanation. While he remains detached and indifferent, everyone else rushes around in a frenzy of incomprehension; even the abbé de Frilair, that past master of worldly 'rationality', is entirely baffled ('This Julien is a strange creature, his action is inexplicable', p. 479). And this incomprehension on the part of the characters was matched by a similar failure of understanding on the part of many of Stendhal's nineteenth-century readers, who, as we have seen, on the whole could make sense of it only by claiming that it made no sense. Faguet, the high priest of the Establishment doctrine of 'realism', the equivalent figure of the official critics of the seventeenth-century Académie, described it as incomprehensible, quite beyond the logic of *vraisemblance*.[45] And Faguet's sense of bewilderment was doubtless accentuated by the fact of the narrator's studious silence. Just as Julien makes no attempt to explain his actions to the people around him, so the narrator makes no attempt to render it intelligible to his readers. The garrulous narrator simply shuts up shop, pulls the carpet from under the feet of the reader, abandons the *doxa* at the very moment it is most needed, for he knows that to make sense of it in these terms would be to betray its meaning.

This silence is, of course, the complete opposite of the silence of the *vraisemblable*. In the most highly developed systems of *vraisemblance*, the norms of the system remain tacit because the writer's confidence in their authority, and in the acceptance of that authority by the reader, is so strong that they do not need to be explicitly named. It is sometimes suggested that this is exactly the case with Stendhal's representation of Julien's crime. Richard Wollheim, for example, commenting on Merleau-Ponty's account of this episode, remarks: 'Merleau-Ponty suggests that much of the tension of Julien's return to Verrières arises from the suppression of the kinds of thoughts or interior detail that we could expect to find in such an account; we get in one page what might have taken up five. If this is so, then it would seem to follow that, for the understanding of this passage, the reader of *Le Rouge et le Noir* needs to come to the book with at any rate some acquaintance with the conventions of the early nineteenth-century novel.[46] Knowledge of those conventions will not, however, help much in this particular case. Stendhal's silence signifies not the tacit acceptance but the disdainful refusal of given codes of *vraisemblance*.[47] It is not that the meaning of Julien's conduct is so obvious that it does not need to be named, but that, in these terms, it is unnameable, except – within a psychological code – as 'mad' or – within a literary code – as *invraisemblable*. This returns us finally to the ironies and paradoxes surrounding the use of the word 'madness' in Stendhal's text (and, moreover, opens on to some of the questions we will encounter in a much acuter form in the work of Nerval). 'Madness', as the construct of its opposite, the discourse of 'reason', is, by virtue of that very fact, strictly unnameable; it can be named, made intelligible, only through a discourse that comes from the other side of 'madness'. Thus, to maintain a certain silence on these matters is to begin to question the hegemony of that discourse; and thereby to pose questions about the foundations and constraints of representation, verisimilitude.

They are in fact exactly the sorts of questions implicit in Stendhal's own revealing remark about the endlessly problematic relations between narration and autobiography:

> I shall find it very difficult to give a rational account of my love for Angela Pietragrua. How does one bring the slightest rationality to a story about so much madness? Where does one begin? How does one make it at all comprehensible? (. . .) By restricting myself to rational forms of narrative, I would be doing too much injustice to my subject (. . .) To be honest, I cannot go on: the subject exceeds the saying of it.[48]

This passage from *Vie de Henry Brulard* could well stand as definitive witness to those points of stubborn resistance in Stendhal's writings to the given stereotypes of representation: the intimacies of the private self lie beyond the resources of narrative embodiment; 'rationality' cannot cope with what, in its own terms, it names as 'madness'; language fails when it is most needed; the authenticity of desire evades the 'injustices' of public discourse by taking flight into silence. 'The subject exceeds the saying of it' . . . This remark, above all, is music to our *avantgardiste* ears, resonating with the distinctive tones of modernism, and in part explains why Stendhal, of all the nineteenth-century novelists, was so regularly exempted from the exhausted tradition of realism by the leading spokesmen of the early twentieth-century avant-garde, from the *Nouvelle*

The Red and the Black *and* The Charterhouse of Parma

Revue Française to surrealism. Gide – always ready to invoke a model for
the urgency of escaping the tyranny of the Model – annexes Stendhal to the
libertarian individualism of 'openness to experience' and the 'gratuitous
act'. Bataille includes *Le Rouge et le Noir* in his short list of privileged texts
which transgress the 'limit' beyond which lies the fundamental
incommunicability of 'experience'.[49] Breton, in a virulent attack on the
language of rationality and the notion of representational art, remarks in
the *Manifeste du surréalisme* that Stendhal's heroes can be seen as
incarnations of active spontaneous life at those moments when the
analytical Stendhalian narrator stops talking about them; 'we refind
Stendhal's heroes when Stendhal loses them'.[50]

Yet perhaps the modernist apotheosis of Stendhal brings with it other
kinds of problem. And, before we turn the clock forward to place Stendhal
in the century to which he truly belongs, we might pause to consider
whether the aesthetics of 'silence' is an adequate response to the dilemmas
Stendhal faced; whether, moreover, it does not itself also risk the very fate
to which it is in principle opposed. For if 'the subject exceeds the saying of
it', what, as Bersani intimates, can we possibly *say* about that [exceeding]?
Logically nothing (silence is uninspectable), but in practice a very great
deal. The paradoxical outcome of Stendhal's silences has been to spawn
critical and interpretative discourse on a large scale; around those gaps the
languages of criticism have garrulously swarmed, usually in the mode of
uncritical celebration. The value, the subversive force, of Silence has
become one of the taken-for-granted stereotypes of our own age. Indeed it
was already such in Stendhal's time. It is almost certainly the case that the
local intellectual source of Stendhal's worry about language was the theory
of Maine de Biran, in particular Biran's insistence on the impossibility of
private 'sensations' obtaining passage into the public categories of language.
But the idea of the excess of subjectivity over language, the notion of an
ineffable 'privateness', deeply resistant to expression, is one of the great
commonplaces of the romantic period as a whole: the romantic subject
speaks endlessly of his own incapacity to speak himself, or rather of the
incapacity of language to speak him, to express his irreducible 'originality'.

We have seen some of the terms in which Stendhal is caught up in the
romantic fictions of uniqueness and originality. But at the same time
Stendhal's ironic consciousness of the complexities he faces was in many
ways far more sophisticated than that of both many of his romantic
contemporaries and his twentieth-century *avant-gardiste* admirers. As
Barthes notes, in what was his last publication ('One always fails in
speaking of what one loves'),[51] Stendhal repeatedly encounters a blockage
in speaking of what is most important to him (his love affairs, Italy, his
heroes' 'aberrations'). Yet that blockage assumes not one form (silence), but
two: either Stendhal can write nothing, or he writes badly; in the latter
case, the inability to speak is a linguistic impotence manifested as a 'fiasco'

of style, whose name is nothing other than the platitude.[52] Silence and
cliché are thus not in a simple relation of opposition, the one a capitulation
to the received discourses, the other their negation. Silence is the other side
of the *idée reçue*, ('received idea'), a symptom of the same malaise. The
incommunicability of silence and the stupidity of the stereotype are sides
of the same coin (in a logic whose paradoxical ramifications we will meet
in a more developed form in Flaubert). This is an important realignment of
the terms in which Stendhal perceived the predicament of self and
language, and carries us well beyond the easy individualism which has
uncritically informed so many other accounts. Barthes's argument,
however, also takes another, and somewhat surprising, turn. It is not in fact
true that 'one always fails in speaking of what one loves'. Stendhal finds a
way out of the repetition of the linguistic and stylistic fiasco. The solution
comes after much delay, after the event: in the magnificent opening pages
of *La Chartreuse de Parme*, or, as Barthes puts it, in the mediation of checked
desire by the 'mythical' structures of narrative. The release of subjectivity
into language, the literary consummation of the pursuit of happiness,
occurs in a narrative structure which has a liberating hero (Napoleon) and
a corresponding hierarchy of positive and negative terms:

> What is required to make a Myth? We must have the action of two
> forces: First of all, a hero, a great liberating Figure: this is Bonaparte,
> who enters Milan, penetrates Italy (. . .); then an opposition, an
> antithesis – a paradigm, in short – which stages the combat of Good
> and Evil and thereby produces what is lacking in the Album and
> belongs to the Book, i.e., a meaning: on one side, in these first pages of
> *The Charterhouse*, boredom, wealth, avarice, Austria, the Police,
> Ascanio, Grianta; on the other, intoxication, heroism, poverty, the
> Republic, [Fabrice], Milan; and above all, on the one side, the Father;
> on the other, Women.[53]

But this version of Stendhal's escape from the double bind of silence and
the stereotype is at once puzzling and unsatisfactory. It is puzzling in that
it does not really square with what Barthes has to say about narrative in
many of his other writings; it is unsatisfactory, because it returns us, in its
own way, to the limiting terms of an aesthetics of individualism. The
impasse of desire before the public categories of language, forever waylaid
and blocked by the fiasco of the platitude, achieves expression in the
'mythic' structure of narrative – that is, in precisely what elsewhere
(notably in *S/Z*) has been exposed as one of the major cultural forms of the
platitude (the 'nauseous' simplifications of the narrative stereotype).
Narrative myth here, however, assumes a new and more positive function;
it has become the occasion of a private therapy, a jubilatory release of
otherwise linguistically blocked emotion. Whereas in *Le Rouge et le Noir*, it

is the complicities of narrative in the rejected terms of specific social representations of subjectivity and desire which lead to a breakdown and a retreat (into 'silence'), in *La Chartreuse de Parme* a miraculous fusion and exorcism are performed. This proposed conjunction of narrative commonplace and the authentic subjectivity of Mr. Myself is odd to a degree. Yet perhaps it is a conjunction that can be used to push the argument in a different direction, and in particular away from the neo-romantic heroisation of Stendhal's 'silences', and also away from the perhaps equally neo-romantic notion of narrative as a kind of private catharsis. *La Chartreuse de Parme* certainly has its mythic structure (precisely of the kind that Barthes himself described in *Mythologies* as the narrative myths flowing from the republican-bonapartist versions of History).[54] But it is also a novel whose power remains unintelligible without reference to its encounter with the public scene of history. It would doubtless be misleading to talk of that encounter as the unproblematical passage of 'real history' into the novel (Napoleon's entry into Italy could be narrativised in a whole number of different, and ideologically determined, ways). But neither does it make much sense to transform the representation of that public scene into a purely private cure. The point about *La Chartreuse de Parme* is that, even as it continues to problematize the relations of 'public' and 'private' (like *Le Rouge et le Noir*, *La Chartreuse de Parme* has its silences), it also, for one brief extraordinary moment, brings the two together. In those opening pages, public event and private feeling are strictly indissociable. We may wish to say that an enabling condition of that connection is the creation of a myth, and certainly sentimental visions of Napoleon exporting the ideals of the French Revolution into Italy require rigorous 'ideological' unpacking. But we should also remember that it was the memory of the historical experience of the Revolution that inspired Stendhal's (short-lived) belief in an art and a language in which personal feelings and collective experience might be brought together (a language 'suitable to the children of the Revolution').

The argument of *Racine et Shakespeare*, it will be recalled, is for an art at once libertarian and modern. But just as the libertarian emphasis is not finally reducible to a code of purely individualist values (it engages a whole politics), so the 'modernist' emphasis does not entail a rejection of mimetic or representational notions of the function of art. What Stendhal rejects is not the idea of representation as such, but outworn forms of representation (the academicist 'imitation of the Model'), in the name of an art that should respond to the challenge of its age. For Stendhal responding to that challenge, holding out the promise of an art that would capture the 'spirit of the age', is directly linked to what he perceived as the dynamic promise of the Revolution. Although not formally systematized as such, *Racine et Shakespeare* proposes a complex representational aesthetic attuned to that dynamic; an idea of art which involves saying both how it is and how it might be, embodying both an actual and a potential within a whole social and historical process. The opening pages of *La Chartreuse de Parme* are a fulfilment, belated and partial, of that promise. We cannot, of course, abstract that beginning from what happens in the rest of the novel, and in particular from that tragic 'fading' effect produced by its strange ending: that rapid narrative dispatch of broken lives into their respective 'silences', or indeed the rapid dispatch of the narrative itself into its own silence. In the gap between the fluent expansiveness of its opening pages and the abrupt curtailment of its closing pages a profound disillusionment is registered; the novel cannot maintain its promise because the history it represents did not. Yet the initial energy of *La Chartreuse de Parme* may require us to be a little more reticent over proclaiming silence as an artistic *solution* to the problems and contradictions Stendhal encountered in the relations between history, language and narrative. It may in fact give an entirely different context for the meaning of silence: that which Stendhal himself evokes, in the words he puts into the mouth of his Academician adversary in *Racine et Shakespeare*: 'Let us remember to respond only with the silence of disdain to these Romantic authors writing to meet the demands of a Revolutionary age'.[55]

Notes

1. I borrow the term 'socio-logic' from R. BARTHES, 'A propos de deux ouvrages de Cl. Lévi-Strauss: sociologie et socio-logique' in R. Bellour and C. Clément (eds), *Claude Lévi-Strauss, Textes de et sur Cl. Lévi-Strauss* (Paris: Gallimard, 1979).

2. G. BLIN, *Stendhal et les problèmes de la personnalité* (Paris: Corti, 1958), vol. 1, p. 299.

3. Cf. J. MÉLIA, *Stendhal et ses commentateurs*, (Paris: Mercure de France, 1911).

4. *Le Journal des débats*, March, 1818.

5. *Le Globe*, August 1827.

6. *La Revue des deux mondes*, Jan. 1843.

7. *La Revue de Paris*, June 1830.

8. *Le Journal des débats*, Dec. 1830.

9. P. MÉRIMÉE *cit.* MÉLIA, *op. cit.*, p. 138.

10. E. FAGUET, *Politiques et moralistes du XIXe siècle*, 3e série (Paris: Société française d'imprimerie et de librairie, 1900), p. 49.

11. STENDHAL, *Vie de Rossini* (ed. Divan), vol. I, p. 284. Except where indicated, all references to Stendhal's works are to the Divan edition, ed. H. Martineau, (Paris, 1927–37). References to the autobiographical writings are to the *Œuvres intimes* ed. H. Martineau (Bibliothèque de la Pléiade, Paris: 1955). [*Editor's note*: references to the text of the novel are to *The Red and the Black*, trans. Catherine Slater, and page numbers are given in brackets after quotations.]

12. *Rome, Naples et Florence en 1817* (ed. Divan, 1956), vol. II, p. 285.

13. *La Revue des deux mondes*, Jan. 1843.

14. Cf. *Racine et Shakespeare*, p. 88.

15. Cf. *The Order of Mimesis*, pp. 41–57.

16. RAPIN, *Réflexions sur la poétique*, cit. Gérard GENETTE, *Figures II* (Paris: Editions du Seuil, 1969) p. 73.

17. H. DE BALZAC, 'Lettres sur la littérature' in *Œuvres diverses* (Paris: Conard, 1940), vol. II, p. 278.

18. J. BAYLEY, *Tolstoy and the Novel* (London: Chatto and Windus, 1968), p. 147.

19. *Ibid.*, p. 150.

20. L. BERSANI, *From Balzac to Beckett* (New York: Oxford University Press, 1970), p. 98.

21. V. BROMBERT, *Stendhal. Fiction and the Themes of Freedom*, (New York: University of Chicago Press, 1968).

22. *Racine et Shakespeare*, p. 318: 'Sterne was only too right: we are nothing but "well rubbed coins" '. On the relation between money and language in Stendhal's thinking, cf. M. CROUZET, 'Stendhal et les signes' in *Romantisme*, 3 (1972).

23. Cf. *Racine et Shakespeare*, p. 210: 'The principal instrument of a people's genius is its language. Of what use is it to a mute to be full of bright ideas? Well, is a man who speaks a language understood only by himself really very different from a mute?'

24. P. BERGER and T. LUCKMANN, *The Social Construction of Reality* (Harmondsworth: Penguin Books, 1971) p. 87.

25. M. CROUZET, *Stendhal et le langage* (Paris: Gallimard, 1981), p. 22.

26. *Ibid.*, p. 18.

27. *Œuvres intimes*, pp. 395, 667.

28. *Racine et Shakespeare*, p. 364.

29. *Rome, Naples et Florence en 1817* (ed. Divan, 1956), p. 89n, p. 224.

30. *Vie de Métastase*, p. 357.

31. MAINE DE BIRAN 'Origine du langage' in *Œuvres*, vol. XII (Paris: Félix Alcan, 1939), pp. 167–213.

32. *Racine et Shakespeare*, p. 24.

33. *Ibid.*, p. 297.

34. *Ibid.*, p. 88.

35. M. CROUZET, *op. cit.*, pp. 288 ff.

36. *Histoire de la peinture en Italie*, vol. II, pp. 132 ff.

37. *Racine et Shakespeare*, p. 165, p. 318.

38. *Ibid.*, p. 88.

39. R. BARTHES, *Le Plaisir du texte* (Paris: Editions du Seuil, 1973), p. 46: 'Every fiction [i.e. "ideological system"] is sustained by a social mode of speech, a sociolect, with which it identifies itself: the fiction is this degree of consistency achieved by a language when it has "taken" exceptionally well and finds a sacerdotal class (priests, intellectuals, artists) to speak it widely and diffuse it.'

40. R. BARTHES, *S/Z* (Paris: Editions du Seuil, 1970), p. 61.

41. Cf. V. BROMBERT, *Stendhal ou la voie oblique* (New Haven and London: Presses universitaires de France, 1954).

42. S. FELMAN, *La 'Folie' dans l'œuvre romanesque de Stendhal* (Paris: Corti, 1971).

43. R. BARTHES, *Le Plaisir du texte*, p. 51.

44. L. BERSANI, *op. cit.*, p. 121.

45. E. FAGUET, *op. cit.*, p. 51.

46. R. WOLLHEIM, *Art and its Objects*, p. 147 (Harmondsworth: Penguin Books, 1970).

47. G. GENETTE, *op. cit.*, p. 78.

48. *Vie de Henry Brulard* in *Œuvres intimes*, pp. 393–4.

49. G. BATAILLE, 'Avant-propos', *Le Bleu du ciel* (Paris: Jean-Jacques Pauvert, 1957), p. 7.

50. A. BRETON, *Manifeste du surréalisme* (Paris: Gallimard, 1972), p. 18.

51. R. BARTHES 'One always fails in speaking of what one loves' in *Tel Quel*, no. 85 (1980).

52. *Ibid.*, p. 35.

53. *Ibid.*, p. 38 [see above, pp. 155 (*Ed.*)].

54. R. BARTHES, *Mythologies* (Paris: Editions du Seuil, 1957), pp. 188–90.

55. *Racine et Shakespeare*, p. 71.

Glossary

BAKHTIN, MIKHAIL (1895–1975) Russian thinker and literary theorist, particularly associated with 'dialogism' (q.v.).

BLUM, LÉON (1872–1950) Socialist politician and man of letters, who led the Popular Front government in 1936 and a socialist government in 1946.

BOURGET, PAUL (1852–1935) Novelist and critic (and friend of Henry James), whose earliest published work was in verse. *Cruelle Enigme* (1885) and *André Cornélis* (1887) secured his reputation as a writer of 'psychological' novels, which was further enhanced by *Le Disciple* (1889), *Cosmopolis* (1893), and *L'Etape* (1902). Later works heavily imbued with Catholic and Royalist sympathies. Now more admired for his critical writings, particularly his *Essais de psychologie contemporaine* (1883), and *Nouveaux Essais de psychologie contemporaine* (1886).

CONDILLAC, ETIENNE DE (1715–80) Philosopher who followed John Locke in analysing the primary role of physical sensations in the development of human mental faculties.

CONGRÉGATION The term was used at the time of the publication of *The Red and the Black* to denote an influential secret religious society of right-wing political views.

CONRAD, JOSEPH, (1857–1924) Novelist of Polish parentage, who spent twenty years at sea before settling in England in 1894. *Lord Jim* appeared in 1900.

CORNEILLE, PIERRE (1606–84) French classical dramatist. *Le Cid*, a tragedy focused on a conflict between love and duty, was first performed in 1637.

DIALOGISM Term from the work of Mikhail Bakhtin (q.v.), who argues that all discourse is in dialogue with prior discourses on the same, given subject, as well as with discourses still to come. Each culture consists in a 'polyphony' of discourses retained in the collective memory (stereotypical discourse and the sophisticated literary text alike), and in relation to which each speaking (or writing) subject has to situate himself or herself in a 'dialogical' process.

DICKENS, CHARLES (1812–70) Prolific English novelist. *Great Expectations* was published in 1860–1.

DIDEROT, DENIS (1713–84) Philosopher, novelist, dramatist, art critic, and editor of the *Encyclopédie* (1751–80), many of whose principal works (*La Religieuse, Jacques le fataliste, Le Neveu de Rameau*, the D'Alembert trilogy) were not published until after his death. *Jacques le Fataliste* (first published in French in 1796) owes a debt to LAURENCE STERNE (q.v.)'s *Tristram Shandy* and is notable for its experimental narrative technique and high degree of narratorial intrusion.

DOSTOYEVSKY, FYODOR MIKHAILOVICH (1821–81) Russian novelist. *The Brothers Karamazov* appeared in 1879–80.

DOXA The Greek word for 'opinion' given new currency by Roland Barthes (see 'Notes on Authors') in his analysis of the *'vraisemblable'* (q.v.) and its dependence on widely shared, normative perceptions of reality.

DUMAS, ALEXANDRE (père) (1802–70) Novelist and dramatist whose complete works number 103 volumes. A leading figure in the Romantics' battle for acceptance on the French stage, notably in *Henri III et sa cour* (1829) and *Antony* (1831). In the latter play the eponymous and rather energetic hero endeavours to elope with a charmed but reluctant Adèle, the neglected wife of an army officer, but ends up stabbing her to death when they are surprised by her husband, thus ensuring that she shall 'belong' to no one but himself.

DURANTY, EDMOND (1833–80) Novelist who edited short-lived review *Réalisme* (July 1856–May 1857) and 'founded' a school of 'Realism' with Champfleury (1821–89), also a novelist, who published a volume of essays entitled *Le Réalisme* (1857).

FAULKNER, WILLIAM (1897–1962) American novelist. *Absalom, Absalom!* was published in 1936.

FIELDING, HENRY (1707–54) English comic novelist. *The History of Tom Jones*, which Stendhal greatly admired, first appeared in 1749.

FLAUBERT, GUSTAVE (1821–88) French novelist best known for *Madame Bovary* (1857) and *L'Éducation sentimentale* (1869).

FREUD, SIGMUND (1856–1939) Austrian founder of psychoanalysis.

GIDE, ANDRÉ (1869–1951) Novelist, dramatist, and critic, winner of the Nobel Prize for Literature in 1947. Considerably influenced by Stendhal, whose two major novels he considered among the greatest in world literature. His only novel *Les Faux-Monnayeurs* was published in 1926.

'HORIZON OF EXPECTATION' Term from 'reception theory' coined by Hans Robert Jauss (at the University of Constance) to denote the range of features expected of a given literary genre (or other literary aspect) by a given readership at a given historical moment. Literary value is measured by 'aesthetic distance' (in Jauss's new use of this old term), that is, by the degree to which a work departs from the 'horizon of expectation' of its first readers.

HUGO, VICTOR (1802–85) Romantic poet, dramatist, and novelist, and the leading figure in the Romantic battle for the French stage, in the course of which the first night of his *Hernani* (1830) proved a triumphant turning-point. *Marion de Lorme*, written in 1829 but censored, was then performed for the first time in 1831: in it the heroine, a courtesan, loves and is loved by DIDIER, who is ignorant of her real identity. When he learns who she is, he spurns her and prefers to die, executed for the capital offence of duelling, even though Marion had slept with a magistrate to secure his pardon. *Ruy Blas*, another verse drama (about the valet Ruy Blas's love for the Queen and his eventual suicide), was first performed in 1838.

IDÉOLOGUES Group of late-eighteenth-century thinkers, disciples of Condillac (q.v.), who included Condorcet, Cabanis, Maine de Biran (q.v.), and Destutt de Tracy (1754–1836). The latter's *Eléments d'idéologie* (1801–5) had a profound influence on the young Henri Beyle. They were concerned to identify how 'ideas' are formed (hence 'idéologie'), and thus were seeking to establish a science of psychology on a physiological basis. Early exponents of a kind of reader-response criticism, they judged a literary work not by its adherence to rules but by the impression left on the reader's reason, sensibility, and imagination.

INTERTEXTUALITY Term coined by Julia Kristeva in 1966 but widely used by other theorists to denote the interdependence of literary texts, placing particular emphasis on the way that one text is always (whether consciously or unconsciously) a patchwork of quotations from other texts.

JAMES, HENRY (1843–1916) American-born novelist who settled in Europe in 1875. *The Princess Casamassima* was published in 1886.

JANIN, JULES (1804–74) An influential literary critic of the mid-nineteenth century, particularly in his role as the weekly drama critic of the *Journal des Débats* for some twenty years (from 1835). The resulting *Histoire de la littérature dramatique* was published in 6 volumes in 1858. Also a novelist and short-story writer, he was elected to the French Academy in 1870.

JANSENISTS Adherents of Jansenism, a religious doctrine derived from the works of Saint Augustine by Cornelius Jansen, or Jansenius (1585–1638) and developed in his posthumously published *Augustinus* (1640). In some respects the Catholic equivalent of Calvinism in that it denies free will and asserts that divine grace is predestined rather than to be earned by good works, its followers (of whom Pascal (q.v.) was the most notable) were characterized by their moral austerity and continuing opposition to the Jesuits.

JOUBERT, JOSEPH (1754–1824) A frequenter of salons and influential moralist who confined his writing mostly to private notebooks, extracts from which were published by Chateaubriand in 1838 (later augmented in 1842).

JOUFFROY, SIMON-THÉODORE (1796–1843) A philosopher and university teacher with particular interest in the observation and analysis of human conduct.

JOYCE, JAMES (1882–1941) Irish author of novels and short stories. *Ulysses* was published on his fortieth birthday in 1922.

JUNG, CARL GUSTAV (1875–1961) Swiss psychologist and psychiatrist noted for his theory of archetypes and the collective unconscious.

JUSTE MILIEU A term to describe those who supported Louis-Philippe (1773–1850; reigned 1830–48), who were thus situated in the 'just centre' between the Republican left and the Legitimists on the right who wanted to restore the Bourbons to the throne.

KLEIN, MELANIE (1882–1960) Austrian-born British psychologist known for her study of child psychology, notably in *The Psychoanalysis of Children* (1932).

LACLOS, PIERRE CHODERLOS DE (1741–1803) Author of *Les Liaisons dangereuses* (1782), an epistolary novel about sexual power-play among French aristocrats.

LAMARTINE, ALPHONSE DE (1790–1869) Romantic poet and later an influential statesman at the time of the 1848 revolution.

LAS CASES, EMMANUEL, COMTE DE (1766–1842) Followed Napoleon into exile on St Helena (1815) but subsequently expelled (1816). Wrote the widely read *Mémorial de Sainte-Hélène* (1822–3), a record of Napoleon's life and expressed opinions in exile.

LE PÈRE GORIOT Novel by Honoré de Balzac (see 'Notes on authors') and published in 1834–5.

LES ÉGAREMENTS DU COEUR ET DE L'ESPRIT (lit. 'The Aberrations of the Heart and Mind') First-person novel (1736) by CRÉBILLON FILS which presents a witty and elegant portrait of contemporary high society and its amorous intrigues.

MAINE DE BIRAN, MARIE-FRANCOIS-PIERRE Originally a disciple of Condillac (q.v.) and a fellow-traveller of the 'Idéologues' (q.v.), later subscribed to Roman Catholicism. In his treatise *De l'influence de l'habitude sur la faculté de penser* (1803) he distinguishes between passive and active 'habits' (or 'sensations' and 'impressions') and emphasizes the importance of 'actively' studying one's own personality as the best means to an understanding of humankind in general.

The Red and the Black *and* The Charterhouse of Parma

MANN, THOMAS (1875–1955) German novelist. *The Magic Mountain* first appeared in 1924.

MANZONI, ALESSANDRO (1785–1873) Italian Romantic novelist and poet, particularly famous for his novel *I Promessi Sposi* (*The Betrothed*), completed in 1827.

MARIVAUX, PIERRE DE (1688–1763) Dramatist and novelist. His two (unfinished) novels *La Vie de Marianne* (1731–41) and *Le Paysan parvenu* (1735–6) may have influenced Fielding (q.v.). Uncertainty of birth is a major theme in both novels, as it is in Fielding's *The History of Tom Jones*.

MEMOIRS OF A TOURIST Stendhal's *Mémoires d'un touriste*, a guide-book enlivened by anecdote and personal comment written in 1837–8 and based on his own travels.

MISE-EN-ABYME Literally a 'placing in the abyss'; a term from medieval heraldry describing the depiction of a shield within a shield (within a shield, etc.) and adopted by André Gide (q.v.) to describe the process of reflecting the literary procedures of a text within the text itself.

MOLIÈRE (1622–73) Comic dramatist. *Le Bourgeois Gentilhomme*, a comedy about bourgeois pretension (in the person of Monsieur Jourdain), was first performed in 1670. *Le Tartuffe*, which derides religious hypocrisy, was first performed in 1664 but prohibited by the king until 1669.

MONTESQUIEU (1689–1755) Philosopher, political theorist, and novelist, best known for his epistolary novel the *Lettres persanes* (1721) and for *De l'esprit des lois* (1721), his study of constitutional government.

MUSSET, ALFRED DE (1810–57) Romantic poet, novelist, and dramatist. *Rolla*, a long poem published in 1833, tells of tragic love and the hero Rolla's suicide.

NATURALISM Term coined by Emile Zola (q.v.) and prompted by Taine's (q.v.) comparison of Balzac's analysis of the human condition to the work of a naturalist. Intended to identify (and publicize) Zola's own principal ambition that the novel should portray human beings as physiological (rather than psychological) entities beset by hereditary and environmental forces.

NODIER, CHARLES (1780–1844) Novelist, short-story writer, critic, and librarian, who hosted the first gatherings of the young Romantic generation at the Bibliothèque de l'Arsenal in Paris.

PASCAL, BLAISE (1623–62) Mathematician, physicist, and religious writer influenced by Jansenism (q.v.) and famous for his *Lettres provinciales* and *Pensées*.

PHENOMENOLOGY A method of philosophical inquiry which focuses on the perceiving consciousness, rather than the perceived object, as the origin and centre of meaning.

POLYPHONY See 'Dialogism'.

POSITIVISM A system of thought in the works of Auguste Comte (1798–1857) in which scientific method is brought to bear in the analysis of human society to the exclusion of all theological or metaphysical concerns. In literary criticism 'positivist' has come to designate critics who examine a literary work predominantly within a biographical, historical, and literary-historical context.

RABELAIS, FRANÇOIS (c.1494–c.1553) Physician, satirist, and humanist, author of *Pantagruel* and *Gargantua*.

RETZ, CARDINAL DE (1614–79) Archbishop of Paris (1653–62) obliged to resign his see for political reasons, and author of the *Conjuration de Fiesque* (1655) and *Mémoires* (published posthumously, 1717).

RICHARDSON, SAMUEL (1689–1761) Novelist particularly noted for his two long, sentimental novels *Pamela* (1740) and *Clarissa* (1747–8).

ROBESPIERRE, MAXIMILIEN DE (1758–94) Lawyer and one of the leaders of the Revolution; virtual dictator during the Terror from 17 Sept. 1793 till his overthrow on 27 July 1794, and guillotined the following day.

ROUSSEAU, JEAN-JACQUES (1712–78) Philosopher, opera composer, novelist, and autobiographer whose *Confessions*, covering his life up until 1766, were written between 1764 and 1770 and published in 1781 (Books I–VI) and 1788 (Books VII–XII).

RUY BLAS See Hugo, Victor.

SAINTE-BEUVE, CHARLES-AUGUSTIN (1804–69) The greatest literary critic in nineteenth-century France, and also a published poet (1829) and author of a semi-autobiographical novel *Volupté* (1834). Began writing for *Le Globe* (1824–7), and then for a variety of newspapers and journals, as well as taking up temporary positions as a university lecturer. Famous particularly for his series of *Portraits* (in the 1830s) and for his *Causeries du lundi*, weekly articles published between 1849 and his death. Appointed to a chair at the Collège de France in 1854.

SAND, GEORGE (1804–76) Prolific and popular Romantic novelist, *Indiana* (1832) being the first of her many successes.

SARTRE, JEAN-PAUL (1905–80) Philosopher, novelist, dramatist, critic, and political commentator. In his first novel *La Nausée* (1938) the hero Antoine ROQUENTIN experiences 'nausea' at his own contingency in the physical world and looks for some way of demonstrating the 'necessity' of his consciousness.

SCOTT, WALTER (1771–1832) Writer of historical novels which enjoyed a great vogue in France during the 1820s.

SHELLEY, MARY WOLLSTONECRAFT (1797–1851) Wife of PERCY BYSSHE SHELLEY and author of *Frankenstein, or the Modern Prometheus* (1818).

STÄEL, MME DE (1766–1817) Early Romantic literary theorist and novelist, author of CORINNE (1807), which is set in Italy and relates the story of a beautiful poetess who dies of grief at losing the man she loves.

STERNE, LAURENCE (1713–68) English comic novelist particularly noted for his *Tristram Shandy* (1759–67), the narrative structure of which is based principally on the art of digression and deferment.

SUE, EUGENE (1804–75) Highly successful author of serialized novels dealing sensationally with Parisian low life, the most famous of which was *Les Mystères de Paris* (1842–3).

TAINE, HIPPOLYTE (1828–93) Philosopher, critic, and historian, who succeeded Eugène Viollet-le-Duc as Professor of Aesthetics and the History of Art at the Ecole des Beaux-Arts in 1864 (till 1883), and one of the leading thinkers of his day. Influenced by the Positivism (q.v.) of Auguste Comte, he developed theories concerning the interdependence of physical and psychological factors ('race', 'milieu', 'moment') which affect cultural and social development and applied these in his studies of art, history, and literature (famously in his *History of English Literature*, 1863), while also influencing subsequent novelists (e.g. Bourget, Zola).

THIBAUDET, ALBERT (1874–1936) Eminent French literary critic, latterly Professor of French literature at Geneva, and author of many works on nineteenth-century writers.

TURGENEV, IVAN (1818–1883) Russian novelist. *Fathers and Sons* was first published in 1862.

VRAISEMBLABLE Lit. 'true-seeming'; a key term in French literary theory since the Renaissance.

ZOLA, EMILE (1840–1902) Self-proclaimed leader of the Naturalist school and novelist famous for his cycle of twenty novels *Les Rougon-Macquart* (1871–93), of which *L'Assommoir* (1877), *Nana* (1880), *Germinal* (1885), *L'Œuvre* (1886), *La Terre* (1887), and *La Bête humaine* (1890) are the best known, and which all trace 'the natural and social history of a family under the Second Empire'. His later novels were principally concerned with social and religious matters.

Notes on Authors

AUERBACH, ERICH (1892–1957) Professor of Romance Philology at Marburg University but forced out by the Nazis in 1935; refugee at Turkish State University, Istanbul, where he wrote *Mimesis* (1946); emigrated to USA in 1947, and joined French Department at Yale University in 1950.

BALZAC, HONORÉ DE (1799–1850) Born in Tours; moved to Paris to study law but in 1819 turned to novel-writing, at first under pseudonyms, later (with *Les Chouans* (1829), his first success) under his own name (to which he added the 'de'). Wrote some 91 novels and stories between 1828 and 1848, among these *Eugénie Grandet* (1833), *Le Père Goriot* (1834–5), *Illusions perdues* (1837–43), and *La cousine Bette* (1847): all these were grouped together for publication as *La Comédie humaine* (1842–8), which was intended as a comprehensive record of French society.

BARBÉRIS, PIERRE (1926-) Following early teaching posts in Aleppo and Beirut (1952–61), taught at the University of Caen and the Ecole Normale de Saint-Cloud, as well as at the Ecole Pratique des Hautes Etudes en Sciences Sociales. Author of a number of important studies of Balzac, such as *Balzac et le mal du siècle* (1970), *Mythes balzaciens* (1972), and *Le Monde de Balzac* (1973). More recent publications include *Aux sources du réalisme* (1978) and *Le Prince et le marchand* (1980) and demonstrate his continued interest in class relations as reflected in literary texts.

BARTHES, ROLAND (1915–80) Father killed in action during the First World War. Moved to Paris with his mother in 1924 and later studied French literature and classics at university. Spent most of the Second World War at sanitoria in the Alps receiving treatment for tuberculosis. After the war, taught French at universities in Romania and Egypt, and from 1960 taught at the Ecole Pratique des Hautes Etudes in Paris. In 1976 appointed to a chair at the Collège de France. Mother died in 1977; and he was run over by a laundry van outside the Collège de France in February 1980. Major critical works include *Le Degré zéro de l'écriture* (1953; *Writing Degree Zero* (1967)), *Système de la mode* (1967; *The Fashion System* (1983)), *Mythologies* (1957, 1970; in English (1972/9)) *S/Z* (1970; in English (1974)), *Le Plaisir du texte* (1973; *The Pleasure of the Text* (1975)), *Fragment d'un discours amoureux* (1977; *A Lover's Discourse: Fragments* (1978)).

BLIN, GEORGES (1917-) Authoritative academic critic, whose main works include *Baudelaire* (1939), *Le Sadisme de Baudelaire* (1948), *Stendhal et les problèmes du roman* (1954), and *Stendhal et les problèmes de la personnalité* (1958).

BOURGET, PAUL (1852–1935) See Glossary.

BROMBERT, VICTOR (1923-) Previously a student and teacher at Yale University, became Henry Putnam University Professor of Romance and Comparative

Literature and Director of the Christian Gauss seminars in criticism at Princeton University and is the author of many important critical works on nineteenth- and twentieth-century French literature, including *Stendhal et la voie oblique* (1954), *The Intellectual Hero: Studies in the French Novel, 1880–1955* (1961), *The Novels of Flaubert* (1966), *Stendhal: Fiction and the Themes of Freedom* (1968), *La Prison romantique. Essai sur l'imaginaire* (Paris, 1975; *The Romantic Prison: the French Tradition* (1978)), and *Victor Hugo and the Visionary Novel* (1984).

BROOKS, PETER (1938–) Tripp Professor of the Humanities at Yale University and Director of the Whitney Humanities Center. Author of several influential studies, notably *The Novel of Worldliness* (1969), *The Melodramatic Imagination* (1976), and *Reading for the Plot. Design and Intention in Narrative* (1984).

CROUZET, MICHEL Previously taught at the University of Picardy and now for over a decade Professor of Nineteenth-Century French Literature at the Sorbonne in Paris; prolific author of comprehensive studies of a wide-range of nineteenth-century writers, especially Stendhal, including *Stendhal et le langage* (1981), *Stendhal et l'italianité* (1982), *La Vie de Henry Brulard ou l'enfance de la révolte* (1982), *La Poétique de Stendhal* (1983), *Raison et déraison chez Stendhal. De l'idéologie à l'esthétique* (1984), *Le Héros fourbe chez Stendhal* (1987), and *Stendhal ou Monsieur Moi-même* (1990).

FAGUET, EMILE (1847–1916) Literary historian and critic, and drama critic of the *Journal des Débats* for twenty years, remembered for his century-by-century survey books of French literature (1885–94) and for the occasional vigour of his critical idiom.

FELMAN, SHOSHANA Professor of French and Comparative Literature at Yale University, and author of *La 'Folie' dans l'œuvre romanesque de Stendhal* (1971), *La Folie et la chose littéraire* (1978; *Writing and Madness* (1985)), *Le Scandale du corps parlant: Don Juan avec Austin, ou la Séduction en deux langues* (1980; *The Literary Speech Act: Don Juan with J.L. Austin, or Seduction in Two Languages* (1983)), *Jacques Lacan and the Adventure of Insight: Psychoanalysis in Contemporary Culture* (1987), and (with Dori Laub) *Testimony: Crises in Witnessing in Literature, Psychoanalysis, and History* (1992).

JEFFERSON, ANN (1949–) Fellow of New College, Oxford, and author of *The nouveau roman and the Poetics of Fiction* (1980), *Reading Realism in Stendhal* (1988), and (with others) *Modern Literary Theory: A Comparative Introduction* (1982; rev. edn 1986); currently editing (with Valerie Minogue) the Pléiade edition of the works of Nathalie Sarraute.

MOSSMAN, CAROL Professor of French at the University of Maryland and author of *The Narrative Matrix. Stendhal's 'Le Rouge et le Noir'* (1984), *Politics and Narratives of birth: Gynocolonization from Rousseau to Zola* (1993), and a number of important articles on Stendhal.

PRENDERGAST, CHRISTOPHER Fellow of King's College, Cambridge, and author of *Balzac: Fiction and Melodrama* (1978), *The Order of Mimesis* (1986), and *Paris and the Nineteenth Century* (1992).

RICHARD, JEAN-PIERRE (1922–) Identified with the so-called Geneva School (Bachelard, Poulet, Starobinski, Rousset *et al.*) and author of major studies of Mallarmé (1961) and Chateaubriand (1967), as well as of countless, highly regarded essays on individual writers published variously in *Littérature et sensation* (1954), *Poésie et profondeur* (1955), *Onze études sur la poésie moderne* (1964), and *Microlectures* (1979, 1984 [*Pages, Paysages*]).

SAINTE-BEUVE, CHARLES-AUGUSTIN (1804–69) See Glossary.

TAINE, HIPPOLYTE (1828–93) See Glossary.

ZOLA, EMILE (1840–1902) See Glossary.

Further Reading

(Included in square brackets are works in French of particular importance or of particular relevance to the critical approaches illustrated above. It should be noted that several items transcend the critical category to which they have been allocated.)

For an earlier selection of critical work on Stendhal, see Victor Brombert (ed.), *Stendhal. A Collection of Critical Essays* (Englewood Cliffs, N.J.: Prentice-Hall, 1962): includes pieces by Martin Turnell, Erich Auerbach, Jean Prévost, Raymond Giraud, Irving Howe, Judd D. Hubert, Léon Blum, Jean Starobinski, Jean-Pierre Richard, Simone de Beauvoir, and Victor Brombert himself.

On *The Red and the Black*, see the volume in the Modern Critical Interpretations series, *Stendhal: 'The Red and the Black'*, ed. Harold Bloom (New York: Chelsea House, 1988): includes pieces by René Girard, Harry Levin, D.A. Miller, Peter Brooks, Ann Jefferson, Margaret Mauldon, and Carol Mossman.

For a useful introduction to a variety of critical perspectives, see *Modern Literary Theory. A Comparative Introduction*, ed. Ann Jefferson and David Robey (2nd edn, London: Batsford, 1986). For further perspectives on the question of realism and representation see Lilian R. Furst (ed.), *Realism* (London and New York: Longman, 1992) in the present series.

[Nineteenth-century reception of Stendhal has been helpfully analysed and illustrated by two important works:

MÉLIA, JEAN *Stendhal et ses commentateurs* (Paris: Mercure de France, 1911).
TALBOT, EMILE *La Critique stendhalienne de Balzac à Zola* (York, S. Carolina: French Literature Publications Company, 1979).]

Selected translations of Stendhal's works

Armance, trans. C.K. Scott Moncrieff (London: Chatto, 1928; reprinted by The Soho Book Company, 1986).
Armance, trans. Gilbert and Suzanne Sale (London: The Merlin Press, 1960).
The Charterhouse of Parma, trans. C.K. Scott Moncrieff and intr. Ann Jefferson (London: David Campbell, 1992).
The Charterhouse of Parma, trans. Margaret R.B. Shaw (Harmondsworth: Penguin Books, 1958).
The Life of Henry Brulard, trans. Jean Stewart and B.C.J.G. Knight (Harmondsworth: Penguin Books, 1973).
Life of Rossini, trans. and ed. Richard N. Coe (rev. edn, London: Calder and Boyars, 1970).

Lives of Haydn, Mozart and Metastasio, trans. and ed. Richard N. Coe (London: Calder and Boyars, 1972).

Love, trans. Gilbert and Suzanne Sale (London: The Merlin Press, 1957).

Lucien Leuwen, trans. H.L.R. Edwards, trans. rev. and ed. Robin Buss (Harmondsworth: Penguin Books, 1991).

The Pink and the Green, followed by Mina de Vanghel, trans. Richard Howard (London: Hamish Hamilton, 1988).

The Red and the Black (under title *Scarlet and Black*), trans. C.K. Scott Moncrieff (first published in 1927; republished in Everyman's Library in 1938 and 1991).

The Red and the Black (under title *Scarlet and Black*), trans. Margaret R.B. Shaw (first published in 1953; republished by Penguin Books (Harmondsworth), 1953).

The Red and the Black, trans. Catherine Slater and intr. Roger Pearson (Oxford: Oxford University Press (The World's Classics), 1991).

To The Happy Few: Selected Letters, trans. Norman Cameron and ed. E. Boudot-Lamotte (first published in 1952; republished by the Soho Book Company, 1986).

Biography

ALTER, ROBERT, in collaboration with CAROL COSMAN *Stendhal. A Biography* (London, Boston, and Sydney: Allen and Unwin, 1980): readable and informative, and the best available in English.

[CROUZET, MICHEL *Stendhal ou Monsieur Moi-Même* (Paris: Flammarion, 1990): now the authoritative French biography of Stendhal.]

MAY, GITA *Stendhal and the Age of Napoleon* (New York: Columbia University Press, 1977): a useful account of Stendhal's life within the context of his times.

Marxism

LUKÁCS, GEORG *Studies in European Realism. A Sociological Survey of the Writings of Balzac, Stendhal, Zola, Tolstoy, Gorki, and others,* trans. Edith Bone (London: Hillway, 1950; republished by The Merlin Press, 1972). Chapter III contains Lukács's famous comparison of Balzac and Stendhal.

'Pre-Structuralist' criticism

(of a biographical, literary historical, thematic, stylistic, formalist, or 'introductory' kind)

ADAMS, ROBERT M. *Stendhal. Notes on a Novelist* (London: The Merlin Press, 1959): still a valuable account of Stendhal, mixing biographical and historical information with perceptive close reading.

[BROMBERT, VICTOR *Stendhal et la voie oblique. L'auteur devant son monde romanesque* (New Haven and Paris: Presses Universitaires de France, 1954): a subtle and influential analysis of Stendhalian irony and the role of the novelist's authorial voice.]

BROOKS, PETER 'Stendhal and the Styles of Worldliness', in his *The Novel of Worldliness. Crébillon, Marivaux, Laclos, Stendhal* (Princeton, N.J.: Princeton

The Red and the Black *and* The Charterhouse of Parma

University Press, 1969): an important account of Stendhal against the background
of the eighteenth-century French novel, in a book which describes itself as
'basically "formalist" in approach' but also as 'making some claim to literary
history', and in which Brooks takes issue with accepted notions of 'realism' and
highlights the limitations of Thematic Criticism (pp. 8–9).

FINCH, ALISON *Stendhal: 'La Chartreuse de Parme'* (London: Edward Arnold, 1984): an
excellent introduction to *The Charterhouse of Parma*, with useful information on the
historical and political background.

HAIG, STIRLING *Stendhal: 'The Red and the Black'* (Cambridge: Cambridge University
Press, 1989): a brief survey of the main features of Stendhal's first major novel.

HEMMINGS, F.W.J. *Stendhal. A Study of his Novels* (Oxford: Clarendon Press, 1964):
includes separate chapters on the major novels, with particular emphasis on their
function as 'imaginary biographies'.

LEVIN, HARRY *The Gates of Horn* (New York: Oxford University Press, 1963): pp.
146–75 contain a useful discussion of Stendhal's realism.

MITCHELL, JOHN *Stendhal: 'Le Rouge et le Noir'* (London: Edward Arnold, 1973): still a
reliable introduction to *The Red and the Black*.

TALBOT, EMILE *Stendhal and Romantic Esthetics* (Lexington, Ky.: French Forum, 1985):
places Stendhal's ideas on art and the 'beau idéal' within the contemporary context.

WOOD, MICHAEL *Stendhal* (London: Elek, 1971): includes separate chapters on
Stendhal's major texts, written in a refreshingly unpompous manner.

Thematic criticism

BERSANI, LEO 'Stendhalian Prisons and *Salons* (*La Chartreuse de Parme*)', in his *Balzac
to Beckett. Center and Circumference in French Fiction* (New York: Oxford University
Press, 1970), pp. 91–139: a valuable account of politics in the novel, which might
usefully complement Victor Brombert's account of 'the poetry of freedom', and
which anticipates Bersani's later psychoanalytic approach to the Stendhalian hero
(see below).

[POULET, GEORGES 'Stendhal', in *Etudes sur le temps humain* (4 vols, Edinburgh and
Paris: 1949–68), iv (*Mesure de l'instant*), 227–51.] An important corrective to
Poulet's view of a 'discontinuous' Stendhal may be read in the final paragraphs
of PAUL DE MAN, 'The Rhetoric of Temporality', in his *Blindness and Insight. Essays
in the Rhetoric of Contemporary Criticism* (rev. edn, London: Methuen, 1983), pp.
187–228.

STAROBINSKI, JEAN 'Stendhal pseudonyme', in his *L'Œil vivant* (Paris: Gallimard,
1961): a classic essay (on the theme of the mask) analysing the paradox of
Stendhal's desire for authorial self-affirmation and his accompanying delight in
pseudonymic self-effacement in the creation of fantasy worlds. Anticipates
psychoanalytic approaches. Part of the essay is available in translation in Victor
Brombert (ed.), *Stendhal. A Collection of Critical Essays*.

Structuralism

GENETTE, GÉRARD 'Stendhal' (first published in 1969), in *Figures of Literary Discourse*,
trans. Alan Sheridan and intr. Marie-Rose Logan (Oxford: Basil Blackwell, 1982):
an important essay calling into question traditional biographical interpretations
of Stendhal's works and stressing the importance of the 'text'.

[Genette, Gérard 'Vraisemblance et motivation', in *Figures II* (Paris: Editions du Seuil, 1969): Stendhal's narration of the shooting of Mme de Rênal is presented as a prime example of 'arbitrary' (as opposed to 'vraisemblable' or 'motivated') narrative.]

Psychoanalytic criticism

Bersani, Leo *A Future for Astynax. Character and Desire in Literature* (Boston and Toronto: Little, Brown & Co., 1976): Chapter IV ('The Paranoid Hero in Stendhal') offers a rich discussion of how 'Stendhal's most profound intention [was] to eliminate the Oedipal stage itself' (p. 116).

[Berthier, Philippe *Stendhal et la Sainte Famille* (Geneva: Droz, 1977): a comprehensive and elegant account of how Henri Beyle's family relationships are 'inscribed' within Stendhal's writings.]

Chaitin, Gilbert *The Unhappy Few: A Psychological Study of the Novels of Stendhal* (Bloomington: Indiana University Press, 1972): Stendhal's novels viewed from a Freudian perspective.

Girard, René *Deceit, Desire and the Novel: Self and Other in Literary Structure*, trans. Yvonne Freccero (Baltimore: Johns Hopkins University Press, 1965): this classic account of the fictional representation of mediated desire (in Cervantes, Flaubert, Stendhal, Proust, Dostoyevsky) contains extensive reference to *The Red and the Black*.

Robert, Marthe *The Origins of the Novel*, trans. Sacha Rabinovitch (Bloomington: Indiana University Press, 1980): offers a Freudian account of the origins of narrative in which *The Red and the Black* features prominently.

Feminism and gender criticism

[Bolster, Richard *Stendhal, Balzac et le féminisme romantique* (Paris: Minard, 1970): Chapter III deals specifically with Stendhal's 'rebellious heroines' and agrees with Clara Malraux (1944) and Simone de Beauvoir that Stendhal is a feminist writer.]

De Beauvoir, Simone *The Second Sex*, trans. H.M. Parshley (New York: Alfred A. Knopf, 1952), pp. 238–48; reprinted in Victor Brombert (ed.), *Stendhal. A Collection of Critical Essays*, pp. 147–56: the classic early feminist text.

Kelly, Dorothy *Fictional Genders. Role and Representation in Nineteenth-Century French Narrative* (Lincoln and London: University of Nebraska Press, 1989): offers analyses of central nineteenth-century texts in relation to their depiction of the 'undecidability of gender'.

Kristeva, Julia *Tales of Love* (first published as *Histoires d'amour* (Paris: Denoel, 1983)), trans. Leon S. Roudiez (New York: Columbia University Press, 1987): feminist and psychoanalytic readings of erotic literature, including 'Stendhal and the Politics of the Gaze: An Egotist's Love' (pp. 341–64).

[May, Gita 'Le féminisme de Stendhal et *Lamiel*', *Stendhal Club*, 20 (1977/8), 191–204: an account of Stendhal's last, unfinished novel, and the role of its heroine as a prototypical urban guerilla.]

Schor, Naomi *Breaking the Chain: Women, Theory, and French Realist Fiction* (New York: Columbia University Press, 1985): post-Structuralist readings of nineteenth-century narratives (including Stendhal's *Lamiel*), which reflect elements of deconstructive, psychoanalytic, and gender criticism.

The Red and the Black *and* The Charterhouse of Parma

Readers and representation

DAY, JAMES T. *Stendhal's Paper Mirror. Patterns of Self-Consciousness in His Novels* (New York, Bern, Frankfurt-am-Main, and Paris: Peter Lang, 1987): a thorough account of reflexivity and 'mise-en-abyme' in Stendhal's novels.

JEFFERSON, ANN *Reading Realism in Stendhal* (Cambridge: Cambridge University Press, 1988): contains separate chapters on *Love, The Red and the Black, Life of Henry Brulard*, and *The Charterhouse of Parma*, with the focus on questions of representation and the role of the reader.

MILLER, D.A. *Narrative and Its Discontents. Problems of Closure in the Traditional Novel* (Princeton, N.J.: Princeton University Press, 1981): Part III ('Narrative "Uncontrol" in Stendhal') discusses the conscious play with plot suspense and the dialectic of 'fixity' and 'freedom' in Stendhal's writing within the genre of the novel.

PEARSON, ROGER *Stendhal's Violin. A Novelist and his Reader* (Oxford: Clarendon Press, 1988): contains separate chapters on the four major novels, with emphasis on reader-response.

Index